ENGAGING EVIL

Methodology and History in Anthropology

Series Editors:
David Parkin, Fellow of All Souls College, University of Oxford
David Gellner, Fellow of All Souls College, University of Oxford
Nayanika Mathur, Fellow of Wolfson College, University of Oxford

Just as anthropology has had a significant influence on many other disciplines in recent years, so too have its methods been challenged by new intellectual and technical developments. This series is designed to offer a forum for debate on the interrelationship between anthropology and other academic fields but also on the challenge to anthropological methods of new intellectual and technological developments, and the role of anthropological thought in a general history of concepts.

Recent volumes:

Volume 36
Engaging Evil: A Moral Anthropology
Edited by William C. Olsen and
Thomas J. Csordas

Volume 35
Medicinal Rule: A Historical Anthropology of Kingship in East and Central Africa
Koen Stroeken

Volume 34
Who Are 'We'? Reimagining Alterity and Affinity in Anthropology
Edited by Liana Chua and Nayanika Mathur

Volume 33
Expeditionary Anthropology: Teamwork, Travel and the 'Science of Man'
Edited by Martin Thomas and
Amanda Harris

Volume 32
Returning Life: Language, Life Force and History in Kilimanjaro
Knut Christian Myhre

Volume 31
The Ethics of Knowledge Creation: Transactions, Relations, and Persons
Edited by Lisette Josephides and Anne Sigfrid Grønseth

Volume 30
Human Origins: Contributions from Social Anthropology
Edited by Camilla Power, Morna Finnegan, and Hilary Callan

Volume 29
Regimes of Ignorance: Anthropological Perspectives on the Production and Reproduction of Non-Knowledge
Edited by Roy M. Dilley and Thomas G. Kirsch

Volume 28
Extraordinary Encounters: Authenticity and the Interview
Edited by Katherine Smith, James Staples, and Nigel Rapport

Volume 27
Durkheim in Dialogue: A Centenary Celebration of The Elementary Forms of Religious Life
Edited by Sondra L. Hausner

For a full volume listing, please see the series page on our website:
http://www.berghahnbooks.com/series/methodology-and-history-in-anthropology

Engaging Evil

A Moral Anthropology

Edited by
William C. Olsen and Thomas J. Csordas

berghahn
NEW YORK • OXFORD
www.berghahnbooks.com

First published in 2019 by
Berghahn Books
www.berghahnbooks.com

© 2019, 2023 William C. Olsen and Thomas J. Csordas
First paperback edition published in 2023

All rights reserved. Except for the quotation of short passages
for the purposes of criticism and review, no part of this book
may be reproduced in any form or by any means, electronic or
mechanical, including photocopying, recording, or any information
storage and retrieval system now known or to be invented,
without written permission of the publisher.

Library of Congress Cataloging-in-Publication Data
Names: Olsen, William C., editor. | Csordas, Thomas J., editor.
Title: Engaging evil : a moral anthropology / edited by William C. Olsen and Thomas J. Csordas.
Description: New York : Berghahn Books, [2019] | Series: Methodology and history in anthropology ; volume 36 | Includes bibliographical references and index.
Identifiers: LCCN 2019003801 (print) | LCCN 2019013694 (ebook) | ISBN 9781789202144 (ebook) | ISBN 9781789202137 (hardback : alk. paper)
Subjects: LCSH: Good and evil--Social aspects. | Philosophical anthropology. | Theological anthropology. | Anthropological ethics.
Classification: LCC BJ1406 (ebook) | LCC BJ1406 .E64 2019 (print) | DDC 302/.17--dc23
LC record available at https://lccn.loc.gov/2019003801

British Library Cataloguing in Publication Data
A catalogue record for this book is available from the British Library

ISBN 978-1-78920-213-7 hardback
ISBN 978-1-80073-640-5 paperback
ISBN 978-1-78920-214-4 ebook

https://doi.org/10.3167/9781789202137

CONTENTS

List of Figures vii

Acknowledgments viii

Introduction 1
William C. Olsen and Thomas J. Csordas

Part I. Evil and Anthropology

Chapter 1. From Theodicy to Homodicy: Evil as an
Anthropological Problem 35
Thomas J. Csordas

Chapter 2. On the Concept of "Evil" in Anthropological
Analyses of Political Violence 51
Byron J. Good

Part II. Evil and Suffering

Chapter 3. Speak No Evil: Inversion and Evasion in Indonesia 71
Andrew Beatty

Chapter 4. Mother Evil in Hell Valley: A Creole
Transvalorization of Evil in Trinidad 95
Roland Littlewood

Chapter 5. Satan on the Old Kent Road: Articulations of Evil
in a Pentecostal Diaspora 111
Simon Coleman

Chapter 6. The Transformation of Evil in Nepal 133
David N. Gellner

Chapter 7. Radical Evil and the Notion of Conscience:
A Buddhist Meditation on Christian Soteriology 156
Gananath Obeyesekere

Chapter 8. Are Spirits Satanic? The Ambiguity of Evil in
Niger 177
   Adeline Masquelier

Part III. Evil and Violence

Chapter 9. Engaging Evil and Excess in Palestine/Israel 199
   Julie Peteet

Chapter 10. The Violence of Evil: A Biocultural Approach to
Violence, Memory, and Pain 225
   Ventura R. Pérez

Chapter 11. The Intention of Evil: *Asram* in Asante 254
   William C. Olsen

Chapter 12. Monsters, Sadists, and the Unspectacular
Torture Experience 275
   Nerina Weiss

Afterword 297
   David Parkin

Authors and Institutions 307

Index 309

FIGURES

1.1	Elementary structure of evil.	41
3.1	Birth of Kala shadow play, Java (Bathara Kala in center).	83
3.2	Javanese shadow play exorcism (with children's clothes draped over top of screen).	84
10.1	Diagram of a biocultural analysis of violence.	230

ACKNOWLEDGMENTS

The editors wish to express their appreciation and gratitude. From its beginning stages, this volume—its scope, content, and scholarly value—benefited from the input, writing, correspondence, and advice of David Parkin. His careful read of drafts and his friendship are deeply valued. The project was first set in motion by previous work of Olsen and through the vision and tenacity of Nancy Scheper-Hughes. Both were involved in organizing the AAA panel sessions, which helped form a foundation for this volume. Tom Csordas was one of the presenters. Nancy's input on evil and violence in this volume may be readily identified. As editors and authors, we express gratitude to the careful reading and comments of two anonymous reviewers and also that of Peter Geschiere. Peter's attention to the ambiguity of evil is especially poignant. Emphasis given to this point thirty-five years ago by David Parkin was expanded, critically applied, and illustrated through Peter's scholarship and his extensive notes.

INTRODUCTION

William C. Olsen and Thomas J. Csordas

> The forces of relative purity, of goodness, of fortune, of life . . . are inextricably linked with the forces of pollution, of evil, of misfortune, and of death.
> —Bruce Kapferer, *A Celebration of Demons*

> Inoculations of evil are crucial to human rights violations because they become part of socially accepted notions of common sense.
> —Carole Nagengast, "Inoculations of Evil in the U.S.-Mexican Border Region"

In this volume, we explore the anthropology of evil as an empirical human phenomenon—an existential/moral feature of human thought and communal or social relations—and the value of evil as a methodological construct—a meaningful tool for comprehending the actions, thought, and coordinated behavior of human communities. Our purpose is to show how evil is situated within culture as a lynchpin of what Cornelius Castoriadis (1998) called the imaginary institution of society, emblematic of the tension between creation and destruction in human affairs. We thus attempt to show the usefulness of treating evil as a descriptive reality where concepts such as violence, criminality, and hatred fall short of capturing the darkest side of human existence. In doing so, we argue that a moral anthropology concerned only with ethical priorities and how people strive to do the right thing lacks depth and is at best two dimensional, or, put another way, misses not only the dark underside of life but also the shades of gray between its blacks and whites.

How do we identify evil, and where does it reside? Epidemics of AIDS, SARS, Ebola plagues, political corruption, state-terror and dirty wars, structural violence and swelling poverty, necro-politics, terrorist massacres, ethnic cleansing and death squads, human trafficking, clerical sex abuse, global slavery, imperial invasions, genocides, and child-soldiers create a tableau of expansive horror and suffering. Evil may appear closer to home as people lose control of financial, political, military, economic, and mystical forces. These events, seen to be both evil in themselves as well as the result of evil conduct, and their locus is difficult to pinpoint insofar as at times they appear structurally anonymous and at other times the works of larger-than-life perpetrators. There is, in addition to these social evils and trends, a more intimate interpersonal evil that though not as visible is equally social and cultural. Here, evil is the operational common denominator of cruelty, abuse, neglect, genocide, betrayal, or domination, which are inherently destructive. This is the everyday evil of personal and subjective problems whether they are explicitly blamed on the malicious intent of others or exhibit the effects of malevolent destructiveness.

This book addresses dimensions of evil in various social settings, including particular kinds of human suffering, and what is done in response. As editors, we eschew any essentialist definition with universal application. Rather, we seek to provide a forum to examine qualifying attributes of what would count as a realization of evil. We argue for a "situational evil," which "identifies the specificity or singularity of evil in discrete events," and which provides contexts for understanding how actors respond to those circumstances (Csordas 2013, 527). With an eye to anthropology's affinity with philosophy, this volume asserts that evil may be pursued from an ontological and existential perspective that enriches and enlivens the empirical and comparative data of ethnography. Cases of genocide and the holocaust, child victimization, organ harvesting, torture, political terror, rape, and murder "constitute anthropology's primal scene" (Scheper-Hughes and Bourgois 2004, 5). These actions may be immediately intuited as evil. In this Introduction, we attempt to explain why this is so and why anthropology should be interested in the topic.

One enduring feature of anthropology is attention to quasi persons and to marginal social circumstances. The range of the anthropological project includes the idiosyncratic as well as the less familiar. We research what is sometimes auspicious and also what may be disturbing. Anthropology informs us of purposive collusion with the occult where victims of sorcery suffer from tumors, menstrual cramping, and TB, but also laziness, alcoholism, addiction, and sterility

(Buchillet 2004). We can read of medicines in Lesotho derived from human body parts used to increase social power and for curing illness (Murray and Sanders 2005); or we may read of dismembered bodies and cannibalism in the Killing Fields of the Khmer Rouge (Hinton 2005). Anthropology tells of "sex thieves" who steal genitalia simply by a handshake (Bonhomme 2016). It shows how eating the roasted flesh of the dead is regarded as an act of compassion toward one's kin (Conklin 2001). Attention to such topics demonstrates "the generalization of moral concern within the discipline" (Fassin 2008, 337) and highlights moral or ethical features of existence including the uncertainty, ambivalence, variation, and ambiguity of social life, human exchange, and meaningful acts (Lambek 2010).

The quintessentially anthropological modus operandum of capturing fundamental aspects of society by attending to its margins is played out in striking and alarming detail by Jean La Fontaine as she writes about alleged Satanists in the UK who are presumed to be occultists, pagans, and witches. Rumored to dwell in both London and the Midlands, these groups are said to advocate the occult as self-proclaimed worshipers of the devil. They are low-income householders reputed to perpetrate clandestine ritual abuse based on creeds fetishized in the allegations of other British populations. By accounts of those who speak of them, they are involved in acts contrary to human sensibilities, and in behaviors that denote "Western society's symbol of the most hideously evil and anti-social form" of abuse, sexuality, and terror (La Fontaine 1998, 80). Their supposed ritual performances and beliefs in *maleficium*, night-witches, support such a premise; and these actions define them as less than human. La Fontaine notes how, "The Satanist of the modern allegations . . . also combines in this image the attributes of two other personifications of the illegitimate and the antisocial: the terrorist and the pedophile. . . . Their combined characteristics added to their inhuman acts make the Satanists the essence of the monstrous stranger" (186). Likewise, the abuses and havoc wreaked by witches in the Bocage region of western France identify a surreptitious network comprised of associations with the malignant and nefarious. French witchcraft is found not merely among extreme marginal cases such as the "irrational" or within a world of "fools and madmen." Rather, witches comprise a furtive and "distant world of the poor, the backward or the insane" (Favret-Saada 1980, 42). The behavior of those who are active in witchcraft goes beyond the irrational, however. As one man in the Bocage said of their vicious actions, "Those I am talking about possess a power to do evil, they make people suffer" (1980, 49).

In another vein, Caton and Zacka (2010, 207) identify photos of torture at Abu Ghraib prison and modes of creativity and suffering. The "grotesque" carnival of torture is a "kind of excess, of too much body or flesh, of the monstrous and the hideous." Some top brass themselves identified the events as "hideous." Others in the George W. Bush administration referred to the photos simply as "disgraceful" or with words that expressed regret. These rhetorical invocations of ugliness and shamefulness converge toward what we would call evil, and their immediacy requires "that we revisit the original urgency of the drive to make 'the social' component of our lives an explicit object of critical inquiry and moral concern" (Wilkinson and Kleinman 2016, 9). We pursue cultural formulations that account for the "perceived ambiguities, puzzles, and paradoxes in human experience" (Geertz 1973, 108). We also agree with Kiernan (1982) that the problem of evil may be insolvable, and for precisely this reason we research meanings and modalities of evil by strategically deploying anthropological tools to optimize the methodological tension between moral engagement and theoretical indifference.

Whatever shock or dismay moves us to turn away from the stark realities of exploitation, horror, dread, and abuse, we are yet compelled to comprehend how such things exist in the contemporary world either as social practices or modes of discourse, and how human life survives at the social margins and discursive limits. We want to know where these things are common and where unusual. Are they identifiable with our own categories of thought and language, or are they beyond description? Are they real or fantasy; routine or spectacle—or maybe both? Are such actions part of a moral and ethical system, or are they its antithesis? Can we realistically identify human behaviors as forms of evil; and can evil be understood in reference to the actions and deeds of human persons? Does anthropology carry a unique charge to report circumstances of evil to the academic community and to the entire world? Is evil—like violence, like madness, like suffering, like pain—a continuum? Political forecasters speak of a deterioration of living conditions under neoliberalism. There appears a "sense of declining fortunes, loss of optimism, and great insecurity" about the future. Ortner notes how these dark moods "must be included in any broad definition of ethnography" (2016, 55). An anthropology of evil is best situated within what Ortner has called a "dark anthropology." Lives wrought with pain and suffering, violence and oppression "very often stand at the center of anthropological work" (Robbins 2013, 448). Engaging evil as an anthropological category implies recognizing evil as something more human than nonhuman. To speak of unspeakable suffering and unmask the face of monstrous destructiveness is not an exoticizing move but a critical exercise in understanding what Jenkins (2015) calls "fundamental human processes."

Yet, with noted exceptions (Parkin 1985; Clough and Mitchell 2001; Ter Haar 2007; Csordas 2013; van Beek and Olsen 2015), anthropologists have been wary of directly addressing evil as such, even while documenting evil or concepts of evil in ethnographic work. It is perhaps because the Christian idea of evil is so hegemonic that even though confronted by a thousand varieties of evil in the field, anthropologists are anxious that their perceptions might be skewed by the Judeo-Christian underpinning of rational thought, so anxious that they are tempted to discount the notion of evil altogether. This is not the case for philosophers, who are less shy of evil—and it is not a foregone conclusion as to whether philosophers are more or less in the thrall of Euro-American intellectual conventions (Badiou 2001; Bernstein 2002; Cole 2006; Dews 2008; Midgely 2001; Ricoeur 1986, 2007; Rorty 2001; Sheets-Johnstone 2008). Their approach, in part, pays close attention to the internal diversity of evil as an ethical, cosmological, ontological, and existential category. Amelie Rorty (2001) identifies multiple subcategories or varieties of evil, each of which expresses incommensurable concerns and has its primary place in a specific outlook, with distinctive preoccupations and questions, theories of agency and responsibility, all of which are historically, contextually, and semantically marked: abominations, disobedience, vice, malevolence, sin, wanton cruelty, immorality, corruption, harm, criminality, sociopathology. Rorty prefers to emphasize the specificity of these multiple forms of evil rather than treating it as a general category, and Lars Svendsen agrees that with respect to evil, "it's a mistake to reduce a manifold of phenomena to one basic form" (2010, 82). He begins with Leibniz's distinction among metaphysical evil inherent in the world's imperfection, physical/natural evil that is suffering, and moral evil that is sin. He subcategorizes moral evil based on the type of motive involved: demonic evil for its own sake; instrumental use of evil means to accomplish a goal that may in itself be good, evil, or neither; idealistic evil perpetrated ostensibly in the name of some presumed good; and stupid or banal evil in the form of thoughtlessness or absence of reflection. Yet the question remains of whether specific forms of evil have something in common, and what we would call that something in common other than "evil."

Anthropologists' wariness about evil may have to do with the risk of essentializing a general category of such existential consequence. This is compounded by deep uneasiness that evil may be a fundamentally or exclusively Christian concept (it is not) and hence inherently ethnocentric, or in a more nuanced sense by unease on the part of anthropologists of Judaeo-Christian background that they may be subconsciously susceptible to a hegemonic Christian idea. Indeed, the figure of Christian evil recurs as problematic in a variety of ways among the chapters of the present volume. For our purposes, it is necessary to observe not only that evil has a role in the imaginary institution of society (Castoriadis 1998), but also that it may have an inherently mythical component. Here, Paul Ricoeur's later essay on evil as a challenge to philosophy and theology is also relevant for anthropology. Ricoeur stresses the contrary but complementary features of sin and suffering in the existential structure of evil: the first is perpetrated and the second undergone, the first elicits reprimand and the second lamentation. At issue for anthropology is "the parallel demonization that makes suffering and sin the expression of the same baneful powers. It is never completely demythologized" (2007, 38).

Recognition of this is the first step in confronting evil from the standpoint of theoretical reflection, and not a reason to shy away from the topic. From a purely quotidian and relatively unmarked position, as Susan Neiman has observed, "Every time we make the judgment *this ought not to have happened*, we are stepping onto a path that leads straight to the problem of evil" (2002, 5). Evil was in question in the aftermath of the great Lisbon earthquake of 1755, and even that ought not to have happened in a good world, and reflection on which led to the modern understanding of natural disasters with no inherent moral content. What is of interest is that currently, more than three hundred years later, we are in the aftermath of the Haitian earthquake of 2010 and the Nepalese earthquakes of 2015. Whereas the question after the Lisbon quake was how such evil could happen, in the present, it is not the quake itself that raises the question of evil. It is the fact that, given the capacities for humanitarian relief in contemporary twenty-first-century society as compared to eighteenth-century European society, we could allow the victims of these quakes to suffer for as long as they have in the aftermath. Hannah Arendt identified a banality of evil. This included Holocaust death camp operatives whose engagement with horrors of genocide saw only minimal levels of brutality even though their work produced body counts and sadistic bodily experiments. To these we can add the short attention span to natural disasters such as earthquakes or the myopia that keeps the suffering of displaced populations out of focus. Insofar as evil flows from the "thoughtlessness" of human agents and their tools of hate and power, Arendt wrote, "What I propose is very simple: it is nothing more than to think what we are doing."

Evil as a Counterpoint in Morality

Especially in the last decade, the place of morals and moral systems has evolved to become a central concern within anthropology. Recognition of morals as part of the social framework and as a legitimate topic for research and writing is provided within several recent pivotal and theoretical arguments. These include D'Andrade (1995); Fassin (2008, 2012); Stroeken (2010); Hallowell (1955); Pocock (1986); Wolfram (1982); Zigon (2008); Humphrey (1997); Overing (1985); Mayer (1981); Parish (1994); Heintz (2009); Laidlaw (2014); Faubion (2011); Lambek (2010); Robbins (2007, 2013); Csordas (2013); Keane (2016); Mattingly et al. (2018); and Kapferer and Gold (2018) to name just a few. Hallowell declared that human society consisted of not only social facts, but also of a moral order. Ethnographic investigation includes coming to terms with intentions, objectives, and motives as well as what people say, comprehend, and believe to be true: something identified as the actor's "moral universe" (Overing 1985, 4). Howell claims that morals include reason, judgment, and ambiguity or confusion. Fortes uses the premise of the morality of the self by noting that the self includes also a recognition of the other or the "stream of social relations." This interchange assumes the individual's "volitional control" over his actions; and these actions mostly conform to social norms and values (Fortes 1987, 122). For Lambek (2000), people make routine assessments of their lives in reflection of ideas that are good. Signe Howell's premise is that anthropology has always held the study of morals as a central focus with the aim of understanding comparative culture and ethics; however, there has been consistent reluctance to identify such concerns as an interest in morals (Humphrey 1997, 6). Howell cites as examples of the anthropology of morals the well-known studies of honor and shame in the Mediterranean and early concerns for the values of crime and custom in the Pacific. One conclusion drawn from these examples is that "humans everywhere are cognitively and emotionally predisposed towards moral sensibility" (1997, 10). We concur with these findings. We find evidence of this moral commonplace in the writings of numerous anthropologists. Social systems contain moral provisions and models for those living within a community or nation. Morality becomes a part of the individual consciousness. For the sake of argument, we might add that morality also includes the acquired attitudes, emotional responses, and individual dispositions of the human person throughout their life span (Zigon 2008, 17). "Embodied morality" is not reviewed by continuous self-reflection. It is embedded in the habitus and done simply as an accepted course of action. Seeking to understand what is most basic to human actions also helps us focus on the foundational precepts of being human (Csordas 2013, 524).

James Laidlaw observes that anthropology has produced a significant number of excellent ethnographic accounts that make fundamental use of moral systems in their descriptive contents. However, though there are notable examples of a moral anthropology, these accounts remain unattached to a continuous stream of internal intellectual argument, such that there is "no anthropology of ethics . . . no sustained field of enquiry and debate. There is no connected history we can tell ourselves about the study of morality in anthropology" (Laidlaw 2002, 311). Laidlaw's premise is that people's conduct is shaped by intentional action in regard to the kind of person they think they should be or become; and this valuation is in conformity with "ideals, values, models, practices, relationships, and institutions that are amenable to ethnographic study" (2002, 327). Wendy James wrote in the 1980s: "Without the presumption of a level at which a conversation on some such fundamental moral principles can at least be sought, I do not see how the tasks of ethnography, and of analytical social anthropology, can be properly carried out" (James 1988, 153). The disciplinary absence may be due to perspectives of moral agency which have been associated more with populations in more complex societies. "The idea of 'morality' *per se* evokes the notion of personal consciousness and the autonomous agent: a figure too often assumed to belong only to our own age and to be quite incompatible with 'earlier' and other supposedly underdeveloped forms of society" (1988, 154). Lacking a clear definition of a locus of moral agency, ethnographic accounts of morals have not produced an "analytical framework for an approach to morals or ethics as such" (Laidlaw 2014, 14).

Yet a moral anthropology, or a study of local moral worlds, appears to be gaining momentum (Csordas 2013). Recent statements claim a moral turn in anthropology can be founded on the "construction of values, and those values' existential implications." A key premise of a "value-related practice in anthropology" is that it involves foundational concerns "with moral forces, but not necessarily in any moralistic sense" (Kapferer and Gold 2018, 8). The turn toward morals and a humanistic anthropology also moves away from previous concerns of power and of modes of resistance in any political and mystical realm. Shifts in anthropology that engage moral discourse are largely driven in part by wider concerns of humanitarianism. Awareness has arisen in the literature regarding the brutality of violence and poverty, "the abjection and suffering of war, the inhumanities of state oppression," and the indifference to outbreaks of terror. Anthropological voices speak against the brutality of oppression and in favor of humanitarian agendas. "Humanitarian discourses and ethics ameliorate the forces of inhumanity," including global forces of techno-capitalism, war, and oppression (Kapferer and Gold 2018, 12–13).

By researching evil, we contribute theoretical and ethnographic support for such a moral analytical framework that is neither necessarily moralistic nor necessarily subject to a vigilante attitude that makes finger wagging attributions of evil. If "most people immediately understand what morality means and what a moral act is without needing definitions" (Fassin 2012, 5), then evil constitutes a portion of human moral thought and conduct, occupying the "negative aspect of any moral system" (Parkin 1985, 3). We recognize that morality infuses human interaction with codes and rules and symbols that sustain even extreme reaches of what it is like to be part of mankind, or the "delimitations of the human" (Pocock 1986, 18). We wish to draw special attention to situations in which evil is inherent in an act of human will and intentionality, particularly when the impact of evil is felt by persons, families, or communities—or where "evil appears as a direct manifestation of the human spirit" (Csordas 2013, 529). Whereas authors writing on moral systems in anthropology have largely passed over the subject of evil, a basic premise to this volume is that "evil is fundamentally implicated in morality and ethics, and all are bound up with meaning" (Csordas 2013, 526). We concur with Kleinman (2011) that personal experiences, including individual freedom and choice, may be active forces for altering moralities in society and even for creating moral crises. Indeed, moral crises and evil are properly viewed as part of the moral system, especially when considering the realm of life that is injurious, harmful, calamitous, disadvantageous, criminal, and which includes human suffering. Evil is often best comprehended when understanding the "boundaries of the good" (Parkin 1985, 3). In response to the query of whether evil is a dimension "undermining morality from below and outside or as intrinsic to morality in a foundational sense," we favor the latter, since "if it wasn't for evil morality would be moot" (Csordas 2013, 525).

From indigenous perspectives, evil may be a category of local thought and action, a moral "descent into the ordinary" (Das 2007, 15). Along with human suffering, evil is also a vital issue that "brings moral debate to the human costs exacted by our social arrangements, economic organization, cultural values, and modes of governance" (Wilkinson and Kleinman 2016, 3). By looking closely at the intersubjective fabric of quotidian living where evil often resides, we "become more fascinated by our mundane struggles to decide between competing imperatives or deal with impasses, unbearable situations, moral dilemmas and double binds" (Jackson 2013, 11). Put differently, it may be said that "anything that can be described in ethical terms involves people's interactions with one another" (Keane 2016, 80). Yet it is often difficult to determine the exact moral framework of the actions of any particular individual. Morals are seldom neutral and, especially in complex circumstances, may be challenged or ignored. Thus, negotiation of the meaning of values and ethics is part of who people are and what they do or do not become. Engaging evil may be useful here since a moral anthropology considers realities of existential lives in conditions and settings of extreme variation. We wish to bring a wider narrative to the "richness of ethical experience that seems to speak to what cannot be said, what might or might not have happened, what might or might not happen, in ways that simply exceed and elude structures of meaning" (Dyring, Mattingly, and Louw 2018, 16).

Beidelman (1986, 201) argues this point from his perspective of living with the Kaguru in Tanzania:

> Each Kaguru struggles to shape a meaningful and expressive world. ... Social and psychic experiences are manifest in a series of dualistic tensions between public and private expression, conformity and individuality, compliance and subversion, and harmony and discord. The notions of imagination and morality ... lie at the heart of these complex correspondences and discrepancies between society and individuals.

Evil enters here as a matter of homodicy rather than theodicy, where living is manifested more in experiential modes than in theocratic frameworks. Zande witchcraft is "not the sole agent of misfortune;" however, since witchcraft is so morally wrong and depraved, "it is the prototype of all evil" (Evans-Pritchard 1937, 56–57). One reason for this perspective is that witchcraft is a deliberately "causative factor in the production of harmful phenomena" in specific physical circumstances and within particular social networks (1937, 72). A witch "cannot send out his witchcraft and leave it to find his victim for itself, but he must define its objective and determine its route" (1937, 36). Parkin claims, "our attempt to understand other peoples' ideas of evil draws us into their theories of human nature: its internal constitution and external boundaries" (1985, 6). Beyond indigenous theories of human nature, for comparative purposes, evil can be seen as a constitutive confrontation with morality in an "immediate existential sense" (Csordas 2013, 525). In this sense, anthropology is positioned to provide a greater perspective on evil and moral systems. "Anthropological approaches that highlight the 'experiential excesses' of ethical life are especially suitable for exposing the ontological indeterminacy of the ethical domain. Many anthropologists would claim that investigations into the 'actual' or empirical are also investigations into the possible" (Dyring, Mattingly, and Louw 2018, 15).

Such reference points signal a move away from political economy and toward the idiosyncratic. Collective reckonings of evil, as in Zande, illustrate this trend. A broadened view of morality, "whether as a way of going about politics by finding evil to be eliminated, including evil people, is, then, part of a larger shift of focus from strategies of power and control to logics of value, all of which follows from the shift to the culturalist framework" (Friedman 2018, 184). Within that framework, the use of evil as an analytical concept may become a working tool within anthropology. In settings such as Azande, evil may provide a flexible moral code in a field of moral actions. This field is often composed of ambiguity and contradictions that involve "struggles and dilemmas that are born of human sociality itself, where partial and temporary agreements are all that is possible, where incompatible viewpoints are the norm, and where scarcity is a permanent condition" (Jackson 2015, 64).

Finally, community morals and religious systems provide explanations of evil. Evil itself implies "a workable set of ethical criteria, normative guides to govern our action" (Geertz 1973, 106). Questions of evil arise when people give meaning to the vicious and contradictory moments of living with pain and suffering, as opposed to the way life ought to have been. We encounter the "strange opacity of certain empirical events, the dumb senselessness of intense or inexorable pain, and the enigmatic unaccountability of gross iniquity" for which there is "no empirical regularity, no emotional form, and no moral coherence" (Geertz 1973, 107–8). Explaining such matters is not equally important in all cultures and societies. People wish to comprehend the meanings of specific evil occurrences and events rather than any expanded explanation of evil on a wider moral platform. Yet morals are enmeshed within living agendas and social systems and within history. As such, morals present a challenge for anthropology to analyze and interpret; but analysis should come from within that experiential context and from history. For Geertz, the "problem of evil" is formed within a worldview involving "the actual nature of the destructive forces within the self and outside of it, of interpreting murder, crop failure, sickness, earthquakes, poverty, and oppression" in a manner that evokes modes of comprehending evil and suffering (1973, 130).

In this volume, chapters by Csordas and by Good address the issue of the place of evil as a viable analytical tool and legitimate concept within anthropology. Csordas claims that evil, minimally defined as malevolent destructiveness, is an inherent dimension of morality. Studies that reject the use of evil as a working construct may have a serious blind spot in examining moral and ethical values and their consequences in action within a culture, including our own. Proposing an anthropological homodicy as an alternative to theodicy, Csordas juxtaposes religious and psychoanalytic analyses of Golding's *Lord of the Flies* to show how supernatural and human cultural phenomenologies of evil can be superimposed on the same scenario and how they can overlap. He also discusses cursing maledictions within Roman Catholic discourse. At least implicitly invoking demonic power, maledictions become vehicles of Satanic influence. They are more than just sinful and may require exorcism. Maledictions as human acts are thus situated at the intersection of culture and the cosmological. Byron Good's chapter reviews the diverse perspectives and assumptions in Western thought that contribute to an understanding of evil. Providing a counterpoint to Csordas, Good critically and skeptically examines the viability of evil as an anthropological tool in a moral sense. He also looks at the decades' long record of state violence and abuses in human rights in Aceh, Indonesia, as a test case to determine the value of the word *evil* as an analytical tool in coming to terms with such events. Good explores anthropological investigations and engagement and interrogates the possibility of moral judgment on what is observed. He asks, "To what end are we as anthropologists to use a language that implies moral judgment as an analytic frame?" His perspective opens consideration of the assumptions that allow anthropologists to assert a status among those qualified to make such judgments in situations such as the violence and trauma in Aceh.

Chaos and Malevolence

Evil is often associated with persons or locales that are incomplete, unholy, unsanctified, or impure. Evil may be seen or unseen, apathetic, full of meaning or appearing entirely gratuitous. Evil may be without form or it may be strategic and cunning. It is mostly associated with unwholesomeness, filth, degradation, fragmentation, decay, defect, and imperfection (Csordas 2013, 527). In many cultures, evil beings or events are sinister, desecrated, and spoiled. Important events, objects, and places require protection and limited exposure to evil influences. Evil may be experienced as uncontrolled power and as full of ambivalent purpose (Geschiere 2013). It may also be transitory, as in Buddhist rituals of exorcism where demons exchange hierarchical order and powers with deities and for a brief time, evil is closely associated with what is pure (Kapferer 1983).

Evil persons are not only misguided or lacking benevolence; they are filled with aberration, moral failing, inexplicable malevolence, and deviance. They may be considered irredeemable in contrast to common criminals whose misdeeds are regarded as capable of rehabilitation. Evil is linked to persons whose existence and identity stand contrary to much of reality and truth. These are cruel beings, dedicating their existence to annihilation and destruction. They bring about dirty wars and death squads, massacres and terror, and their works are graphic, painful, and meaningful to all. Evil brings abandon to the life of the soul; it induces suffering and a degradation and humiliation that disrupt any desire to exist. Through evil, one may wish to never have been born. When criminal, their misdeeds are considered unspeakable, inciting notions of horror, such as child molestation, necrophilia, and genocide. The gravity of such actions compels heads of state, the ICC, or the United Nations to declare certain actions as crimes against humanity rather than as acts of war and modes of terror. Evil persons are often portrayed as having lives that "should not be." These are persons who represent the "very worst of all badness." This description of evil resonates with the idea that evil is "inversion of the ideal of order itself" (Pocock 1985, 47).

Some authors contend that paradoxes and ambiguities of evil become reality because of personal will or the intentionality of the person. Human intentions can create circumstances of privation and moral indigence that descend to the level of evil because of their severity. A lyrical rendition of this theme is given by John Milton as Paradise becomes lost to humans due to their first disobedience by way of a forbidden tree, which brought "death into the world, and all our woe." In such a scenario, the universe is often predisposed to both good and evil, and one of these powers becomes a distinct and experiential reality based upon the actions of humans in relation to one another. The example of the Dinka from East Africa illustrates how senselessness and avaricious intent thwarts the will of divinity and brings about the more selfish results of men and women. For the Dinka, an archetypical people experienced no death and had sufficient food to eat based on a daily allotment from Divinity. One day, while pounding millet, the woman decided out of greed to plant more millet than was permitted. Her inattention resulted in striking Divinity with a hoe. Now offended, Divinity retreated into the sky, severed the rope between heaven and earth, and left humans to contend with suffering, sickness, death, and laboring for food (Lienhardt 1961, 29). This scenario is repeated in Navajo where "chaos is the general state of affairs" in an existence known as Lower World, which happened before any contemporary time and space. The suffering and evil of primordial chaos persist in the current Navajo world and are captured within the realm of community living in which a range of moral options provides a basis for living and experience. "In such a context, it should come as no surprise that the ideal state of *hozho* is part of a continuum, the other end of which is *hochxo*, evil, ugly, worthless." Life in the present is "orderly and operates according to rules of reciprocity" when the moral system is not disturbed through infractions of personal greed, lust, or volatility. This life stipulates "beauty, harmony, good, happiness, and everything that is positive"; and such values are known by all and are expected to be experienced as part of daily life (Frisbie 1987, 3–4). Violations of the cosmic order are inherently *hochxo*, or evil.

In Africa, evil is commonly associated with "wildness, deviance, terror, destruction, chaos, unbridled passions and sexual lust, and predatory forces. Evil effects or substances may be found in the barrel of a gun as well as in pureed vegetables and pulp cereal given to a young child" (Van Beek and Olsen 2015, 2). Malevolent beings, such as demons, witches, spirits, and so on, become the personification of evil and assert evil and nefarious intentions of ill will. Grace Harris captures the question of morality, sorcery, and geography as she describes Taita responses to witchcraft. "A sorcerer violating fundamental morality transgressed against human decency. A neighborhood full of undetected sorcerers was on the verge of ceasing to be a viable moral community" (Harris 1978, 29). When such horrendous and powerful forces become personified, intentional suffering of others is also identified, defined, and understood. In turn, identifying and personifying evil allows the moral community to "engage them in dialogue and reflect on the boundaries of humanity" by calculating the very dimensions of evil (Parkin 1985, 23).

Evil rhetoric in Kaguru resembles what is found throughout the continent. "Belief in witchcraft is a mode of imagining evil, judged harmful, bad, and beyond any moral justification" (Beidelman 1986, 138). Kuranko witches are predatory and cannibalistic. They consume vital organs of their victims; and they channel away the life blood of victims through the back or neck. Witches are considered evil because they are seen to epitomize the worst in women and to bring about anxiety and weakness in men (Jackson 1989, 94). Each African scenario epitomizes how evil is personified; and then the evil entity is attributed with the capacity for evil or "wonton destructiveness," which may also be "punishable by other humans and/or by divinities" (Parkin 1985, 21). The moral imagination constructs the witch as an inversion or negation of the moral concept of the person. This descriptive mode is active throughout Africa. It is a contextualizing mode of comprehending that which is reprehensible and bad enough to be called evil.

Intentional suffering is also a quality of modern genocide and political torture. Hinton's definition of political terror and torture differs from genocide in that the latter presents a sustained attempt to annihilate a collectivity (Hinton 2002, 6). We may see all these aspects of cruelty, however, within a continuum of evil since they all involve repetitive intention to inflict pain and suffering in a way that is wantonly destructive. Wanton forms of destructiveness serve to remind us of the limitations of anthropology's central precept, notably cultural relativism. In this volume, we seek an alternative position, one that allows anthropology to condemn the horrendous acts of brutality, political cruelty, and the evil of induced suffering. In her chapter on Turkish torture of Kurdish rebels, Nerina Weiss identifies the 1980s as a "period of barbarism." Torture was linked to identity, nationhood, and heroism. It was also purposeful and intensely intersubjective. An example is given of a guard who deliberately attempts to break a victim (Yusuf) by falsely stating that, while in prison, the man's wife has taken her own life by setting fire to their house. The fire also kills their four-month-old son. The guard then burns the only photo kept by the prisoner of his family. Yusuf's breakdown involves the onset of symptoms of neuroses and severe illness. His therapist later describes the process as "*onskabsfuld* (evil), horrible, and horrendous" (Medical file of a Turkish male political activist, October 1985).

Medical anthropology provides illustrations of evil in this regard. When disease is given meaning like this, symptoms may be regarded as disruptive in a social sense as well as a personal sense. Relations may include spirits, ancestors, witches, and deities, as well as the network of ties to family and neighbors. Presumptions of "sent sickness" may prevail. Investigations into such events often identify a perpetrator, but they also seek out the meaning of the act itself. Why him as a victim? Or, why you as a culprit? Especially when the disease brings death, realities of sickness are very often identified as acts of evil. Such a "personification of evil" recognizes the intent of the perpetrator as a deliberate provocation of suffering and pain. Victims' lives become broken and shattered. Human entities who are extended kin or community invoke the powers of witchcraft or sorcery. The result may be death and disease, but the mystically acquired power of known peers does the work of demons and malevolent spirits. Spirits may have the greater powers, whereas humans are often the vessels of wrath, misery, and destruction.

Olsen's chapter notes that evil is a foundational principle for understanding Asante perceptions of some forms of disease, notably those that are identified in Western culture as modes of mental illness. Even more indicative of evil is the childhood disease known locally as *asram*. Symptoms of *asram* are nearly always delivered via witchcraft. But it is the intentionality of the witch that makes the deed particularly nefarious. Asante say of such illnesses that the child is the being who is most valuable to the future of the family and lineage; and thus the child's death is most likely to bring the greatest measure of grief and suffering. Infant death also obliterates the anticipation that a life's work will be fulfilled by that child, including the care of elderly parents. *Asram* is also particularly evil since it extinguishes all apprehension of *nkrabea*, which is the destiny of the being made by deity before the infant was born. As such, *asram* is an attempt to counter the work of Nyame (God) and also of the future. Due to the likelihood of infant illness and child mortality, evil remains an intermittent and recurring suspicious force within the lives of young couples and their families and neighbors. Those suffering may also be exposed to the "vulnerability of intimacy" (Geschiere 2013) and its associations with evil and witchcraft, as certain herbalists are perpetrators of *asram* in attempts to counter the disease by the sale of their herbs. Geschiere's premise of the close associations between intimacy and witchcraft in Africa are seen in the Ghana example. Evil is ambiguous when it becomes manifest in relations of family. African witchcraft is found among kin or close neighbors. Yet relations of trust are constantly shifting, making evil highly situational. Kin may represent amity; but they may also be the bearers of deep sorrow. Asante episodes of *asram* show how kinsmen are rarely completely outside the realm of evil.

The "motiveless evil" of South Asian mythology may also be captured in descriptions of sorcery in Sri Lanka. "The horror of torture, like that of sorcery, is the turning against the victim, as the instruments of pain, of all that is familiar, pleasurable, safe, and secure. . . . In both torture and sorcery, rationality and reason are engaged to the service of painful destruction." When such misery threatens a person, "experiences of sorcery indicate the transmutation of a life world into a space of dangerous and threatening realities and ultimately into a space of death" (Kapferer 1997, 192). Evil is a declaration "on the other," claims Obeyesekere. The word invariably implies reprehensible conduct; and once applied, we presume those persons may revisit that behavior "on us." Obeyesekere's chapter invokes Kant's notion of "radical evil" to portray characters whose acts are so heinous that their course of action lacks all "guilt, remorse, repentance, and conscience." They thus acquire the character of "resentiment," a term taken from Nietzsche to pertain to "motiveless evil," such as seen in the character Iago in Shakespeare's *Othello* or Angulimala in Buddhist Sri Lankan myths the *Suttas*. With the idea of a motiveless evil at large in the world, we are close to coming full circle back to chaos. "Resentiment" is experienced within those who have committed atrocious and extensive modes of evil: killings, rape, and the like. Buddhism frames dilemmas such as: What sorts of Karma await such evil persons? Why do sinners prosper and the good suffer? Why must the good face such disappointment and strife? In the long term, Karma may ultimately claim the Evil soul. But the process is long, and may entail multiple rebirths. Such mythical tales may also have their parallels in the contemporary world when the tyrant thrives while the just man remains a perpetual victim. Yet evil is no less present when "good" forces descend into the use of torture and brutality to punish those associated with an evil head of state, such as Saddam Hussein, Efrain Rios Montt, Juvenal Habyarimana, Charles Taylor, and Muammar Gaddafi.

Divinities and Demons

How does evil exist in a world created and overseen by a benevolent deity? Reconciling a merciful or loving God with a world of suffering, evil, and death has caused confusion, disbelief, and indifference toward that Deity. The problem of theodicy implies that there is a "source to the victim's indisposition" or predicament of evil, implying there is an "agent responsible" for suffering and pain (Kiernan 1982, 288). Where such a Being is omnipotent, or is known to embody sympathy, the perceived contradictions are especially puzzling. Robin Wright describes the lives of Baniwa in Northwest Amazon, including a description of the world of humans. This world is "irredeemably evil" in that it is comprised of "wicked people" (*maatchikwe*) and because it is a place of pain (*kaiwikwe*) and a place of rot (*ekukwe*). Much of the world's abasement is due to the abundance of witches and sorcerers. They contaminate the world and make it intrinsically a flawed place of existence. The world and all of human existence are "flawed by evil, misfortune, and death" (Wright 2004, 85).

One intriguing answer to this line of philosophical inquiry comes from the Nupe of northern Nigeria. Like nearly all other African cosmologies, the Nupe are monotheistic. God is all-powerful and all-knowing. God is literally the creator of all things, including evil. "Good and evil are both laid into the same creation, as are the various sources of evil—malevolent spirits, disease, witchcraft" (Nadel 1954, 12). In this setting, "the deficiencies of the world are taken for granted" rather than as a source of puzzlement and dread. "The only problem in Nupe theology is the actual power of evil, not its origin" (Nadel 1954, 12). And the presence and potency of evil are assumed because of the distance of Deity from the world created by Deity. For the Nupe, the question is not why does evil exist or why did God not create a more perfect world. Instead, moral dilemmas surround the fact that the distance between humans and God too often leads to suffering, disease, and death. Why is God so unresponsive to the human condition? For the Nupe, the answer is because God has only limited interest in the world and its problems. The Nupe world was created with an implied potential for evil; and evil things "slip into it by chance." Thus, Deity created a world that included a possibility for evil, and "the actual evils are a consequence of the 'world left to itself,' that is, of accident and unpredictable circumstances" (Nadel 1954, 36).

A similar perspective comes from Malaysian Sufism. Orthodox Muslims proclaim that everything that exists comes from God. Without God, nothing exists, and God is in everything equally and wholly. The entirety of this divine scenario includes belief and devotion. But it includes also treason, sin, infidelity, and evil (*jabat*). The creation and explanation of evil are circular in Muslim Malaysia. "Evil as a cosmic force invades and causes suffering and so explains it" (Bousfield 1985, 206). They do evil because they are created with an inherited ability to be evil. Evil exists because it was meant to exist. "The destructive intentions both initiate Evil and are initiated by it" (Bousfield 1985, 206).

The relation between evil and divine will is played out within several of our chapters. Littlewood's chapter describes Mother Earth, a psychotic cult-leader in Trinidad who identifies herself with multiple personalities—including deity—and who has gathered a community of followers that likewise identify with her pathological personality and set of laws and rules. "Mother Earth is Nature. She is the Devil, the Black, the Mad, the Left-Handed, the Witch, the Naked, the victim of Interference" (Littlewood 1993, 134). Mother Earth's declarations and persona display what "should not be" as they proscribe a self-imposed mantel to "combat mistaken doctrines of our existing religions." She is the Devil and "represents Life and Nature, in opposition to the so-called Christian God" and in defiance of the principles of Science and Death. She opposes churches, prisons, education, money, politics, urban life, contemporary morals, and well-informed opinions. Her personal revelations disclose the End of the world, where her own powers will make the blind see, the crippled walk, and will implement cures for all diseases. Mother Earth is an "inversion" to order in all her exactitude. She and her followers revere the "left" while God inhabits the "right." "Bad" is exchanged for good; and conventional obscenities have become the common lexicon. This vocabulary centers upon the whims of a woman who, in flesh and blood, is regarded by her community as "the source of all life." Evil is empowering in the sense where it inhabits space and structures that are contrary to a life lived otherwise.

We see the theme of the ubiquity and possible omniscience of evil realized within the lives and moral framework of Yoruba migrants in two Pentecostal congregations in London. Coleman's chapter brings awareness to the flexibility of evil, including its "ability to inhabit every nook and cranny of people's lives, and indeed to emerge in contexts where variations of excess, imperfection, and incompleteness are uncovered." Ambiguous evil is found in Christian populations of Yoruba in London, where it expands to fill a globalizing moral world of Nigerians, Pentecostals, and those living in new settings of immigration. Evil reflects attitudes derived from history, culture, and the new realities of British life as experienced by those who are both outsiders by origin, and insiders by legal and political appropriation. It becomes a versatile trope of discourse about the demonic, with a character that transforms the moment as it responds to a plurality of possible applications and meanings. Open accusations of witchcraft evil in

Nigeria become more circumspect in London as immigrants adapt to a Christian community that frames evil and the Devil in ways that may be more restricted. Evil enters Pentecostal practices not only as a topic of frequent and expressed concern but also as part of a more general morality that is an inherent "modality of action" (Csordas 2013, 535). Church congregations in London promote an altered sense of community. "Intimacy brings not only protection but also danger" (Geschiere 2013, xxii); and new intimacies stimulate a new, Christian discourse about who is evil. Coleman's chapter shows us a shifting geography of evil that allows its terms to be applied to changing times, places, and populations.

Evil spirits and conceptions of evil have become everyday features of Islam in southern Niger. The moral code resonates with a "demonization of local spirits" who advocate theft, immorality, and other loathsome actions. Masquelier's chapter reveals a transitioning Muslim cosmology, including a proliferation of spirits whose character has evolved from the mysterious and wild in the 1980s. Spirits are known to inflict infertility, paralysis, and skin rashes upon victims. Spirits today are more deliberate in attacking children. Spirits especially attack young girls who ignore religious injunctions and leave their bodies uncovered. These girls thereby experience a threatened sexuality. Demonization of spirits by Muslim clerics does not marginalize these evil entities. Rather, they assume a more active, if ambiguous, place in community life. Evil spirits now take up a more robust identity within a continuing religious crusade between God who is good and Satan who is evil.

Ambiguous and duplicitous characters who personify evil are demonstrated in Beatty's chapter on Indonesian history, culture, and contemporary shadow plays. The goddess Durga gives birth to Kala, an evil figure who embodies misfortune and bad luck. Kala and evil are eventually expelled from the cosmos. But in the process, modes of disorder, chaos, and calamity befall human communities swept up in her wake. In more recent times, the powers of the state emerged within the scenario of this morality play. Witch-type figures have assumed evil personas of history and mythology. Mob violence, mutilation, and body dismemberment are the results of a contemporary politics of state terror. The characters assume the destructiveness of Kala's armies as the political ideology of the Right asserts a violent agenda in attempts to vanquish evil foes of the Left. Suharto himself becomes incorporated into the mythological charter, and new characters of evil appear on the fringes of the everyday: headhunters, tricksters, monsters that hunt the shadowless noonday. In this scenario, ambiguous evil characters of contemporary politics correspond to evil characters of history and drama.

The personalization of evil has broad application. Nietsche's despair captured this breadth when he said, "Are we not straying, as through an infinite nothing? Do we not feel the breath of empty space?" In this vein, Julie Peteet draws attention to a "misery committee," which limits food intake for Palestinians, imposing "excessively calibrated punishment and deprivation." When asked about his condition, one Gaza resident responded, "I am breathing but not alive." A living, personified being representing all forms of evil may be superfluous in this form of living death. In the post-Enlightenment West, where rationality, skepticism, evidence, and proof form much of the worldview and consciousness of the self, the notion of personified evil carries less impact for an individual's moral career. Explicit evil appears to be limited mostly to analogy or symbol, while implicit evil is instantiated in mute existential despair.

Structural and Political Violence

Is evil part of the quotidian world surrounding us? Is evil ordinary? Violence and suffering are found in the home as well as the warzone. Sometimes they exist in both settings at once, as for the Salvadoran women discussed by Jenkins (2015) who were often refugees from the brutality of the civil war and the brutality of their husbands, as political and domestic violence amplified one another in a cycle of extreme distress. Suffering and depravation are part of a daily routine for large global populations experiencing lower ends of economic and income strata. Paul Farmer has articulated how violence is embedded in the structure of social relations insofar as "social inequalities based on race or ethnicity, gender, religious creed, and—above all—social class are the motor force behind most human rights violations. In other words, violence against individuals is usually embedded in entrenched structural violence" (2003, 219). Of the 31,000 children under age five who die each day globally, over half die because of hunger-related causes. Other similar numbers show that poverty kills by limiting health care access. Realities of structural violence negatively impact the daily lives of millions. This includes examples of AIDS cases in Nigeria, where the morality of the disease illustrates the deepening gulf of income inequalities, modernity, and new wealth (Smith 2014).

Can some violence be identified as evil? Modes of structural violence and poverty include the world's greatest extremes of disease and mortality, lack of education, homelessness, powerlessness in resources and mobility, "a shared fate of misery, and the day-to-day violence of hunger, thirst, and bodily pain" (Kleinman 2000, 227). Parkin notes, "Suffering may be culturally defined, but is never lacking. The predicaments are therefore many" (Parkin 1985, 23). Anthropologists claim that some populations make a personification of evil, showing evil to be the result of a named perpetrator with an identifiable victim—an individual or a community. Varying modes of excess, depravation, and even disease may be the results. A scenario of evil intent and personal suffering makes for familiar struggles among humans and also between humans and spirits or God. Intentions aside, what is to be made of those predicaments in anthropology where known persons and communal living constantly embrace suffering and pain, death and decay, abandonment and loss? This "space of death" has itself become a kind of moral struggle with perpetual uncertainty about life or death, health or sickness, with increasing degrees of uncertainty. Anthropology now lives with that space; we seek to understand its place in history and within a global political economy.

While most forms of evil involve violations of individuals and collective bodies, not all violence is evil. Evil does not exist solely in terms of graphic and physical abuse, assault, or infliction of pain. It includes assaults on the meaning of life and death, on agency, on personhood and dignity. Evil attacks the ontological security of the victim's attachment to the world. Cannibalism, kidnapping, disappearances, dissections, sadism, sexual abuse, domestic violence, torture, containment, immobility, extinction, and annihilation may be regarded as examples. There are many social and political realities that render ordinary people vulnerable, wounded, and afraid. In times of political chaos or natural disasters, people disappear, and fears and allegations of kidnapping and murder for organs proliferate. They surface from the "political social imaginary"—where state bio-power and necro-politics occupy a zone between the real and the imagined.

Recent accounts of violence call for "anthropological witnessing." Scholarly distance in the name of cultural analysis and relativism may be criticized. In those episodes where the ethnographer is a witness to torture, rape, ethnic killings, hate crimes, child abuse, ethnic violence, victim eradication, and the like, the witness is called upon to render of voice of condemnation within their writing. Academic and scientific accounts should yield to broader descriptions of violence as modes of terror. State sanctioned violence and terror are included in this equation. State killings and violence by Rios Montt in Guatemala, the on-going slaughters in El Salvador, and the Killing Fields of Cambodia are examples of where anthropology has played its hand in exposing the terror of the state. A state killing apparatus often works in times when the larger population is "immunized by means of a small inoculation of acknowledged evil in order to protect it against the risk" of wider encroachments from a minority group. Such myth-building, says Nagengast (2002), serves to identify the offending population, what they have done to offend, and what the state must do to eradicate the problem. Authors in the present volume claim that such occasions of state violence may be reasonably identified as circumstances of evil due to the purposeful plan to cause suffering and to bring about the annihilation of one community by the state.

Ordinary evil as structural violence is abundant in the lives of squatters and sharecroppers who inhabit sugar plantations around Alto do Cruziero in northeast Brazil. Political terror, oppressive social conditions, and poverty have a deep impact on the body and its functions. The aftermath of colonial farming and the more recent military dictatorship in the 1960s and 1970s rendered the northeast as a "zone of abandonment" (Biehl 2005). For those at the miserable end of Brazilian political economy (Scheper-Hughes 1992, 229–30), the impact of violence—including tactics of dirty wars—is both devastating and routine. Ordinary evil in Brazil's Northeast is seen through structural violence: military tactics include the disappearance and targeting of subversives and agitators of the state. Such events have become routine and expected. "Among the people of the Alto, disappearances form part of the backdrop of everyday life and confirm their worst fears and anxieties—that of losing themselves and their loved ones to the random forces and institutionalized violence of the state." These circumstances created a moral environment of emotional indifference at the sudden death of young children, such that mothers do not mourn the death of a child unless the child reaches an older age, an age that is not so strongly associated with the politics of poverty, death, and disease. Meanwhile, people generally "keep their peace despite the everyday violence of drought, hunger, sickness, and unnecessary death" (Scheper-Hughes 1992, 507–8).

In a review of decades of Apartheid, Adam Ashforth identifies the mechanics of the South African state as enacting modes of power, one of which was evil in its intentions to inflict pain and suffering. The state murdered, segregated by race, and forced legal separation and inaccessibility to power of millions of native South Africans. In fact, the "system was evil. . . . For to name evil is to identify power, the power to cause harm, and the attribution of evil to a political system is not independent of the modes of attributing evil to the other powers that shape the fortunes of everyday existence. When these powers are also invisible, epistemological problems proliferate" (Ashforth 2015, 373). Apartheid evil was an everyday matter, the quotidian source of essentially all forms of misfortune which had negative impact upon black people. "No one doubted that the System was evil, it was spoken of as a generalized source of suffering and misfortune" (Ashforth 2005, 268).

Julie Peteet's chapter in this volume claims that evil is found also within the routine and within structural configurations without always being "excessively violent." It may be revealed in "mundane quotidian acts of subjugation, degradation, and petty violence" that are found in Palestinian relations with Israel. Israeli modes of power create perceptions of the Palestinian that include irrational, pathological, and unlawful. The state reinforces modes of subordination and hierarchy that "infantilize and humiliate to the point of despair." Knesset decisions, she claims, create a schema that epitomizes Palestinian agendas and political action as "irrational, pathological, and beyond the pale of lawful response" and involves an abandonment of human rights. These tactics thereby legitimize a severity in administrative dominion, one that presumes "responses to the evil nearby."

There is a point at which structural and political violence shade into one another, where everyday violence becomes overt armed conflict, and at worst becomes routine as in contemporary Syria, Iraq, and Afghanistan. Colonial and post-colonial political forces become active vectors of violence and evil during years of civil war between FRELIMO and RENAMO in Mozambique (Englund 2002, 2006). Social and economic elite display animosity, indifference, duplicity, and self-aggrandizement within the political sphere. Leaders who began the Civil War on one side of the conflict became aligned with the opposite side because of cleavages in ethnicity and within forces of a rising national economy. Self-serving and duplicitous public officials became the foundation of rumors of massive levels of cholera within the water supply, the killing of school children, wide extractions of human blood from patients in public hospitals, and the trade in body parts and blood for money on the international market. An economy of death soon reappeared. Corpses of the dead were then used to repay foreign donors all interest on the national debt. The outcome was the result of war and its aftermath, economic forces imposed by outside foreign agents, a rising democratic landscape, and perceptions of the state as an actor based on its own self-interests.

Evil in everyday actions is vividly portrayed in the chapter by Perez, who claims evil "as an obscuring mechanism to acts of violence" since it "challenges our hope that the world makes sense." Violence in Mexican border towns was historically less episodic and spectacular and more systematic and every day. The "landscape of evil" encompassed a public space of well-established modes of suffering: rape, torture, murder, and human-trafficking. Also common to the region were malnutrition and poverty. Members of renegade political groups and labor organizations disappeared. Perez argues that Ciudad Juárez may be identified as a contemporary "death zone," where "the politics of civility and democratic conflict have been erased." Ciudad Juárez is also synonymous today with Narco violence and death.

If "evil refers to various ideas of imperfection and excess seen as destructive" (Parkin 1985, 23), and if excess and its trepidations are "represented via the complex and often horrific imagery of evil" (Mitchell 2001, 3), what illustrates the excess and imperfection of evil more than genocide and the Holocaust? Or human trafficking and slavery? Or dirty wars? Or state terror? In these cases, evil becomes invisible to the perpetrator or community of killers because of the perceived moral necessity for killing. Scheper-Hughes and Bourgois (2004, 2) have argued that violence "defies easy categorization." It may be sudden, or well planned. Violence may be state-sanctioned, or it may be contrary to the laws of the state. Violence may be headline news, or it may be invisible to the entire population. Thus, the everyday violence of infant mortality, slow starvation, disease, despair, and humiliation that "destroys social marginalized humans with even greater frequency are usually invisible or misrecognized." Moreover, most "violence is not deviant behavior, not disapproved of, but to the contrary is defined as virtuous action in the service of generally applauded conventional social, economic, and political norms" (Scheper-Hughes and Bourgois 2004, 5).

Political and economic developments often give rise, historically, to questions of exclusion and even possibly eradication. Eliminating the problem population through torture and killing has sometimes been the presumed resolution. Peacetime violence, including small wars and invisible genocides, is no less excessive and evil. The range of excess and evil related to killing and forms of violence constitute what Scheper-Hughes and Bourgois have termed a genocidal or violence continuum. This continuum "refers to the ease with which humans are capable of reducing the socially vulnerable into expendable nonpersons and assuming the license—even the duty—to kill, maim, or soul-murder" (Scheper-Hughes and Bourgois 2004, 19). Recent publications on the ethnography of violence show that violence, while shocking and alarming, may certainly have a normative place within society and society's moral system. Violence is as cultural as other common acts in society, such as political elections or weekend sport. The reality of a cultural bedrock provides the act of violence with its power to create havoc. It is what makes it so disturbing.

Conclusion

Authors in this volume address a subject much too long excluded from wider anthropological discourse. Evil has been avoided because its presumed associations with Western history and Christian society are loaded with social baggage. Disengaging from those contexts appeared too difficult. Other anthropologists claim evil belongs in the realm of metaphysics and should remain unobserved. They argue that research focus should remain on acts of brutality, such as violence, rape, and murder. These concepts are sufficient to portray the realities of cruelty. Evil has been denied and rejected by anthropologists as an indefensible subject of study rather than embraced and highlighted as a human reality within the purview of anthropology. The range of topics in this volume supports a broader application of the concept in anthropology. Insofar as evil and moral behavior very often imply one another, we affirm that the topic has value as anthropologists write of moral systems. Evil certainly defines the boundaries of humanity; and it distinguishes ex-human and post-human from the bestiary of other creatures. Realities of unresolved warfare, brutality, senseless death, dull violence, sorcery, and mystical harm and suffering demand anthropological attention because they exist within our own orbit of experience. We can then ask: Do we find in the attribution of evil "the other" who is also ourselves?

We do not anticipate this volume will put an end to the challenges in anthropology of glossing behavioral meanings and translating linguistic elements from different cultures with the word "evil." We certainly have no vested interest in making this process an easy one. Translation of cultures endures as the work of anthropology no matter what theory may remake its horizons. We do remain convinced that a moral anthropology will increasingly refine its work at the nexus of judgement and human experience on the one hand and political economy and power relations on the other. As a sustaining framework in individual and community involvement and knowledge, moral anthropology calls for a fuller comprehension of moral systems as they are played out in life stories of gender, violence, terror, witchcraft, myth, religion, and so forth. Operative within such systems, and included as integral to moral codes, is evil.

William C. Olsen, Georgetown University

Thomas J. Csordas, UC San Diego

References

Ashforth, Adam. 2005. *Witchcraft, Violence and Democracy in South Africa*. Chicago: University of Chicago Press.
——— . 2015. "The Meaning of 'Apartheid' and the Epistemology of Evil." In *Evil in Africa*. Edited by William C. Olsen and Walter van Beek, 364–80. Bloomington: Indiana University Press.
Badiou, Alain. 2001. Ethics: *An Essay on the Understanding of Evil*. London: Verso.
Beidelman, T. O. 1986. *Moral Imagination in Kaguru Modes of Thought*. Bloomington: Indiana University Press.
Bernstein, Richard. 2002. *Radical Evil: A Philosophical Interrogation*. Cambridge, MA: Polity.
Biehl, Joao. 2005. *Vita*. Berkeley: University of California Press.
Bonhomme, Julien. 2016. *The Sex Thieves*. Chicago: Hau Books.
Bousfield, John. 1985. "Good, Evil, and Spiritual Powers: Reflections of Sufi Teachings." In *The Anthropology of Evil*. Edited by David Parkin, 194–208. Oxford: Blackwell.
Buchillet, Dominique. 2004. "Sorcery Beliefs, Transmission of Shamanic Knowledge and Therapeutic Practice among the Desana of the Upper Rio Negro Region, Brazil." In *In Darkness and Secrecy*. Edited by Neil Whitehead and Robin Wright, 109–31. Durham, NC: Duke University Press.
Castoriadis, Cornelius. 1998. *The Imaginary Institution of Society*. Cambridge, MA: MIT Press.
Caton, Steven, and Bernardo Zacka. 2010. "Abu Ghraib, the Security Apparatus, and the Performativity of Power." *American Ethnologist* 37: 203–11.
Clough, Paul, and Jon Mitchell, eds. 2001. *Powers of Good and Evil*. New York: Berghahn Books.
Cole, Philip. 2006. *The Myth of Evil: Demonizing the Enemy*. New York: Praeger.
Conklin, Beth. 2001. *Consuming Grief*. Austin: University of Texas Press.
Csordas, Thomas. 2013. "Morality as a Cultural System?" *Current Anthropology*. 54: 523–46.
D'Andrade, Roy. 1995. "Moral Models in Anthropology." *Current Anthropology*. 36: 399–408.

Das, Veena. 2007. *Life and Words*. Berkeley: University of California Press.
Dews, Peter. 2008. *The Idea of Evil*. Oxford: Blackwell.
Dyring, Rasmus, Cheryl Mattingly, and Maria Louw. 2018. "The Question of Moral Engines." In *Moral Engines*. Edited by Cheryl Mattingly, et al., 9–36. Oxford: Berghahn Books.
Ellis, Stephen, and Gerrie Ter Haar. 2004. *Worlds of Power*. Oxford: Oxford University Press.
Evans-Pritchard, E. E. 1937. *Witchcraft, Oracles, and Magic among the Azande*. Oxford: Oxford University Press.
Englund, Harri. 2002. *From War to Peace on the Mozambique-Malawi Borderland*. Edinburgh: Edinburgh University Press.
———. 2006. *Prisoners of Freedom*. Berkeley: University of California Press.
Farmer, Paul. 2003. *Pathologies of Power*. Berkeley: University of California Press.
Fassin, Didier. 2008. "Beyond Good and Evil?" *Anthropological Theory* 8: 333–44.
———, ed. 2012. *A Companion to Moral Anthropology*. Oxford: Wiley-Blackwell.
———. 2012. "Introduction." In *A Companion to Moral Anthropology*. Edited by Didier Fassin, 1–19. Oxford: Wiley-Blackwell.
Faubion, James. 2011. *An Anthropology of Ethics*. Cambridge, UK: Cambridge University Press.
Favret-Saada, Jeanne. 1980. *Deadly Words*. Cambridge, UK: Cambridge University Press.
Fortes, Meyer. 1987. *Religion, Morality and the Person*. Cambridge, UK: Cambridge University Press.
Friedman, Jonathan. 2018. "Situating Morality." In *Moral Anthropology*. Edited by Bruce Kapferer and Marina Gold, 182–98. New York: Berghahn Books.
Frisbie, Charlotte. 1987. *Navaho Medicine Bundles or Jish*. Albuquerque: University of New Mexico Press.
Geertz, Clifford. 1973. *The Interpretation of Cultures*. New York: Basic Books.
Geschiere, Peter. 2013. *Witchcraft, Intimacy and Trust*. Chicago: University of Chicago Press.
Hallowell, Irving. 1955. *Culture and Experience*. Philadelphia: University of Pennsylvania Press.
Harris, Grace. 1978. *Casting Out Anger*. Cambridge: Cambridge University Press.
Heintz, Monica. 2009. *The Anthropology of Moralities*. New York: Berghahn Books.
Herzfeld, Michael. 1985. *The Poetics of Manhood*. Princeton, NJ: Princeton University Press.
Hinton, Alex. 2002. "Dark Side of Modernity." In *Annihilating Difference*. Edited by Alex Hinton, 1–40. Berkeley: University of California Press.
———. 2005. *Why Did They Kill?* Berkeley: University of California Press.

Humphrey, Caroline. 1997. "Exemplars and Rules." In *The Ethnography of Moralities*. Edited by Signe Howell, 25–47. London: Routledge.
Jackson, Michael. 1989. *Paths Toward a Clearing*. Bloomington: Indiana University Press.
———. 2013. *The Wherewithal of Life*. Berkeley: University of California Press.
———. 2015. "The Reopening of the Gate of Effort." In *Anthropology and Philosophy*. Edited by Sune Liisberg, Esther Oluffa Pedersen, and Anne Line Dalsgard, 61–75. New York: Berghahn Books.
James, Wendy. 1988. *The Listening Ebony*. Oxford: Oxford University Press.
Jenkins, Janis H. 2015. *Extraordinary Conditions: Culture and Experience in Mental Illness*. Berkeley: University of California Press.
Kapferer, Bruce. 1983. *A Celebration of Demons*. Bloomington: Indiana University Press.
———. 1997. *The Feast of the Sorcerer*. Chicago: University of Chicago Press.
Kapferer, Bruce, and Marina Gold. 2018. "Introduction." In *Moral Anthropology*. Edited by Bruce Kapferer and Marina Gold, 1–26. New York: Berghahn Books.
Keane, Webb. 2016. *Ethical Life*. Princeton, NJ: Princeton University Press.
Kiernan, J. P. 1982. "The 'Problem of Evil' in the Context of Ancestral Intervention in the Affairs of the Living in Africa." *Man* 17: 287–301.
Kleinman, Arthur. 2000. "The Violences of Everyday Life." In *Violence and Subjectivity*. Edited by Veena Das et al., 226–41. Berkeley: University of California Press.
———. 2011. *Deep China*. Berkeley: University of California Press.
La Fontaine, J. S. 1998. *Speak of the Devil*. Cambridge, UK: Cambridge University Press.
Laidlaw, James. 2002. "For an Anthropology of Ethics and Freedom." *The Journal of the Royal Anthropological Institute* 8: 311–32.
———. 2014. *The Subject of Virtue*. Cambridge, UK: Cambridge University Press.
Lambek, Michael. 2000. "The Anthropology of Religion and the Quarrel between Poetry and Philosophy." *Current Anthropology* 41: 309–20.
———. 2010. "Toward an Ethic of the Act." In *Ordinary Ethics*. Edited by Michael Lambek, 39–63. New York: Fordham University Press.
Littlewood, Roland. 1993. *Pathology and Identity*. Cambridge, UK: Cambridge University Press.
Lienhardt, Godfrey. 1961. *Divinity and Experience*. Oxford: Oxford University Press.
Mayer, A. C., ed. 1981. *Culture and Morality*. Oxford: Oxford University Press.
Mattingly, Cheryl, et al., eds. 2018. *Moral Engines*. New York: Berghahn Books.
Midgely, Mary. 2001. *Wickedness*. 2nd ed. London: Routledge.
Mitchell, Jon. 2001. "Introduction." In *Powers of Good and Evil*. Edited by Paul Clough and Jon Mitchell, 1–16. Oxford: Berghahn Books.

Murray, Colin, and Peter Sanders. 2005. *Medicine Murder in Colonial Lesotho*. Edinburgh: Edinburgh University Press.

Nadel, S. F. 1954. *Nupe Religion*. London: Routledge and Kegan Paul.

Nagengast, Carole. 2002. "Inoculations of Evil in the U.S.-Mexican Border Region." In *Annihilating Difference*. Edited by Alex Hinton, 325–47. Berkeley: University of California Press.

Neiman, Susan. 2002. *Evil in Modern Thought: An Alternative History of Philosophy*. Princeton, NJ: Princeton University Press.

Ortner, Sherry. 2016. "Dark Anthropology and Its Others." *Hau: Journal of Ethnographic Theory* 6: 47–73.

Overing, Joanna. 1985. "Introduction." In *Reason and Morality*. Edited by Joanna Overing, 1–28. London: Tavistock.

Parish, Steven. 1994. *Moral Knowing in a Hindu Sacred City*. New York: Columbia University Press.

Parkin, David. 1985. "Introduction." In *The Anthropology of Evil*. Edited by David Parkin, 1–25. Oxford: Blackwell.

Pocock, David. 1985. "Unruly Evil." In *The Anthropology of Evil*. Edited by David Parkin, 42–56. Oxford: Blackwell.

———. 1986. "The Ethnography of Morals." *International Journal of Moral and Social Studies* 1: 3–20.

Ricoeur, Paul. 1986. *The Symbolism of Evil*. Boston, MA: Beacon.

———. 2007. *Evil: A Challenge to Philosophy and Theology*. London: Continuum.

Robbins, Joel. 2007. "Between Reproduction and Freedom: Morality, Value, and Radical Cultural Change." *Ethnos* 72: 293–314.

———. 2013. "Beyond the Suffering Subject: Toward an Anthropology of the Good." *Journal of the Royal Anthropological Institute* 19: 447–62.

Rorty, Amélie Oksenberg. 2001. "Varieties of Evil." In *The Many Faces of Evil*. Edited by Amélie Rorty, xi–xvii. London: Routledge.

Scheper-Hughes, Nancy. 1992. *Death Without Weeping*. Berkeley: University of California Press.

Scheper-Hughes, Nancy, and Philippe Bourgois. 2004. "Introduction." In *Violence in War and Peace*. Edited by Nancy Scheper-Hughes and Philippe Bourgois, 1–32. Oxford: Blackwell.

Sheets-Johnstone, Maxine. 2008. *The Roots of Morality*. College Station: Pennsylvania State University Press.

Smith, Daniel Jordan. 2014. *AIDS Doesn't Show Its Face*. Chicago: University of Chicago Press.

Stroeken, Koen. 2010. *Moral Power*. New York: Berghahn Books.

Svendsen, Lars. 2010. *A Philosophy of Evil*. Champaign, IL: Dalkey Archive Press.

Ter Haar, Gerrie, ed. 2007. *Imagining Evil*. Trenton, NJ: Africa World Press.

Van Beek, Walter, and William C. Olsen. 2015. "Introduction." In *Evil in Africa*. Edited by William C. Olsen and Walter van Beek, 1–28. Bloomington: Indiana University Press.

Wilkinson, Iain, and Arthur Kleinman. 2016. *A Passion for Society*. Berkeley: University of California Press.
Wolfram, Sybil. 1982. "Anthropology and Morality." *Journal of the Anthropological Society of Oxford* 13: 262–74.
Wright, Robin. 2004. "The Wicked and the Wise Men." In *In Darkness and Secrecy*. Edited by Neil Whitehead and Robin Wright, 82–108. Durham, NC: Duke University Press.
Zigon, Jarrett. 2008. *Morality*. Oxford: Berg.

PART I
―――――
Evil and Anthropology

Chapter 1

FROM THEODICY TO HOMODICY

EVIL AS AN ANTHROPOLOGICAL PROBLEM

Thomas J. Csordas

What should an anthropological theory of evil look like? First, it would have to recognize evil as both an analytical/etic and empirical/emic category relevant across cultures. That is, on the one hand, anthropologists would recognize evil as a concrete possibility in human relations, and on the other, ethnographers would document indigenous formulations of evil and lexical equivalents or approximations of words for "evil." Second, such a theory would be based on existential considerations, with the understanding that in some instances, evil could constitute a generalized mode of being, recognized as more or less common in a society, and in others, evil could be a characteristic or quality of particular actions or series of actions. Third, an anthropological theory would have to confront the ambiguity in understanding evil's locus and source as human or cosmological (supernatural or preternatural) and the manner in which this duality plays out in different societies and scenarios.

Finally, a theory of evil would require a minimal working definition that could survive comparison across modes of thinking and cultural contexts. The notion of malevolent destructiveness is the minimal definition that I prefer and propose. It is preferable, for example, to making evil a synonym of, and hence redundant with, violence, which is at least at first glance more easily identified empirically. Yet violence does not happen by itself—what matters is by whom and against whom it is committed. Moreover, if it is possible to refer to "violence in the most morally neutral sense of the term," as Derrida does in discussing the human subjection of animals (2008, 25), then what other than evil would we name the criterion under which the moral neutrality of violence is abrogated? Insofar as it is even possible to articulate phrases such as "justifiable homicide" or a "just war," it is evident that although all evil may be violent, not all violence is evil, and the problem of defining evil as such remains unaddressed (for valuable anthropological treatments of violence, see Das et al. 2000; Scheper-Hughes and Bourgois 2003).

Concern with evil is prompted in part by the current surge of interest in morality among anthropologists. If such an interest has not existed until now—and that is debatable—is it not pretentious to claim unselfconsciously that we are qualified at this moment to invent a moral anthropology? Such a move, if we are serious, means that we had better be prepared to confront and engage not only cultural relativism, which can be debated in a more or less theoretical and intellectually neutral manner, but also the far thornier issue of moral relativism. Cultural relativism is itself a moral stance that anthropologists like to think promotes tolerance; moral relativism is a challenge to the definition of morality that invites existential vertigo. The emerging anthropological models—moral anthropology, anthropology of morality, local moral worlds, anthropology of ethics (Csordas 2013)—presume actors who recognize moral challenges and want to make the morally best choice. They tend neither to theorize nor to address evil as such. Yet to elide the issue of evil is to dodge the question of morality; for in a sense, *if it wasn't for evil, morality would be moot*, or at least there would be far less at stake. This is the case whether one understands evil as undermining morality from the outside or as intrinsic to morality in a foundational sense. Does evil exist; and if so, in what sense? Does it make a difference to distinguish ontological, cultural, discursive, or personal understandings of evil in relation to morality? Is it possible to be/do evil and not know it? Under what conditions can evil be perpetrated in the name of good or god?

Writing at the beginning of the twenty-first century, philosopher Amélie Rorty (2001) observed that contemporary ethics and moral philosophy had "taken the high road," with philosophers formulating all kinds of moral ideals and discussion of moral evaluation while paying little attention to the "Dark Side." In presenting a compendium of the Western canon of thought on evil, Rorty herself declines to refer to evil as a generic category while accepting it as an umbrella concept, invoking the image of a messy family genealogy reminiscent of Wittgenstein's (1973) notion of family resemblance that recognizes multiple strands of commonality across different uses of a word without generic identity among the meanings of that word. A few pages later, she writes, "Evil may not be an ontological category or natural kind, but it seems a fundamental feature of human psychology that . . . we are revolted by actions that we classify as 'abominable,' 'evil,' 'inhuman'" (2001, xv). In the meantime, since this cautious and somewhat ambivalent take on the status of evil, there appears to have been a resurgence of interest in evil among philosophers (Badiou 2001 [1998]; Bernstein 2002; Cole 2006; Dews 2008; Midgely 2001; Ricoeur 2007; Sheets-Johnstone 2008; Svendsen 2010), while the new wave of anthropological writing on morality continues on what Rorty called the high road.

When I began to consider this issue, my intent was in part to point out the relative silence of current anthropological literature on the topic of evil and pose the question of whether this silence is sustainable (Csordas 2013). Upon presenting my argument that a critical engagement with the concept of evil is requisite in a cross-culturally valid approach to morality before an audience of anthropologists and other social scientists, I was surprised that the response included considerable apprehension and even resistance. One colleague asserted that evil is a purely mythological concept that should stay that way, and that raising the question of evil is dangerous, like letting a genie out of a bottle. Another colleague claimed that evil is a metaphysical category, and that it is better to focus on material categories such as murder, genocide, torture, rape, and slavery. But *as soon as one asks what these forms of abuse have in common*, one is hard pressed to find a more precisely descriptive word than *evil*. In this respect, it is less productive to frame the question in terms of an opposition between evil as a metaphysical category and other more material categories than to recognize evil as a general category with specific instances, or at least a useful umbrella concept (Rorty 2001; Svendsen 2010). My point in recalling these objections is that, given their reflex skepticism as to whether a critically refined concept of evil is necessary to understanding morality, the desire to keep this genie in its bottle may be less a matter of intellectual prudence and more a failure of intellectual nerve. The failure of nerve in demurring to name evil as such is ironic insofar as anthropologists display plenty of courage in addressing specific instances of violence, depravity, and their consequent suffering. In sum, it is critical to examine the cultural constitution of ethical life and the social foundations of morality, but to continue acknowledging only the good does not go beyond good and evil, it only sidesteps a problem that anthropology, for the most part, finds disturbing.

Whence the readiness to dismiss evil as a mythological or metaphysical category rather than elaborating it as a moral or existential one? It is in part due to a sense that evil is a "Christian concept" and therefore necessarily ethnocentric. This element of the problem was expressed in an email exchange among contributors to the present volume when Gananath Obeyesekere wrote that "as far as I know there is no notion of EVIL in the Buddhist tradition and I am not sure how you can relate it to the more complex traditions of Hinduism and Buddhism. EVIL seems to me to be such a Christian turn." Presentation of the word in all capital letters already presumes an objectified and essentialized evil, doubtless of little use anthropologically. Yet this comment raises a series of significant questions for how anthropology addresses evil. If Buddhism and Hinduism do not have an elaborated notion of evil, do they not have some formulations that bear a family resemblance to evil as malevolent destructiveness; and is it necessary that we find a notion similar to evil elaborated universally across religions in order for it to be useful? If evil is such a Christian turn, does this imply that evil is only relevant within Christianity and specifically in the way that Christianity elaborates it? Even more consequential from an anthropological standpoint, if Buddhism and Hinduism as religious systems do not elaborate evil, does this imply that evil cannot be perpetrated in Buddhist and Hindu societies? The Rohingya refugee crisis unfolded in a Buddhist society, Myanmar, whose government declared that people should not use the name "Rohingya"—do they also have the prerogative to abjure us from using the term *evil* in connection with this situation on the grounds that theirs is a Buddhist society? Finally, the comment refers specifically to religious systems. Does this imply that the anthropological study of morality cannot formulate a category of evil in human terms not beholden to religion? Wouldn't that miss the opportunity to challenge the hegemony of that very Christian notion of evil to which Obeyesekere refers? In fact, given that evil or its cognates are broadly identifiable across cultures (evidenced in the contributions to the present volume), the anthropological reticence may stem less from a concern that evil is inherently Christian than from an uneasiness that, since the Christian concept of evil is hegemonic in Western civilization, our own analytic purview might be occluded by a lingering veil of Christian sensibility. The appropriate response, I suggest, is not to abjure the concept, but to insist that critical reflection be applied in deploying "evil" in a way that is not beholden to Christian presuppositions or the presuppositions of any other religious system. Indeed, Nietzsche (1967) argued that the very concept of evil originated as a product of class antagonism.

It would be naïve to think that overcoming this lingering hegemonic sensibility can be achieved with a snap of the fingers. In any case, to argue that evil be excluded from the study of morality on the grounds that it is necessarily mythological, metaphysical, or religious is to invoke a line of thinking applicable to morality itself. Nietzsche asserted, "'Every evil the sight of which edifies a god is justified': thus spoke the primitive logic of feeling—and was it, indeed, only primitive?" (1967, 69). He thus points to the facility with which evil can be transposed into goodness not only in the mythological primitive but the secularized modern mentality. Alain Badiou (in commenting on Levinas) claimed, "Every effort to turn ethics into the principle of thought and action is essentially religious" (2001, 223), thus suggesting that a foregrounding of morality and ethics such as that currently proposed in anthropology may already fall under the category of the religious, even prior to including within it a critical assessment of evil. It is in this context that we must face that there is within the existential structure of evil a challenge for anthropology parallel to the challenge for philosophy and theology identified by Ricouer, namely "the parallel demonization that makes suffering and sin the expression of the same baneful powers. It is never completely demythologized" (2007, 38). The structural duality of sin and suffering in itself affirms that an anthropology of morality must acknowledge at its very source the enigma of evil. This does not simply mean that an anthropological approach to morality must execute comparative, cross-cultural study. It also requires a specification of how an anthropological approach to morality itself defines evil as a demythologized human phenomenon. Is there a better dichotomy (or continuum) than good/evil, such as benevolent/malevolent or life-affirming/destructive? Would we be satisfied with a morally neutral "dangerous" instead of evil?

Given the challenge of defining evil as a demythologized human phenomenon, we can usefully recall David Parkin's distinction among three senses in which we typically use the word evil: "the moral, referring to human culpability; the physical, by which is understood destructive elemental forces of nature, for example earthquakes, storms, or the plague; and the metaphysical, by which disorder in the cosmos or in relations with divinity results from a conflict of principles or wills" (1985, 15). These are all traditionally implicated in the problem of theodicy, but the first takes priority in a study such as ours. Moreover, when we refer to a human phenomenon, it is critical to take "phenomenon" in the specific sense of what appears in perception of self and other, relations and actions within the intersubjective lifeworld, and what comes to apperception in the process of meaning-making. As anthropologists concerned with meaning, we are not obligated to understand evil as a thing or substance (if it were, it would have to be as a noxious existential secretion), neither as a cosmological force or ontological element of the universe (whether personified or not). For Geertz, "the problem of meaning" was defined by "the existence of bafflement, pain, and moral paradox" (1973, 109). The problem of (or about) evil is the same sort of problem, closely related to but not the same as the problem of suffering and, in Geertz's words, "concerned with threats to our ability to make sound moral judgments. What is involved in the problem of evil is not the adequacy of our symbolic resources to govern our affective life, but the adequacy of those resources to provide a workable set of ethical criteria, normative guides to govern our action" (1973, 106). In other words, evil is fundamentally implicated in morality and ethics, and all are bound up with meaning.

Insofar as meaning, morality, and evil are fundamentally human phenomena, and recognizing that neologism and barbarism are close kin in language, I want to say that, as anthropologists rather than theologians, our concern is not with theodicy but with homodicy. The difference between understanding evil as a cosmological force and a human phenomenon is vivid in a comparison between two famous literary doctors: Faust and Jekyll. The real-life model of Faust is said to have been a disreputable alchemist, what a more recent era would call a mad scientist. Parkin has observed: "Mephistopheles represented to Faust not just evil, but an experience that could not be obtained by either divine or secular means. The devil for, let us say, the reckless, brave, and foolish here offers a third world" (1985, 19). In this scenario, evil is a force external to humans, a cosmic force that, personified as the devil, has its own agenda, motives, and modus operandum. It can be negotiated within the sense of making a Faustian bargain, but it can also be prevailed against and even tricked so that the protagonist takes on a heroic cast as a representative of humanity independent of both god and the devil. Recall that though Marlowe's Faust loses his soul, Goethe's Faust is saved in the end. Even Marlowe's doomed Faust has moral qualms and second thoughts throughout, maintaining some identity as a sympathetic, if tragic, figure.

Our other literary doctor is less ambiguous, a better example of evil as a purely human phenomenon. The mad scientist Dr. Jekyll was not compelled by the limits of knowledge and wisdom to seek a supernatural solution to his quest for enhanced pleasure and human fulfillment. For him, excess was transmuted into malevolence as he literally became addicted to evil. By the end, one has to suspect that the potion did not actually transform the mild and moral Dr. Jekyll, but in fact brought out Mr. Hyde as his true self—monstrous and evil. If an anthropological study of morality is addressed to the question of what it means to be human—synonymous with the question of defining human nature—this possibility of evil cannot be dodged. The likelihood that Jekyll did not initially realize that he was flirting with and then succumbing to evil enhances the tragedy and, for us, defines the conceptual ground upon which an anthropological approach to morality can be constructed.

Let us take one more step toward defining this ground. Building on the minimal anthropological definition of evil as malevolent destructiveness that I proposed above, let us add an elementary structure to that destructiveness. The basic insight is that evil can have its locus at either a collective or interpersonal level, and that its mode of agency can be active or passive. These two dimensions generate an elementary structure as depicted in figure 1.1, with full acknowledgment of structuralism's identification of the importance of binary opposition in human culture and consciousness. The distinction between collective and interpersonal is, in the first instance, a matter of scale, but it is also of consequence that evil perpetrated at the interpersonal level can more readily remain secret, darkness that remains in the dark. The distinction between active and passive in this instance is between hatred as onrushing annihilation and disregard as a careless turning away, where "careless" is understood as both without caution and without care. The two-by-two table generated by this elementary structure

	Collective	**Interpersonal**
Active	Genocide	Murder
Passive	Environmental degradation	Abandonment

Figure 1.1 Elementary structure of evil. Figure created by the author.

can be populated by ideal types of genocide as active collective evil, murder as active interpersonal evil, environmental degradation as passive collective evil, and abandonment as passive interpersonal evil.

This formulation of an elementary structure is provisional, and certainly we could and would have to elaborate the contents of each of the cells. One pertinent question already evident is how to treat the passive evil of disregard, first of all with respect to whether evil resides in intention or in consequence. The example of environmental degradation is a consequence that can be described as evil, but the industrialists whose explicit intention is to maximize profits do not necessarily also have the intention of degrading the environment. Passively not knowing the results of one's actions is not an excuse, but it is a problem for the theory of evil. Is not knowing the same as being unaware? Does the question of why one does not know come into play along with questions of denial, repression, and self-deception? Opening the door to such questions is as far as we can go here, and it comes with the anthropological formulation of evil as a human phenomenon fundamentally bound up with the problem of meaning.

Lord of the Flies

The idea that evil is a human phenomenon to be understood in human terms rather than a religious notion does not preclude the study of evil in religious settings. Quite the contrary, it invites a perspective that incorporates or encompasses evil in both religious and secular contexts, including contexts defined by Christianity. In this section, I want to illustrate the fact that even when one can agree that evil is present in a scenario, it is subject to various interpretations with respect to whether its source is human or divine, natural or supernatural, with consequent modulations in how evil is constituted as a meaningful human phenomenon. The scenario I will consider is the one portrayed in William Golding's novel *Lord of the Flies*. The central image here is undoubtedly Christian, since this appellation is one found in the Bible and refers to Satan. The scenario in the novel most definitely includes malevolent destructiveness in existential immediacy, and is subject to radically different interpretations, two of which I will compare. The first is presented by psychoanalyst Nathalie Zaltzman in the opening chapter of her book *L'Esprit du Mal*, entitled "Children are Pigs." The second is by a Roman Catholic priest who is both a theologian and an exorcist and uses a film version of *Lord of the Flies* in a course on exorcism he teaches to seminarians. In brief, in the psychoanalytic interpretation, evil is understood under the sign of *regression*, while in the exorcistic interpretation, evil is understood under the sign of *possession*.

The plot of the novel centers on a group of young boys stranded on a tropical island when the plane carrying their school chorale crashes and leaves all adults dead. Tragedy ensues as the boys succumb to fear and malevolent destruction, first killing a wild pig and then two of their own comrades. Granted that the Lord of the Flies is an appellation of the devil in the Judaeo-Christian tradition, both the psychoanalytic and Catholic interpretations are unequivocally in accord that the fictional scenario bears a deep truth about evil. Zaltzman begins by challenging Freud's observation that although taboo as ritualized prohibition has remained a constant throughout the development of culture and civilization, totemism as collective identification with a symbol eventually became archaic and obsolete. She sees the realistic vividness of the conch and the severed pig's head as totems uniting one group of boys around reasonable coexistence under the sign of the word and language and another around what I would call malevolent destructiveness under the sign of action and murder. This is a form of psychic regression, but neither to a previous state of culture nor to an earlier developmental stage of the individual. It is a narcissistic regression that is both individual and collective; in fact, it has to do precisely with the place of the individual in the group in the context of a dehumanization that goes counter to the work of culture as it takes place both in psychoanalysis and in, optimistically, the progression of human history.

In fact, there is here a radical difference from either the primitive or childish states of being because both are highly moralized. The presences of the word, of the father, and of ritual means of observation, expiation, creation, and commemoration are already present in both states. Indeed, even the instance of murder is marked and ritualized. Zaltzman suggests instead that in the kind of regression portrayed in Golding's scenario, something new emerges. We could certainly call it a state of being (Dasein in Heidegger's sense), a state characterized as unrestrained and uninhibited malevolence—or in abbreviated form, evil. This regression produces, generates, or projects an image of itself that is simultaneously its existential concreteness, and that phenomenological kernel constitutes a deity, a purely originary crystallization of evil. *Originary* is the word I use to capture Zaltzman's emphasis that this is not a derivative being in the sense that the Christian Satan is a fallen angel, never more than a creature. Golding captures the essential nature of this spirit when he has it say to the protagonist just before the moment of his murder, "I am part of you. Intimately part of you, intimately."

The Catholic priest with whom I spoke taught a course in systematic theology about exorcism to seminarians, the syllabus of which included viewing contemporary films and learning to analyze the scenarios presented from the standpoint of an exorcist intent on identifying demonic influence. These films included not only the genre about actual exorcism, though such films are frequently based on actual cases (e.g., *The Exorcist*, *The Exorcism of Emily Rose*, *The Rite*, *The Conjuring*), but also several others in the plots of which the priest attempted to teach students to identify patterns of evil (*Emerald Forest*, *Eyes Wide Shut*, *Lord of the Flies*). The priest uses the film version of Golding's novel to illustrate a pattern of possession in which vulnerability induced by trauma is exploited by demons to gain purchase on the traumatized person.

To be precise, if after their rescue an exorcist were to interview the plane-wrecked boys who succumbed to violent impulses, they might provide a narrative that some of what they did was accidental or perhaps just a game. But in thinking like an exorcist,

> You have to divorce the narrative from the particular line of behavior. And carefully trace what is perhaps the most important thing to look for, and that is destruction. Most especially murder. That's what you trace.... What's important is that you see the possessed person drawn into what the liturgy refers to as Satan's Fruits. He is the father of lies and the father of murder. And all the boys do to describe this will be one kind of lie or another. Simon attacked us, or Piggy we didn't mean it, or Jack was an idiot, or . . . I'm not listening to that. I have to plug my ears when I'm listening to a narrative and watch only for the things that show me if demons are present here. The rule of thumb is destruction. Destruction of relationships, destruction of human lives, destruction of property, people, things, destruction of emotional life, interior life, faith, confidence in one's self, psychological health, it's about destruction. (Catholic priest—personal interview)

Through taking a close personal history, this priest would have to focus on tracing demonic activity and not listen to explanations that would obscure demonic influence.

In the story, the exorcist observes a progression from enshrining a pig's head on a stick to placing the head in a cave with one of the dead pilots, and the pig begins to speak. A child trauma specialist interviewing the boys after their rescue might say that this is hallucination brought on by severe deprivation and separation anxiety, but it's right after the pig begins to speak that the murders start. So from the standpoint of an exorcist, "This is an example of a possession. And even though the boys are now back and they are out of the influence of that island and whatever happened there, it doesn't for an instant mean that their contact with the demonic first made there is finished. They brought it back with them" (Catholic priest—personal interview). What psychotherapy and exorcism do have in common is recognition that an unresolved issue remains unresolved until a person does something about it—but what the "it" is remains radically different.

This kind of exegesis provides an insight into the indigenous ontology and rationality underlying the practice of Catholic exorcism. It is an ontology in which evil is an active, agentive presence that can be identified if one knows what to look for. Evil appears in the interstices of everyday life, in the all but invisible folds of the ordinary. This is why the term "preternatural" is more accurate than "supernatural" for describing the phenomenology of exorcistic practice. I use the term phenomenology in its precise sense of the phenomenon as something that appears in reality and indeed defines reality, because evil is an empirical phenomenon for the exorcist. Moreover, it is an intersubjective phenomenon insofar as what is interpreted as evil is understood to be so because it takes the form of an "ontological entity" that is personal in nature, and not at all in normal circumstances "intimately a part of you." There is no question of the collective in this drama of the individual soul and the kind of relationship it has with the divine: devotion or domination, intimacy or bondage, nurturance or destruction, authority or rebellion, word or action, benevolence or malevolence.

Malediction, Exorcism, and Evil

In the preceding section, I examined a scenario of malevolent destructiveness, comparing an anthropocentric (psychoanalytic) and theological (Roman Catholic) account. In this section, I will examine a circumstance entirely within a religious setting in which human and supernatural agencies are understood to inform and interact with one another. A widespread practice in which human malevolence is mingled with powers beyond the human is malediction, or cursing. It is best to begin by considering the word "malediction" in the simple sense (if there is ever such a thing) of speaking evil or evil-saying. The idea of evil—*male*—is conceptually, existentially, morally, and cosmologically complex, so I want to focus first on the saying—*diction*. Consider first an explicit utterance in what seems to me the relatively straightforward form of "hurling epithets." This phrase is felicitous, to use a word reminiscent of John Austin's reflections on speech acts, because the notion of hurling emphasizes the physical, embodied, material aspect of malediction as a rhetorical performance. The same recognition of the physicality of utterance is needed to understand why the children's retort to the bully, "Sticks and stones may break my bones, but names will never hurt me," is simply wrong. Names are hurtful insofar as they are no less material than sticks or stones when they are hurled and hit their mark.

Malediction in the form of hurling epithets is not as simple as it may at first seem, however. There is a fundamental difference between the utterances "You bastard!" and "Go to hell!" The first expresses malevolence or ill will with reference to an imputed personal characteristic that bespeaks illegitimacy. The second, as watered-down and secularized as it may be in colloquial usage, has reference to a supernatural and cosmological domain that remains deeply resonant even in secular settings and across religious traditions. In short, the malediction "You bastard!" is an insult. "Go to hell!" is a curse. The difference is not only one of degree, but one of fundamental type.

The supernatural/cosmological dimension tapped by full blown malediction opens onto the existential/moral question of whether evil—specifically the motivation of hatred and destruction—is a function (or perhaps better said, a modality) of the human or the divine. In this section, I will bring to the table one ethnographic fact about malediction that can serve as an occasion of reflection on this issue. The fact comes from my research on Roman Catholic exorcism in the United States and Italy. In both settings, exorcists encounter not only the extraordinary action of demons, but also the effects of curses imposed by other people—and the two are sometimes closely intertwined. In Italy, there is a deep-seated cultural elaboration of curses in everyday life, with the possibility of spoken curse (maledizione), a curse placed in an object that can come in contact with the intended victim (fattura), and the curse that can be transmitted by a malevolent or envious glance of the evil eye (malocchio). There is the social presence of the witch (fattuchiera or strega) and the magician or wizard (mago or stregone). Exorcists in North America also report such practices and practitioners, at least among certain segments of the population and in relation to certain dark forms of occult practice or the non-Christian religion of some immigrant groups.

The key ethnographic fact I want to emphasize is how the notion of malediction penetrates to and is deeply implicated in the practice of exorcism. While its associated practices may be considered superstitious by the Church, they are still recognized as dangerous and not to be dismissed or taken lightly. Often, this follows a cultural script, such as (especially in Italy) customary antipathy between mother-in-law and daughter-in-law. More important for the present discussion is how the exorcist is just as likely to encounter a curse as an evil spirit. How does the religious system construe this form of human aggression and malevolence in relation to demonic aggression and malevolence?

The answer appears to be that malediction is coopted by and subsumed under demonic activity in a particular way. They are not two separate problems encountered by the exorcist, for in practice, the ritual charge of the exorcist is not to counteract spells but to cast out demons. Neither is it necessarily understood that the witch or wizard operates by conjuring an evil spirit to perpetrate harm on a victim. Instead, the hatred manifest in the curse "opens the door" to demonic activity—one might interpret this in a more phenomenological sense by saying that hatred *is* a door through which Satan acquires access or gains purchase on lives. In this sense, malediction may not have a direct effect, but creates or exploits a weakness or vulnerability to demonic affliction in the victim. By the same token, the perpetrator of the curse becomes, wittingly or unwittingly, an agent or pawn of Satan to the peril of his/her own soul. The one who curses may not explicitly invoke the devil, but implicitly invites the devil. In this way, malediction may be understood as superstitious, but nevertheless thought to have a real and negative spiritual effect that transcends the realm of human emotion and agency.

The ethnographic fact of malediction subsumed under demonic affliction in contemporary Catholic exorcism offers the opportunity for reflection on the problem of evil. Evidently, malediction is subordinated to the cosmological struggle between good and evil as embodied and personified in God and Satan. This is a religious message of exorcism and also part of its commentary on the presence of evil in the world of today. As an element of therapeutic process, it may have the effect, beneficial or not, of displacing a certain amount of responsibility and guilt in a fraught interpersonal situation within the lived experience of a demonically afflicted person. More broadly, it raises the question of whether evil is an individual trait or an ontological entity. If the latter, is it personified as a kind of sentient being? This touches on the difference between saying someone is an evil person, that someone is evil incarnate, or that someone is possessed by evil. If we start from the human side, add the ontological, and personify that, we get demonology. If we start from the religious side, challenge faith, and humanize that, we get sociopathy. In one case, the explanation of evil requires a supporting theodicy; in the other, an acknowledgment of what we can only call homodicy.

Ontology and Evil

These considerations bring us to the observation that anthropologists have taken a keen interest in ontology in the past few years, to the point where some have advertised an "ontological turn" in the discipline's attempt to understand culture and experience (Holbraad and Pedersen 2017). This is in part connected with a new willingness to entertain a dialogue with philosophy as a discipline and recognition that anthropology and philosophy often ask the same questions. I think this is a good thing in general, and I am of the opinion that the only real difference between philosophers and us anthropologists is that we have data, the data of ethnography. When it comes to ontology, however, I am not convinced anthropologists are equipped to address it, and this is evidenced by the squeamishness of addressing in particular the question of evil even in recent discussions of morality. It is even more relevant in discussions of ontology, where if anthropologists are serious about the matter, they can hardly avoid the question of the existence of evil in human affairs.

Indeed, the alternate interpretations of *Lord of the Flies* according to *regression* and *possession* raise the question of whether evil knows itself as such unless it has a contrast (love, care) against which to confirm itself. Perhaps pure evil does not know itself as such if it is malevolent destructiveness unchecked and unselfconscious, entirely outside the work of culture. Zaltzman's exposition suggests that it exists as a force and symbol, not a mode of being in the world because it is a deity in its own primordial right, a singularity and not a fallen angel fully aware of its origin as a creature of God. In the exorcist's version, Satan is irredeemable because of an irrevocable exercise of free will; in the psychoanalytic version, the question of redeemability never arises because the deity is generated directly from the human psyche. Moreover, as a fallen angel, Satan is entirely part of the work of culture, not only a foil for the divine but integral to it, as in the magical realist novel *Mulata* by Miguel Asturias, in which the inevitability of European conquest of autochthonous South American deities was made clear in the revelation that the Christian God and devil were fully in collaboration to ensure the Conquest. Within the ritual world defined by exorcism, where we encounter *malediction* intimately intertwined with *possession*, the curse goes beyond mere sin, which is anything that challenges divine will and opens one to demonic vulnerability but can be dealt with via the sacrament of confession. Uttering the curse is sin but also a malevolence that partakes of the demonic form and hence comes under the purview of the exorcist. It exists at the juncture of the cosmological and anthropological.

Cultural elaborations of evil that include the divine, supernatural, preternatural, or magical do not require an ontological commitment on the part of the anthropologist. Variations of malevolent destructiveness offer empirical instances of and for the kind of imaginative free variation that phenomenology prescribes as a method, helping to describe the constitution of reality as an existential phenomenon, and hence a distinctly human phenomenon. Further examination of the implications and consequences for lived experience of the kinds of scenarios I have considered here can contribute to the cultural phenomenology of evil, or the understanding of evil as a meaningful human phenomenon.

Thomas J. Csordas, UC San Diego

Acknowledgments

My research on Roman Catholic Exorcism was supported by a grant from the Social Science Research Council's initiative on New Directions in the Study of Prayer.

References

Asturias, Miguel Angel. 1982. *Mulata*. Translated by Gregory Rabassa. New York: Dell.
Badiou, Alain. 2001 (1998). *Ethics: An Essay on the Understanding of Evil*. London: Verso.
Bernstein, Richard. 2002. *Radical Evil: A Philosophical Interrogation*. Cambridge, MA: Polity.
Cole, Philip. 2006. *The Myth of Evil: Demonizing the Enemy*. New York: Praeger.
Csordas, Thomas J. 2013. "Morality as a Cultural System?" *Current Anthropology* 54(5): 523–46.
Das, Veena, Arthur Kleinman, Mamphela Ramphele, and Pamela Reynolds, eds. 2000. *Violence and Subjectivity*. Berkeley: University of California Press.

Derrida, Jacques. 2008. *The Animal That Therefore I Am*. Edited by Marie-Louise Mallet. Translated by David Wills. New York: Fordham University Press.
Dews, Peter. 2008. *The Idea of Evil*. Oxford: Blackwell.
Geertz, Clifford. 1973. *The Interpretation of Cultures*. New York: Basic Books.
Holbraad, Martin, and Morten Axel Pedersen. 2017. *The Ontological Turn: An Anthropological Exposition*. Cambridge, UK: Cambridge University Press.
Midgely, Mary. 2001. *Wickedness*. 2nd ed. London: Routledge.
Nietzsche, Friedrich. 1967. *On the Genealogy of Morals*. Translated by Walter Kaufmann and R. J. Hollingdale. New York: Vintage Books.
Parkin, David. 1985. "Introduction." In *The Anthropology of Evil*. Edited by David Parkin, 1–25. Oxford: Blackwell.
Ricoeur, Paul. 2007. *Evil: A Challenge to Philosophy and Theology*. London: Continuum.
Rorty, Amélie Oksenberg. 2001. "Varieties of Evil." In *The Many Faces of Evil*. Edited by Amélie Rorty, xi–xvii. London: Routledge.
Scheper-Hughes, Nancy, and Philippe Bourgois, eds. 2003. *Violence in War and Peace: An Anthology*. Oxford: Blackwell.
Sheets-Johnstone, Maxine. 2008. *The Roots of Morality*. College Station: Penn State University Press.
Svendsen, Lars. 2010. *A Philosophy of Evil*. Champaign, IL: Dalkey Archive Press.
Wittgenstein, Ludwig. 1973. *Philosophical Investigations*. 3rd ed. Translated by G.E.M. Anscombe. New York: Pearson.
Zaltzman, Nathalie. 2007. *L'Esprit du Mal*. Paris: Editions de l'Olivier.

Chapter 2

ON THE CONCEPT OF "EVIL" IN ANTHROPOLOGICAL ANALYSES OF POLITICAL VIOLENCE

Byron J. Good

When Bill Olsen wrote to invite me to join the discussions that led to this book, I responded in an email: "I have qualms about the use of moral categories in anthropological analysis, but I am tempted to join this fine group. I work in settings of serious violence. I have avoided confronting the question of when to use the term evil in this context, and to what end. But this remains an open and important issue." My intuition, which made its way into my abstract for that discussion, was that anthropologists should indeed investigate how persons in other societies use a concept (or concepts) akin to "evil," and in what contexts and how this term translates to diverse Euro-American concepts of evil. The importance of studying local moral systems and concepts that might be translated as "evil" seems to me noncontroversial; the project is important and largely unrealized. However, the abstract for the original discussion framed the issue differently: "The 21st century is fraught with evil," it began. "Evil resides at local, national, and international levels. . . . How is evil recognized? What is the impact of evil upon a community or a nation? How is evil normalized, maintained or restricted?" In that framing, evil was not placed in quotation marks, as a local category. Evil was represented as a taken-for-granted reality in the world, as well as an analytic category for anthropology. Here, my intuition was to reject this implied claim, to raise broad questions about the place of moral categories within anthropological analysis, but more specifically to reject the use of "evil" as an anthropological category. This chapter began as a reflection on that immediate intuition about the place of evil in anthropological analyses.

The Introduction to this volume provides a more nuanced framing of the issues: "We explore the anthropology of evil as an empirical human phenomenon—an existential/moral feature of human thought and communal or social relations—and the value of evil as a methodological construct ..." (Olsen and Csordas 2019). But questions concerning the nature of "evil" as an "empirical human phenomenon" and whether evil, which I consider a moral construct, should serve as an analytic category for anthropology are still raised by this framing. My intuition remains to question these basic premises. This chapter, then, is an attempt to explore this intuition from a number of perspectives.

A few more words by way of introduction: I consider myself a deeply engaged medical, psychological, and psychiatric anthropologist. For the past decade, much of my life has been consumed by collaborating with colleagues in Indonesia attempting to build improved mental health services in their communities: in Aceh, following the great tsunami of 2004 and the peace agreement that ended a civil war; and in Yogyakarta, where our group is trying to develop an evidence-based mental health services model to provide care for a population of 3.5 million people with approximately thirty psychiatrists. I am driven in part by my horror at listening to stories of torture of men, women, and children in Aceh, and by my shock and sense of outrage at seeing persons with psychotic illness living in chains or confined to tiny rooms or cages without receiving any regular medical care. For me, this work is not lacking in moral import. I am not troubled about talking about social justice and care for the poor and disadvantaged as a motivating force for my work, and although I have some qualms about the universalizing claims of human rights discourse, that discourse has become a powerful force for political change in Indonesian society and for advocacy for persons with severe mental illness around the world. Why then am I troubled by the potential for "evil" to be used as a category within anthropology? Why is my initial intuition so strongly against making this category central, even in settings of mass violence and killings such as those that engulfed Indonesia in 1965, or in discussing the systematic torture of Acehnese civilians by Indonesian special forces? These are the questions I reflect on briefly in this chapter.

My data come from working in Indonesia for the past twenty-two years, and in particular the work Professor Mary-Jo DelVecchio Good and I did in postconflict communities in Aceh following the December

26, 2004, tsunami that killed approximately 180,000 people, which led in turn to the signing of the Helsinki peace accords on August 15, 2005, ending a decade and a half of a bloody conflict between Indonesian military forces and those of the Free Aceh Movement.[1] In November 2005, we began consulting for the International Organization for Migration (IOM) concerning mental health strategies in previously high conflict areas of Aceh. By February 2006, we were accompanying IOM research teams into villages of three districts of Aceh to conduct a survey designed to guide IOM in launching post-conflict mental health programs, to which we were deeply committed for five years, work which continues in other forms today.

The survey we helped lead produced an outpouring of stories of violence and torture enacted by the Indonesian military. In one village, our interviewers left in such shock that Jesse Grayman, our then graduate student, collaborator, and coordinator of the IOM survey, arranged for the organization to send a mobile mental health team for a visit to this village. This visit turned out to be critical for the mental health intervention project we helped IOM design. Our notes and memories from that visit give a small picture of the phenomena that open questions about how to write and think anthropologically about conflict and violence.

On February 15, 2006, we joined a group of Acehnese doctors and nurses, including a deeply committed local psychiatrist, and a guide who was a former leader of the Free Aceh Movement (Gerakan Aceh Merdeka—GAM), in a caravan of four-wheel drive vehicles, marked with the blue and white symbols of IOM, up into the hills of North Aceh.[2] We passed untended rice fields and overgrown pinang gardens and burned out hulks of houses along the side of the deeply rutted, muddy road, finally stopping in a shabby village center, with a few nearly empty shops, where people had begun to gather, expecting our visit. We were greeted with coffee, cigarettes, and small talk, which gradually turned more somber as people began to refer to the events of the conflict. After a short time, we walked to the *meunasah*, the village center, where we were met by a tall, thin man in his forties wailing loudly as his friends tried to support him. The doctor preceded him up the stairs to a large, open room, where the two sat, facing each other, surrounded by a growing crowd of villagers, and opened his "trauma clinic." My scribbled handwritten notes report the following:

> In April of 2004, men in black shirts came at 4 a.m. and accused this man of being a spy for GAM. They beat him, bound his hands and legs, tied a plastic bag over his head, suffocated him, hung him on a pole like a goat, beat him many times, smashed his head, and left him for dead.

The villagers found him and released him. But since then, he can't sleep, he can't work, he can't take care of his family, and he cries constantly. The doctor took control, grabbed his hands, said a prayer with him, calmed him, took his blood pressure, and gave him an injection of a sedative, and the man is soon sleeping quietly.

Thunder and lightning accompanied a tropical downpour, as one by one, villagers came to speak with the doctor. A woman tells her story. Her husband was taken in 1990, he was cut open, his heart was taken out, he was killed in front of her and her children. Her child had a gun put to his throat. She has a pain in her heart, she feels sad, easily frightened. She was dragged by the soldiers, then fell unconscious. She still feels pain in her back. They killed her husband in front of her daughter and her children. Her daughter was covered by a cloth, so she didn't have to see. They cut off his ear and put it in the *meunasah*. She doesn't know where his head was put. She suddenly makes a joke, and the mood lightens.

A woman approaches the doctor crying, telling how she was tortured, her toenails torn out, beaten. TNI (the Indonesian military) members kept asking her where GAM is. She didn't know. Her husband was taken, her house was burned, and even now, she doesn't know where her husband is, though this happened in 2004. He wasn't a GAM member, but he was accused and tortured, as they asked, "Where is GAM? Where are the weapons?" She was suspected of cooking food for GAM. A second group of soldiers came and asked her, "Where is the flag of Indonesia? Why don't you report to us?" She finally escaped to the forest, where she hid for seven days and nights, afraid she would be beaten again.

And so the stories went on, for nearly five hours—until the doctor had had all he could take and asked a trainer from the local soccer team to massage him. We all relaxed for a bit, then took our leave.

Mary-Jo and I spent five years leading a project that took mobile teams of doctors and nurses up into these conflict-affected villages to listen to stories and provide mental health care. Like many anthropologists who work in such settings, we heard unfathomable stories of violence and cruelty, producing images that live with us until today. We heard stories of remarkable resilience, of women defending men and their houses (M. Good 2015). Villagers commented on the cruelty or evil (*jahat*) of the Indonesian soldiers involved in the violence, although this was not central to most discussions. And we had the enormous satisfaction of watching communities recover—in what was a genuine "*post*conflict" setting—and watching those who had suffered lasting trauma respond to treatment and put the horror of the events into their past. Like all who have worked in such settings, we were not left unscathed by the horror of what we heard.

Listening to stories of terror and violence—many more graphic than I am willing to commit to writing—raised for me, particularly intensely during the time I was going into the field with our Acehnese mental health teams, fundamental questions about human nature, about human propensity for cruelty, as well as about the social organization of violence and links between subjectivity and organized violence. It would not be difficult to describe the events we heard about in Aceh—or other examples of violence that haunt Indonesia, Indonesians, and those of us who work there to this day—as "evil." Why, then, my intuition not to analyze these phenomena as an anthropology of evil? Is it simply that I come to these issues primarily as a psychological anthropologist, rather than via the anthropology of morality? Or are there other reasons, both theoretical and personal, to support my initial intuition? Given the limits of this chapter, I want to place for brief discussion several issues that deserve more time and reflection. I do so in conversation with two primary texts: Amélie Rorty's *The Many Faces of Evil* (2001) and Judith Butler's *Giving an Account of Oneself* (2005).

In the Preface to her remarkable sourcebook, *The Many Faces of Evil*, Amélie Rorty observes that most philosophers and ethicists these days focus on the virtues and on rational means for determining right actions. "Few ethical theorists," she writes, "have anatomized varieties of sheer wickedness or discussed the lures of sin, evil, immorality, cruelty" (2001, xi). The "Dark Side," she says, has been left for legal theorists, psychologists and psychiatrists, social scientists, filmmakers, and novelists. The same focus on virtue over the "Dark Side" has been true for many who argue for an "ethical turn" in anthropology (Zigon and Throop 2014, 2). Indeed, most notably perhaps, Robbins's (2013) call for "an anthropology of the good" is juxtaposed precisely to an anthropology that attends to "the subject living in pain, in poverty, or under conditions of violence or oppression" (448). Robbins caricatures a large body of work as constituting the "suffering slot" in anthropology. "Suffering slot ethnography," he argues, "is secure in its knowledge of good and evil and works toward achieving progress in the direction of its already widely accepted models of good" (2013, 456). While use of the term "suffering slot" is rhetorically understandable, such an argument fundamentally misrepresents the struggle of many anthropologists who work in settings of violence or postconflict to make sense of what they have seen. In the process, this term also demeans those with whom many anthropologists work. If indeed there is to be an ethical turn within anthropology, it ignores, at its peril, the "Dark Side," pain, poverty, violence, and oppression, as well as those who suffer their consequences.

In any analyses of the kind of violence I describe above, I personally begin with an assumption that human nature and our social worlds are profoundly irrational, that any ethics of principles and rational logics fails to address adequately the irrational, and that anthropologists should be included among those who reflect on the Dark Side. I thus strongly support the overall thrust of this volume. The question is whether the language of evil is the most useful way to pursue such reflections. I am interested, on the one hand, in the status of "evil" as a phenomenological and conceptual category, and, on the other, in the relationships between psychological and social analyses of such cruelty and violence and moral analyses. These are the issues I want to take up here.

Rorty's collection is a reminder of the enormous conceptual diversity of evil historically in the broad set of traditions that have contributed to Western philosophical and religious reflection. Her brief but piercing Introduction to the volume and the rich set of historical documents she gathers together demonstrate extraordinarily diverse, often sharply conflicting understandings of "evil," ranging from Manichean views of the essential duality of the universe, or the Gnostic understanding of the war between Darkness and Light, to the early Hebrew tradition in which the Jewish community related to God as the giver of laws and prohibitions, with evil conceived as the breaking of God's laws.[3] Augustine and early Christians saw the willful, lustful body at war with the good; Luther understood humans as essentially and hopelessly depraved, rescuable only by the enormous grace of God. More modern, equally diverse formulations include romanticized visions of evil, as well as evil represented by the cruelty of everyday life—including Hannah Arendt's important, albeit controversial, arguments about the banality of evil. Evil is thus variously associated, as the works Rorty has gathered together show, with disobedience or disorder, with sin and vice, with willfulness, waywardness, and everyday cruelty, with individual acts as well as bureaucratic structures, each contributing to a complex vocabulary for evil. Rorty sides in the end with Nietzsche's view of the hazards of dichotomizing Good and Evil, which potentially reduces the rich language we have for types of cruelty, violence, and immorality under an implied unitary conception of evil. She strongly supports, however, explorations of diverse phenomena of the Dark Side and engagement with the philosophical and religious traditions that provide moral framing for efforts to understand their place in the world.

My point in briefly noting the fundamental diversity of concepts of evil is to argue that an anthropology of evil cannot simply provide rich reflections on particular examples of what the author assumes all will immediately intuit as evil—the holocaust and other mass killings, the slave trade, racism, child victimization, torture, and so on—assuming this constitutes an analytic field and a mode of analysis, without positioning the discussion of evil relative to fundamentally different understandings of what this term refers to. Such an anthropology cannot be "secure in its knowledge of good and evil," as Robbins claims the anthropologists of "suffering" are, cannot simply provide thick descriptions of that which we assume will provoke horror, but must instead be positioned within existing discourses. This critique is, of course, only an entrée to a broader conversation of the kind evoked in this book. However, it is important to recognize that what any given anthropologist—or others concerned about these issues—intuits to be the meaning of "evil" may vary widely from any other (cf. Fischer 2012).

This leads to my second point. Individual intuitions about moral concepts vary enormously, and are by no means completely predictable based on knowing what religious or moral tradition the individual has grown up in. They are not simply reflections of cultural norms and values, or culturally constituted moral systems. While debates about the relationship between the individual and a culture have been central to the history of psychological anthropology, it is quite clear, from Sapir's earliest brilliant formulations, that individuals vary widely in how they appropriate, adapt to, respond to, and react against a cultural tradition and its claims, including its system of religion and morality, whether implicit or explicit.[4]

The degree of individual differences in ethical intuitions has often been brought home to me quite forcefully when engaging medical students, residents, or physicians about ethical complexities of their work. One brief example:

I was teaching a tutorial with six medical students in the "Doctor-Patient" course in Harvard's New Pathway curriculum some years ago. Our task for the tutorial was to discuss two cases: in one case, a baby born with severe birth defects was kept alive through fairly heroic interventions by the physician team, though the parents were ambivalent at best about keeping the baby alive; in the second, physicians resisted the wishes of the parents to undertake extreme measures to keep such a baby alive. Students argued back and forth about what physicians should do in cases such as these. I soon realized students were simply restating their own positions, but none was being swayed by arguments or seemed interested in changing their position. So I stopped the conversation, asked that each student in turn tell the group what in their own life histories led to their intuition about what the physicians should do in such cases. I recall a Mexican

American student saying that he grew up in California in a religious Catholic family, and that through his whole life, he has been committed to physicians saving and maintaining life as a primary value. A young woman whose family came from India said she still spends time with extended family members there, often sees great poverty, and feels that the amount of money spent on keeping these babies alive is a kind of obscene use of resources. A third, a young man from a Jewish family in greater Boston, said simply that he has always felt the parents should have the autonomy to decide in cases like this, that they will have to live with the outcomes and should be able to choose. When each student had reflected on where his or her intuition about what physicians should do in such cases had come from in their own lives, they fell silent. Students understood the validity of the positions being argued by their classmates, given their life experiences, and no longer seemed to feel the need to convince others of their own position in the discussion.

Of course medical ethics has arisen in hospitals and clinical settings to help clinicians and institutions make decisions, in large part because of the diversity of individual intuitions—by physicians and medical staff, patients and families, and others involved in care and reimbursement—about issues of moral import. Indeed, one might argue that this is the primary value of medical ethics as employed in clinical settings.

For the purposes of this chapter, three implications might be noted. First, we need to seriously question the assumption that when an anthropology of evil is discussed that an author can assume a consensus about the meaning of the term "evil" or that "we" know intuitively what "we" are talking about when using the term. However philosophically framed, intuitions about moral categories such as right and wrong, but even more for the category evil, will vary widely among those who use the term.

Second, for anthropologists in this conversation, it matters in what ways we have individually experienced religious and moral systems in our own lives for what our intuitions will be, including whether and how to use moral concepts in anthropological analysis. To what extent do we conceive moral systems as shaping our understandings of the good and that which gives meaning to our lives, for example, and to what extent do we experience (or have we experienced) moral systems as oppressive? Such questions open onto views of moral systems as fundamentally diverse as those theorized by Freud and Durkheim. Are ethical systems largely about controlling dangerous sexuality and aggression, or do ethical systems grow out of, represent, or help produce social solidarity (to caricature these positions)? For the Nietzsche of *On the Genealogy of Morals*, Judith Butler writes, "The institution of law compels an originally aggressive human to turn the aggression 'inward,' to craft an inner world composed of a guilty conscience and to vent that aggression against oneself in the name of morality" (2005, 14). The point here is that the very intuition about using ethical terms such as "evil" as analytic categories for anthropology depends in part upon our own experiences of moral systems.

Third, my own intuition expressed in the opening of this chapter grows out of—at least in part—my experience growing up as an Illinois Mennonite farm boy, heir to a great tradition of pacifism and the importance of serving those most in need, but equally heir to the great Protestant revivalist preaching tradition of Billy Sunday and Billy Graham and a host of great evangelists. Evil in this world is sin, and its consequences terrifying; I often experienced the "local moral world," in my colleague Arthur Kleinman's (2006) terms, as oppressive, and "what really mattered" an issue of profound anxiety. Anthropology has been a great release from this tradition, and psychoanalysis a means of dealing with its marks. Little wonder, perhaps, that I am suspicious of the use of "evil" as a primary tool within my own anthropological vocabulary.

But what about the horrors of political violence, which clearly exemplify the Dark Side of human experience? Is this a setting for engaging an anthropology of evil? How do we best write about violence in ways that provoke at the same time a sense of terror of the unfamiliar and an awareness of uncanny familiarity? Anthropologists who work in settings of extreme violence are quite far from being "secure in [our] knowledge of good and evil," as Robbins (2013) seems to think. Our work in Aceh was haunted by knowledge of religious, ethnic, and state violence around the archipelago—violence associated with the fall of the Suharto regime and the outbreak of burnings of Chinese communities and rapes of Chinese women; religious and ethnic violence in Ambon and Poso; a terrifying set of "ninja" killings akin to classic witch hunts in East Java (Siegel 2006); and spontaneous mob violence against those suspected of criminal acts in urban settings such as Jakarta. And these in turn provoked memories of the murderous history of killings in 1965–66 when Suharto and the military launched killings of "Communists," which killed upwards of one million Indonesians in one of the least known mass killings of the twentieth century, so richly portrayed in Robert Lemelson's stunning documentary *Forty Years of Silence: An Indonesian Tragedy* (2006) and Josh Oppenheimer's acclaimed film *The Act of Killing*

(2012). Oppenheimer's film has the ability to make viewers feel the uncanniness of the presence of the distant past: those engaged in the killings of 1965 are still present, literally, anxious to be remembered, gleeful in reproducing their acts, eventually haunted, but, above all, still present. Lemelson's film reminds us that past is still very present for those who suffered, for those for whom the violence has been routinized and reproduced, both bureaucratically by the labeling of those who are *anak PKI*, children of Communists—an example, perhaps, of Arendt's "banality of evil"—and through reenacted violence in local communities.

It seems relevant here to make note of Eric Santner's (1990) discussion of holocaust films in postwar Germany. The third chapter of this book provides reflections on "Screen Memories" associated with Edgar Reitz's film *Heimat—Eine Chronik in elf Teilen*, or "Heimat—A Chronicle in Eleven Parts." Though not noted by Santner, the focus on *Heimat* (home, homeland) resonates immediately with Freud's writing on the uncanny, the *unheimlich*. Santner's analysis of one moment in the film, when there is a shift from an "otherwise all-pervasive black and white" to vivid color, is particularly relevant for our thinking about what analytic concepts should be employed in our writing about violence. Santner writes that "not unlike an intrusion of the primary processes into the order of the secondary processes, these moments may indeed draw attention to the film *as* image and so fulfill the function that the Russian formalists saw as the poetic function par excellence, namely the removal of objects from the automatism of perception" (1990, 61). He quotes Victor Shklovsky (1965), "The technique of art is to make objects 'unfamiliar,' to make forms difficult, to increase the difficulty and length of perception because the process of perception is an aesthetic end in itself and must be prolonged." At the same time, Santner argues, such moments in the film may have the opposite effect, "to constitute objects as *familiar*," allowing them to enter into "the intimate sphere of interiorizing recollection (*Er-innerung*)." Anthropologists face the same challenge. It is possible through our telling to make acts of violence appear so distant as to be utterly other. At the same time, our recursive telling of stories can produce an unintended familiarity. An important question for those of us who write about violence as we have witnessed it or heard it reenacted in narratives is how to capture both a sense of the "unfamiliar" in violence and the uncanny sense of its familiarity. For this, we may also ask whether and in what ways the language of "evil" enables such writing.

Listening to stories of violence and torture from those who have suffered evokes complex responses in those of us who are engaged witnesses. These range from feelings of shock or terror to a sense of deep admiration for the ability of humans to live with and overcome such violence in the Ordinary (in Veena Das's [1997] terms, borrowed from Cavell), to remain human, reject victimhood, find ways to put terror in the past. It opens our awareness also, however, to rage and the desire for revenge, to wondering how those who commit such violence could do so, and eventually to projective identification, to sensing in oneself how such perverse violence could be possible, evoking an eerie recognition not only of terror but also of the presence of what Freud called the death drive.

Working in Indonesia these past twenty-two years has made me reflect far more than I had on the powerful effects of historical violence, colonial violence, the killings of 1965, as well as current forms of violence, spectacular and banal. These have affected how I think about human nature, about both Indonesian and American societies, about political and bureaucratic structures and events, and about moral responses to violence as well. I find myself increasingly trying to theorize the power of the irrational, the unspeakable, and that which is profoundly hidden, the stranger within, which motivates and organizes our individual lives and our politics. And it is here, perhaps counterintuitively, that I find Judith Butler's *Giving an Account of Oneself* (2005), first delivered at the University of Amsterdam as the Spinoza Lectures, to be useful and challenging for any discussion of violence and evil.

The fundamental project of this set of lectures was to ask how we can conceive of individuals as ethical beings if we presume an unconscious or a barred self, if we presume that the motives for many of our acts are largely outside our knowability, that we are charged with giving an account of ourselves when much that underlies our actions as subjects, including enacting or experiencing violence, is unknowable. "If it is really true that we are, as it were, divided, ungrounded, or incoherent from the start, will it be impossible to ground a notion of personal or social responsibility?" Butler asks (2005, 19). The lectures propose to provide a positive answer to this questions: "I will argue otherwise by showing how a theory of subject formation that acknowledges the limits of self-knowledge can serve a conception of ethics and, indeed, responsibility." The book elaborates the question and sketches a set of answers. For me, the questions are more important than the answers she elaborates. How can we approach the morality of actions if we presume a powerful and active unconscious on the part of actors? Butler argues explicitly that this question is critical both for addressing those who enact and those who experience violence.

Butler begins with a complex theory of subject formation that is grounded in psychoanalysis:

> The one story that the "I" cannot tell is the story of its own emergence as an "I" who not only speaks but comes to give an account of itself. In this sense, a story is being told, but the "I" who tells the story, who may well appear within the story as the first-person narrator, constitutes a point of opacity and interrupts a sequence, induces a break or eruption of the non-narrativizable in the midst of the story. (2005, 66)

This of course challenges not only our claims to make moral judgments concerning settings in which we work, but also our efforts, as anthropologists, to understand narratives that are told to us. How do we listen to narratives of selves in the face of the "eruption of the non-narrativizable"? To what end are we as anthropologists to use a language that implies moral judgment as an analytic frame—versus one that focuses on psychological processes? And from what position do we make moral judgments? "Recognition cannot be reduced to making and delivering judgments about others," Butler writes (2005, 44).

> The scene of moral judgment, when it is a judgment of persons for being as they are, invariably establishes a clear moral distance between the one who judges and the one who is judged. . . . Although I am certainly not arguing that we ought never to make judgments, I think that it is important, in rethinking the cultural terms of ethics, to remember that not all ethical relations are reducible to acts of judgment and that the very capacity to judge presupposes a prior relation between those who judge and those who are judged. (2005, 45)

This line of argument is critical as we attempt to understand the horrifying enactment of violence—to understand, as well as make ethical judgments about, those who engage in violence. How are we to listen to so-called perpetrators of violence? How are we to make sense of motives and of what become vicious local moral worlds? In what way is the language of evil, used in anthropological analysis of violence, a means of "judgment of persons for being as they are," a way of establishing "a clear moral distance between the one who judges and the one who is judged"? Does such judgment preclude actual investigation and analysis of how individuals find themselves enacting the violence in which they are engaged? Butler's line of argument is also critical for understanding the response of those who are the primary victims of violence. "It is always possible to say, 'Oh, some violence was done to me, and this gives me full permission to act under the sign of 'self-defense,'" Butler writes (2005, 100). "Many atrocities are committed under the sign of a 'self-defense' that, precisely because it achieves a permanent moral justification for retaliation, knows no end and can have no end. Such a strategy has developed an infinite way to rename its aggression as suffering and so provides an infinite justification for its aggression" (2005, 100–1). But of course this is only one example of responses to personal or historical violence and traumatic memory.

For many, responses to violence were not reduced to retaliation or even to charges of evil. It is clear in Aceh that losses associated with the tsunami were easier to manage, through religious practice, than those resulting from the violence, even though the magnitude of the losses suffered were often greater for those whose families were swept away by the tsunami. Acehnese regularly use the religious terms *pasrah* (surrender, acceptance) and *ikhlas* (sincere—in ones moral commitment to accepting what God has given), as well as *sabar* (patience) (see Samuels 2012, ch. 3 for full discussion; cf. Samuels 2010) to describe the process of working through trauma or loss (see also Good and Good 2017). This was more difficult for those who suffered violence or torture by the Indonesian military as part of the conflict. Many we interviewed expressed continued anger for what they had suffered—and many Acehnese feel that only a genuine acknowledgment of the human rights violations would allow them to come fully to terms with the violence. "If you know someone has done something to you, and they come into your house and say, 'I did such and such, I'm sorry,'" a former GAM leader told us, "the matter would be easily finished. But if that person comes into your house and sits with you, but does not acknowledge what he has done, how can the matter be finished?"

In all of this work, I am concerned that the language of evil suggests "making and delivering judgments about others," in Butler's terms (2005, 44), rather than engaging the opacity of the self and both the horrifying otherness and uncanny familiarity of the violence as described to us by those with whom we and our mental health teams worked in Aceh. It seems to me at the very least that if the term is to be used by anthropologists, both the personal meanings of the term for the anthropologist "making the judgment" and the relation of this judgment to understanding the psychological and social dimensions of those engaged in what is perceived as evil need to be explored richly. I remain personally reluctant to use evil as an anthropological concept.

I find myself increasingly interested in "haunting" as a conceptual frame, one that has a potential for complex relations to local languages of morality, as well as both the psychological and the political (Good 2015, forthcoming). I have suggested that a "hauntology," drawing on Derrida's *Specters of Marx* (1994), analyses based in Freud's elusive concept of the uncanny (Freud 2003 [1919]), and formulations in cultural studies of analyses of the spectral (Del Pilar Blanco and Peeren 2013), may be particularly useful in analyzing memories of historical violence that remain at the edges of awareness and the appearance of powerful ghosts or specters of both past and future.

Avery Gordon's *Ghostly Matters: Haunting and the Sociological Imagination* (originally published 1997), particularly the Introduction to the new edition (published in 2008), provides a rich language for analyzing what we experienced in Aceh, but also for exploring how histories of violence are embedded in language and political structures and erupt into awareness.

> Haunting was the language and the experiential modality by which I tried to reach an understanding of the meeting of force and meaning, because haunting is one way in which abusive systems of power make themselves known and their impacts felt in everyday life especially when they are supposedly over and done with (slavery, for instance) or when their oppressive nature is denied." (2008, xvi)

She described haunting as

> an animated state in which a repressed or unresolved social violence is making itself known, sometimes very directly, sometimes more obliquely.... The whole essence ... of a ghost is that it has real presence and demands its due.... Haunting and the appearance of specters or ghosts is one way ... we are notified that what's been concealed is very much alive and present. (2008, xvi)

Drawing on this work, I suggest we consider a "hauntological ethics" that may provide an alternative to an ethics of good and evil, providing both a way of positioning our own ethical critique as anthropologists and our intuiting and investigating the experiences of those in the societies in which we work. As ethical subjects today, anthropologists, particularly American anthropologists ferrying back and forth across diverse local worlds, are haunted by an awareness of the profound inequalities of wealth and access to resources with which we live, by an awareness that in our names terrible violence is being enacted toward many in the world, and that we live amidst structures of privilege resulting from a history of violence, slavery, racism, colonialism, and gender violence. A hauntological ethics asks how we can possibly live moral lives among such haunting. It is perhaps the awareness that we live in times that "no ethics, no politics ... seems possible and thinkable and just" that has made anthropologists in recent times to turn to notions such as aspiration and hope.[5] If the fundamental issues of the unconscious, of irrationality, violence, and historical memory are not made central to this work, if it does not engage the Dark Side and its ghosts, the "ethical turn" will fail to address the most critical issues facing anthropologists.

It is not clear to me that the language of evil is the most useful way to address such issues. I am, however, grateful to have the opportunity to reflect critically on these issues and on how we as anthropologists link ethical and ethnographic reflection in responding to the settings in which many of us now work.

Byron J. Good, Harvard University

Notes

1. Discussion of this work is found in Good, Good, and Grayman 2010; Good 2012, 2015, forthcoming; Good and Good 2013; Good, Good, and Grayman 2015.
2. A version of this event is told in Good, Good, and Grayman 2015, 387–89.
3. Michael Fischer added the following note in the margins while reading and commenting on this essay: "But those laws, crucially, are matters of interpretation by the community—viz. the parable of Moses asking God for a sign to prove his interpretation right, God moving a mountain, and the community saying that doesn't matter because the law was given to us at Mt. Sinai, and God laughing saying 'my children have defeated me'—God gave the 10 Commandment Tablets, and man broke them into pieces and had to reconstruct them (a parable common to Judaism and Islam—see Fischer and Abedi, *Debating Muslims*, 1991). Or in Jewish mysticism, evil is located in the incapacity of the human to absorb all of the *sefirot* (components of the divine), a kind of alienation of knowledge from its fruits (the story of the Garden of Eden and the tree of knowledge)." This should serve as a reminder that each of the positions noted here is simply a gesture to very complex traditions represented—and misrepresented—by historical discussions of evil.
4. The fullest available elaboration of Sapir's thoughts on these issues is available in Sapir's reconstituted lectures, assembled by Judith Irvine (Sapir 2002).
5. Jonathan Lear's (2006) notion of "radical hope" is relevant here.

References

Butler, Judith. 2005. *Giving an Account of Oneself*. New York: Fordham University Press.

Das, Veena. 1997. "The Act of Witnessing: Violence, Poisonous Knowledge, and Subjectivity." In *Violence and Subjectivity*. Edited by Veena Das, Arthur Kleinman, Mamphela Ramphele, and Pamela Reynolds, 205–25. Berkeley: University of California Press.

Del Pilar Blanco, Maria, and Esther Peeren, eds. 2013. *The Spectralities Reader: Ghosts and Haunting in Contemporary Cultural Theory*. New York: Bloomsbury.

Derrida, Jacques. 1994. *Specters of Marx: The State of the Debt, the Work of Mourning, & the New International*. New York: Routledge.

Fischer, Michael M. J. 2012. "Science." In *A Companion to Moral Anthropology*. Edited by Didier Fassin, 395–412. Oxford: John Wiley and Sons.

Fischer, Michael M. J., and Mehdi Abedi. 1991. *Debating Muslims: Cultural Dialogues in Postmodernity and Tradition*. Madison: University of Wisconsin Press.

Freud, Sigmund. 2003 [1919]. *The Uncanny*. New York: Penguin.

Good, Byron J. 2012. "Theorizing the 'Subject' of Medical and Psychiatric Anthropology." The 2010 R. R. Marett Memorial Lecture. *Journal of the Royal Anthropological Institute* 18(3): 515–35.

———. 2015. "Haunted by Aceh: Specters of Violence in Post-Suharto Indonesia." In *Genocide and Mass Violence: Memory, Symptom, and Recovery*. Edited by Hinton and Hinton, 58–82. Cambridge, UK: Cambridge University Press.

———. Forthcoming. "Hauntology: A Personal and Theoretical Genealogy." *Ethos: Journal of the Society for Psychological Anthropology*.

Good, Byron J., and Mary-Jo DelVecchio Good. 2017. "Toward a Cultural Psychology of Trauma and Trauma-Related Disorders." In *Universalism without Uniformity: Explorations in Mind and Culture*. Edited by Julia L Cassaniti and Usha Menon, 260–79. Chicago: University of Chicago Press.

Good, Byron J., Mary-Jo DelVecchio Good, and Jesse Grayman. 2015. "Is PTSD a 'Good Enough' Concept for Postconflict Mental Health Care? Reflections on Work in Aceh, Indonesia." In *Culture and PTSD: Trauma in Global and Historical Perspective*. Edited by Hinton and Good. Philadelphia: University of Pennsylvania Press.

Good, Mary-Jo DelVecchio. 2015. "Acehenese Women's Narratives of Traumatic Experience, Resilience and Recovery." In *Genocide and Mass Violence: Memory, Symptom, Recovery*. Edited by Devon E. Hinton and Alexander L. Hinton, 280–300. Cambridge, UK: Cambridge University Press.

Good, Mary-Jo DelVecchio, and Byron J. Good. 2013. "Perspectives on the Politics of Peace in Aceh, Indonesia." In *Radical Egalitarianism: Local Realities, Global Relations*. Edited by Felicity Aulino, Miriam Goheen, and Stanley J. Tambiah, 191–208. New York: Fordham University Press.

Good, Mary-Jo DelVecchio, Byron J. Good, and Jesse Grayman. 2010. "Complex Engagements: Responding to Violence in Postconflict Aceh." In *Contemporary States of Emergency: The Politics of Military and Humanitarian Interventions*. Edited by Didier Fassin and Mariella Pandolfi, 241–66. New York: Zone.

Kleinman, Arthur. 2006. *What Really Matters: Living a Moral Life Amidst Uncertainty and Danger*. Oxford: Oxford University Press.

Lear, Jonathan. 2006. *Radical Hope: Ethics in the Face of Cultural Devastation*. Cambridge: Harvard University Press.

Olsen, William C., and Thomas J. Csordas. 2019. "Introduction." *Engaging Evil: A Moral Anthropology*. (This volume.)

Rorty, Amélie Oksenberg, ed. 2001. *The Many Faces of Evil: Historical Perspectives*. New York: Routledge.

Robbins, Joel. 2013. "Beyond the Suffering Subject: Toward an Anthropology of the Good." *Journal of the Royal Anthropological Institute* 19: 447–62.

Samuels, Annemarie. 2010. "Remaking Neighbourhoods in Banda Aceh: Post-tsunami Reconstruction of Everyday Life." In *Post-Disaster Reconstruction: Lessons from Aceh*. Edited by Matthew Clarke, Fanany Ismet, and Sue Kenny, 210–223. London: Earthscan.

———. 2012. "After the Tsunami: The Remaking of Everyday Life in Banda Aceh, Indonesia." PhD dissertation, Leiden University.

Sapir, Edward. 2002. *Edward Sapir: The Psychology of Culture. A Course of Lectures*. Reconstructed and edited by Judith T. Irvine. Berlin: Mouton de Gruyter.

Santner, Eric L. 1990. *Stranded Objects: Mourning, Memory, and Film in Postwar Germany*. Ithaca, NY: Cornell University Press.

Shklovsky, Victor. 1965. "Art as Technique." In *Russian Formalist Criticism: Four Essays*. Translated by Lee T. Lemon and Marion J Reis. Lincoln: University of Nebraska Press.

Siegel, James T. 2006. *Naming the Witch*. Stanford: Stanford University Press.

Zigon, Jarrett, and C. Jason Throop. 2014. "Moral Experience: Introduction." *Ethos: Journal of the Society for Psychological Anthropology* 42: 1–15.

PART II

Evil and Suffering

Chapter 3

SPEAK NO EVIL

INVERSION AND EVASION IN INDONESIA

Andrew Beatty

The Root and the Flower

How and where does evil emerge? Under what conditions is it recognized? When is it named? When denied? Questions about evil revolve around origins: false starts, botched creations, damaged childhoods, mutations, and, archetypally for some of us, original sin, "man's first disobedience and the fruit/Of that forbidden tree, whose mortal taste/ Brought death into the world, and all our woe." So Milton (1674) had it. But the birth of evil is not just a Puritan hang-up. Everywhere, the *how* and the *where* questions quickly revert to a nagging *why*, as if only a first cause—or a final cause—could resolve the mystery. So the scrutiny of conscience or crime leads inevitably back to some prior condition that will make sense of the whole. The root of all evil.

That urge to understand is the driver. For as Weber insisted, the problem of evil is ultimately a problem of meaning. You can't deal with it until you understand its origin and raison d'être. It's also a problem of attribution. Is evil "in the nature of things," part of the System, as Manicheans, conspiracy theorists, and Christian apologists propose? Without evil, no good, no choice, no freedom, no redemption, no material world. Hence Augustine's doctrine of *felix culpa*, the Fortunate Fall. Or is evil a stain to be expunged forever from human nature and society, as assorted Utopians would have it? Do we have only ourselves to blame? Made bad, can we be remade good?

Philosophers, bishops, and political thinkers tend to come at these big questions from first principles. What was in God's mind when he created the serpent? Could he have done better? Could he have created a being who always freely chose the good? Or, in a secular frame, how can a diversity of competing interests be accommodated in a just social system, the evils of oppression avoided, and a better kind of citizen created?

To the anthropologist, first principles are always question-begging in that they lack the context that would give precise meaning to the terms. Without knowing what counts locally as evil, without knowing what makes up a person or a good life, we can't bring into focus the bigger picture. We begin, necessarily, with the local. Yet even in the smallest, remotest communities, in the midst of individual suffering, it is the big questions that loom, generalities answering to particulars. That confrontation of scales—microcosm and macrocosm—is part of what makes the problem of evil so compelling. The fascination is in the working out of Last Things in the small print of everyday life.

In this chapter, I want to look at how the problem of evil, locally conceived, is reconfigured under the pressure of conversion and the incorporation of small-scale societies into the modern state. On this broader stage, how does evil change shape and meaning? How is the primordial updated? Where now is the serpent?

Java and Nias: Locating Evil

To explore these questions, I consider two Indonesian societies: one tribal, mostly nonliterate; the other a settled agrarian civilization. To put a name to them: Nias, a heavily forested island, nominally Christian, in the Indian Ocean; and Java, a chain of volcanoes, cities, and crowded plains, mainly Muslim with a deep heritage of Hinduism, syncretic mysticism, and a pantheon Allah shares with the ancestors, sprites, and monsters. In neither setting is there a simple translation of the English word "evil," or even of "bad." The Niha for bad is *lö sökhi*, "not good."[1] There's no separate term for evil. In the Niha Bible, when God says, "It is not good that the man should be alone; I will make him a helper as his partner," he uses the same formula as when he tells Adam, "of the Tree of Knowledge of Good and *Not Good* thou shall not eat."

In Javanese, *apik* means good, nice, attractive, while its antonym *elek* means bad, nasty, evil, and ugly, the moral and aesthetic overlapping. Again, no specific word for "evil." But let's not forget that *our* word has a number of meanings, ranging from a generally deplored condition—as in "the evil of poverty"—to what theologians call "natural evil"—earthquakes and epidemics—to the moral evil exemplified in certain crimes held to be against the order of things and which place miscreants beyond the pale of normal humanity. In many, perhaps most, societies, there are distinctions more or less of this kind, with different sorts of diagnosis and remedy—legal, ritual, and therapeutic—even if they aren't named or get lumped together, as in our word "evil." The greater variation is found in the *locating* of evil, whether in persons, moral careers, systems gone awry, the spirit world, or some grander cosmic scheme. Is evil *out there* or *in here*? One of my themes will be that what makes evil a problem is its ambiguous locality, its slipperiness and unboundedness, above all, its sticky attachment to the self. Unlike the merely bad, wrong, or dangerous, evil is often represented and experienced as chaotic, gratuitous, off the scale, irreducible to human schemes. Hence Yahweh's taunt to Job: "Canst thou draw out Leviathan with a hook?" (Job 41:1 KJV). Indeed, one reason evil fascinates is because it is incalculable, escaping the neat formulation of moral codes and mechanical explanations. "Lack of a word for it" might be said to illustrate the elusiveness of evil rather than, as some prefer, pointing to its cultural relativity.

The Headhunter, a Necessary Evil

In both Nias and Java, nonetheless, evil has an epitome, a figure that stands for death as much as evil. In Java, it's the spirit ogre Bathara Kala, the misbegotten son of Bathara Guru (Shiva) and Durga. In Nias, where I shall begin, the new religion provided a ready-made villain in Satan, but the Evil One—or the Not Good One—never really caught on. The Bible translator had assigned a mischievous spirit named Afökha to the role of fallen angel; but in two years filled with mischief, not to say evil, I rarely heard the Prince of Darkness name checked. No, in Nias, the repository of fear and horror, the thing people dreaded, was the headhunter, *emali*. (In Niasan, to "scream in terror," *fa'emali*, means "to shout *headhunter*.") In whatever era— from pre-Colonial to the present—the headhunter was an ever-present danger, real or imaginary. But—and this is where the problem begins—raiding and headhunting were authorized by the ancestors. If you wanted to win glory as a warrior, reinforce a house, or give a dead chief a proper send-off, you needed a skull (Fries 1908). Killing was hideous, to be sure, but good things came from bad. Headhunting was a necessary evil. What excused it in the old morality was the fact that, in the generalized exchange of predation, harm to others was matched by risk to yourself, for the raiders, though instruments of terror, were themselves potential victims, as were their families. This is the crucial point, psychologically, ethically, and—as we shall see—historically. The menacing outsider was a version of yourself; so to take a head, you first had to *become other*, shedding your humanity. Before setting out, raiders would lap blood from a pig's trough, then gird themselves with crocodile-hide and tusked helmets. Once in character, they were free from scruple. They were cruel, as a tiger is cruel, but blameless—neither malevolent nor morally at fault. Which is why ritual indemnity, a license to kill, applied whether the victim was an armed opponent or an innocent child alone in the fields. The mode of action (not to overtheorize it as "ethical stance") was not defined by the pendulum swing of feuding, with honor robbed and recovered: honor had little to do with it. Between killing and revenge (*sulö*, "repayment") was a blind spot, a conceptual gap through which men ran like beasts—so, at least, they remembered it many years later (Beatty 2015).

The blind spot contained a paradox. Headhunters were the supreme outsiders, the bogeymen; but that faceless terror was also yourself. So what did you see in the mirror? Decent citizen and family man or cold-blooded killer? We can point to the tricks of evasion: ritual separation, symbolic metamorphosis, the uniform of death. But the puzzle remains, as it does with any official denial of inhumanity, whether fog-of-war euphemism or bureaucratic fudge. It is less the images of the demonic that perplex than those of the demon off duty: the camp commandant enjoying Beethoven after work, the torturer playing with his children, the tyrant at prayer. How can someone be both human and inhuman? Psychologically, by projection and categorical inversion of the opposing self; sociologically, by whatever cultural and social apparatus makes this possible. In the run-up to the Spanish Civil War, warming up for later horrors, Franco used the brutal Foreign Legion to put down an insurrection in Asturias, arguing that the left-wing workers—fellow Spaniards—were barbarians like the Moroccans he had spent years terrorizing (Preston 2000, 16). Acts of cleansing savagery were noble and necessary. During the Civil War, the priests blessed his cannons.

We demonize others, but it's ourselves we have to live with; and for that there are always ways and means. Moral duplicity—distinct from mere hypocrisy—often rests on a duplex morality, hence the conventional markers of ethnic slurs, separation walls, intercaste rules, and stigma. The Nias case, as we shall see, required a splitting of the self, not just a change of uniform or shuffling of roles. It complicates the perennial conundrum of human iniquity, reminding us that—however easy ideology makes it—*psychologically*, denial is difficult because humans are singular, if morally double. I cannot pretend to solve this "enigma of enigmas," to use a phrase of Ricoeur (1967) in his book on evil. What I *can* do is offer some insight into what it takes to recognize in the other your demonic double; to say, as Prospero says of Caliban at the end of *The Tempest*, "this thing of darkness I acknowledge mine." I can do this because exactly a century ago, something of the kind happened, quite suddenly, in Nias when a Protestant conversion movement known as the Great Repentance swept the island. It started in a village close to the dingy port of Gunung Sitoli, where the Rhinish missionaries had toiled for half a century without success. By 1915, they had won only a few hundred converts, poor families whose faith was bartered for pennies and medicines sent by parishes back home in the Rhineland. The German missionaries, and especially the Dutch administrators, were quite cynical about these converts, seeing them as spiritual benefit scroungers. But they were soon to get a shock.[2]

Dutch conquest of the East Indies' Outer Islands had come three hundred years after first landfall in Java. Under the Cultivation System, Java had become the most profitable colony in the world. But Nias was too remote and too poor to be of interest to the colonial capital. At the time of conquest in 1906, the only thriving export was slaves, traded with north Sumatra. Gold was needed for bridewealth and feasts of merit, and the quickest way to get it was by selling captives. In the late nineteenth century, lust for gold caused a spike in raiding that led to the depopulation of large tracts of the south and to the militarization of bordering areas. Villages were fortified with palisades and booby-trapped trenches; sentries guarded the approaches. Fear of the headhunters was compounded by fear of slavers. But the enemy was also within. As late as the 1980s, old men still recounted stories of betrayal carried out by their younger selves, half-boasting, half-lamenting that they "ate" their relatives for gold.

The slave trade fed the system of competitive exchange and the prestige economy, though in spirit it was the exact opposite, flouting the rule of good measure, the precise calibration of debts and merit, and the balancing of the books over a lifetime that would allow a feastgiver to die peacefully and pass to the ancestral Valhalla (Beatty 1992). In the moral calculus, taking what did not belong to you was the cardinal sin. To gain something for nothing, to steal, even to profit, was to offend the ancestors and risk the afterlife. Gold, the prize, came to embody a contradiction between the rule of equity in internal exchange and the rapacity of the external market. The most desirable commodity was tarnished. Luckily, there were detox rituals to transfer guilt to a scapegoat, a slave who was beheaded, clad in the owner's filthy gold.

The ambivalence that gold excited can be read in a myth, still told, of a sow that ate humans and excreted gold. In the nineteenth century, the whole island became something of a golden sow, devouring humans and churning out wealth. In the twentieth century, the pig passed to the Dutch, which explains both *their* riches and the poverty of Nias. It's an apt metaphor for exploitation, a scatological symbol of avidity and disgust, perhaps self-disgust, but also a peculiarly Niasan example of wishful thinking, for the golden sow is a forbidden fantasy of something for nothing, wealth without origin.

Such was the moral framework on the eve of conquest.

The Discovery of Evil

Conversion unfolded a series of paradoxes: a heavenly something for an earthly nothing, a deal with the divine "costing not less than everything," a Fortunate Fall waiting to happen. It was the world turned upside down, a new way of thinking for the New People, as converts were called. Yet tradition had paved the way in the nexus of exchange and in concepts of wickedness, redemption, and salvation. Long before the Bible came, changing everything and nothing, Niha already knew damnation and resurrection (*femaoso*, the ritual "raising" of a dead chief). Two generations after the Repentance, watching the chief of Orahua review his feasting history from his deathbed, it was hard to see where the old ended and the new began. "Away with your damned hallelujahs!" he yelled at the priest, while his followers rose to air their grievances, clearing his path for transition. But where was he headed?

Cosmological ambiguity was there from the outset. The missionaries had seized on cultural parallels to leaven scriptural translations with local concepts, sometimes reinforcing, but mostly inverting the old values. Honoring thy father and mother, a basic tenet of life in Nias, turned out to have its origin in the Bible: it was headlined as a commandment. Yet, perplexingly, the wooden ancestor figures that filled Niha houses were damned as idols. Rules against short measuring and adultery—standard Niha themes—turned out, like a host of other dos and don'ts, to have a more specific source than Ancestors Anonymous. In the missionaries' hands, everything was foreseen and scripted, yet bathed in a different light. This could be reassuring, but mostly it was unsettling, like discovering someone you thought you knew was really someone else—an analogy that could apply to the whole conversion process. The force of prohibition and the doublethink of translation effected an othering, or doubling, of the self. In becoming a new person, you discovered you were—or harbored within yourself—someone else, and that someone else was evil.

Translation preempted the present by rewriting the past. The German missionaries' simple task had been to find local equivalents, a Niha word for *heilig* or *Himmel*. But for the target audience—the translated—the effect was more complicated: a known word with a solid reliable meaning suddenly shifts ground or acquires a double meaning, only one of which is authorized. *So'aya*, "one who uses spells" (a sorcerer), becomes "the Lord." *Horö*, "war," "enmity," "crime," becomes "sin." Sometimes the old sense persists awkwardly alongside the new. Your affines, traditionally called "Those who own us" (*Sokhö ya'ita*), now have to share this epithet with God. Elderly men and women who scrutinize entrails and set bones are upgraded to Hebrew prophets (*sama'ele'ö*). The word for taboo, *moni*, goes for "holy." The Holy Bible, in turn, is called the Tabooed Scripture. But the old use of *moni* is forbidden, if not forgotten. Taboos are tabooed. By repetition of the new meanings, the world known to ritual and accessible through ritual is hollowed out; commerce with the dead becomes impossible. But that unnameable, invisible realm, the source of blessing and curse, is still there, replenishing or withering crops, exerting an influence for good or ill, but no longer manipulable or knowable. The whole relation to knowledge is inverted. In the Garden of Eden, evil was a *product* of knowledge, the fruit of that forbidden tree. Ignorance was bliss. For Niha, the discovery of evil required them, perversely, to unlearn what they had known, the world of the ancestors, sacrifice, and raiding. Almost everything in the past was forbidden. It had become literally unspeakable.

This was translation as linguistic estrangement, obliging people to *unknow*, or know in a different way, what they had known before. In the Niha Bible, native concepts, personages, even local history found a role, at once familiar and strange. In the retrofitted cosmos, the spiritual luster craved by chiefs became the radiance of God. The struggles between heathens and Hebrews prophesied the conversions and defections of contemporary Nias. Egyptian plagues recurred in the epidemics that ravaged the island after World War I. What should have been a bad fit—a desert creed for a forest people—turned out to be startlingly apt.

Yet the Bible was not yet the handbook for Niha converts that it would become. It was not until the Dutch garrison had established control that the freighted words struck home; the message as it were *rediscovered* as a version of their own past and present predicament. An overwhelming sense of *déjà vu* probably accounts for the converts' scriptural zeal. Naturally, the missionaries saw in it God's hand. Yet without the colonial cataclysm, the prophetic threats and promises would not have made sense. Biblical tales of sin, dispossession, and restoration now had a new experiential truth. The Book of Job was, and remains, a favorite, a primer on cosmic injustice. But at the time of the mass conversions, the most popular story was "Samson and Delilah," a tale of national defeat and sacrificial redemption. Apart from the strikingly relevant symbolism of magical hair (which recalled chiefly luster), for Niha, the story had a peculiar resonance, a sting. In repudiating their own tradition, Niha converts had brought the temple crashing down on their heads. Triumph over the enemy was a kind of defeat.

The Spectacle of Evil

So how did the Great Repentance begin? The trigger was a retreat held to celebrate the fiftieth jubilee of the mission. Missionary Rudersdorf, deploring the lack of conscience among his flock, demanded from them an extended period of reflection on their sinfulness, threatening "expulsion from the Last Supper, should they not repent and change their lives" (Hummel & Telaumbanua 2007, 157). Excommunication meant exclusion from the religious community and refusal of the sacraments: a terrible penalty for converts who had broken with their pagan kin. It suggested the humiliating refusal of one's portion at feasts and implied social ostracism, the severest sanction short of execution. The threat worked. Converts flocked to Rudersdorf's classes. They read (or listened) and pondered their sins. Native evangelists carried the message to other districts. Here's how one missionary remembers the events (Kriele 1927, 95–96):

> The course taken by the revival was more or less the same everywhere. People were seized by terrors of conscience, suddenly feeling themselves inescapably confronted with the divine holiness. The sense of sin and guilt overwhelmed them with elemental force, and it seemed as though a sentence of annihilation were being passed on their whole life. As one

of the missionaries wrote at the time, "The fear of God is passing over our island." They cried to God for forgiveness, but could not feel that this was enough. An irresistible force drove them to the missionaries. Crowds streamed to the mission house in a way our workers had never experienced. For weeks and months they were able to do little else but hear confessions all day . . . . Terrible revelations were made; matters which had taken place twenty or thirty years before were brought to light. Unsparingly, they stripped the masks from their faces, caring for nothing but to be free of the load which oppressed them. Many trembled all over and stood as if crushed before the missionary, who only needed now to direct them to the consolation of the Gospel, to the Cross of Christ.

"Annihilation" seems the right word, for conversion brought a rejection of all that it meant to be Niha, a word that encompassed both human and Niasan. Venerable practices like sacrifice, ancestor worship, headhunting, and plunder—all that made for a good life—were abandoned along with the household gods, who were torn from their fixtures and burned on bonfires that lit up the hills. Morally, this was year zero.

Orahua, in the center of the island, experienced these events a full decade later, and then again, in successive decades, like a relapsing illness. Repentance was not self-limiting. The trouble was that you could not erase the past: the past was yourself. The headhunters had gone, but now the threat was within, its evulsion a collective horror. Whereas in the north, the movement was driven by confession, a talking cure, in Orahua, penitence was mute. Converts created a theatre of cruelty, a spectacle of evil in which the *self*—not the other—was demonized. Before astonished congregations, reprobates reenacted their "crimes" in trance, establishing their innocence by acting out their guilt. But this wordless mime was not quite confession, not quite deliverance.

What protected them from revenge was the innocent automatism of the dumbshow, the sense that the compulsion came from outside. As spiritual contagion spread through the audience, witnesses felt compelled to join in, leaping onstage to rape, rob, or kill, even seizing the original victim in pantomime violence. Here, truly, was a return of the repressed. Acting on buried impulses and memories, penitents claimed to know little of what had passed. And victims could only forgive them, embracing them in their tears. Yet because the catharsis was inarticulate, incomplete, the embers of memory were not extinguished, and symptoms would again break out every few years. These revivals were always wordless: each new phase named for its primary symptom. After the first Repentance came the Shivering, a few years later the Jumping, and then, most memorably, the Laughing, when whole congregations rocked with laughter as if at some endless cosmic joke. As Freud (2003) first noted in a famous essay, the uncanny is marked by compulsion and repetition. The techniques of salvation—laughing, jumping, shivering—were in each case repetitive and compulsive. A symptom that still occurs in revivals today—the beat goes on—is rhythmic speaking in tongues. Niha called it the "new language." What did it mean? A veteran of the last Repentance in the 1960s said to me, "We didn't understand. It was like your language, it meant nothing. Only God understands." But *who* speaks or acts in these sessions? The ancestors, the Holy Spirit, the crowd, your former self? Does agency lie outside or in? Can you ventriloquize yourself? Is the new language, void of meaning, a figure for the silence of God?

In the Repentance, the duality that Freud sees as belonging to the uncanny, the sense of ourselves as obscurely double—Jekyll and Hyde—is dramatized. The incorporated, dormant past is once again externalized, brought to light. But the penitent is neither one thing nor the other, neither old Adam nor new person. And that blurring of boundaries, of times and tenses, of agency and identity, is what creates the uncanny effect: the queasy automatism and sense of horror that stands out as the dominant emotion, both in eye-witness reports and in recollection.

The acting out, the making visible, is critical. In his book on the uncanny, Royle notes "a special emphasis on the visual, on what comes to light, on what is revealed to the eye. The uncanny is what comes out of the darkness. . . . 'To make the invisible visible is uncanny' (de Man)" (2003, 108). Niha today speak of the past as a time of gloom and darkness, and of God as Light.[3] They understood Samson's blindness. But if the reenactments were startlingly visual—a spectacle of the self as other—what was actually *seen*, what kind of insight achieved? Royle insinuates a troubling thought: "At some level the feeling of the uncanny may be bound up with the most extreme nostalgia or 'homesickness'" (2003, 2).

Nostalgia for the forbidden, a misremembrance of things past—was this what thwarted the Repentance and explained its recurring symptoms? (One thinks of Freud's dictum: "Hysterics suffer mainly from reminiscences.") Or was it that the suppression of the ancestors, and of one's own ancestrally hallowed acts, merely "displaced them to the realm of psychology," as Terry Castles writes of Enlightenment rationalism. "By relocating the world of ghosts in the closed space of the imagination, one ended up supernaturalizing the mind itself" (Castles, cited in Davis 2007, 7).

Unlike revivalist cults elsewhere, inspiration did not lead to rebellion. Blindness did not lead to insight. The muteness of the confession and its ritual containment meant that the movement gained no political traction. Instead, the Pentecostal fire was self-consuming. The millennium fizzled out. The head of the mission who had proclaimed the greatest awakening in Asia later declared that fundamentally nothing had changed (Müller-Krüger 1968, 281).

And yet, of course, it had. For conversion, which came through the discovery of evil and a new conception of the self, was the pathway into a differently shaped cosmos. From being the center of the world, tribal Nias would diminish to a speck on someone else's horizon. And for the Niha themselves, a silent role as extras near the end of the cosmic drama. ("When is the End coming?" people would ask me.) Henceforth, it was the unconverted who replaced raiders as the archetypal "outsider," *niha baero*, a word that came to mean "pagan," "unbeliever." But believers, too, remained tainted, their salvation uncertain. In the new dispensation, Old Nias was incorporated as original sin, the indelible evil that barred full admission to Christendom. As one man lamented to me, "We here at the edge of the world are God's stepchildren. Unlike you, we shall never enter the kingdom of heaven."

Java: Containing Evil

The case is rather different in Java, where a blend of religious traditions—Muslim, Hindu, and native Javanese—has spawned a rich philosophical discourse on morality (Beatty 1999, 2009). And yet, as we shall see, recent events show a certain resemblance with Nias. Evil and misfortune are personified in Kala, son of the goddess Durga. His story is told in a shadow play, The Birth of Kala, which provides both an account of the origin of evil and a manual of how to deal with it—diagnosis and cure. As Stephen Headley (2000) has shown, at the climax of the play, the puppeteer, who briefly incarnates Vishnu (*Wisnu*, in Javanese), recites an ancient cosmogonic text that releases Kala's victims from his power and expels him from the village where the play is being performed. The monster cannot be killed, but his fangs can be drawn. The Kala story is unique in several respects. Unlike other plays in the tradition, it merges Hindu mythology with a native creation myth; it is performed in daylight, when Kala stalks his prey; and it has a ritual purpose: it is an exorcism. The theory is simple: because evil has an origin, it can be rooted out.

In Banyuwangi, on the eastern tip of Java, where I carry out fieldwork, this is the only shadow play traditionally performed, and it has a special local significance. Remote from palace and barracks, the eastern cape was a political outlier, a place of exiles and malcontents. (An independent kingdom was destroyed by the Dutch in 1768.) The containment of power, whether for good or evil, was and still is a problem. Here, the classical models of Javanese statecraft elaborated by Geertz (1968) and Anderson (1990) do not apply. Instead of the exemplary center, with the ruler as axis of the world, power is dispersed among sacred locations: caves, groves, and ruins haunted by rebels and sages. Their shrines are controlled by caretakers and mystics who are able to tap the networks and scan the relics for contemporary meanings. Anderson's classical model has a radiant center, but no perimeter: power fades with distance, like the signal from a telephone mast. In Banyuwangi, the problem of accumulation and containment takes a different form. Without center or periphery, power is kept from leaking away or running wild not by centripetal ritual but by constructing a temporary boundary (Beatty 2012a). This is what villagers do in domestic and community rituals, marking out an enclosure, whether of woven leaves, Koranic prayers, or by pacing out a boundary. This is the firewall tested by Kala.

Like other figures of the shadow play, Kala (depicted in figure 3.1) is both *out there* and *in here*, demon and disposition—a conscious ambiguity that separates reflexive Java from regressive Nias. In Javanese philosophy, the puppets are a gallery of human types. To watch them is to recognize oneself and one's neighbors. But Kala is anomalous, disruptive of any scheme. He came into being when his father, Guru (Shiva), riding on an ox behind his consort Uma/Durga, becomes aroused but fails to connect with her. The god's semen falls into the ocean, boiling up to create a monster who unleashes evil and death upon the world. Ricoeur's notion of "pre-ethical" evil as defilement, a "symbolic stain," seems apposite (Ricoeur 1967, 26); but so too is Douglas's (1966) structural conception of pollution. Guru's effusion is, supremely, "matter out of place," the primal sin for which all humans must pay. As a sage admonishes the lecherous god, "this all started because you chose the wrong time and place to begin" (Headley 2000, 39). As Headley explains in his presentation of a Central Javanese performance, Kala's victims are soiled, hexed (*sukerta*, from *suker*, "dirt"). Kala himself helpfully adds: "For those who hear it, that word means those who bear the mark have an impaired and tainted destiny" (Headley 2000, 45). The exorcism is a purification. Such is the case in Banyuwangi, too, though at the

Figure 3.1 Birth of Kala shadow play, Java (Bathara Kala in center). Photograph by the author.

extremity of Java, beyond the reach of any palace, there's a special emphasis in performance on the spilled seed as *power without a container*, danger distilled.

The young Kala develops an unhealthy appetite for human flesh when some blood accidentally gets into his soup. "Mm, what was that in the soup today, Ma?" he asks Durga. To limit his cravings she offers him a restricted menu of children born in certain birth combinations: twins, an only child, boy-girl-boy, and others born out of place or away from home. All these are tainted and designated for death; the goal of the exorcism to remove impurity and danger. In figure 3.2, the clothes of participating children are draped over the screen.

At the end of the show, they gather behind the screen and pull a pandanus string, the other end held by the puppeteer, unraveling an empty leaf basket (a container without content: inversion of the problem to be solved), releasing them from Kala's power. The performance, known as *ruwatan*, refers to this act of freeing: an exorcism.[4]

Hosted by worried parents, the event combines deadly serious themes with ghost-train comedy. Kala himself is a gurgling buffoon, the cause of superstitious thrills rather than genuine terror. But the moment of exorcism is a solemn pause in the levity. The burning of incense, the descent of Wisnu, and the incantation of mantras by

Figure 3.2 Javanese shadow play exorcism (with children's clothes draped over top of screen). Photograph by the author.

the puppeteer are tense with significance. At any rate, parents of twins—a dish fit for a demon—are eager to stage the event, preferring not to take the risk.

Evil Unleashed: A "Witch Craze"

Here, then, in contrast to Nias, is a moral framework that requires no double standard, no self-denial. Evil is conceptualized, acknowledged, put on stage, and managed. It's all good, clean fun. Yet Java, too, has had its periodic convulsions and strife—famously, its Year of Living Dangerously. When Java runs *amuk* (a Javanese word), Kala escapes the bounds of the play. Indeed, we are forewarned of the possibility; for, like Brechtian drama, the plot violates the distinction between audience and characters. The host's family even figure among the puppets, while the puppeteer, in his screen avatar, chases the burping ogre through the village on his quest for victims. (In Bomo, a poor village further south, when funds are lacking for a full performance, the local magician, dressed as the monster, *recites* the Kala myth, then chases twins, triplets, and other edible combinations round the village, Benny Hill style.) Once Kala is loose, like the genie, he's very hard to put back in the bottle.

Which is what happened as my second period of fieldwork in Java ended in 1997, just before the fall of the dictator Suharto. A "witch craze" broke out that led—over the next year—to the lynching of over one hundred people across the district.[5] When the first case occurred in a village near where I was living, I heard the news from a carpenter who had been working there. Over the remains of a neighborhood prayer-meal, he related the events with grim satisfaction—how the victim had been dragged out and cut down, how a mob had burned down the house—and he pronounced the death a "cleansing." But his audience disputed whether the victim could really be a sorcerer and whether black magic (*sihir*) was a fiction, as the headman protested, or an undeniable fact. Such was the view of the carpenter, who as neighborhood imam carried influence. In his words, which seemed to express a dogma, "It may not be disbelieved."

In the next weeks, reports of other attacks followed, always in a haze of rumor and contradiction. Victims were reputed sorcerers or preachers, madmen or vagrants; killers were neighbors or outsiders, security agents or masked ninjas. It was disturbing but not extraordinary; no one imagined what would follow: the deaths, the curfews, the investigations. No one expects the Spanish Inquisition. And yet, paving the way, a blasphemy trial in a nearby town caused riots, stoking official panic and public anxiety about the unrest spreading. Anonymous phone calls reached outlying villages, leaflets were dropped in mosques. Briefly, the road to Banyuwangi was sealed.

Before the witch hunt was in full swing in 1998, and the whole district frantic, I had made my exit. There being no on-the-spot accounts by trained observers, most views of what happened—my own included—depended on hearsay and rumor-fed press reports. By the time proper research was begun, stories had been told to reporters, policemen, independent commissions, and to villagers by and about themselves so many times that the actuality—whether said, done, or imagined—was scarcely recoverable. You might say the same of the Great Repentance; but among miserable sinners, there was nothing more to hide—that was the point.

Explanations of the witch craze have been wildly diverse, with conspiracy theories to the fore: that instigators were Suharto's men spreading chaos, or jihadis bent on liquidating the infidel, or *anti*-Muslim provocateurs blackening orthodox parties as a threat to pluralism.[6] A surplus of theory contrasted with a dearth of first-hand information. In a pattern that Nils Bubandt (2001), writing of other conflicts, calls an "epidemic logic," external factors—local radio and media speculation, security warnings (social media had hardly begun)—kindled local fears and reprisals, producing the dreaded outcomes.

Only two accounts derive from anthropological research and both reject conspiracy. The Cornell anthropologist James Siegel, who conducted interviews in 2000, divines an existential crisis. The collapse of the Suharto regime left people bewildered. Totalitarian surveillance had *created* its subjects, but the mirror in which people saw themselves defined, and recognized themselves as citizens, suddenly clouded. In the rural hinterland, on the edge of the state, agency became obscure, so obscure that villagers suspected even themselves of being witches: repositories of malignity in the Africanist sense (Siegel 2006, 124; Evans-Pritchard 1937). Paraphrasing, one might say that the occult powers of the state—the right over life and death—passed to those who had ceased to belong to it. Witchcraft supplanted statecraft. The victims of mob violence were scapegoats—evil externalized and eradicated—and the witchcraze a scattershot, preemptive strike. As in the anticommunist pogroms of the 1960s, killing became a way of establishing one's innocence. But mutilation and dismembering, literal overkill, only served to emphasize the futility of the quest and the virulence of contagion.

Siegel's thesis might conceivably fit the capital, Jakarta, with its Orwellian ministries and legions of spies, or the intricate hierarchy of the traditional sultanates. But there were no "witch" killings in Jakarta or Jogja. The violence erupted where the ruler's gaze never determined identity or everyday experience. Siegel's theory ignores the history and geography that made the area what it is: the proximity to Hindu Bali, the 250-year lag in colonization and the imposition of Islam, the distinct regional culture which not for nothing is called Osing, the vernacular word for No, a one-fingered salute to the political center.

Against Siegel's poststructuralist analysis, a young Australian scholar, Nicholas Herriman (2014), offers older-style evidence. In 2001, he carried out twelve months of fieldwork south of Banyuwangi, sampling affected villages in every subdistrict, doing interviews (150 of them), and checking press reports against police records. The facts, thus constituted, showed that in nearly every case, alleged sorcerers and their victims were known to one another. Suspicions followed the familiar trail of grudges and misfortunes. The pattern was normal for sorcery-related killings in Java. No need for ninjas, the deep state, or Derridean specters. What was abnormal was the scale, which Herriman attributes to the loosening of the state. People seized the opportunity to take revenge and exact community justice on alleged deviants just as they had always done when disorder permitted. They joined in because of peer pressure or because they could get away with it. This is what they told Herriman, and this is what the facts, assembled from name lists, interviews, and court judgments, amply confirmed. Herriman's forensic presentation and his trenchant dismissal of half-baked theories are compelling ("I could find no evidence for this" chimes like a mantra through the text). Yet any reconstruction, however firmly grounded, will leave ethnographic lacunae. There is a distance between act, report, and interview that cannot be factored out, and layers of linguistic complexity—Indonesian (the language of officialdom), Madurese, and Javanese in at least two regional variants—that cannot show through. The difficulty of constructing a sufficient narrative, of recovering motivation, situated thought, and emotion in formal interviews with strangers—all without personal knowledge of lives or circumstances—obscures what lies *behind* the facts, which are not, in any case, neutral evidence but constructions by interested parties *after the fact*. An ethnographic hinterland, a history of relations, cannot be denied for lack of present evidence. In Banyuwangi, people get ill, bear grudges, and don't ordinarily take revenge—least of all, on behalf of others. Rules of avoidance and norms of harmony mean that personal quarrels rarely ramify, even within a family. Why, then, did something long tolerated become suddenly intolerable, bad enough for murder? Why *these* particular individuals, these aggressors, these victims? Why would hundreds join in a killing? Why the extreme savagery? And why did some villages—such as Bayu, my own home-from-home—escape the violence? What checks and balances protected Bayu but failed in Kenjo or Kabat? We are back with the origin questions.

The Presence of the Past

It is possible to reconcile the two approaches. Herriman nails the proximate causes—strange illnesses, grudging suspicions; Siegel explains the paranoia. But equally, each theory undermines the other. As in any conflicted history, the reconstituted facts must, in part, be *post hoc* rationalizations, shaped for diverse audiences, including the tellers themselves. Give the cops what they want, and don't let them think we are gullible rustics. As Siegel (2006, 146) puts it, "citing disputes thus normalizes the uncanny," whereas the uncanny is what needs to be explained. Siegel's political model is misplaced (by several hundred miles), and his recipe for evil confuses sorcery with witchcraft and witchcraft with spirit possession. Yet, eventually, his finger lands, I'm pretty sure, on the right spot, the sore point, if not the root of evil (2006, 161–62). It has to do with the relation between present and past; and to anyone familiar with Indonesia, it will seem all too obvious, though the case could only be made through intimate narrative engagement, not factual accounting or abstract speculation. Faulkner's weighty comment on the defeated American South comes to mind: "The past is never dead," he opined, "it's not even past." The historic defeats of the Confederate South, Republican Spain, Indonesian communism, and pagan Nias all have in common a stifled, unspeakable history, a broken timeline bisected Before and After. In Nias, the reference point was the Great Repentance; in Java, the coup of 1965. The anti-communist massacres of that year, with up to a million dead, were a pivotal moment, shaping national and village politics ever since.

Banyuwangi, a communist stronghold, suffered twenty-five thousand dead (Cribb 1991, 10). The army and Muslim organizations may have led the killings, but in the back-country, every village had its homegrown, black-clad death squad and its quota of victims. Complicity—often born of fear—was widely shared. Yet the fear that ruled the countryside back then was less of the communists (who mostly were *not*) than of the people afraid of the communists: the vigilantes. The modus operandi of nighttime raids, road blocks, and mutilations was the template for the later witch craze in which, once more, it was fear of the men in black that prevailed—hence the panicky talk of ninjas and outside forces (Retsikas 2006). But terror is a double-edged sword. The horror that the vigilantes inflicted came back to haunt them. The retired killers, some of whom I knew well in the 1990s, have tended to die badly—at least, that's how others like to see it—and their deaths are usually explained by the law of karma. Tapan of Bayu was found dead in a ditch, covered in ants; Rapi'i fell mute and died, unmourned, during my last stay. The more reflective, which is not to say guilty, expect a cosmic reckoning. For there's no escaping *cakra manggilingan*, the wheel of fortune. In the old Javanese saying, what goes around comes around. Yet, as I often observed in late night conversations, any talk of blame arouses a vague anxiety, for who in this affair was innocent? Natural justice—a tidy end, if also a sticky end—turns out to be one more evasion.

A Political Exorcism

So where is Kala in this story? In popular cosmology, ghouls and sorcerers belong to Kala's army; and in the classical dualist symbolism, they are among the "figures of the left" (*pengiwa*): the *sinister*, one might say, whereas the Islamic line, descending from Adam, comprises the figures of the right (Beatty 1999, 107–8; Pigeaud 1967–70, I: 151). In a perversion of the traditional order, which allows some legitimacy to the left-hand Indic line, the *political* left became demonized, and factional killings equated with witch-cleansings. It was to the "sinister" line that communists were assigned in 1965. Propaganda made their mass destruction into a preordained exorcism, a purification ushering in the restoration of order under Suharto; the New Order, as it was called. The recent witch hunt lacked this catch-all deviant category, but the political context was no less crucial even if the victims were less determinate. In the months after Suharto fell, Kala-exorcisms took place in cities across Java (Headley 2004, 453–73).

It might seem, then, that when circumstances require, Javanese can conveniently project their demons outward, making of Kala and his tribe an external enemy where philosophy once made him a human symbol. But the ravenous terror that gripped Banyuwangi during the witch craze suggests the projection is not entirely successful. Like the Great Repentance in Nias, the legacy of past massacres, revived in contemporary lynchings is, unavoidably, a return of the repressed: the victims who keep coming back to be killed. Siegel calls it "the repetition of an historical event, one never assimilated and therefore repeated" (Siegel 2006, 162). In monstering the Other—whether communists, magicians, or misfits—Javanese evade their demons, whitewashing their terrible past. Unlike Kala, these demons cannot be exorcised because they mostly have no face or name; their referent is a "thing of darkness none acknowledge" as their own.

All this is relatively new in Indonesian history: evil has burst its bounds and run riot. Yet the framing of evil—or rather the way it has of slipping through the frame—is not new; for evil has always been a threshold phenomenon—of interleaving realms, categorical borders, and fugue states. The sperm that finds no womb; the monster that hunts in the shadowless noon; the headhunters, half-men, half-animal: all are dangerous because of their vague dislocation, their haunting semipresence. Like the spirit world that governs it, evil is on the fringes of the everyday, elusive but palpable, most potent when sensed rather than seen or grasped. Its evocation in spectacle is paradoxical, displacing; and what can be more deranging than the trauma of conversion or the black ops of the shadowy state? For these new kinds of evil, neither prayer nor mantra will suffice.

Conclusion

Let me end with some comments that bring together three interrelated aspects of evil: its structural dimensions, its affective quality, and its essential mystery. In my Indonesian examples, evil consists in harm inflicted by and upon others who are *more* or *less* than human: ninja, headhunter, monster, communist, sorcerer: an other who is always, potentially, oneself. Hence the ritual format, the off-putting fancy dress, the mutilations. In his book *Religion and Its Monsters*, the Bible scholar Timothy Beal writes that "monsters are in the world but not of the world. They are paradoxical personifications of *otherness within sameness* . . . threatening figures of anomaly within the well-established and accepted order of things. They represent the outside that has gotten inside" (Beal 2001, 4—original emphasis). My Indonesian cases express Beal's formulation, which also gives us an angle on their contrasting figurations, a perspective on evil that is neither theological nor rooted in Christian or Islamic cosmologies. Javanese exorcism plays on the outside/inside motif from the beginning: the spilt seed, the puppeteer channeling Vishnu, the domestication and ejection of Kala from the village. Ritual patrols the borders and expels what has "gotten inside." But this tidy arrangement breaks down with the unraveling of the New Order. Evil in the contrasting Nias case is constructed on a separation of human and monster/headhunter achieved through doubling and denial.[7] But conversion leads to an interiorization of the distinction, a move from inside-out to outside-in. The monstering of the self.

Whatever its primeval origin and its protean forms, evil is conjured *between people*—humans acting inhumanly; not between people and God, as is the case with sin. Yet it is the otherworldliness, the garish supernatural light, that discovers or creates evil and that distinguishes it from ordinary wrongdoing. That discovery, in turn, is an *emotional* response, not a cool assessment or moral reckoning. Evil is in the heart of the beholder: a reaction of fear, loathing, or horror. It is the disclosure that, in turn, produces the uncanny effect, the jolting sense of dislocation, *déjà vu*, or supernatural doubling. As Royle puts it:

> The uncanny has to do with the sense of a secret encounter . . . an apprehension, however fleeting, of something that should have remained secret and hidden but has come to light. But it is not "out there," in any simple sense: as a crisis of the proper and natural, it disturbs any straightforward sense of what is inside and what is outside. The uncanny has to do with a strangeness of framing and borders, an experience of liminality. (2003, 2)

The Abrahamic traditions that refract evil through sin, humanizing it, mostly miss the outlandish, hair-raising, monstrous character of evil conveyed by the Indonesian examples (though Job's Leviathan fits the bill). In the Western tradition, this incalculable effect finds expression not in orthodoxy but in imaginative works that escape or defy doctrine: *Moby Dick*, *The Turn of the Screw*, *Macbeth*—figurations of evil that hover mystifyingly in paradox, plumbing depths, inverting perceptions (*Fair is foul, foul is fair*), confounding black and white, inner/outer distinctions. The transgressing of boundaries that produces the uncanny means that evil defies reckoning, a just apportioning of blame. However sensational, however banal, evil remains an unfathomable mystery.[8] Yet it has definable contexts and its recognition obeys a distinct psychobiological mechanism, raising hairs, making the flesh creep. Crucial to both my cases, a generational gap—a mute incubation period—prepares the way for a terrifying eruption of the past. And this return, in the Gothic conception, is uncanny. The German word—Freud's word—is *unheimlich*, "unhomely," an etymology that could fruitfully be explored in an ethnographic context where *pernah*, Javanese for "feeling at home," "comfortably placed," is both a salient emotion and a primary social objective (Beatty 2019). Beal writes: "Monsters are personifications of the *unheimlich*. They stand for what endangers one's sense of at-homeness, that is, one's sense of security, stability, integrity, well-being, health and meaning. They make one feel *not at home at home*. They are figures of chaos and disintegration *within* order and orientation" (2001, 5—original emphases). In both Java and Nias, evil is a phenomenon of dislocation, being out of place, no longer at home in the world. Kala may be dismissed for a while, the headhunter banished, but efforts to root out evil must end in failure, for evil no longer has a root, if it ever had.

Andrew Beatty, Brunel University London

Notes

1. The people of Nias are called Niha ("human," Niasan).
2. Information on the Great Repentance (*fangesa dödö sebua*) is mostly buried in missionary archives and journals. Among examples consulted: Anonymous 1916, 1917; Müller 1931. Hummel and Telaumbanua (2007) is a theological PhD dissertation. Information on Orahua and Central Nias, where the Repentance happened much later, is based on

fieldwork from 1986–88 and 2011. Beatty 2012b, an article on conversion and emotion, offers a fuller account.
3. Beatty (2015, 97–98) contains a comic sermon on this theme.
4. Between 1992 and 1997, I watched and recorded segments of half a dozen Kala shows, in villages around Banyuwangi. The stories (*lakon*) differ in certain respects from the classical versions (Van Groenendael 1992). I have also drawn on Headley's presentation of a performance in Central Java (2000) and his erudite study of cosmology (2004).
5. I use the popular terms "witch hunt" and "witch craze" loosely; but, strictly, "there are no practitioners who perform destructive magic as a result of inherited ability. In other words, Javanese society knows of sorcerers but not of witches" (Koentjaraningrat 1985, 419; Geertz 1960, 107). Siegel (2006) disagrees.
6. For several months, regional press reports and unofficial notices were collated in daily online blogs. For a sample of academic discussion, see Retsikas 2006; Van Dijk 2001. My own small speculation (Beatty 1999, 259) was disproved by Herriman's work (2014), which supersedes all previous studies.
7. As Parkin puts it, "the term 'evil' when applied to monsters denotes a field of human impossibilities" (1985, 12).
8. "Ah the mysteries of virtue! The mysteries of evil!" concludes the narrator of *Durga/Umayi*, Mangunwijaya's novelistic transposition of the Kala myth to modern Indonesia (Mangunwijaya 2004, 168).

References

Anderson, Benedict. 1990. *Language and Power: Exploring Political Cultures in Indonesia*. Ithaca, NY: Cornell University Press.
Anonymous. 1916. "Eine religiöse Erweckung in Nias." *Berichte der Rheinischen Missions-Gesellschaft*: 250–51.
———. 1917. "Die Erweckungsbewegung auf Nias." *Berichte der Rheinischen Missions-Gesellschaft*: 7–10, 40–44, 173–74.
Beal, Timothy K. 2001. *Religion and Its Monsters*. London: Routledge.
Beatty, Andrew. 1992. *Society and Exchange in Nias*. Oxford: Clarendon Press.
———. 1999. *Varieties of Javanese Religion*. Cambridge, UK: Cambridge University Press.
———. 2009. *A Shadow Falls: In the Heart of Java*. London: Faber & Faber.
———. 2012a. "Kala Defanged: Managing Power in Java away from the Centre." *Bijdragen tot de Taal-, Land- en Volkenkunde* 168: 173–94.
———. 2012b. "The Tell-Tale Heart: Conversion and Emotion in Nias." *Ethos* 77(3): 295–320.
———. 2015. *After the Ancestors: An Anthropologist's Story*. Cambridge, UK: Cambridge University Press.

———. 2019. *Emotional Worlds: Beyond an Anthropology of Emotion.* Cambridge, UK: Cambridge University Press.

Bubandt, Nils. 2001. "Malukan Apocalypse: Themes in the Dynamics of Violence in Eastern Indonesia." In *Violence in Indonesia.* Edited by Ingrid Wessel and Georgia Wimhöfer. Hamburg: Abera.

Cribb, Robert, ed. 1991. *The Indonesian Killings of 1965–1966: Studies from Java and Bali.* Clayton, Victoria: Monash University.

Davis, Colin. 2007. *Haunted Subjects: Deconstruction, Psychoanalysis and the Return of the Dead.* Basingstoke: Palgrave Macmillan.

Douglas, Mary. 1966. *Purity and Danger.* London: Routledge & Kegan Paul.

Evans-Pritchard, E. 1937. *Witchcraft, Oracles and Magic among the Azande.* Oxford: Oxford University Press.

Fries, E. 1908. "Das 'Koppensnellen' auf Nias." *Allgemeine Missions-Zeitschrift* 35: 73–88.

Freud, Sigmund. 2003. *The Uncanny.* Translated by David McLintock. Harmondsworth: Penguin.

Geertz, Clifford. 1960. *The Religion of Java.* Chicago: University of Chicago Press.

———. 1968. *Islam Observed: Religious Development in Morocco and Indonesia.* Chicago: University of Chicago Press.

Headley, Stephen. 2000. *From Cosmogony to Exorcism in a Javanese Genesis: The Spilt Seed.* Oxford: Oxford University Press.

———. 2004. *Durga's Mosque: Cosmology, Conversion and Community in Central Javanese Islam.* Singapore: Institute of Southeast Asian Studies.

Herriman, Nicholas. 2014. *Witch-hunt and Conspiracy: The "Ninja Case" in East Java.* Clayton: Monash University Publishing.

Hummel, Uwe, and Tuhoni Telaumbanua. 2007. "Cross and Adu: A Socio-historical Study on the Encounter between Christianity and the Indigenous Culture on Nias and the Batu Islands, Indonesia (1865–1965)." PhD dissertation, Utrecht University.

Koentjaraningrat. 1985. *Javanese Culture.* Oxford: Oxford University Press.

Kriele, Ed. 1927. "The Nias Revival." *International Review of Missions* 26(61): 91–102.

Mangunwijaya, Y. B. 2004. *Durga/Umayi.* Translated by Ward Keeler. Seattle: University of Washington Press.

Milton, John. 2005 (1674). *Paradise Lost.* Ed. David Scott Kastan. Indianapolis: Hackett.

Müller, T. 1931. *Die "grosse Reue" auf Nias. Geschichte und Gestalt einer Erweckung auf dem Missionsfelde.* Gütersloh: Bertelsmann.

Müller-Krüger, Theodore. 1968. *Der Protestantismus in Indonesien.* Stuttgart: Evangelisches Verlagswerk.

Parkin, David. 1985. *The Anthropology of Evil.* Oxford: Blackwell.

Pigeaud, Th. 1967–70. *Literature of Java.* 3 vols. The Hague: Martinus Nijhoff.

Preston, Paul. 2000. *Comrades! Portraits from the Spanish Civil War.* London: Fontana Press.

Retsikas, Konstantinos. 2006. "The Semiotics of Violence: Ninja, Sorcerers, and State-Terror in Post-Soeharto Indonesia." *Bijdragen tot de Taal-, Land- en Volkenkunde* 162: 56–94.

Royle, Nicholas. 2003. *The Uncanny*. Manchester: Manchester University Press.

Ricoeur, Paul. 1967. *The Symbolism of Evil*. Translated by Emerson Buchanan. Boston, MA: Beacon Press.

Siegel, James T. 2006. *Naming the Witch*. Redwood City, CA: Stanford University Press.

Van Dijk, Kees. 2001. *A Country in Despair: Indonesia between 1997 and 2000*. Leiden: KITLV Press.

Van Groenendael, C. M. V. 1992 "Is There an Eastern Wayang Tradition? Some Dramatis Personae of the Murwakala Myth of the 'Eastern' Tradition." *Bijdragen tot de Taal-, Land- en Volkenkunde* 148: 309–15.

Chapter 4

MOTHER EVIL IN HELL VALLEY

A CREOLE TRANSVALORIZATION OF EVIL IN TRINIDAD

Roland Littlewood

Mother Nature
She say she be so evil
Evil, evil, evil
Mother, Mother, Mother be so evil
—Extempore song from Pomme Cythère, one of Mother Earth's biological sons

Hell Valley, the Valley of Decision, is not really a valley at all: more a slight declivity on the twenty-mile track between the two villages on the north coast of Trinidad.[1] In the evening, on a clear night, the lighthouse on the neighboring island of Tobago might be seen, but otherwise, nothing obviously manmade remains along the coast except the deserted remnants of scattered hamlets that fifty years ago were inhabited by a local African Caribbean peasantry who worked on the small and now-abandoned coffee, cocoa, and copra estates. The often obscured track is known as the Turnpike, but government intentions to turn it into a metaled road along the coast were abandoned years ago: both villages are reached by existing roads from the interior that end in each village.

Few now pass along the track, perhaps a hiking group of secondary school children or the occasional eccentric mystic seeking out the group who have built their community here. From the path, one can look down on a lawn cropped by two goats, a wooden house—the last survivor of the original village—and a group of "African" style huts. Across the front boards of the house, rough painting proclaims

"Hell Valley—the Devil live here." A silk cotton sapling, to the locals the mark of African sorcery, grows against the house. Around the settlement, the land has been cleared and planted with a wide variety of local cultigens—banana, yam, coffee, tobacco, dasheen, coconut, and so on. Beyond the cultivated area, the track disappears once more into the bush on each side through which it continues onto a village in the West, to Pinnacle in the East, both around ten miles away. To the North, a cliff descends from the track down to the sea where a rocky shore harbors two boats carved and built by the Earth People.

Trinidad's national history is typical of the anglophone Caribbean—settlement by the Spanish in the fifteenth century, then by the French with the establishment of sugar slave plantations, conquered by the British, the end of slavery and economic decline, nineteenth-century Indian immigration, local internal government, labor unrest in the 1930s, independence in 1962. Since the early twentieth century, its oil industry has been exploited and the standard of living is high, supposedly the third highest in the Americas after the United States and Canada; certain rural areas excepted, concrete houses, electricity, piped water, and metaled roads are standard. Secondary education is compulsory and the oil revenues have allowed the establishment of a steel works and large construction and other industries. The labor intensive agricultural cultivation of sugar, coffee, cocoa, and *ground provisions* has been effectively abandoned and the bulk of "local" food is brought in to anglophone Trinidad from the smaller and poorer islands to the north.

In the northeast of the island, the mountains of the Northern range, the geographical continuation of the South American Cordillera, rise from the sea to three thousand feet. They were occupied only in the late nineteenth century by the exslaves, isolated families who established a "reconstituted peasantry" (as Mintz calls it) of small *estates* of coffee and cocoa in the lower reaches—"behind God's back"—growing coconuts and provision in the narrow littoral.

Few Trinidadian people have not heard of the Earth People, a small community established on this coast. In a country familiar with the millennial religious response of the Shouter Baptists, and with the Rastafari movement, a recent import from Jamaica, the Earth People remain an enigma. Their appearance, from the villages to the capital Port of Spain, causes public outrage, for their most outstanding characteristic is that they go about naked. Public opinion favors the view that these young men, carrying staves and cutlasses, and with the long matted dreadlocks of the Rastas, are probably crazy—if not the whole group, then their leader, Mother Earth, whose visions once gave birth to the movement and who accompanies their marches to town. Each dry season, the group leaves the coast for Port-of-Spain, walking naked or with short kilts of sacking, to pass on to other people their message and to gather new recruits from the poorer working-class areas east of the capital, areas that appear to have missed out on Trinidad's new oil wealth. Communication, however, is hampered by the Earth Peoples' nakedness, their characteristic language with their deliberate and frequent use of obscenities, and Mother Earth's striking doctrines. She announces to Trinidadians, a largely devout if hardly a church-going population, that God does not exist but that she herself is the Biblical Devil, the Mother of Africa and India, Nature incarnate.

In 1973, after Trinidad's brief Black Power "uprising," when she was thirty-nine, she left Port-of-Spain along with some of her children and her then partner, to settle in one of the deserted hamlets of the coast overlooking a rocky bay and a long curving beach bisected by a river that, laden with mangroves, slowly entered the sea as a modest delta between the overgrown coconut groves, now abandoned except for occasional forays by fishermen from the two villages to gather copra.

The family had been Spiritual (Shouter) Baptists, and they continued to "pick along in the Bible" as she puts it, fasting like others in Lent and interpreting the visionary import of their dreams. After the birth of twins in their wooden hut in 1975, Jeanette experienced a series of revelations. She became aware that the Christian doctrine of God the Father as Creator was untrue and that the world was rather the work of a primordial Mother who had created the original race of black people, once hermaphrodite, the Race of the Mother, the Race of Africa and India. But Her rebellious Son reentered his Mother's womb to steal her power of creation and succeeded in modifying part of her creation to produce the white people, the Race of the Son, the Race of Death. The whites, acting as the Son's agents, once enslaved the blacks and have continued to exploit them. The Way of the Children of the Son is the Way of Death, of technology, cities, clothes, schools, hospitals, factories, and wage labor. The Way of the Children of the Mother is the Way of Nature: a return to the simplicity of the Beginning, a simplicity of nakedness, cultivation of the land by hand and with respect, of gentle and nonexploiting human relationships.

The Son, in his continued quest for the power of domination, has recently entered into a new phase. He has succeeded in establishing himself in black people and is also on the point of creating nonhuman people, both robots and computers. The Mother, who has borne all this behavior out of Her love for him, has finally lost patience. She is about to end the current order of the Son in a catastrophic drought and famine, the End, a destruction of the Son's work through the agency of his own Children, after which the original state of Nature will once again prevail.

Jeanette herself, the human woman, is a partial incarnation of the original Mother who will fully enter into her at the End. Her task now is to assist the return to Nature by establishing a community on the coast, Hell Valley, the Valley of Decision, to prepare for the return to the Beginning and to "put out" the truth to her people, the black nation, the Mother's Children. She has to combat the mistaken doctrines of our existing religions—Christianity and Islam—which revere the Son over the Mother, and to correct the distorted teaching of the Bible. For She herself is the Devil and represents Life and Nature, in opposition to the so-called Christian God who is really only her Son, the principle of Science and Death. As the Devil, she is opposed to churches and prisons, education and money, politics and urban life, contemporary morals and fashionable opinions.

The exact timing of the End is uncertain, but it will come in Jeanette's physical lifetime. Then Time itself will cease, disease will be healed, the blind see, the deaf hear, the crippled walk, and the Nation will speak one language. The Son will return to his own proper planet, the Sun, really a planet of ice, which is currently hidden from us by Fire placed there by the Mother.

Since her revelations, which mark the Beginning of the End, in 1975, Mother Earth's family has been joined by a small number of black Trinidadians, often old friends and neighbors from town, young men who sometimes bring their girlfriends and children to come and "Plant for the Nation." The community has a high turnover, and while over fifty people have been associated with the Earth People, when I stayed with them in 1981–82, there were twenty-three young men living in the Valley of Decision with perhaps twenty close sympathizers in town, some of whom come each year and spend some time in the Valley.

The Inversion of Customary Symbols

For the observer, one of the most striking things about the group is just how "nonevil" they are in any conventional sense of everyday international English. The group are quiet, placid, humorous, generous, and, on the whole, nonquarrelsome. It is in their idiom that they have turned upside down many customary usages.

As God is "right" in normative discourse, the Earth People revere the "left" and interchange the meanings (though not in direction), and they are aware of the association of the "left" with the progressive side in politics. Hence, "Are you all left?" and "All left!"—their customary salutations, often made with a clenched fist. "Bad" is exchanged for "good": "This fish broth real bad, give me some more." Conventional obscenities are the Natural words and should always be used, for Mother Earth is herself the Cunt of all, the source of all life.

Such inversions (Needham 1979) are generally restricted to a few key terms and then in a recognized ideological sense. Thus, to stub one's toe on a tree root and say, "That felt good," would occasion puzzlement and *picong* (satire), but maybe also lead to a discussion of one's particular values. The inevitable confusion between standard and community uses of these terms, such as happens particularly among new members, leads to general merriment and teasing, part of the process of *humbling yourself* on entering the community.

The Earth People are dealing with a problem that faces any new religion or alternative dispensation that emerges out of an existing and dominant religious tradition—here Christianity. If you accept that the old religion was in some ways valid, you can attack it for its individual hypocrites who have failed to live up to their professed ideas (just as Christianity did with the Hebrew religion). You can take the earlier doctrines and consider them only a partial manifestation of the real but new truth (Christianity again, and also Islam in relation to Christianity itself). Or you can take the old religion as having deliberately concealed some of its truths or made them available in only a disguised form (as with "cargo" and "nativist" cults, and other colonized responses to missionary Christianity). To a variable extent, you have to dismiss the old truths altogether, arguing they have been superseded or reconceptualized by the new dispensation (Christianity maintaining it fulfilled the old Hebrew Law in spirit rather than in letter, Islam in criticizing Christianity for having elevated its prophet into a God).

The Earth People use all these various possibilities. They retain the old Christian schema of a Creator (God in Christianity, the Mother for the EP), whose close adherent or offspring rebels against the Creator as an Adversary (Satan in Christianity, the Son for the EP).[2] The Son/Sun elision used by Mother Earth seems to reemphasize the fact that the earth is getting nearer the sun, becoming hotter,[3] and is about to be shriveled up, presumably through the Son's mistaken agency, though that is not elaborated (oil, the vital blood of Nature, is being drained away). Enough is enough! The Creator, sensing (or proposing) the end time is near, incarnates themselves into human form (Jesus in Christianity, Jeanette among the Earth People): so Jesus *is* God, and Jeanette *is* the Earth Mother. The old terms are retained by transvalorization, but "God" now becomes the subordinate principle—not the Father, but the incestuous Son rebelling against his parthenogenic Mother and raping her. Because Christianity has presented this schema in a Bible written already *upsided down*, the new dispensation has to invert the inversion to get back to the original truth, and it takes on Christianity's term for its rebellious principle, the Devil, but one which now names the benign Creator. The Earth People still retain much of the original biblical phraseology, but understood in its inverted sense: "I am the Way, the Truth and the Life," proclaims Mother Earth.

A Problem of Evil

What representations presage Mother Earth's rebellious Son? The parent–child relation already describes the orisha–human pair in Trinidad's African-derived *shango* religion, as in Christianity where humans are the Children of God. Her Son has only gained his power through The Mother, to whom he remains subordinate; in some ways, he recalls an erring Black son, akin perhaps more to his Mother than to the human Society he brings into being. He is identified with the Christian God and with Jesus, and in the earlier days of the movement, before a clear opposition to Christianity emerged, Jeanette's partner Cyprian was called the Good Shepherd, a common name for Jesus in both Shouter Baptism and shango and which may be adopted by core members of either group.

Although Mother Earth now styles herself as the Devil, her attributes as The Mother—preeminence and autochthoneity—are closer to those of the Christian's God than they are to those of their Devil. The latter has hardly been an important figure anyway in West Indian Christianity. In West Africa, the Devil was identified by the missionaries in the power Eshu, the male trickster, probably because Eshu was associated with the erotic and with fire. In Trinidad, Eshu retains his phallic characteristics and association with thresholds, as in Brazil where he becomes a "negative spirit" (Simpson 1980). Herskovits (1958) suggests that the Satan of Afro-America retains the ludic characteristics of the trickster, and local Christianity emphasizes our unregenerate nature rather than the attraction of the Evil One who, if he appears at all, does so in the form of the carnival masquerade figure *jabjab* (*diable-diable*), more prankster than devil.[4]

The ordering of moral power distinguishes what we might call "should be" from "should not be." In the West, at least, this distinction is closely aligned with the actual ontology of our world: "what should be" is to an extent "what is," although "what is" may alternatively be taken as a relatively neutral battleground for moral forces. (To talk in this way of "what should not be" is quite clumsy, but we cannot automatically resort to the conventional notion of "evil," for this, of course, is the term that, in Mother Earth's inversion, stands for "what should be.") "What should not be" may be equated with some preexistent ground as to be a formed or residual Nature (as in South Asian religions), or alternatively as coequal and coeternal with "what should be" in "what is" (Manichean dualism), or as a fallen variant of the original order (Western monotheism). After Parkin (1985), we may gloss these ideal types as monist, dualist, and semidualist. But in any actual tradition as practical, including the universal religions, we are likely to find a mélange of coexisting explanations.

How does the world of "what should not be" continue to intrude into the world of "what should be" or "what is"? It may be contingent on the recalcitrant moral evolution of our world, or in God's testing of us, or from the Devil, or else through the individual (sin), through others (witchcraft), or just from the stars or even by sheer chance. Dominant social groups define themselves through the moral order of "what should be": frequently with "what is." That their (to us historically located) institutions are identical to the eternally sacred is for them self-evident. Subdominant sectors are aligned to "what should not be": in the West to Evil, or later to the prehuman or the elemental. Thus, the European cleric has on occasion taken both women and Blacks as morally close to the powers of Evil, while the nineteenth-century biologist saw them as an undifferentiated Nature out of which males and Whites have evolved. The subdominant (sometimes with dissidents from the dominant group who are no longer convinced of the universal truth or of their own personal fit with it) start from this ascribed identity, to affirm themselves, relative to the dominant order, in a variety of different ways:

1. Taking themselves as the true exemplars of dominant values, which are not (or no longer) located in the dominant group: for example radical European Puritanism (Quakers, Anabaptists) and those Afro-American sects which preach a Black God (such as Ras Tafari, Black Muslims).
2. Arguing that the dominant values are flawed in some way: insurgent Christianity and radical Puritanism in its secular shift.

3. Recognizing the dominant system as inevitable, but seeing it as somehow misconceived: a rare and essentially "pessimistic" position, that of some Gnostics, the romantic diabolists, and the Frankists.
4. Emphasizing a more complex variant of the dominant values so that different levels of knowledge, different moral dispensations, are simultaneously true: Gnostics, Kabbalists. This may be associated with an emergent or evolutionary "monist" perspective (Marxism or the Hermetic corpus of *high science* [European magic] in Trinidad).
5. Just accepting the subdominant position: untouchables among the Hindus, and the baptized peoples of the European empires—on the surface at least.
6. Rejecting the dominant values altogether as fundamentally misconceived. This of course cannot be absolute, for within any system, the possibility of innovation is limited to those things already recognized as alternative or equivalent, between which a new choice is made. Nevertheless, the "feel" of total rejection is common to the participants' own experience of their actions, even while we might argue that their perspective retains close affinities with positions 1 and 2, as for Jamaican Ras Tafari or Philadelphia Move whose discourse remains essentially biblical.

If we take the oppositional sensibility as an intermittent set of psychological, moral, and social rebellions against the established order, we will not be surprised to find many of these alternatives coincide with, or succeed, each other within the same oppositional movement; in the case of Ras Tafari, the Jamaican Native Baptists plus the continuing African and *high science* knowledge together with a conscious Black countertradition, and with African anticolonialism.

Mother Earth's frank and radical identification with the Devil cuts across many of the justifications and apologies of those oppositional ideologies still tied to Christianity. She freely adopts the most prejudiced (the more prejudiced the better) imagery of the standard "what should not be." In Afro-American English, *evil* and *bad* already carry a defiant and slightly self-parodying sense, egalitarian and demotic. It is thus a short step to radicalize their perversity as central. In Hell Valley, the term *evil* also refers to everyday life. When Breadfruit's preparation of a fish soup is praised as "fucking evil," this is not so far removed from the Pinnacle villagers' cheerful tribute to puncheon rum as "wicked," or the urban Trinidad matrons' exasperated but ultimately accepting—if wry—description of the local tearaways as "bad an' wort'less, ai' no behaviour."[5]

Similarly, Hell ("Heaven" is not a term used by the Earth People) returns us to the original Life. As Karl Rahner suggests, the Western notion of hell has always contained some sense of the deep, the elemental, the ancestral: "When we think of man entering hell we think of him as establishing contact with the most intrinsic, unified and deepest level of the reality of the world" (1962, 22). Such "weak" usages of evil, hell, and the Devil playfully contravene the conventional "strong," moral, usage. They are never entirely lacking in a conscious desire *épater le bourgeois*, which for me when in the Valley recalled Baudelaire, Swinburne, and Aleister Crowley. There is, quite simply, enormous fun in the rather delicious pursuit of "evil."

At the same time, personal identification with these terms does articulate a major cognitive alternative. A reaffirmation of subdominant values argues: "If this then is evil, what is your good?" Much of what can be read as antinomian high spirits or lurid fascination is arguably a forced choice for the nondominant in a rigidly dual system, as for those anticolonial rebels in the Cook Islands who marked themselves with "the sign of Satan" (Burridge 1971, 22). (To which we may compare the rural Guatemalan revering of Judas.) Simpson (1978, 217) argues that the black slaves of the Caribbean regarded the Devil as "a friend in need," and Worsley (1970) recalls that among wartime Melanesian cults, "Djaman [German] was favoured as an anti-Government tongue." Madam Blavasky is supposed to have said to Yeats, "I used to wonder and pity the people who sell their souls to the Devil, but now I only pity them. They have to have someone on their side," like the Devil supplicated by the infamous Canon Docre in Huysmans's *Là-Bas*: "Mainstay of the Despairing Poor, Cardinal of the Vanquished, King of the Disinherited" (1891, 246). Michael Taussig (1980) considers such an identification with the enemy's enemy in his book *The Devil and Commodity Fetishism in South America*: the Afro-American peasants of the Colombian plantations and the Quechua-speaking peasants working Bolivian tin mines both invoke the Devil to increase their production, but to do so is ultimately to be blighted. Taussig argues, "The Devil is a stunningly apt symbol of the alienation experienced by peasants as they enter the ranks of the proletariat." While Irene Silverblatt (1987) sees this Devil as one imported by the whites to represent indigenous traditions, recalling the transformation of Eshu by the missionaries, Taussig takes the Devil as a representation of competitive relations of production but also as standing for black people themselves. The Columbian peasant can lend himself to the Devil temporarily, but this is self-defeating; unlike Mother Earth, he is seeking palliation, a temporary accommodation. Whether the

Devil could be said to have served as a symbol of black resistance in the Caribbean before Mother Earth is uncertain. Rastas and Black Muslims alike use the term "devil" for the whites, but George Simpson (1980) briefly cites a ganja-using group in Jamaica whose members called on the Devil and sought possession by "fallen spirits."

The Son/Sun

In everyday conversation, Mother Earth uses "Sun" and "Son" almost interchangeably. In Christianity, the association (in English of course a homophone) is not uncommon: solar representations of God or his son Jesus derive from St. John's Gospel and the Book of Revelation. Fire, of course, characterizes not only the light of the Gospel, but also Hell, whose proud Lucifer, the Son of the Morning, is another, albeit rebellious, son. Fire is also popularly assimilated to other attributes devalued by Mother Earth—anger, sickness, sexuality, jealousy— while the converse of light, darkness, is an attribute of both the Devil and the European's colonial image of Africa.[6]

In its permanence and power, the Sun is a powerful everyday representation of "what is" and "what should be." On occasion, it has served as an emblem for the oppressed, as it did for Spartacus's insurgent Kingdom of the Sun. Morton (1952) claims that by the third century AD, the Sun had come to represent the "millennial aspirations of the dispossessed," only to be co-opted back into the establishment by Diocletian and thence into state Christianity. If the Sun seems vital to natural power, how can Mother Earth relinquish it so easily to the whites? In part because, whatever the tourist image of the bountiful sun, the experience of agriculture in the Caribbean is not, as in gloomy Britain, waiting on the reluctant sun but an active protection against this omnipresent and destructive solar power— skin-darkening, energy-drawing, madness-inducing (Littlewood 1993). *Shade trees* have to be planted to give plants shelter from the sun so that they can grow, and the earth appears virtually self-fecundating. For the Earth People, the Son's planet is, confusingly, really the Planet of Ice; its apparent heat has been placed between the Sun and the Earth to obstruct his return to our planet when he is finally expelled. The heat then comes from the Earth itself; at the Miracle, the Beginning of the End, The Mother made this heat come closer to the Earth to redeem us physically. "When you body more free, is to develop more heat—which is power," says Jeanette. This employs the local Hot-Cold idiom in which our everyday labor produces heat that saps our energy and that we attempt to reduce by working less or by taking a diuretic bush tea (Littlewood 1993). Uniquely among country people, the Earth People do not take a cooling and continue to work when they are really heated:

> The Sun suppose to be putting back inside of you, not drawing! You can feel it "drawing" yes, because of the spirit which is in your flesh which is not able to stand the heat. You cannot stand it because your body become weak to your own self which is the fire. Your body is make up out of fire. Without that fire in your body, your body is not living. So now that heat that is returning, your body have to build again because you have to take off the clothes. And when the clothes is off, your body will start receiving the elements as the animals. Wild animals take the heat and you cannot take it? You are clothed with clothes which not belongings to you so then your body becomes weak. The sun you suppose to be able to take it, as the animals do, the birds do. Now I will put it this way: not until yourself spirit keep coming closer to the flesh by your nakedness, your living, your thinking, then there is nothing that will bother you, neither heat nor cold, because your body will be mature for that. (Mother Earth audio-recorded on my last visit to her in 1982)[7]

An opposition of Sun to Moon in European and Amerindian mythologies usually parallels one of Male to Female (but sometimes the converse). For the Earth People, the Moon—the womb of the Earth, which was penetrated by the Son—was then expelled to become the planet we see: "Corruption had entered She, and She had to spit it out," says Mother Earth. Eliade has suggested that this affinity of the Moon and the Earth, both in opposition to the Sun, is simply experientially obvious. Colonial slaves, like the earlier Caribs, used the moon for registering plantation work periods, and lunar cycles of animal and plant growth are still recognized by local field workers. In Trinidad, men associate the moon with women's inconstancy, with their natural fecundity and menstruation: the very word "moon" may refer to their genitals (Lewis 1983, 41). As with other rural Trinidadian women, Mother Earth maintains that her menstrual periods are synchronous with the moon, whose waxing and waning are associated with the intermittent passage of its energy to the earth.

She talks of the Sun and Moon simply as principles rather than sensible objects[8]—"they ai' planets; they is life"—but their properties retain those of the planets we see. "Everything has its meaning, its sign, everything carry its spirit," says Mother Earth the semiotician. She rejects the heliocentric arrangement of the planets. When I drew it in the dust of her hut in the course of our debates, she was indignant. "This is madness! You turn the children upside down. How could the planets be before the Earth when it brings forth?" Jakatan concurred:

"How teachers give you the true facts now?" Like the local villagers, they regard the American moon-shot as an elaborately faked exercise, for could the womb permit men born of her to return once again?

Conclusion

I have continued to use the older term *inversion* in spite of suggestions (Needham 1980) that *opposition* might be more appropriate: inversion does not only describe the latent possibilities of the system but conveys the physical sense of overturning institutions so characteristic of the participants' experience. In brief, explanations of symbolic inversion, such as the Good to Evil transposition, have been offered by observers and participants from diverse perspectives, which we may gloss according to three broad Western modes of characterizations; psychological, sociological, and cognitive.

Psychological: the return of the repressed, as elaborated in psychoanalytical and literary theory (Scheff 1979). The inversion may be regarded alternatively as a "reaction formation" of the socialized individual to the recognition of his physiological drives (Freud 1937). There may be a conscious cultural elaboration of some type of catharsis or discharge of tension to restore equilibrium, usually associated with a quantifiable conception of sin or gross matter, which can penetrate boundaries—we find it in the Jewish rituals of the scapegoat, excretion before prayer, the treatment of illness by enema, or the "purging" of the house at Passover. Theories of catharsis in drama, following Aristotle, stress the resonance (Mimesis) of the dramatic role with the personal experiences of actor and audience, in extreme situations, both may run amok together in the deviant role (Geertz 1966). A tentative psychophysiological basis for this type of experience has been elaborated in Smith and Apter's Reversal Theory (Apter 1982).

Sociological: inversion is presented by a culture as the alternative to the established order and, as it is typically both temporary and allowed only in certain specific ritual contexts (or limited to a powerless minority), it reaffirms the boundaries of control and thus cements the existing system (Gluckman 1962; Babcock 1978). While orthodox Jews are usually forbidden to play cards or get drunk, these two activities are tolerated and even encouraged on two specific days in the year; similarly, the blood of humans or animals is scrupulously avoided at all times, except at circumcision when it may actually be sucked. In communities where the idea of cannibalism is totally repugnant, the homicide may be purified by ritual ingestion of the deceased's liver (Goody 1982). Inversion thus marks a principle by constrained contravention of it.

Cognitive: both the "psychological" and "sociological" approaches are functional and static: they emphasize the homeostasis of a given system; inversion is either the catharsis of undesirable elements or the passage between two equivalent and coexisting systems (Babcock 1978). Similarly, the antinomian individual who contravenes the norm gives unity to a simple bipolar system (Peacock 1968). Inversion may, however, be innovative in that certain patterns can, as it were, hot up latent contradictions, by overt statements and actions, inverting the normal schema in certain areas (represented by a chiasmus in the polythetic classification). Symbolic inversions can be regarded as intellectual tools that have the potential to enlarge the conceptual repertoire (Turner 1974). Although oppositions may be a dominant mode of symbolic ordering, their inversion provides the basis for change. The apparent paradox is resolved at an implicit "higher" level—simple oppositions become the means by which a more sophisticated, radical, and universal conceptualization may be attained (Babcock 1978). As the original symbolic schema was closely related to the social order, the weakening of this schema in some is likely to lead to a greater autonomy of ideology from specific environmental and political determinants and thus perhaps to more "internalized" and individualized values: when Jesus denied that plucking corn on the Sabbath was *work*, he implied a new dispensation in which "the Law was broken in Form to be fulfilled in Spirit."

It is perhaps too early to characterize any Universalist influence for Mother Earth.[9] Certainly her overturning of the dual classification in certain areas allows the Earth People, like the Rastas, to escape from an externally imposed system of values. Her rejection of binarism, her interpenetration of black and white, and of male and female, appear to offer us all a more universal dispensation than the more limited ethnic redefinitions of Ras Tafari:

> They want me to believe in Fadam
> And forget my Mother is the Eve-am
> For She who is my Mother
> She who be so evil
> For evil is the garden
> The garden is the Eve-am
> Eve is the evil
> Evil, evil . . .

Roland Littlewood, University of London

Notes

1. I stayed in 1981–82 in Pinnacle Village, carrying out a study on local medicines, while spending increasing time in Hell Valley ten miles along the Turnpike [a pseudonym, like Pinnacle] (Littlewood 1993). The name the "Valley of Decision" is biblical in origin (Joel 3:14), the decision being that of the deity at the Last Judgement. I use "Creole" here to refer to African European culture and population in Trinidad as opposed to Indo-Trinidadian. This account uses some material from Littlewood 1984 and 1993 and is in the "ethnographic present": after Mother Earth died in the 1980s, the community dissolved into four groups, a small one staying on the original site and pursuing the original way of life. Mother Earth's immediate biological sons and daughters live in Never Dirty, a poor eastern area of the capital Port-of-Spain; a group led by Mother Earth's last partner, Jakatan, are in a village along the coast and work as nature guides for ecological tourists; and a dispersed collection in Port-of-Spain retain but little of the original fervour—the first three all still following varying bits of the original teaching.
2. The term "Adversary," adopted from Christianity, is jokingly used among the Earth People themselves to refer to one inside the group who contravenes your immediate wish or practice. Thus Pumpkin, at two years old and the youngest member of the community, is jokingly known as "The Adversary." This negation of a negation is not taken too far in practice: thus "the original Adversary" (the Christian Devil) should, if logic was pursued all the way through, be a prime example of the community's values rather than a temporary nuisance. And yet, in a way, he is, for another person, not personally aggrieved by the child's thoughtless behaviour, and will say approvingly, "Pumpkin come real natural now": i.e., he is adhering to the group's ideals of the countersocial though this may be personally inconvenient.
3. This was in 1975, and thus long before international concerns with global warming.
4. My colleague, Rebecca Lynch, working now in the same area of Trinidad, tells me that in the 2010s, the Devil plays a more important role in the local moral universe: presumably under the influence of evangelical Protestantism such as Pentecostalism, which has dichotomised the religious universe of the 1980s, where a multitude of spirits and afflictions were regarded as morally neutral or as due simply to heedless human perversity or indeed as frank folklore, but not as metaphysical evil.
5. By the 1990s, "evil" had become a term of approbation among young black Britons and North Americans, and then among young adults more generally, fusing with the transvalorizations of punk music.
6. Not just the colonist but the missionary. I recall from my brother's stamp collection a prewar triangular from east or central Africa inscribed "Light in Darkness."

7. Consistent anyway with my usual fieldwork practice, I did not take camera or tape machine until my final visit when I had become anxious about obtaining a full record of the group. To my relief, they accepted my equipment as a compromised necessity for communicating with the external world.
8. Cf. Levine (1978) who suggests that African-descended cultures in the Americas have always had a "this worldly" physical location of Heaven and Hell, which proceeds from traditional West African societies.
9. But we might note her affinities with the evangelical (individualized) turn in Christianity in Trinidad and with ecofeminism. It is significant that one successor group (Note 1) have moved into environmental tourism and turtle preservation. When I was with the group, one member had a dream that Mother Earth interpreted as Nature saying, "Kill no more of my children [turtles] or something bad will happen." Until then, the Earth People, like the Pinnacle villagers, had caught and eaten the local turtles.

References

Apter, M. J. 1982. *The Experience of Motivation: The Theory of Psychological Reversals.* London: Academic Press.

Babcock, B. 1978. *The Reversible World: Symbolic Inversions in Art and Society.* New York: Cornell University Press.

Burridge, K. 1971. *New Heaven, New Earth: A Study of Millenarian Activities.* Oxford: Blackwell.

Freud, S. 1937. *The Ego and the Mechanisms of Defence.* London: Hogarth.

Geertz, C. 1966. "Religion as a Cultural System." In *Anthropological Approaches to the Study of Religion.* Edited by M. Banton. London: Tavistock.

Goody, J. 1982. *Cooking, Cuisine and Class.* Cambridge, UK: Cambridge University Press.

Gluckman, M. 1962. *Rituals of Rebellion in South-East Africa.* Manchester: Manchester University Press.

Herskovits, M. 1958 (1941). *The Myth of the Negro Past.* Boston, MA: Boston Press.

Huysmans, J. K. 1891. *Là-Bas.* English translation, 1972 edition. New York: Dover.

Levine, L. W. 1978. *Black Culture and Black Consciousness: Afro-American Folk Thought from Slavery to Freedom.* New York: Oxford University Press.

Lewis, G. 1983. *Main Currents in Caribbean Thought: The Historical Evolution of Caribbean Society in its Ideological Aspects 1493–1900.* Kingston: Heinemann.

Linton, R. 1943. "Nativist Movements." *American Anthropologist* 45: 230–40.

Littlewood, R. 1984. "The Imitation of Madness: The Influence of Psychopathology upon Culture." *Social Science and Medicine* 19: 705–15.

———. 1993. *Pathology and Identity: The Work of Mother Earth in Trinidad.* Cambridge, UK: Cambridge University Press.

Morton, A. L. 1952. *The English Utopia.* London: Lawrence and Wishart.

Needham, R. 1979. *Symbolic Classification.* Santa Monica, CA: Goodyear.

———. 1980. *Reversals.* Henry Myers Lecture, Royal Anthropological Institute, London.

Parkin, D. 1985. "Introduction." In *The Anthropology of Evil.* Edited by D. Parkin. Oxford: Blackwell.

Peacock, J. 1968. *Rites and Modernisation: Symbolic Aspects of Indonesian Proletarian Drama.* Chicago: Chicago University Press.

Rahner, K. 1962. *On the Theology of Death.* London: Nelson.

Scheff, T. 1979. *Catharsis in Healing, Ritual and Drama.* Berkeley: University of California Press.

Silverblatt, I. 1987. *Moon, Sun and Witches.* New Haven, CT: Yale University Press.

Simpson, G. E. 1978. *Black Religions in the New World.* New York: Columbia University Press.

———. 1980. *Religious Cults of the Caribbean.* Puerto Rico: Institute of Caribbean Studies.

Taussig, M. 1980. *The Devil and Commodity Fetishism in South America.* Chapel Hill: University of South Carolina Press.

Turner, V. 1974. *Dramas, Fields and Metaphors.* Ithaca, NY: Cornell University Press.

Wilson, B. 1973. *Magic and the Millennium.* London: Paladin.

Worsley, P. 1970. *The Trumpet Shall Sound.* London: Paladin.

Chapter 5

SATAN ON THE OLD KENT ROAD

ARTICULATIONS OF EVIL IN A PENTECOSTAL DIASPORA

Simon Coleman

Introduction: Studying Evil

Evil provokes unease among anthropologists of religion. In common with discussions of asceticism (Cannell 2006), it runs the risk of haunting rather than energizing our analytical frameworks, exposing awkward remnants of Christian influence. Reflecting on such ambivalences, Thomas J. Csordas asks whether our readiness to dismiss evil as a metaphysical category rather than exploring it as a moral or existential one is connected with deep worries over appearing ethnocentric (2013, 526). On the other hand, as David Parkin points out, "It is precisely because the term has been so loose analytically that it has been able to reveal so much empirically" (1985, 2).

Parkin's distinctions among three varieties of evil illustrate the flexibility that he is describing and promote a nuanced approach to the topic that reveals its convoluted relationships to socially sanctioned assumptions of normalcy and mutual accountability. The presence of "excess" is said to prompt responses such as witchcraft accusations that target the wealthy, the powerful, and the highly visible in society (see also Clough and Mitchell 2001); "imperfection" is typically manifested through illness, caused by the malevolent will of another person; finally, "incompleteness" implies the unsettling of an ideal or planned course of life through misfortunes such as untimely death or lack of fertility (Parkin 1985, 18). These examples indicate the general principle that evil may be seen as "the negative aspect within any moral system" (Parkin 1985, 3; Van Beek and Olsen 2015, 2). We therefore see how evil will likely shift its character and location according to changing circumstances and aspirations. Furthermore, just as human motives tend to be mixed, variously concealed, and not always clear to the protagonists in a given situation, "negativity" adopts many tones and shades: van Beek and Olsen refer to the "gray zones where evil may transition into something that is not evil" (2), especially in cultural contexts, frequent in Africa, where spiritual beings in general are not regarded as inherently good or bad (11). Ideological ambiguities are evident even within Christianity, the religion from which the category of evil is often said to have derived most obviously (Taylor 1985). No definitive judgment can be made as to whether Christian thought is monist or dualist in its explanations of the presence of malevolent forces in the world. Lionel Caplan therefore characterizes this religion's theodicy as "semi-dualist" (1985, 111; see also Parkin 1985, 9), indicating the complexity of Christianity's attitudes toward the interactions of divine, satanic, and human agencies.

These questions of multifaceted moralities are deeply relevant to the form of Christianity that I focus on in this chapter. They highlight what is frequently at stake theoretically and methodologically in studying Christian debates over the origins, ontological status, and varieties of the demonic. In recent years, the burgeoning anthropology of Pentecostalism and charismatic movements (Coleman and Hackett 2015) has constructed evil as a highly dynamic analytical object in at least two interlinked ways, both of which have helped to form a vibrant subfield of study focused on trying to understand the current growth of spirit-filled Christianity in many parts of the world. The metaphors underlying these analyses—those of "rupture" and "occultation" respectively—reinforce Parkin's observations on "excess," "imperfection," and "incompleteness" and raise further significant questions about agency, but also shift the scale and operations of evil (as well as those of studying evil) more explicitly into wider questions of transnational mobility and political economy.[1]

According to one perspective, Pentecostalism globalizes by pushing Christianity's semi-dualism in the direction of a combative cosmology oriented toward establishing distance from previous cultural and religious forms. The sociologist José Casanova's well-known claim that Pentecostalism is "an uprooted local culture engaged in spiritual warfare with its own roots" (2001, 437) has parallels with Birgit Meyer's (1999) analysis of religion, modernity, and diabolical imagery among the Ewe of Ghana. Meyer notices that talk about demons and the Devil in Pentecostal churches occurs in a context where incorporation into the modern capitalist economy has produced ambivalences toward older, reciprocal, often familial relations. Under such circumstances, "Pentecostalism ... enables people to move back and forth between the way of life they (wish to) have left behind and the one to which they aspire. ... By offering discourse and ritual practices pertaining to demons, believers are enabled to thematise continuously the 'old'" (Meyer 1999, 212). Similar tendencies are highlighted by Joel Robbins, who sees Pentecostalism as a "culture against culture" (2004, 127) that deploys such mechanisms as baptism and the use of an ascetic code embedded in increasingly dualistic schemas to contrast God and the Devil, past and present, church and the world. Robbins's broader point is that these orientations prompt rupture with previous assumptions about spirits, but do so without requiring entirely new ways of perceiving human and divine worlds: the old spirits are assumed still to exist, but their moral charge is turned from potentially positive to decidedly negative. Pentecostalism encompasses rather than entirely abandons the spiritual expressions of older cosmological schemas, and pursues its morally reforming agenda all the more effectively for doing so.

(Post)modernity and its discontents are also invoked in another influential analysis of the salience of evil in contemporary Pentecostalism, contained in Jean and John Comaroff's depiction of "occult economies," which they see increasingly in operation around the world (1999; also 2001). This notion has close resonances with Parkin's category of excess, since it refers to cases where people appear to gain wealth without engaging in overtly productive activity, leading to accusations that insidious forces can account for such accumulation (Comaroff and Comaroff 1999, 282). The Comaroffs draw on a number of illustrative ethnographic cases, including Prosperity-oriented forms of Pentecostalism in southern Africa, where they argue that people search for almost magical means to achieve material aspirations, and yet, at the same time, demonize those who *do* appear to succeed. Thus "the salvific and the satanic are conditions of each other's possibility" (Comaroff and Comaroff 2001, 26; also Lindhardt 2009, 44), reflecting neoliberal economic conditions where wealth creation is mysterious, remote from visible processes of production, and retreating from workers' grasp in a runaway world characterized by unpredictable demands for flexibilized labor (Comaroff and Comaroff 1999, 294).

In different ways, these writers depict a Pentecostalism that both inhabits and seeks to define—indeed, to operate through—mobility and change. "Rupture" broadly emphasizes movement away from the past, while "occultation" stresses the moral and social consequences of lack of an experience of meaningful movement. Taken together, these two metaphors are suggestive of complementary, positive, and negative dimensions of globalization, while focusing on a form of Christianity that is chronically oriented toward the idea of reaching out into wider cultural and religious fields. In such an ideological context, and acknowledging considerable variations within Pentecostalism itself, discourse about the demonic expresses moral judgment but may in addition become a ritual and narrative catalyst, justifying fundamental transformation of the self and others, albeit in ways that acknowledge what Meyer (1999) sees as people's simultaneous involvement in old and new ways of life. What also emerges strongly is a sense that Pentecostalism has the capacity to deploy what Englund has called "indeterminacy of scale in arguments about the occult" (2007, 296; see also Geschiere 1997). Evil is no longer tied only to small-scale relationships—the kind highlighted by more traditional work on witchcraft and the evil eye (e.g., Macfarlane 1985, 58)—and may also become a commentary on relationships at relatively distant or even remote scales of operation or imagination.

My ethnographic focus in this chapter is on Pentecostals for whom questions of scale, mobility, connections with wider social and cultural fields, and relationships between old and new do indeed take on particular resonances, and whose lives are permeated by discourses around the presence of evil in intimate as well as more distanced social and material realms. I draw on fieldwork that Katrin Maier and I have conducted on members of the Redeemed Christian Church of God (RCCG), most of them identifiable as Yoruba, located in two congregations (or parishes) in London.[2] Our informants are situated in aspirant but sometimes precarious diasporic circumstances—generally born in or with parents from Nigeria, keenly aware of their status as migrants to the UK, and perhaps still seeking legal permission to remain. Their cultural and geographical horizons extend tenuously in varied but patterned directions, mediated by familial, work, and congregational relationships and imaginaries: around the UK and into Europe but more often between London and Nigeria, and across known and unknown parts of the metropolis itself.

One striking dimension of our informants' awareness of evil is the latter's ubiquity combined with its flexibility, its ability to inhabit every nook and cranny of people's lives, and indeed to emerge in contexts where variations of excess, imperfection, and incompleteness are uncovered. Evil traverses the full, globalizing "moral geography" (Krause 2015) of Nigerian, Pentecostal, diasporic lives, and it both reflects attitudes derived from people's background and comes to express the concerns of those who are still self-consciously dealing with the consequences, risks, spatial confusions, and opportunities afforded by mobility. It would be wrong, however, to see such ideas about evil as always being expressed in systematic ways: the very plasticity of demonic discourse allows it to be instantiated as appropriate and according to context, and sometimes in ways that would appear mutually incompatible if directly juxtaposed. Evil enters Pentecostal practices not only as a topic of frequent and expressed concern but also as part of a more general morality that is an inherent "modality of action" (Csordas 2013, 535).

To be sure, apotropaic themes as well as worries about evil as a kind of contagion frequently emerge in our fieldwork, as might be expected; however, what I also wish to uncover is a dimension that is less emphasized in the literature, at least in the way I want to express it: the social and cultural "productivity" (compare Robbins 2009) of discourse about evil among such Pentecostals. Such discourse incorporates but also goes beyond what is conventionally designated in the literature as "spiritual warfare" (e.g., Hackett 2013), while thematizing both scale and territorial possession in its imagery.

My argument is that—in the context of a faith that reaches out into other cultural, social, and spatial worlds—identifying and engaging the presence of evil (with all its nuances) becomes a mode of *articulation* with the capacity to take on powerful ideological dimensions among Christians whose social and cultural location within Nigerian or British society remains unclear. "Evil articulations" often transcend or bypass the close interpersonal ties more conventionally associated with, say, witchcraft accusations. In addition, they are not primarily about the rejection of the old (as expressed by rupture discourse), but rather about asserting a moral claim over newly occupied social, cultural, and religious environments. To articulate with rather than accuse thus implies less a desire to create social distance in a context of already close-knit social competition, and more an attempt to achieve a form of ideological encompassment—to create a common scale of value among apparently disparate groups. It enables Christians to project themselves morally, imaginatively, and ritually into institutional contexts that are often denied to them in their host society, as well as into wider, transnational spheres of operation.

My image of projection as a form of articulation has some resonances with Rijk van Dijk's notion of "social catapaulting" (2009), which he uses to describe the ways in which Ghanaian migrant churches provide a context for members not only to cushion economic and social blows that follow from having moved from home, but also to engage markets as a means of providing evidence of faith and personal conviction. Interestingly, van Dijk is not arguing that such entrepreneurial activity demonstrates unfettered agency on the part of the individual; rather, churches may "bounce" people into new situations, applying pressure on them to take advantage of perceived opportunities. In turn, I see RCCG discourse relating to evil as a form of *moral* catapaulting, promoting the sense that the host society contains environments that invite moral and sometimes ritual intervention. Such opportunities may also become mini tests—indices of the degree of commitment of the Christian. Intervention of this sort does not necessarily involve direct confrontation with host society; rather, it may involve articulation at a distance, promoting a sense of participation in the lives of people who may have no idea that they are being targeted.

In the following, I situate Maier's and my informants literally and metaphorically within the complex diasporic landscapes and horizons they inhabit, before tracing various dimensions of evil that touch their lives. I explore the invocation of evil as a form of articulation—with spatial, social, moral, cultural, and indeed political dimensions. Evil emerges in my analysis as a loose discourse, scaling up and down, sometimes sharply dualist and sometimes semi-dualist. Its flexibility is key to its shifting but continued salience, and to its capacity to act as a means of articulation with a wider social environment on the part of people who are still attempting to find their place in diaspora.

Between Lagos and "Little Lagos"

Peckham, a suburb of southeast London, has a history reaching back to Roman times, but its reputation from the 1960s has been marked rather more by oscillations between urban decay and social regeneration. The North Peckham Housing Estate became nationally notorious in 2000 when a young Nigerian boy, Damilola Taylor, was stabbed to death on his way home by youths who were only much later convicted of manslaughter. The suburb is one of the most ethnically diverse parts of the UK, with a population that is around 35 percent black African, according to the 2001 national census. It is sometimes known in local parlance as little Lagos—an area studded with Nigerian food stores, hair and nail salons, barber shops, clothes stores, travel agencies, law firms, mosques, and churches. Unsurprisingly, then, Peckham and nearby parts of south and east London such as Catford, Camberwell, Deptford, Southwark, Thamesmead, and Woolwich are where many of Katrin's and my informants live—places that provide relatively cheap accommodation and access to work, though not parts of the city in which they necessarily wish to remain in the long term. These suburbs contrast markedly with the opulent downtown surroundings of Mayfair and Knightsbridge, where more prosperous Nigerian residents of the city—those typically involved in banking and the energy sector—prefer to invest.

Nigerians constitute one of the largest immigrants groups in the UK, their population formed originally by students who came before independence was gained in 1960, then boosted by those seeking to escape decades of political unrest and, from the 1980s, the instability of the oil economy. Today, perhaps 180,000 Nigerians live in Britain (Office of National Statistics 2013), and well over half of that figure dwell in London. A growing public profile is tempered by a reputation that is decidedly mixed. West African immigrants in Europe are regularly featured in the media in connection with child trafficking and state benefit fraud (Coleman and Maier 2011). In 2010, the celebrations of the fiftieth anniversary of Nigeria's independence from Britain prompted lukewarm responses from local commentators, including a piece by a BBC journalist with the damning title: "Nigeria at 50: 'Nothing to Celebrate.'"[3] The article told a well-worn story of corruption and squandering of resources by an oil-rich postcolonial state. At the same time, Nigerians are firmly embedded within British school and university systems, and the very failure of Nigeria's education to meet the demands of a youthful population continues to push ambitious people (or children of motivated parents) overseas.[4] Furthermore, as celebrated by the online news source *Nigeria News Today*, a publication oriented to readers within and beyond the country, at the last UK general election, four members of parliament were of Nigerian descent.[5]

Our choice of two RCCG congregations in which to conduct fieldwork reflected the complex social, economic, and cultural location of contemporary Nigerian migrants in London. One parish, which we call Tower of God,[6] is located on the Old Kent Road, an important thoroughfare linking central London with the southeast of the city.[7] Tower of God was among the first of the RCCG parishes planted in the UK in the early 1990s, but its itinerant origins have traced the contours of the mini Nigerian landscape within London that I sketched above: its head pastor began preaching in a business center in Woolwich before transferring his fledgling group of followers to a Methodist Church in Peckham, where he was permitted to hold worship services when the regular congregation was not using the building. Finally, the move was made to a crumbling building in the Old Kent Road in Southwark, with a hall big enough to hold some 180 people. The congregation consists of a few hundred members, many aged—in common with the RCCG generally in the UK—between twenty-five and fifty.[8] Most have low-paid jobs in restaurants, hospitals, nurseries, and post offices, though some also run their own businesses, often in parallel to paid employment (Maier 2012). The ambitions of members are expressed not only by their busy work lives but also by the ownership of their church, which was bought with funds provided by the congregation. The Old Kent Road itself contains numerous churches, including a handful of other RCCG parishes, and the head pastor of Tower of God half joked, half prophesied to us: "There is nothing accidental with God. . . . God must be saying something. . . . With time this Old Kent Road is going to be changed to Church Road. I think that's the only thing I can say!"[9]

While Tower of God is situated in a relatively modest building located in a busy high street, the other congregation in our study, Jesus House, occupies a more impressive and purpose-built edifice that is nonetheless situated in rather out-of-the way surroundings—part of a faceless industrial estate in Brent, a suburb in the northwest of the city. The church was founded as a plant of a parish in Lagos in 1994, and moved around London before being located in its warehouse-like building with reflective glass plates on the outside and numerous offices, a bookstore, a café, and a large hall. Three services are run every Sunday, and members of Jesus House, who number several thousand, not only tend to have better paid jobs than those at Tower of God, they often come from all over London and beyond. The group's premises are off the beaten track, but they embody powerful spatial ambition: the main foyer boasts a stylized world map (with Africa at the center) placed on a wall behind the reception desk alongside clocks telling the time in London, New York, and Beijing. Jesus House acts as a coordinator of Europe-wide events for the RCCG, and twice a year it plays a central role in orchestrating the Festival of Life conference, normally located in the massive Excel exhibition halls in East London. The Festival attracts some thirty thousand participants and features the Church's General Overseer, Enoch Adeboye, as its main speaker. Jesus House for All Nations (to employ its full title) also encompasses its own form of cosmopolitanism by including semi-independent, French- and Portuguese-speaking networks within its church-based activities. In addition, it presents something of a public face for UK-based RCCG members in relation to other organizations in London and beyond. Congregation members still rejoice in the fact that Prince Charles came to celebrate his fifty-ninth birthday on their premises in 2007, while in 2001, head Pastor Agu Irukwu (a barrister and former investment banker) was chosen as "Britain's Most Inspirational Black Person" in a national competition.[10]

At the background to the activities of both of these congregations is their affiliation to a denomination that not only forms one of the most active 'black majority' Churches in London,[11] but is also known across a much wider Pentecostal landscape for its mission to bring back the gospel to what is seen as the spiritually degenerate continent of Europe (Ukah 2005). Such church-planting is aided by a denomination-wide strategy of saturating city spaces with parishes wherever possible, contributing to the remarkable aspiration of ensuring that no person on earth will be more than five minutes travel time away from one of its venues. Today, some forty or more countries in Europe have RCCG churches, part of a total membership estimated at over a million (e.g., Harris 2006, 222).

The story of RCCG's emergence as a transnational organization provides a powerful narrative of accelerated spatial dissemination. The RCCG was founded in Christian-dominated southwestern Nigeria in 1952, but remained an insignificant, inward-looking, holiness group until it was taken over in 1981 by Pastor Adeboye, a university lecturer and applied mathematician. As Peel (2008; drawing on Ukah 2008) observes, if the 1980s and 1990s constituted a period when the condition of the Nigerian nation went from bad to worse, the RCCG went from strength to strength through presenting itself as an alternative social formation, promoting Nigeria's true destiny as a Christian nation (Marshall 2009, 180, 209). Expansive ambition combined with a degree of encapsulation is still embodied in the RCCG's spiritual and social center, Redemption Camp (also Redemption City), situated about thirty kilometers outside Lagos along the Expressway to Ibadan. Behind a guarded entrance lies a self-contained community marked by an atmosphere of urbanity, order, wealth, and education (Maier 2012). It represents a material embodiment of Adeboye's strategy from the 1980s of complementing the RCCG's long-standing holiness orientation with a more outward-looking, consciously modern, "Prosperity" outlook, promoting the idea that Christianity and worldly success, personal discipline and public affluence (and influence), are not incompatible.

While the RCCG message of order and aspiration resonates in Nigeria, it has also played a powerful ideological role in the lives of members who have migrated to Europe and North America. Ukah (2005, 319) describes the denomination's expansion as inserting itself into multifaceted flows already being created by mobile networks of Nigerian migrants. He notes: "Mobilities are . . . the engines of transformation of the RCCG" (Ukah 2005, 325). In this sense, the forces of political economy and Pentecostal valorization of movement have been mutually compatible. However, there is a vital further dimension—and limitation—of the Pentecostal diaspora as it is lived out by RCCG members in the UK and other parts of Europe. Even in Jesus House, which boasts a membership made up of people representing some forty different nationalities, the congregation remains dominated by Nigerians. This situation points to a form of involuntary encapsulation rather different from the planned isolation represented by Redemption Camp, and indicates that the RCCG currently still maintains a dual identity as ethnic enclave and cosmopolitan corporate entity (Ukah 2009, 121). It also takes us back to our central consideration of the spatial, social, cultural, and legal position of RCCG members in diaspora, and to the moral geography that they inhabit but which they also hope to reform and refashion. We can now turn back more explicitly to the question of evil, to its locations and articulations in the lives of the congregation members whom Katrin and I encountered in the suburbs of London.

The Devil Is in the Diaspora

These words of Pastor Bankole[12] give a vivid sense of how evil might be encountered by our informants:

> Dreams can show the future, and types of bondage. A dream about climbing a mountain and not being able to reach the top means that one is bound by evil powers operating [as] a stumbling block in one's life. A dream where one sees oneself in primary or secondary school, means he [or] she is bound by the spirit of setback because one ought to see oneself ahead, doing a PhD or being a professor. When someone gets a dream like this, they are lucky, because that means God shows then clearly what's going on and wants them to be delivered.[13]

Like many fellow believers, the pastor is intensely interested in dreams—experiences that mediate between personal consciousness and supernatural communication. Powerful dreams alert the person to a spiritual crisis beneath the surface of things that requires interpretation and then action, including deliverance through the Church.[14] Along with other potentially ambiguous encounters whose origins (divine or demonic) cannot always be known, they require the exercise of discernment: between good and bad, opportunity and temptation. They also appear in this example to have a deeply spatial quality, oriented around a mountain and a school—both environments that express aspiration that can be blocked by evil forces, but which are also sufficiently generic to apply to the lives of believers in Nigeria or Europe.

Pastor Bankole's words point to a landscape of religious encounter that goes far beyond the boundaries of any church building. In doing so, he echoes Kristine Krause's (2015) depiction of how spatially and spiritually informed imaginaries among Ghanaian Pentecostals in Europe bring together a cluster of orientations: toward inner self, immediate surroundings, and the wider world respectively. Krause notes that experiences of diaspora, filled with a frequent sense of displacement, provoke acts of "moralizing the world," according to which the believer feels empowered to evaluate their surroundings, inscribing constructions of moral superiority or inferiority on to many of the spaces they encounter. A Pentecostal moral geography is therefore also a relational geography, directed toward others even as it is "part of crafting the ways of being a person and belonging somewhere" (Krause 2015, 77).

Parallel assumptions are evident among the RCCG informants whom Katrin and I have encountered, for whom migration frequently involves a search for what James Doubleday, describing a similar population in London, calls "achieving a sense of home by receiving their goodly heritage" (2008, 85). Gaining one's rightful heritage may, in these terms, be linked with a sense of destiny (2008, 13), and one that can be promoted precisely by living in a megacity such as London. John Peel argues that the message of the RCCG draws on a wider Yoruba notion of *olaju*, enlightenment, carrying the connotation that: "Progress depends on opening oneself to the wider world, forward movement on spatial enlargement" (2000, 317). His analysis meshes well with Doubleday's discussion of how his Yoruba Pentecostal informants in London articulate a sense of urban space as open, porous, constructed through social interconnection, with the "space-ness" or capacity of places reminiscent of the Yoruba metaphorical market-place (2008, 64; Coleman and Maier 2013, 10). But such capacity can also be challenged by certain forms of evil that may considerably narrow one's horizons.

In the following, I divide up informants' encounters with evil into three modalities. The following are not exhaustive, but indicate ways in which the presence of evil is detected at different scales of experience and imagination. All three have a spatial dimension and overlap with—though they do not precisely correspond with—Krause's Pentecostal moral geography of self, surroundings, and world. The first two—disciplines and translations—help to create the ideological and ritual conditions under which the third—articulations—may take place.

Disciplines

As Christians who combine holiness and prosperity orientations, RCCG members learn constantly to monitor their actions and attitudes. For instance, Michael, a man in his thirties who had lived a secular life in Nigeria before he migrated but who was now a frequent attender of Tower of God, recounted his struggles with remaining celibate in the UK for some eight years while he looked for a wife; whenever he felt temptation becoming too much, he combined more obviously spiritual efforts with going for a walk or jogging until the urge subsided.[15] Another informant, Mary, testified to her routine of coming back home from work tired each day, but still submitting herself to the duty of making food for her husband.[16] Many similar examples could be cited, and their power lies in their very banality, their capacity to cover all areas of life from the overtly spiritual to the deeply domestic, because the two cannot clearly be distinguished. In such a context of expectation, going for a cleansing run or cooking for a husband are not merely submissions to forms of Church authority and ideology; they are also embodied assertions that one's body and one's consciousness are sites of important spiritual struggle. Thus a woman noted rather starkly in a cell group meeting, "If we are suffering, it's also because the devil especially attacks believers. He doesn't need to attack nonbelievers because they are going to hell anyway."[17]

There is nothing unusual about Christian concerns over personal piety, but for our informants, they also constitute specifically Pentecostal experiences of self in an environment that is a space of frequent temptation. One informant, Emmanuel, told us:

> As a Christian man: Watch what you see. Learn to turn your eye immediately. I tell you. Tell yourself: "Eye, I bind you, you must not look in that direction again!" You may not say or do anything . . . but you are already committing sin. And by the time those thoughts become accumulated, it's trouble.[18]

Emmanuel's admonition—to himself as much as to anybody else—works on a number of levels. The anonymous city is rendered a place of dangerous sights and sites, in this case associated with lust, and so the Christian subject is required to engaged in an intriguing practice of double vision, to "watch what one sees," with watching implying a spiritually and morally informed monitoring of an urban Pentecostal habitus. In this narrative, watching triggers an internal dialogue that voices an inwardly directed form of deliverance discourse. If the "evil eye" stereotypically implies an act of malevolence directed toward another person, here the "unregulated eye" becomes a medium of temptation of the self, and one that must be controlled through self-disciplining watchfulness.

Many of our informants link self-disciplining to the active cultivation of another form of Pentecostal enskilment, and one that we encountered above: that of discernment. The assumption is that the holy Christian is both relatively shielded from Satanic attacks and more receptive to divine communication. The supernatural can be experienced in numerous ways—through visions, dreams, external or internal voices, encountering apparent coincidences that are actually signs or miracles—and as Rose, a young married woman from Tower of God, told us: "Like Satan, God is a spirit. They can both speak to us. And it is up to us to listen to one or the other." But it may not always be immediately obvious how these two voices can be distinguished, and that is when discernment must come into play. Rose continued that Satan can even inhabit the hearts of one's children, indicating not only that Satan has the capacity to act through humans, but also that at times those humans might still be people who are close at hand.

In practice, the fragility but also the flexibility of the sociospiritual environment inhabited by believers is revealed as people balance piety with necessity. Michael explained how he navigated his way through dangerous situations by "closing off" aspects of himself. As a graphic artist, he was forced, for instance, to work with photos of a rock musician that featured tattoos he did not approve of. However, he argued, "His photo doesn't affect me, it doesn't communicate with me. I do it, get my money, and go."[19] He exhibited similarly selective decision-making in dealing with a close acquaintance:[20]

> I have a friend. . . . He doesn't know much about Christ, but he is morally sound. . . . He does some things like smoking, drinking . . . those are the things that I don't pick from his behavior. Other good things I pick, educating or morals, great ideas. He fornicates. Those are the things I don't like.[21]

Translations

Elsewhere (Coleman and Maier 2011), Katrin and I have noted how many of our informants live in a diasporic metropolitan space that we call London-Lagos, involving a form of cultural and social habitation of both cities that involves maintaining links with family and friends in the Nigerian city, and occupying an ideological and moral milieu made up of connections as well as tensions between the two cities. London is a space of relative order and opportunity, but deep secularity. Lagos may be chaotic and corrupt, but it provides public spaces in which Christianity can flourish without apology. Thus, "translation" refers to the ways in which believers, both consciously and unconsciously, perceive, experience, and negotiate a dual form of dwelling. And for the purposes of this chapter, the most significant question is how evil is both transmitted and transformed in the move to the UK.

Translation can have both linguistic and spatial referents, as revealed in the following extract from a sermon by a pastor of another RCCG Church on the Old Kent Road. As he described six satanic weapons that his listeners must look out for, Pastor Babatunde warned them against the phenomenon of "satanic burial":[22]

> They put bits of your hair in a coffin and evil words are spoken. People who are manipulated like that go mad. . . . People in the West think this madness is caused by stress, which is correct, but there are evil forces behind that stress. Your hair represents your glory.

This is just one of many examples we encountered of demonic imagery that would be perfectly at home in Nigeria, reflecting worries over enemies alongside concerns over the integrity of a body whose margins are seen as vulnerable. But, at the same time as he transfers demonic discourse from a West African to an English context, the pastor is also translating such language into Western terms of understanding, only to then dismiss the adequacy of the latter. In his view, the Western etiology of stress has a certain logic, but it cannot comprehend the deeper social and spiritual causes of what Parkin (1985) would term "imperfection." Another incident mentioned in the same sermon embeds supernatural causation within a prosaic English context, that of a local subway station. In describing another Satanic weapon—wooden effigies—the pastor notes: "When someone loses blood, the figure has been cut with a knife; a man in Catford walked up and down the platform at the station as if waiting for the train; when it came, he jumped on the rails." The police might conclude that the man was suffering stress leading to suicide, but the Christian knows—discerns—that other forces are at work.

While Pastor Babatunde speaks openly with his congregation about such matters, this kind of discourse is unlikely to be invoked with secular English interlocutors, unless under the special circumstances of conversionist testimony. Interviewing an RCCG member from Germany, Katrin was told that Westerners "don't like to talk about the Devil and evil power. And the fact that you don't talk about it doesn't mean it is not there!"[23] On the other hand, when chatting with Rose, whom she came to know well, Katrin was given an unexpected glimpse into the Rose's spiritualized reading of her new country of residence. In discussing plans for a picnic, Katrin asked Rose whether she liked to go to the beach. Rose replied that she was scared of the sea, and at one point was afraid that she herself might be a water spirit, a Mami Wata. Rose's response indicates a degree of past uncertainty about her own spiritual status, but also goes beyond conventional Christian talk of God, Jesus, the Holy Spirit, and the Devil into a wider and more differentiated spiritual cosmology—all applicable within an English as much as a Nigerian landscape.

Clearly, our informants make numerous distinctions between the UK and Nigeria as places in which to live and worship. Apart from those already mentioned, an obvious difference is the degree to which Islam forms an obvious rival in much of West Africa, whereas in Europe both religions must contend with racism and secularity. However, the processes of translation I have highlighted indicate the continued salience of West African categories of evil powers, and their embeddedness in diaspora. They say less about how such categories might be taken to apply to wider English society itself.

Articulations

In his analysis of Ghanaian Methodist migrants to London, Mattia Fumanti (in press) talks of his informants' struggles to gain legal status. Lack of official recognition is mitigated and challenged, however, by performances of "virtuous citizenship," through which believers can claim a space in a postcolonial context via hard work and adherence to the law. For these migrants, the Methodist Church provides a venue through which they can care for others, whether Christian or not—although among British Methodists, the encapsulation of Ghanaian "ethnic" fellowships is also seen as a potential problem of governance.

RCCG members do not belong to a comparably venerable ecclesiastical institution, but they perform their own versions of virtuous citizenship through advocating disciplined lifestyles that prioritize education, employment, and advancement within conventional channels of recognition. Both Jesus House and Tower of God work extensively with local authorities, including police, and engage in a degree of ecumenical and charitable activity. And yet RCCG activists' articulations with other institutions are tempered not only by relative ethnic encapsulation, but also by unease with aspects of British culture and morality. The virtuosity of their citizenship not only incorporates a characteristic Pentecostal desire to reach into and reform wider society, it also draws on a strong hierarchy of values in which aspects of Christian Nigerian culture are clearly superior to those extant in much of the UK. This stance is expressed nowhere more strongly than in the fields of gender and sexual politics. The head pastor of Tower of God, a mild-mannered man, complains to his congregation:

> Among the temptations and sins in the UK is fornication. The Devil attacks marriages in particular in this part of the world. Dads are marginalized in school, children are told to give invitations "to your mum." That is among other things because there are so many single mothers. Also, there is gay marriage—Adam and Steve.[24]

Others express their views still more forcefully, claiming it is the Christian's duty to fight against "Sodom," but there is also a more general politics of gender at play, as expressed in the words of a young woman, Faith: "We are not from the Western world. Here, the man wears the skirts now. I have even heard an African woman say to her husband: 'The baby is crying, why don't you take it?'"[25] Her remark recalls Mary's comment, mentioned above, concerning the duty of the disciplined woman to care for her husband. There are many other ways in which our informants feel excluded from British customs, including those tolerated in more liberal churches, but sexuality and gender issues provide a striking example of such struggles because they touch on so many issues, including marriage, reproduction, and encounters with medical institutions (Coleman and Maier 2011).

Such relative alienation does not, however, prevent church members from feeling responsibility for, and a desire to participate in, local or national life in Britain or even Europe. As Adan remarked, explaining his migration and his desire to be a part of life in England and Germany: "I was having a good work in Nigeria. . . . I took care of parents, siblings, and friends. I was not open to travel to Europe. . . . Nigeria didn't want to let me go, too. But there were still some people who wanted me to go higher."[26] Here, he links his move to a distinct sense of personal destiny, and one that is based away from West Africa.

The hope for RCCG members such as Adan is that one day even the Prime Minister might be both a Christian and of Nigerian origin, and so be in a position to change the moral climate of the country. Occasions such as Prince Charles's visit to Jesus House indicated a form of public recognition and legitimation that is highly desired. However, for the time being, other methods may be employed to create a sense of moral entrepreneurship. While expressive of a strong sense of responsibility for British others, these do not necessarily require direct confrontation with the host society. Rose voiced a sentiment echoed by fellow believers: "Our behavior will do it if we are not bold enough to approach people directly."[27] Thus, action that combines spiritual discipline and civic virtue is assumed to have its own performative effect. Responsibilities may also be assumed through specific forms of prayerful practice, including those that are almost reminiscent of "beating the bounds" of a given geographical area. Pastor Babatunde told us of his strategies of praying and fasting for people in his local area, but also walking with congregation members into estates in Southwark and praying against such Satanic activities as violence, robberies, poverty, and the breaking up of homes. His method of "reaching out," which has echoes in other RCCG parishes, is reminiscent of Kevin O'Neill's (2015) depiction of Guatemalan "Pentecostal politics" as performed through ritual practices that create alternative forms of Christianized citizenship, according to which prayer itself is indeed regarded as participation in civic and political terms.[28]

What I am describing is an unusual set of articulations, to be sure, where both distance and proximity are expressed via actions "at one remove" from conventional engagement and interlocution. But the effectiveness of such action is also indicated by mentioning an occasion when it was replaced by more direct forms of seeking a ritualized connection. Katrin attended the regular RCCG Carol Service event in Trafalgar Square, Central London, in December 2008.[29] At first, the adoption of the tropes of a traditional British Christmas event attracted a largely white crowd—though interestingly not many parishioners from RCCG congregations. The woman distributing leaflets with song lyrics explained to Katrin that such music was being used as a means of creating connections with the population at large, since the RCCG does "not want to be black all the time, they want to blend into society and reach out." The strategy seemed to be working, until the leader of the event asked those gathered to turn to a neighbor and utter a phrase commonplace in a Nigerian (and indeed a Pentecostal) context: "Jesus is the reason for the season." The result was puzzlement, nervous laughter, and a rapidly dispersing crowd.

Concluding Remarks

If the anthropology of evil has been haunted by traces of Christian discourse, it has also—particularly in discussions of witchcraft—regularly been visited by the specter of another problematic theoretical debate: that of functionalism. My argument in this chapter has certainly been that ideas and practices relating to the Satanic are expressive of complex and shifting scales of experience among diasporic members of the RCCG; furthermore, I see such discourse as potentially having a morally catapaulting effect, enabling a sense of moral participation in, and even encompassment of, aspects of British institutional life.

I am not, however, presenting a vision of Christians whose only rationale (conscious or unconscious) for engaging in congregational activities is to mitigate a sense of marginalization from wider society, and nor am I suggesting that individual believers are trapped within ideological frameworks that determine their actions. We saw, for instance, how Michael engaged in delicate ethical negotiations in his work and leisure, establishing certain accommodations among different economic, social, and spiritual demands. Furthermore, although I have not developed the point in this chapter, we also need to see membership of an RCCG congregation as itself a product of ethical and social negotiation, sometimes linked more for instance to friendship or romantic networks than to overriding commitment to a single denomination (Doubleday 2008).

At the center of my analysis of evil has been the metaphor but also the materiality of location—linked to such dimensions as scale, diaspora, landscape, and the demands of urban living in London, Lagos, and "London-Lagos." The shifting coordinates of people's lives are made salient not only through RCCG strategies of expansion or Pentecostal distinctions between physical and supernatural realms of reality, but also by the everyday labor of establishing places to work, worship and perhaps achieve some kind of destiny. In such a context, evil retains an identity as the negative aspect of a broader moral system; and yet, as we have seen, the system itself takes on shifting shapes and scales, just as the assertion of negativity can sometimes lead to forms of opportunity—articulations that constitute positive aspirations rather than mere accusations in relation to the expanded world in which believers find themselves.

Simon Coleman, University of Toronto

Notes

1. For older ethnographic work relating to the political economy of discourse relating to the demonic, see, for example, Taussig (1980).
2. This research was supported by a grant from NORFACE, and most of the fieldwork took place between 2008 and 2010, with some subsequent visits. Much of the work was carried out by Maier under the supervision of Coleman (Maier completed her PhD at the University of Sussex in 2012), though some was conducted jointly or by Coleman alone. Both researchers visited southwestern Nigeria in 2009, following up kinship and friendship networks of London-based church members.
3. Robin Denselow, "Nigeria at 50: 'Nothing to Celebrate,'" *BBC News*, 24 September 2010, http://www.bbc.co.uk/news/world-africa-11398020.
4. "Education in Nigeria," *WES World Education News + Reviews*, 7 March 2017, http://wenr.wes.org/2013/07/an-overview-of-education-in-nigeria/.
5. Beth Hart, "Meet Four Nigerian MPs in the UK Parliament," *Legit*, accessed 7 November 2018, https://www.naij.com/435290-meet-four-nigerian-mps-in-the-uk-parliament.html.
6. While Tower of God is a pseudonym we have given to the parish where we studied on the Old Kent Road, there is little possibility of concealing the identity of Jesus House, given its location, size, and function in the UK.
7. See also Maier 2012, chapter 2.
8. See also Hunt and Lightley 2001; Ukah 2009.
9. Interview, 24 May 2010.
10. "Pastor Agu Irukwu of RCCG Jesus House London chosen as 'Britain's Most Inspirational Black Person'—Competition organized by Mayor of London and Metro," *Bella Naija*, 31 October 2011, http://www.bellanaija.com/2011/10/pastor-agu-irukwu-of-rggc-jesus-house-london-chosen-as-britains-most-inspirational-black-person-wins-54-of-votes-competition-organized-by-mayor-of-london-boris-johnson-and-metro-newspaper/.
11. Though the RCCG's headquarters and highest concentration are still in the Lagos area, it had over six thousand parishes worldwide in 2002 (Ukah 2005) and probably possesses many more now. In the UK, it has an estimated two hundred branches, around one hundred of them in London (Burgess, Knibbe, and Quaas 2010).
12. A pseudonym, in common with other mentions of RCCG members in this chapter, with the exception of Pastor Agu.
13. Interview, 07 June 2009.
14. For an overview of deliverance practices in Nigeria, see Hackett (2013).
15. Conversation, 15 August 2009.
16. Testimony night, 20 August 2009.
17. 24 October 2008.

18. Interview, 25 July 2009.
19. Conversation, 16 August 2009.
20. Conversation, 18 July 2008.
21. Krause (2015) notes that her Ghanaian informants build up an "inner space" as they monitor moods, praying, and discernment. The parallels with our Nigerian informants are clear, and it is worth adding that this is a space that the person takes with them as they move through the unpredictable, "external" spaces of London.
22. 21 November 2008.
23. 07 June 2009.
24. Sermon, 24 April 2009.
25. Interview, Feyi—29 May 2009.
26. Conversation, 05 May 2009.
27. Conversation, 15 August 2009.
28. O'Neill's and Fumanti's notions of religious citizenship, rooted in virtue and ritual respectively, thus come together in such action.
29. 15 December 2008.

References

Burgess, Richard, Kim Knibbe, and Anna Quaas. 2010. "Nigerian-initiated Pentecostal Churches as a Social Force in Europe: The Case of the Redeemed Christian Church of God." *PentecoStudies* 9: 97–121.

Cannell, Fenella, ed. 2006. *The Anthropology of Christianity*. Durham, NC and London: Duke University Press.

Caplan, Lionel. 1985. "The Popular Culture of Evil in Urban South India." In *The Anthropology of Evil*. Edited by David Parkin, 110–27. Oxford: Blackwell.

Casanova, José. 2001. "Religion, the New Millennium, and Globalization." *Sociology of Religion* 62: 437.

Clough, Paul, and Jon Mitchell, eds. 2001. *Powers of Good and Evil: Social Transformation and Popular Belief*. Oxford: Berghahn Books.

Coleman, Simon, and Katrin Maier. 2011. "Who Will Tend the Vine? Pentecostalism, Parenting and the Role of the State in 'London-Lagos.'" *Journal of Religion in Europe* 4(3): 450–70.

———. 2013. "Redeeming the City: Creating and Traversing 'London-Lagos.'" *Religion* 43(3): 353–64.

Coleman, Simon, and Rosalind Hackett, eds. 2015. *The Anthropology of Global Pentecostalism and Evangelicalism*. New York: New York University Press.

Comaroff, Jean, and John Comaroff. 1999. "Occult Economies and the Violence of Abstraction: Notes from the South African Postcolony." *American Ethnologist* 26(2): 279–303.

———. 2001. "Millennial Capitalism: First Thoughts of a Second Coming." In *Millennial Capitalism and the Culture of Neoliberalism*.

Edited by Jean Comaroff and John Comaroff, 1–56. London: Duke University Press.

Csordas, Thomas. 2013. "Morality as a Cultural System?" *Current Anthropology* 54(5): 523–46.

Doubleday, James. 2008. "Yoruba Londoners: Transnational Pentecostalism, Personhood, Destiny and Success." PhD dissertation, University of Cambridge.

Englund, Harri. 2007. "Witchcraft and the Limits of Mass Mediation in Malawi." *Journal of the Royal Anthropological Institute* (N.S.) 13: 295–311.

Fumanti, Mattia. In press. "Interdisciplinary Approaches to Cultural Citizenship and Migration." In *Routledge Companion to Anthropology*. Edited by Simon Coleman, Susan Hyatt, and Ann Kingsolver. New York: Routledge.

Geschiere, Peter. 1997. *The Modernity of Witchcraft: Politics and the Occult in Postcolonial Africa*. Charlottesville: University Press of Virginia.

Hackett, Rosalind. 2013. "Discourses of Demonization in Africa and Beyond." *Diogenes* 50(3): 61–75.

Harris, Hermione. 2006. *Yoruba in Diaspora: An African Church in London*. New York: Palgrave, Macmillan.

Hunt, Stephen, and Nicola Lightly. 2001. "The British Black Pentecostal 'Revival': Identity and Belief in the 'New' Nigerian Churches." *Ethnic and Racial Studies* 24(1): 104–24.

Krause, Kristine. 2015. "Orientations: Moral Geographies in Transnational Ghanaian Pentecostal Networks." In *The Anthropology of Global Pentecostalism and Evangelicalism*. Edited by Simon Coleman and Rosalind Hackett, 75–92. New York: New York University Press.

Lindhardt, Martin. 2009. "More than Just Money: The Faith Gospel and Occult Economies in Contemporary Tanzania." *Nova Religio* 13(1): 41–67.

Macfarlane, Alan. 1985. "The Root of All Evil." In *The Anthropology of Evil*. Edited by David Parkin, 57–76. Oxford: Blackwell.

Maier, Katrin. 2012. "Redeeming London. Gender Self and Mobility among Nigerian Pentecostals in London." Unpublished PhD dissertation, University of Sussex.

Marshall, Ruth. 2009. *Political Spiritualities: The Pentecostal Revolution in Nigeria*. Chicago: University of Chicago.

Meyer, Birgit. 1999. *Translating the Devil: Religion and Modernity among the Ewe in Ghana*. Edinburgh: Edinburgh University Press.

O'Neill, Kevin. 2015. "Politics of Prayer: Christianity and the Decriminalization of Cocaine in Guatemala." In *The Anthropology of Global Pentecostalism and Evangelicalism*. Edited by Simon Coleman and Rosalind Hackett, 214–27. New York: New York University Press.

Parkin, David. 1985. "Introduction." In *The Anthropology of Evil*. Edited by David Parkin, 1–25. Oxford: Blackwell.

Peel, John. 2000. *Religious Encounter and the Making of the Yoruba*. Bloomington: Indiana University Press.

———. 2008. "Foreword." In *A New Paradigm of Pentecostal Power: A Study of the Redeemed Christian Church of God in Nigeria*. Edited by Asonzeh Ukah, xix–xxiv. Trenton, NJ: Africa World Press.

Robbins, Joel. 2004. "The Globalization of Pentecostal and Charismatic Christianity." *Annual Review of Anthropology* 33: 117–43.

———. 2009. "Pentecostal Networks and the Spirit of Globalization: On the Social Productivity of Ritual Forms." *Social Analysis* 53(1): 55–66.

Taussig, Michael. 1980. *The Devil and Commodity Fetishism in South America*. Chapel Hill: The University of North Carolina Press.

Taylor, Donald. 1985. "Theological Thoughts about Evil." In *The Anthropology of Evil*. Edited by David Parkin, 26–41. Oxford: Blackwell.

Ukah, Azonzeh. 2005. "Mobilities, Migration and Multiplication: The Expansion of the Religious Field of the Redeemed Christian Church of God." In *Religion in the Context of African Migration*. Edited by Afe Adogame and Cordula Weissköppel, 317–41. Bayreuth: Eckhard Breitinger.

———. 2008. *A New Paradigm of Pentecostal Power: A Study of the Redeemed Christian Church of God in Nigeria*. Trenton, NJ: Africa World Press, Inc.

———. 2009. "Reverse Mission or Asylum Christianity: A Nigerian Church in Europe." In *Africans and the Politics of Popular Cultures*. Edited by Toyin Falola and Augustine Agwuele, 104–32. Rochester, NY: University of Rochester Press.

Van Beek, Walter E. A., and William C. Olsen. 2015. "Introduction: African Notions of Evil: The Chimera of Justice." In *Evil in Africa: Encounters with the Everyday*. Edited by William C. Olsen and Walter E. A. Van Beek, 1–26. Bloomington: Indiana University Press.

Van Dijk, Rijk. 2009. "Social Catapulting and the Spirit of Entrepreneurialism: Migrants, Private Initiative and the Pentecostal Ethic in Botswana." In *Traveling Spirits: Migrants, Markets and Mobilities*, Edited by Gertrud Hüwelmeier, and Kristine Krause, 101–17. New York: Routledge.

Chapter 6

THE TRANSFORMATION OF EVIL IN NEPAL

David N. Gellner

Disease, undeserved suffering, unexpected misfortune, hunger, crop failure, early and untimely death—all agree that these are in some sense "evils" and that humans must struggle to overcome them. But what is the immediate cause of such suffering?

Material drawn from fieldwork in Nepal over more than thirty years suggests the rather unfashionable conclusion (unfashionable within social and cultural anthropology at any rate) that, in the Nepalese context at least, there is an intense battle going on between two radically different and competing answers to this question. At the broadest level of generality, these two answers reflect two worldviews and two sets of assumptions, which may be labeled (for convenience, and with caveats) "traditional" and "modernist" respectively. The battle between these two worldviews is not an equal one. The modernist side has the education system, the power of the state, and the prestige of international organizations on its side. But the modernists do not have everything their own way; the traditional view appears to be embedded in the fabric of peasant lifeways and is much further from eradication than the modernists would wish. (I call the latter viewpoint "traditional" rather than "traditional*ist*" because it is not ideologically driven in the same way as the modernist one.)

The traditional view seeks the origin of misfortunes in mistakes or malicious action, whether because people have failed to propitiate the right gods, spirits, and ancestors, or, sometimes, because malign individuals—witches—have sent misfortune that must be dealt with by ritual and sacrifice. Modernists—politicians, activists, educators—think that the causes of misfortunes lie in ignorance and poverty and that the path to overcoming them leads through the application of science, especially medicine, education, and the adoption of democratic reforms. They see belief in witches and supernatural causation as on a par with the suppression of women and the practices of untouchability: morally wrong, ignorant, and "backward." Furthermore, the belief in witchcraft has the paradoxical result of bringing about the very things it fears (victimization, social discord).

Since my argument is likely to be misunderstood as a simplistic modernization narrative (whereas it is in fact *about* the modernization narrative), the following caveats are necessary. It is no part of the present argument that an ultimate victory of modernism (whatever that might look like) is either necessary or inevitable. Nor is it any part of the argument that the two paradigms are homogeneous, hermetically sealed, internally consistent, or symmetrical; it is in fact possible for some people to hold versions of both positions either simultaneously or seriatim in different contexts. It *is* part of the argument that a focus on competing representations of evil is productive and illuminating.

I intend to explore this clash between different conceptions of evil through a particular incident, in which a woman, suspected of being possessed by a witch, was killed in the process of exorcism, and the killers (her husband and the medium conducting the exorcism) were tried and sent to jail. This incident brought the traditional and modernist views of witchcraft into stark and unavoidable conflict. The term "ontology" has been used in a variety of ways in recent anthropological writing and debate (Carrithers et al. 2010; Kelly 2014); on any definition, it is fair to say that these two worldviews imply different ontologies (i.e., radically different theories about what kinds of things exist and can exist, and a radically different attitude to questions of explanation and blame). The two positions also presuppose different stances toward time and narrative, in that the traditional point of view sees evil as endemic and liable to erupt at any moment, whereas the modernist believes in its gradual and progressive eradication.

It is important to stress that this clash of viewpoints is not a struggle between two easily identifiable sets of people. Nor is it the case that so-called superstitions necessarily decline when people move to the cities; urbanization and modernization may in fact lead to an increase in witchcraft and sorcery, as has long been known.[1] I have written elsewhere (LeVine and Gellner 2005) about modernist assumptions within reformist Buddhism, namely the claims that Buddhism, rightly understood, is rationalist, egalitarian, and scientific. In that context, also, a large number of viewpoints are possible; it is a mistake to assume that all advocates of reform within Buddhism adopt a strongly modernist position. Some do so, but many do not. In a similar way, the same is true in this context. By no means do all of those who earn their living in what might be designated the modernist sector of the economy (as doctors, teachers, or development professionals, for example) adopt an aggressively antisuperstition stance.

Strong and Weak Senses of "Evil"

In a landmark volume edited by David Parkin, *The Anthropology of Evil* (1985), it was generally agreed that there are two senses of the term "evil" in modern English: a weak sense, in which it was no more than a synonym for "bad" or "misfortune"; and a stronger sense, in which it is used in an emotive and condemnatory way to refer to people who are beyond the pale, who epitomize badness in ways that "normal" humans, frail though they may be, do not. We can distinguish these two senses as $evil_w$ and $evil_s$. This distinction does not map neatly on to the different worldviews I have outlined above (and of course languages other than English often do not have a distinction between "bad" and "evil"). Adherents of the traditional view generally believe in both strong and weak senses: there are both occasional $evil_s$ people and manifold $evils_w$ in the world. An enormous amount of ritual and religious practice in Nepal is aimed primarily at warding off generalized $evils_w$ and thereby ensuring health and prosperity, very thisworldly ends.[2]

Like adherents of the traditional view, modernists in the Nepali context may also believe in both kinds of evil. For example, Nepal has a long tradition of leftist politics that sees "feudalism" and "patriarchy" as social evils, often embodied in the figure of the moneylender, who is portrayed in much street theatre and other literature as $evil_s$. Nepali Maoists have frequently denounced and occasionally humiliated or killed landlord moneylenders, believed to be the embodiment of evil in the Marxist analysis of rural backwardness.[3] But it is probably fair to say that, on balance, the modernist view is that $evil_s$ is rare and most of what people face, and what society needs to deal with, is a plethora of $evils_w$.

In addition to general agreement in *The Anthropology of Evil* about the dual sense of "evil," there was an interesting standoff between two of the contributors to that collection, David Pocock and Alan

Macfarlane. Pocock (1985) held that for most people in modern Britain, the stronger sense still possesses meaning and is used for people such as child molesters and rapists. But, according to Pocock, there is also a minority view that denies the existence of radical evil and assumes instead that, properly understood, no person is really evil. Macfarlane (1985), by contrast, basing himself on historical evidence going back to the seventeenth century, particularly his own and his collaborators' work in the village of Earls Colne in Essex, as well as on Thomas (1971), asserted that for four centuries, if not longer, what Pocock characterizes as the minority view has been, at least in England, the dominant view. In other words, in England, compared to most other societies, the concept of radical evil was largely absent. There were evils$_w$, but no evil$_s$. Even in the seventeenth century, there was no Inquisition in England, so that "the terror of evil was not encouraged" (Macfarlane 1985, 69). Sacrifices and other ritual means were conspicuous by their absence in seventeenth-century Earls Colne. On the rare occasions when the word "evil" was used, it referred to the mundane misfortunes and crimes of everyday life and was not used in the strong sense. Today, Macfarlane argued, evil$_s$ has been banished to the realms of science fiction (or, he might have added, crime fiction).

How might these two arguments be reconciled? As Parkin points out in his introduction, "it is precisely because the term does have such strong connotations in modern Britain that it is sparingly used" (1985, 6). Everyday life is indeed secularized to the point where most people do not expect to confront evil$_s$ in it, and the word "evil" is rarely used for evil$_w$ any more (as Macfarlane argued). Rather, evil is shocking and interesting precisely because one does not expect it to happen to oneself: it is represented in crime dramas and appears in news reports on TV. Yet, as Pocock argued, most people still have a need to be able to contrast the taken-for-granted moral and predictable world in which, in the developed world, we mostly expect to live with, on the other hand, the horrors or evil of the child abuser, serial killer, or terrorist. Judges in rare murder cases do feel the need to call on the word. From time to time, the belief in evil$_s$ produces its object, as in the moral panic about Satanic abuse of children in the UK in the late 1980s (La Fontaine 1998).

The difference between modern Britain and modern Nepal is that, for the majority in Nepal, ordinary life is not secularized (though pressures to secularize are present, and secularizing messages are pushed through education and development programs).[4] Nepal is, in Weberian terms, still enchanted. Enchantment is not a hobby (crystal therapy), entertainment (*Buffy the Vampire Slayer*, *Harry Potter*, *The X-Files*), or an esoteric path for a minority who define themselves as in opposition to mainstream society (Greenwood 2000).[5] It is rather a mundane fact of everyday life. Educated Nepalis know that there are parts of the world where belief in spirits is largely absent or at best ironic. They believe that, as educated people, they should not believe in witches, and they expect Westerners not to believe in them. When confronted by such phenomena in the company of a foreigner, they are very likely to turn to the foreigner and say, "Of course, you don't believe in all this." Yet a very considerable number of educated Nepalis do in fact believe in them; very often, they believe in them because they have had experiences that can only or best be explained by these beliefs. Their belief is ironic, tinged with doubt. For many of their countrymen, on the other hand, there is no irony and even mentioning witches is to be avoided for fear of attracting their attention.

In making the claim that modern Britain is predominantly secularized, one must immediately guard against misunderstanding. It is plainly true that there are many people who attend churches where the literal existence of spirits, both evil and good, is taken for granted. And yet, as Charles Taylor (2007) has persuasively argued in *A Secular Age*, his impressive and influential reworking of the Weberian disenchantment thesis, affirming religious belief in the modern world is a very different stance from what it was in the age of faith. Furthermore, today—firm believers in the spirits and possession apart—most people possess what he calls a "buffered self," sheltered from attack or subversion by misfortune or the transcendent, as opposed to the "porous self," always vulnerable to such invasion, that was taken for granted before secularization.[6]

The ethnographic case that I describe here depended, implicitly, on a "porous" view of the self. It brought traditional and modernist views into headlong confrontation. The courts upheld, unequivocally, the modernist side and sent those who espoused the traditional view to jail. We are not, therefore, dealing with a situation where official proceedings provide support to witchcraft beliefs and witch hunts, as in early modern Europe and some places in twentieth-century Africa (Behringer 2004, 222–23). Subsequently, a feature film was made. Despite being based only loosely on the events, and perhaps precisely because it was a work of the imagination, the film was able to represent events without taking sides, with psychological depth, and in such a way as to be susceptible to both traditional and modernist interpretations. For this reason, it is, I suggest, worth considering the film in some detail as well.

The Setting

Nepal regularly makes it into the bottom rungs of world tables for poverty and underdevelopment. It is therefore hardly surprising that there is a powerful discourse of development in the country. Politicians have, for many decades, been promising to "unleash all-round development," "turn Nepal into the Switzerland of Asia," "develop Nepal like Singapore," and so on. As Pigg says, "For Nepalis, modernity is not an abstraction" (1996, 172). On the contrary, it is built into the structure of their everyday lives; for many, it is a career.

Thus, a considerable aid and development "industry" has developed in Kathmandu (Hindman 2013) with offshoots in other towns. A whole class of Nepali intermediaries have sprung up who work in development and find it far more congenial—more modern, less corrupt, less bound in to traditional hierarchies, as well as more rewarding both financially and in other ways—than the more secure career and guaranteed pension of government service (Heaton Shrestha 2002, 2010). The growth of this development industry, its failures and embedding in ongoing corruption and unaccountability, have led to a considerable number of analyses and critiques over the years, both by Nepalis and by foreigners.[7]

Not finding sufficient work inside Nepal, many ordinary Nepalis have migrated abroad in increasing numbers: it is estimated that at least 10 percent of Nepal's 28 million people are working outside the country at any one time.[8] About half of all Nepali households are reckoned either to have a member currently abroad or someone who has returned from working abroad (Sharma et al. 2014, 32). The sufferings of many Nepali workers in the Gulf countries have long been known in Nepal; anyone who flies into Kathmandu, changing planes in Dubai or Doha, is likely to observe a coffin being offloaded along with their luggage.[9] Working conditions in Qatar became a worldwide issue following a series of exposés in the *Guardian* in 2014, which revealed how the stadiums being readied for the football World Cup in Qatar in 2022 were costing the lives of many Bangladeshi, Indian, and Nepali workers.[10]

With many ordinary and rural Nepalis now working in the Gulf, Thailand, Malaysia, and South Korea, and many ordinary Nepalis able to access cable TV, the gap between Nepal and other countries is now evident not just to a privileged elite, but to the broad mass of the people. That gap is not only visible on TV, cinema, laptop, or mobile screens. Kathmandu is home to a significant number of foreigners, who are not swallowed up by the sheer size of the capital as in Delhi. In addition to tourists, religious seekers, students, trekkers, and mountaineers, there are diplomats and "expatriate" aid professionals, both the well-heeled family types brought in by international aid organizations (Hindman 2013) and younger individuals who turn up and find more casual employment for a year or three (Norum 2015).

Kathmandu is also a major migration destination within Nepal, as well as for migrant labor from India. What used to be sleepy, exotic, Hindu-Buddhist agro-cities—the centuries-old temples and palaces of their city cores designated World Heritage sites—have now merged into a crowded Asian megacity with slums, traffic jams, high-rise apartment blocks, water shortages, and up to sixteen hours per day of scheduled "loadshedding" (as electricity cuts are called in Nepal).[11] The Kathmandu Valley had an urban population of less than 200,000 in the early 1950s, which grew to nearly 600,000 in 1991, and over 1.4 million in 2011. The facilities of the capital (hospitals, schools) and the push factor of the Maoist insurgency/civil war from 1996 to 2006 meant that many people from the hills of Nepal resettled in the capital. The Newars, who are the Kathmandu Valley's original and historic inhabitants (Gellner and Quigley 1995), are now a minority in their own homeland. Large numbers of people, many of them recent migrants to the city, now live cheek by jowl with neighbors of different ethnic groups and castes.

The Kathmandu Valley has an array of different types of healing system on offer that I have summarized in a list of nine main types (Gellner 2001, 237): biomedical, Ayurvedic, Unani, ritual, astrological, imported healing cults (such as the Japanese Seimeikyo and Christianity), mixed treatment (ritual/Ayurvedic/astrology) by Tantric healers, possession healing (by shamans or mediums), and herbalism.[12] Some of these are remote or rare (Unani), so the actual choice facing most people is, in practice, reduced to four: the biomedical (either a pharmacist, "compounder," or doctor), the astrological, the ritual healer (all male), or the medium (predominantly female) or shaman (mostly male). There are cases where different specialists cross-refer (a healer may tell a patient to see a doctor; a doctor may judge that the complaint is best dealt with by a healer). It is the mediums, shamans, and healers who specialize in (among other things) diagnoses of witchcraft. The following case, of a Newar Farmer-caste woman, is typical:

> I felt very weak for nearly three months and consulted the doctor, but it was not helpful. Then I went to the healer, a deo-ma [i.e., a medium, literally "god-mother"], who said it was due to the bokshi's bigar [witch's

"spoiling"]. The healer beat me first to elicit a reply from the witch as to why she was troubling me, then when that did not work, she asked my husband to do so and he beat me very badly, threatening to break my bones. I was so weak after that, I could not even stand up. But while it was going on I felt no pain as it was the bokshi [witch] and not me, who was really being beaten. Finally, the healer made that witch speak through me and she promised to leave me alone after that. I vomited when I got back home and maybe the bigar came out that time. We think the bokshi is from my husband's side of the family since we live in my mother's house. She only had three daughters and no sons and my husband is one of three sons, so I am taking care of my mother's property with him. It could be a case of jealousy as his brothers did not inherit much and we are better off than they. (Dietrich 1998, 92)

The Case of Gita and Sarasvati

The ethnographic case to be discussed occurred in Maitidevi, Kathmandu, a part of the city where migrants from the Nepalese hills outnumber indigenous Newars. Accusations of witchcraft, and the treatment of women so accused, are topics that come up fairly frequently in the Nepalese press. Most often it is the case of a widow in the Tarai region in the south of the country, usually poor and low caste, who has been accused of being a witch, attacked, forced to eat feces, and sometimes killed. Those who attack the woman in question are usually neighbors and sometimes relatives. In contrast, the case to be described here occurred in the heart of the capital city, Kathmandu.[13]

Late on the evening of 7 May 1997, a medium, a woman called Gita K. C.,[14] was treating another woman, Sarasvati Adhikari, who was suspected of being possessed by a witch. In order to make the witch speak and identify herself, Gita, aided by Sarasvati's husband, Ganga Bahadur, and the landlord and landlady of the house where Gita was living, beat and burned Sarasvati with a hot rice spatula. Mohan Mainali, a journalist, was renting an apartment downstairs. Hearing pitiful sounds, "like a dog being run over," he twice went upstairs to remonstrate with them, but they insisted that they were not hitting (*pitnu*) Sarasvati but rather attempting to help her (*upacar garnu*). Since he feared that the police would either respond slowly or accuse him of involvement, and since he had to leave town for work early the next day, he asked his brother to phone a feminist activist friend, Shobha Gautam, in the morning. Gautam came, with journalist Amrita Lamsal and other activists, and they brought along the police from the local station. They found Sarasvati lying on the top floor on a straw mattress with her wrists bound with a rope. Her two big toes were also tied with black thread. Boiling water had been poured on her legs and her tongue had been branded with the spatula. Eventually, the police took Sarasvati to Bir Hospital. Her children, a daughter of around ten and a son of about six, were taken to the NGO, CWIN (Child Workers of Nepal).

Early the next morning, Sarasvati died from her injuries. By the following day, when the death certificate was signed and the body released, a large crowd had gathered outside the hospital and they formed an impromptu demonstration, accompanying Sarasvati's body to the Pashupati temple for cremation. There were placards protesting against violence against women and condemning superstition. Gita, Sarasvati's husband, the landlord, and the landlady were all arrested and charged with murder. In due course, they were all sent to jail, the landlord for only a month, the landlady for four years, the husband and Gita for longer.[15]

The reporting of the case demonstrated considerable divergences. The article by Bel Bahadur Bhujel (1997), written while the court case was still going on, includes a long and rambling account of Gita's childhood and young adulthood, the main point of which is to demonstrate her immorality (lack of respect for seniors, habit of thieving at every opportunity, failure to stay with her husband, and manipulative promiscuity in relations with men). The emotive and loaded language of this part of the article does not inspire confidence in the rest of Bhujel's account. Be that as it may, Bhujel asserts that there was a love affair between Gita and Ganga Bahadur, that Ganga Bahadur believed that it was thanks to Gita's mantras that he had succeeded in getting a job as a security guard at the US Embassy, and that together they had planned the murder of Sarasvati.

The Film *Mukundo* (*Mask of Desire*, 1999)

Assessing and disentangling representations of these events is made more complex by the fact that a highly regarded feature film was based loosely on these events (Sherpa 1999). The screenplay was by Kesang Tseten, who later established a reputation as a documentary filmmaker. The filmmaker in this case was Tsering Rhita Sherpa. Unfortunately, *Mukundo* came out at a time when Nepal was perhaps not yet ready for such a film and it played for only a few days to virtually empty cinemas in Kathmandu.

As noted in a review in *Nepali Times* (Anonymous 2000), the film has a mythic quality. The review compares it to *Black Orpheus*, "where an extraordinary event is made plausible by [its] setting against the Dionysian background of the Rio Carnival." The opening of the film is an exorcistic séance, realistically depicted, in which a woman, evidently possessed by a witch, is breathing heavily and being treated by Gita (played by Mithila Sharma), who also begins to breathe fast and to beat the possessed woman with a grass broom. As usual on such occasions, family members and others are present. Gita has a priestly attendant, who we later learn is her brother. He is represented as a Vaishnava Brahmin wearing a dhoti.[16] The séance over, he chides Gita to eat, and we see him calling her back to her vocation to help suffering humanity. She, on the other hand, is clearly troubled and oppressed by having to treat so much human misery. Later, we learn that she had a failed marriage to a mentally disturbed young man who committed suicide.

The frame of healing having been established, the film switches to the story of Sarasvati (Gauri Malla) and her husband Dipak (Ratan Subedi) (as the Ganga Bahadur character is called in the film). The setting for the film is the old royal city of Patan (Lalitpur). The couple live with their two daughters in a rented apartment off a small courtyard with a well, a Buddhist shrine (chaitya), Newar neighbors, and peeling election posters stuck on the brick walls of the courtyard's houses. Dipak works as a security guard and, when his night duty is finished, he cycles home every morning past the medieval palace (a UNESCO World Heritage site) at the center of the city. He is portrayed as a simple family man, previously a successful footballer who still likes to keep fit. Sarasvati is pregnant and would like to give him a son.

Sarasvati meets a holy man while worshipping in the eerily empty nineteenth-century temples of Shankhamul, just outside the old city and next to the River Bagmati. The holy man tells her to worship the goddess Tripura to obtain a son, which she duly does. A son is born, but soon falls ill. Sarasvati is sure the illness has come because she has not thanked the holy man or the goddess. Dipak insists they must go to the hospital where they are given medicine and told to come back if the baby does not improve. Sarasvati goes off to consult the holy man and he advises her to pray hard and to go to a medium of the goddess Tripura, but he warns her that there is also a risk in doing so. Dipak, urged by his wife that they must do something to save their son, goes in search of the medium.

He finds the medium, Gita (Mithila Sharma), and observes her healing. Dipak and Sarasvati go back to the doctor, who gives them more medicine and says, "If this doesn't work, there is nothing further we can do." Dipak comes round to the idea of consulting the medium. But before they can do so, the boy dies. Dipak's mother has come to help with the birth, but the death of the child brings out serious tensions between mother-in-law and daughter-in-law, with Dipak caught between them. Sarasvati falls into depression. She and her mother-in-law accuse each other of being possessed by a witch. Sarasvati asks Dipak to take her to the goddess; she blames herself for not thanking the goddess for the gift of the baby. She declares herself ready to be healed and cleansed, however much the healer may beat her.

When his mother departs for the village one day, Dipak takes Sarasvati to see Gita, where the healing session in fact involves no beating. The next day, Sarasvati seems to be better. Meanwhile, Gita is suffering and is unable to cure; the patients are sent away for the day. Her brother reminds her of her vocation to save suffering humanity and to give up all human passions and attachments. She retorts that she did not ask to be chosen. Is he just afraid that he will lose "all this" (i.e., the income and way of life) that her healing provides?

Gita goes out in search of Dipak and Sarasvati's apartment, spies him leaving for work, and goes up to meet Sarasvati. Gita speaks about love, and Sarasvati protests that she understands nothing of what Gita is saying. But when Dipak is home and Sarasvati is relating Gita's visit, she divines that Gita spoke about love so much because she lacks it in her own life. Friendship and a kind of love triangle develop. Sarasvati is convinced she is ugly in comparison with Gita. They have arranged to go together to see the local festival of Matsyendranath. But Sarasvati complains of feeling unwell and insists that Gita and Dipak go to see it without her. It gets late as Gita tells Dipak the story of her marriage at sixteen and how her husband, not ready for marriage, sick and weak, committed suicide. People blamed her for his death. She was afflicted by whatever he had. Doctors couldn't heal her. A guru diagnosed possession, and she slowly started to recover. She learned how to help others.

Dipak and Gita get caught in the rain, and return to Gita's house for tea. When Dipak finally returns to his apartment, Sarasvati is waiting in the dark and accuses Gita of being a witch, of seeking to seduce Dipak away from her. Meanwhile, Gita is continuing to have difficulties healing and is again called back to her duty by her brother, who tells her that she cannot have room for the mother goddess if she has impure feelings inside her. Sarasvati is also disturbed and fearful that her husband is having an affair. Dipak sends his and Saravati's daughters to his mother. Sarasvati goes to see Gita and asks her to heal her, because it all started with "the mother." Gita tells her to come back with her husband at the appointed time.

Gita prepares herself for the evening séance, praying to the goddess Tripura to help her heal this time. Outside, the festival of Matsyendranath is under way, with drumming and dancing, huge crowds following the chariots of the gods. Dipak and Sarasvati come to sit before Gita incarnating the goddess. The film ends with Gita working herself up into a frenzy. She seems to be losing her power, but then redoubles her efforts. She slaps Sarasvati and binds her toes and wrists. Sarasvati fights back and bites Gita. Gita declares that there is a witch and beats Sarasvati in order to exorcize the evil spirit inhabiting her. The two women fight in the darkness. We hear Dipak's voice calling out that it is dark. The film ends.

Those with prior knowledge of the case on which the film is based will no doubt have assumed that the film ends with the death of Sarasvati. Other Nepalis to whom I have shown the film (in a village setting) are less sure and admitted that they were puzzled by the ending, which is indeed somewhat ambiguous. Nevertheless, they were generally intrigued by the film, appreciating its representations of family life (interactions with the children; mother-in-law–daughter-in-law tussles) and empathizing with the situations portrayed. They interpreted Gita's increasing failure to heal, as her brother does in the film, to her "base passions," in particular to her falling in love with Dipak. And, not surprisingly, having been exposed to many such messages in schools and development meetings, some of them thought that the film aimed to teach its audience about the dangers of "superstition" (*andhavisvas*).[17] This indeed seems to have been the director's intention (to warn of the misuse of religion).

The subtle psychological portrayal and superb acting both of healer and of the sick, the ambiguity about who is a witch and who is to blame, means that if there is a message, it is not a blunt one, and people can bring to the film different points of view, both modernist and traditional and possibly several in between. Evil exists (the child dies, his mother becomes bitter and dies), but is it a case of $evil_w$ or $evil_s$? Does the child die because his mother fails to keep her part of the bargain with the gods? Or is it merely ignorant thinking on her part that makes it so?

It has been suggested to me that the possibility of romance between Dipak and Gita was the invention of the filmmaker "since films require some spice." But the suggestion of an affair is already there in Bhujel's journalistic account (which may have influenced the writer of the screenplay, though he claims only to have seen one small newspaper article about the original case). The possibility of a love triangle is firmly dismissed by the journalist Maila as nothing more than rumor (1997, 80).

Modernist Campaigns against Witchcraft

Peter van der Veer (2014) has pointed out how South Asia and China diverge quite remarkably in their paths to modernization. In China, religion has been overtly attacked and rejected wholesale. The destruction and mayhem of the Cultural Revolution was only the culmination of a long tradition of anticlericalism and attempts to impose a religion-free worldview on a "superstitious" populace. In South Asia, by contrast, political liberation has come very frequently in religious garb. Gandhi is the obvious example, but there were alternative versions that also combined religion and political resistance. Even the secular Nehru, while anticlerical in his sentiments, did not translate that into policy. Indeed, being "secular" in the Indian context often means simply not being highly partisan, and supporting all religions, rather than being hostile to religion as such (Bhargava 2010).

In Nepal, which was an officially Hindu kingdom until 2007, outright opposition to religion is even rarer than in India (where there is, at least, a minority rationalist tradition, now severely embattled: see, for example, Ramachandran [2015]). While it is not compulsory to declare one's faith in God, as for politicians in the US, neither is religion taboo for Nepalese politicians, and many have an active interest in spirituality, the gods, and obtaining whatever divine assistance they can. Despite differing views on the importance of religion, and a tolerant public sphere, there is universal agreement that some parts of traditional culture constitute "social evils" (*samajik vikriti*) which therefore need to be abolished and/or reformed. Foremost among these evils are beliefs about untouchability (that some castes are inherently impure and should not be interacted with; that women are impure during menstruation), about widow remarriage (that however young a woman is, once widowed she should never remarry), and about witchcraft (that community action should be taken against "known witches").[18]

Already, in Nepal's first general law code of 1854, considerable restrictions were put on any healer seeking to diagnose witchcraft (Macdonald 1976). Today, it is illegal to accuse anyone of being a witch or wizard, or to attempt to chase them out of their homes on such a charge, to boycott or torture them (section 10B of the current General Law Code). Various feminist organizations campaign against witchcraft accusations and try to pressure policemen and civil servants in the affected areas to apply the law. They point out that the victims of such accusations are never rich or well placed, but rather tend to be the poor, the low caste, and those with little support in society.

In *Endless Atrocities: Women Survivors of Witch Accusation* (Ansari 2014), many harrowing testimonies, mostly from women who have been beaten and worse for being witches, attest both to the fear people have of the witch's power and to the sufferings of those who are suspected of being witches. In some cases, the accusations come from closely related family members, often when there is a property motive.[19] Mohna Ansari asks:

> Who are accused of witchery? The rich and influential women are not accused of being a witch, but Dalit, widow (single women), elderly, poor, illiterate, and marginalized women are. Similarly, introvert, physically ugly or those who cannot afford make-up, those who lead an extremely difficult life physically and mentally, and those women who have been perceived as a threat to the elite are accused of practising witchcraft. (Ansari 2014, 34)

On this view, the cause is ignorance, lack of education. Bring the light of education, and all will be solved. Describing similar cases, under the headline "Witch-hunting: Medieval Barbarity Continues to Blight the Landscape of New Nepal," journalist Mallika Aryal writes:

> Nepal has been a party to the Convention on the Elimination of All Forms of Discrimination against Women since 1991. ... Witch-hunting is an extreme form of gender violence and the reason it is not taken seriously is because the victims are usually from marginalised communities. Nepal's gender movement has made amazing strides, but it has done little for this community of victims. Activists in Kathmandu can push for laws against witch-hunting while those in the field can work to spread awareness against the medieval superstitions that target these women. The Nepal Police, too, needs to include a chapter on how to address crimes related to superstition in their training manuals. (Aryal 2009)

In other words, action against the traditional view of evil is based on grounds of equality, human rights, and progress. It is a moral campaign, founded on appeals to justice and equity. Education and awareness campaigns are the means to that end.

Conclusion

On the one side, there is the traditional assumption that humans are capable of causing physical suffering to others, sometimes by wishing them harm and carrying out harmful rituals, sometimes inadvertently, just by looking at them. On the other, there is the modernist belief in science, including in the social sphere. These are incommensurable worldviews and different moralities; in one sense, the advocates of each are living in different worlds, with wholly different assumptions about unseen forces, causation, blame, and redress. Except that the two worlds collide and impact on each other. The state may and does try to intervene in some cases, but that, in itself, does not eliminate the belief in mystical causation, nor the assumption that the majority of those who are guilty of harming others in this way are women, usually postmenopausal women.[20] The current success and expansion of Christianity in Nepal may have a lot to do with its ability to combine both worldviews. It accepts the existence of evil spirits, but offers a progress-oriented, modern-seeming (and cheaper) route to overcoming them (Fricke 2008; Gibson 2015).

Durkheim famously declared: "There are no religions that are false. All are true after their own fashion" (Durkheim 1995, 2). He also stressed the importance of deviant behavior for defining a community (1982, 98–101). Anthropology, traditionally, has generally taken both lines—the interpretive and the functionalist—in its approach to witchcraft and other similar beliefs and practices. The classic mode of reconciling these different views of personhood, causation, morality, and what kind of forces exist "out there" and within ourselves is to combine Evans-Prichard's *Witchcraft, Oracles, and Magic among the Azande* (1937) and Lévi-Strauss's essays, "The Sorcerer and His Magic" and "The Effectiveness of Symbols" (Lévi-Strauss 1963, chapters 9 and 10). The magical worldview is, from the lay point of view, as coherent a set of assumptions as any other one might live by; there are sufficient explanations for the failure of any theory or oracle built in to the worldview to prevent any hard falsifications. The Azande are skeptical about particular healers or medicines, and know that we live with imperfect knowledge in a complex universe. Failures on particular occasions to predict or explain do not call the system as a whole into question. Particular healing successes can be explained, following Lévi-Strauss, by seeing the sorcerer as a master therapist, able to manipulate metaphors and persuade the patient to adopt a more positive frame of mind, which is itself a large part of the healing process.

This conventional anthropological reconciliation of traditional and modernist views on sorcery presupposes that mental forces exist, that maliciousness exists, and that maliciousness may indeed have real effects on other people, but it disallows that malicious thoughts on their own can cause someone to fall ill. Witchcraft accusations, on the conventional view, are a kind of metaphor for dealing with neighbors and relatives, or for coping with rapid social change and/or globalization. No doubt there have been plenty of advances that nuance the understanding of ritual since the days of Evans-Pritchard and Lévi-Strauss.[21]

Modernists know in advance that those who believe in witchcraft must be wrong. Some anthropologists, in reaction, deny that informants can ever be wrong (only other anthropologists and Western thought since the Enlightenment can be wrong) and ask us to open ourselves to the possibility that the entities posited by indigenous thought might, on their own, explain how social life goes on in the places where anthropologists work. In the present case, that means trying to empathize with taken-for-granted beliefs that spirits do possess people and that old women bewitch others and cause their cattle to stop giving milk and their children to die. While that is indeed a necessary part of the process of attempting to understand the course of events in cases such as Sarasvati's, it surely cannot be the end point or the conclusion of the enquiry. For one thing, there are, and have always been, local skeptics who do not subscribe to these explanations; "belief" is not uniform or equally shared.[22]

The genius of the film *Mukundo* is that—despite the filmmaker having an agenda to show the misuse of religion—it understands this. It is not simple propaganda pushing the messages of international aid agencies. It portrays the different characters in equal depth, as well as the powerful emotions of longing, fear, and envy that motivate them in a fairly standard family situation. The audience can read what happens in terms both of $evil_w$ and of $evil_s$, in terms of tradition or of modernity, and in such a way that all the characters appear as victims in different ways. Whether reconstructed, so far as is possible, through the accounts of those who observed it, or viewed through the lens of the film, the Sarasvati case was profoundly social, as well, of course, as political, in that it went to court and generated political protest.

The modernist campaigns against witchcraft accusations are attempts to get people to think and moralize differently, and to conceptualize evil, time, and personhood in new and different ways. It is a campaign led by feminists that is, on the face of it, about rights.

But it carries along with it a very different and new moral ontology, which posits persons—men, women, and children—as equal, rights-bearing, and autonomous individuals in a world supposed to be devoid of malign spirit attack and susceptible of continual improvement. The contrast with the deeply social and hierarchical zero-sum world of "distributed" and "porous" persons—whose identity, fortune, and misfortune is deeply implicated with that of their close kin, deceased ancestors, and the family gods—could not be more stark.

David N. Gellner, Oxford University

Notes

I am grateful to Basanta Maharjan for help in fieldwork and tracing materials. I thank D. P. Martinez, D. Parkin, C. Letizia, A. de Sales, A. Lamsal, I. Gibson, F. Gurung, and M. Clarke for helpful suggestions on earlier drafts. They are not to be blamed for the result, for which I take sole responsibility. Fieldwork in Nepal since 1982 has been supported by a number of bodies, among them the Leverhulme Trust, the British Academy, and the ESRC. The most recent ESRC grant was for research into "Caste, Class, and Culture" [ES/L00240X/1].

1. Cf. Geschiere (1997) who refers to "the modernity of witchcraft." There does not seem to be in Asia, as the Comaroffs describe for Africa (1999), the widespread idea that the prosperity of those who flourish economically under modern conditions is due to powerful sorcery or witchcraft.
2. In so far as Africanists imagine that Asian religions adopt an "'otherworldly' posture" (e.g., Van Beek & Olsen 2015, 5), this is an error and gives a very misleading impression of what most ritual and religious practice in South Asia is actually about.
3. See Adhikari (2014) for an account of the Maoist revolution. For a very readable account of two young communists' attempts to radicalize Nepalis (Thangmis) in the village of Piskar, in the years leading up to a notorious massacre there in 1984, see Shneiderman (2010). On the brief Maoist uprising in May 1971 in Jhapa, just over the Nepalese border from Naxalbari in India, in which eight "class enemies" were eliminated, see Thapa (2004, 26–27). On the Maoist use of song and theatre, see De Sales (2003), Mottin (2010), and Stirr (2013).
4. This is not to deny that there are social pockets or enclaves within modern Britain where nonironic belief in possession and demons is to be found. But the overall contrast remains valid.
5. Behringer (2004, 231–32) identifies Jacob Grimm and Jules Michelet as the originators of the romantic view of premodern witches.
6. See Daniel (1984) for a classic account of the "porous" self in South Asia.

7. It would be impossible to cite all the literature in the anthropology of development in Nepal, but the following should be mentioned: N. Shrestha 1998; A. M. Shrestha 1999; Pigg 1992, 1996; Pandey 1999; Lim 2008; Leve 2001, 2007; Gellner 2015, forthcoming; Fujikura 2013.
8. Labor permits issued to those seeking to work abroad by Nepal's Department of Foreign Employment have increased by over one hundred fold in the twenty years between 1993 and 2013. In the early 1990s, only a few thousand were issued a year; now it is nearing half a million a year (Sharma et al. 2014, 46). Permits are not needed for work in India.
9. See Rai (2016) who records that on average, 1500 workers leave each day for the Gulf and Malaysia, and three bodies are flown back "shrink-wrapped and stuffed into plywood boxes."
10. A series of three films by Kesang Tseten also portray the lives of Nepali workers in the Gulf vividly. See also publications by Tristan Bruslé (2009, 2012).
11. After more than a decade in which life adapted to loadshedding schedules, it suddenly came to an end late in 2016 when a new managing director of the Nepal Electricity Corporation was appointed, Kulman Ghising, who was determined to remove corruption, tackle leakage, and import more electricity from India. Ghising's popularity in Nepal is probably second only to the captain of the national cricket team.
12. On healers and mediums in Nepal (mainly the Kathmandu Valley), see Coon (1989), Pigg (1995), Gellner and Shrestha (1993), Gellner (1994), Dietrich (1998), and Harper (2014). On shamanism in Nepal there is an enormous literature, too large to summarize here.
13. I have described the case briefly before on the basis of press accounts (Gellner 2001, 246–47).
14. K. C. is a common surname in Nepal, standing for Khatri Chhetri. Since *Khatri* refers to lower-status Chhetris, who are offspring of non-Chhetri mothers, the use of the English letters as an abbreviation is a way to make the surname sound more honorific.
15. I am grateful to Mohan Mainali and Amrita Lamsal for being willing to share their painful memories of this case with me.
16. Some small ethnographic observations: It is unusual, not to say highly unlikely, that the attendant of a medium would be an orthodox Brahman as suggested here (also, Vaishnava Brahmans are very rare in Nepal). Furthermore, the séances are shown as taking place on the ground floor, open to the courtyard, whereas they always happen upstairs on the first floor where there is more privacy.
17. On the invention of the term "superstition" in the South Asian context, see Bharati (1970). On superstition and healing in school textbooks, see Gellner (2004), and in development discourse about health, see Pigg (1995, 1996).

18. Animal sacrifice is another traditional practice seen as thoroughly reprehensible by some, but quite acceptable by others, and therefore the object of considerable debate (Gellner, Hausner, and Letizia 2016).
19. For a book-length case study of a case of this sort in Rajasthan, India, see Carstairs (1983).
20. Before 1951, the Ranas filled their palaces with concubines, who were often seized from the Tamang villages around the Kathmandu Valley. Dietrich (1998, 251) cites a retired concubine who claimed that such girls were often raped, accused of witchcraft, and killed.
21. For example, Humphrey and Laidlaw (1994) and Houseman and Severi (1998). Elsewhere, I argue that any attempt to build a general theory of ritual cannot be based on a single paradigm case, and must acknowledge at least three contrasting stances toward ritual and the sacred (Gellner 2001, chapters 3–4).
22. For a justly acclaimed account that negotiates these epistemological traps in a sophisticated manner, see Favret-Saada (1980).

References

Adhikari, A. 2014. *The Bullet and the Ballot Box: The Story of Nepal's Maoist Revolution*. London: Verso.
Anonymous. 2000. "Mask of Desire [Review of "Mukundo"]." *Nepali Times* 7. Retrieved 4 January 2019 from http://nepalitimes.com/news.php?id=10859%20-%20.VGYWtstyb-Y#.VnF46cso2Uk.
Ansari, M. 2014. "Witch-hunting and Legal Remedy." In *Endless Atrocity: Women Survivors of Witch Accusation*, 33–36. Kathmandu: CARE/Sancharika.
Aryal, M. 2009. "Witch-hunts: Medieval Barbarity Continues to Blight the Landscape of New Nepal." *Nepali Times* 482 (25 Dec). Retrieved 4 January 2018 from http://nepalitimes.com/news.php?id=16636#.VnFlasso2Uk.
Behringer, W. 2004. *Witches and Witch-Hunts: A Global History*. Cambridge: Polity.
Bharati, A. 1970. "The Use of 'Superstition' as an Anti-Traditional Device in Urban Hinduism." *Contributions to Indian Sociology* (n.s.) 4: 36–49.
Bhargava, R. 2010. *The Promise of India's Secular Democracy*. Delhi: Oxford University Press.
Bhujel, B. B. 1997. "Boksi jharne nihunma dhamini Gitako cartikala." [The plot of medium Gita under cover of exorcizing a witch.] *Satyakatha* 3(21): 5–24.
Bruslé. T. 2009. "Who's in a Labour Camp? A Socio-economic Analysis of Nepalese Migrants in Qatar." *European Bulletin of Himalayan Research* 35–36: 154–70.

———. 2012. "What's New in the Gulf? New Technologies, Consumption and Display of Modernity among Nepali Workers in Qatar." *e-migrinter* 8: 59–73.

Carrithers, M., et al. 2010. "Ontology Is Just Another Word for Culture." [GDAT Manchester 2008.] *Critique of Anthropology* 30(2): 152–200.

Carstairs, G. M. 1983. *Death of a Witch: A Village in North India, 1950–1981.* London: Hutchinson.

Comaroff, J., and J. L. Comaroff. 1999. "Occult Economies and the Violence of Abstraction: Notes from the South African Postcolony." *American Ethnologist* 26(2): 279–303.

Coon, E. 1989. "Possessing Power: Ajima and Her Medium." *Himalaya* 9(1): 5. digitalcommons.macalester.edu/himalaya/vol9/iss1/5.

Daniel, E. V. 1984. *Fluid Signs: Being a Person the Tamil Way.* Berkeley: University of California Press.

De Sales, A. 2003. "Remarks on Revolutionary Songs and Iconography." *European Bulletin of Himalayan Research* 24: 5–24.

Dietrich, A. 1998. *Tantric Healing in the Kathmandu Valley.* Delhi: Book Faith India.

Durkheim, E. 1982 [1894]. *The Rules of Sociological Method.* Translated by W. D. Halls. New York: The Free Press.

———. 1995 [1915]. *The Elementary Forms of Religious Life.* Translated by K. E. Fields. New York: The Free Press.

Evans-Pritchard, E. E. 1937. *Witchcraft, Oracles, and Magic among the Azande.* Oxford: Clarendon.

Favret-Saada, J. 1980. *Deadly Words: Witchcraft in the Bocage.* Cambridge, UK: Cambridge University Press.

Fricke, T. 2008. "Tamang Conversions: Culture, Politics, and the Christian Conversion Narrative in Nepal." *Contributions to Nepalese Studies* 35(1): 35–62.

Fujikura, T. 2013. *Discourses of Awareness: Development, Social Movements and the Practices of Freedom in Nepal.* Kathmandu: Martin Chautari.

Gellner, D. N. 1994. "Priests, Healers, Mediums, and Witches: The Context of Possession in the Kathmandu Valley." *Man* (n.s.) 26(1): 27–48.

———. 2001. *The Anthropology of Buddhism and Hinduism: Weberian Themes.* Delhi: Oxford University Press.

———. 2004. "Children's Voices from Kathmandu and Lalitpur, Nepal." *Journal of Asian and African Studies* 68: 1–47.

———. 2015. "Rituals of Democracy and Development in Nepal." In *Governance, Conflict and Development in South Asia: Perspectives from India, Nepal and Sri Lanka.* Edited by S. Hettige and E. Gerharz, 99–127. Delhi: Sage.

———. forthcoming. "Masters of Hybridity: How Activists Reconstructed Nepali Society." *Journal of the Royal Anthropological Institute* (n.s.).

Gellner, D. N., and U. S. Shrestha. 1993. "Portrait of a Tantric Healer: A Preliminary Report into Curing Traditions in the Kathmandu Valley."

In *Nepal: Past and Present*. Edited by G. Toffin, 135–47. Paris: CNRS. (Republished as chapter 9 in Gellner 2001.)

Gellner, D. N., and D. Quigley, eds. 1995. *Contested Hierarchies: A Collaborative Ethnography of Caste among the Newars of the Kathmandu Valley, Nepal*. Delhi: Oxford University Press.

Gellner, D. N., S. Hausner, and C. Letizia, eds. 2016. *Religion, Secularism, and Ethnicity in Contemporary Nepal*. Delhi: Oxford University Press.

Geschiere, P. 1997. *The Modernity of Witchcraft: Politics and the Occult in Post-colonial Africa*. Charlottesville: University of Virginia Press.

Gibson, I. 2015. "Suffering and Christianity: Conversion and Ethical Change among the Newars of Bhaktapur." DPhil dissertation, University of Oxford.

Greenwood, S. 2000. *Magic, Witchcraft and the Otherworld: An Anthropology*. Oxford: Berg Publishers.

Harper, I. 2014. *Development and Public Health in the Himalayas: Reflections on Healing in Contemporary Nepal*. London: Routledge.

Heaton Shrestha, C. 2002. "NGOs as *Thekadar* or *Sevak*: Identity Crisis in Nepal's Non-governmental Sector." *European Bulletin of Himalayan Research* 22: 5–36.

———. 2010. "Activists and Development in Nepal." In *Varieties of Activist Experience: Civil Society in South Asia*. Edited by D. N. Gellner, 181–216. Delhi: Sage.

Hindman, H. 2013. *Mediating the Global: Expatria's Forms and Consequences in Kathmandu*. Stanford, CA: Stanford University Press.

Houseman, M., and C. Severi. 1998. *Naven or the Other Self: A Relational Approach to Ritual Action*. Leiden: Brill.

Humphrey, L., and J. Laidlaw. 1994. *The Archetypal Actions of Ritual: A Theory of Ritual Illustrated by the Jain Rite of Worship*. Oxford: Clarendon.

Kelly, J. D. 2014. "The Ontological Turn: Where Are We?" *HAU: Journal of Ethnographic Theory* 4(1): 357–60.

La Fontaine, J. S. 1998. *Speak of the Devil: Tales of Satanic Abuse in Contemporary England*. Cambridge, UK: Cambridge University Press.

Leve, L. 2001. "Between Jesse Helms and Ram Bahadur: Women, NGOs, 'Participation,' and 'Empowerment' in Nepal." *PoLAR: Political and Legal Anthropology Review* 24(1): 108–28.

———. 2007. "'Failed Development' and Rural Revolution in Nepal: Rethinking Subaltern Consciousness and Women's Empowerment." *Anthropological Quarterly* 80(1): 127–72.

LeVine, S., and D. N. Gellner. 2005. *Rebuilding Buddhism: The Theravada Movement in Twentieth-Century Nepal*. Cambridge, MA: Harvard University Press.

Lévi-Strauss, C. 1963. *Structural Anthropology*. New York: Basic Books.

Lim, F. K. G. 2008. *Imagining the Good Life: Negotiating Culture and Development in Nepal Himalaya*. Leiden: Brill.

Macdonald, A. W. 1976. "Sorcery in the Nepalese Code of 1853." In *Spirit Possession in the Nepal Himalayas*. Edited by J. Hitchcock and R. L. Jones. Warminster: Aris and Phillips.

Macfarlane, A. 1985. "The Root of All Evil." In *The Anthropology of Evil*. Edited by D. Parkin, 57–76. Oxford: Blackwell.

Maila, V. 1997. "Andhavisvasko adma hatya." [Murder Under the Cover of Superstition.] *Tathyakatha* 47: 70–90.

Mottin, M. 2010. "Catchy Melodies and Clenched Fists: Performance as Politics in Maoist Cultural Programs." In *The Maoist Insurgency in Nepal: Revolution in the Twenty-first Century*. Edited by M. P. Lawoti and A. K. Pahari, 52–72. London & New York: Routledge.

Norum, R. 2015. "The Hypersocial: Transience, Privilege and the Neo-colonial Imaginary in Expatria, Kathmandu." DPhil dissertation, University of Oxford.

Panday, D. R. 1999. *Nepal's Failed Development: Reflections on the Mission and the Maladies*. Kathmandu: Nepal South Asia Centre.

Parkin, D. ed. 1985. *The Anthropology of Evil*. Oxford: Blackwell.

Pigg, S. L. 1992. "Inventing Social Categories through Place: Social Representations and Development in Nepal." *Comparative Studies in Society and History* 34(3): 491–513.

———. 1995. "The Social Symbolism of Healing in Nepal." *Ethnology* 34(1): 17–36.

———. 1996. "The Credible and the Credulous: The Question of 'Villagers' Beliefs' in Nepal." *Cultural Anthropology* 11(2): 160–201.

Pocock, D. 1985. "Unruly Evil." In *The Anthropology of Evil*. Edited by D. Parkin, 42–56. Oxford: Blackwell.

Rai, O. A. 2016. "Killed in the Line of Duty." *Nepali Times* 790 (8 Jan).

Ramachandran, S. 2015. "Rationalist Thinkers under Attack in India." *Asia Times* (5 Oct). Retrieved 4 January 2019 from http://atimes.com/2015/10/secular-thinkers-under-attack-in-india/.

Sharma, S., S. Pandey, D. Pathak, and B. Sijapati-Basnett. 2014. *State of Migration in Nepal*. Kathmandu: Centre for the Study of Labour and Mobility. www.ceslam.org.

Sherpa, T. R. 1999. "Mukundo (Mask of Desire)." Screenplay K. Tseten. Mahankal, Nepal: Mila Productions/NHK.

Shneiderman, S. 2010. "Creating 'Civilized' Communists: A Quarter of a Century of Politicization in Rural Nepal." In *Varieties of Activist Experience: Civil Society in South Asia*. Edited by D. N. Gellner, 46–80. Delhi: Sage.

Shrestha, A. M. 1999. *Bleeding Mountains of Nepal: A Story of Corruption, Greed, Misuse of Power and Resources*. San Jose: Authors Choice Press.

Shrestha, N. 1998. *In the Name of Development: A Reflection on Nepal*. Kathmandu: Educational Enterprises.

Stirr, A. 2013. "Tears for the Revolution: Nepali Musical Nationalism, Emotion, and the Maoist Movement." In *Revolution in Nepal: An*

Anthropological and Historical Approach to the People's War. Edited by M. Lecomte-Tilouine, 367–92. Delhi: Oxford University Press.

Taylor, C. 2007. *A Secular Age*. Cambridge, MA: Harvard University Press.

Thapa, D., with B. Sijapati. 2004. *A Kingdom under Siege: Nepal's Maoist Insurgency, 1996–2004*. London: Zed.

Thomas, K. 1971. *Religion and the Decline of Magic*. London: Weidenfeld and Nicholson.

Van Beek, W. E. A., and W. C. Olsen. 2015. "Introduction: African Notions of Evil: The Chimera of Justice." in *Evil in Africa: Encounters with the Everyday*. Edited by W. C. Olsen and W. E. A. van Beek, 1–26. Bloomington: Indiana University Press.

Van der Veer, P. 2014. *The Modern Spirit of Asia: The Spiritual and the Secular in China and India*. Princeton, NJ: Princeton University Press.

Chapter 7

RADICAL EVIL AND THE NOTION OF CONSCIENCE

A BUDDHIST MEDITATION ON CHRISTIAN SOTERIOLOGY

Gananath Obeyesekere

>Whatever is done with love always occurs beyond good and evil.
>—Friedrich Nietzsche, *Beyond Good and Evil* (1966), aphorism 153

"Evil" is a slippery term. Nowadays, it is used sometimes explicitly and at other times implicitly in much of the Anglophile world to designate a special form of malevolence whether or not it is contrasted with the term "good." The contrastive set "good" and "bad" is used all the time, and in Sri Lanka, one could reasonably translate this set as *honda* and *naraka*. Thus, we would say of a person who has committed some wrong as someone who does not understand *honda-naraka*, even though *naraka* can in more formal discourse refer to "hell," which is impossible with the English term "bad." By contrast, "evil" can easily be rendered as "badness" in popular discourse and as "hell" in joking relationships ("I had a hell of a day"), but it would be difficult to say, "I had an evil day." It seems one cannot easily render "evil" and "bad" as synonyms, although there is no law against it. However much "evil" can be used in popular usage ("he doesn't know the difference between good and evil"), the word "evil" carries with it an "essence," as it were, a connotation of extreme malevolence or irremediable badness. It is this sense of "evil" that Nietzsche tried to convey when he spoke of those trapped in "good and evil" and the need to go "beyond good and evil." That sense of essence is conveyed by George W. Bush when he spoke of the "evil empire," implicitly identifying a whole society or societies with the archetypal "evil" empire that

Hitler erected. It is that extreme sense of Evil that I want to consider here. And although protagonists of evil may not use that word, *we* might label such expressions as "evil." The irony here is that those whom we designate as evil often reject that word and might well insist our use of the "e word" is false and misses the essential nobility and goodness of those human beings whom we had the temerity to label as evil. *We* might think Hitler and his compatriots were evil, but those compatriots would deny it and turn our sense of evil upside down with substitute labels, such as Aryan—or, like Eichmann, affirm that one was doing ones duty by following orders, and it is we who might say Hitler is nevertheless "evil," even a form of the "banality of evil," if such a beast exists. The Eichmann problem is once you claim you are only doing your duty, then there is no need to impute Evil to the Other. The Eichmanns (Arendt 2006) of the world are probably found in some form or other as silent participants in the normality of everyday terror, the common enough embourgeoisement of evil.[1] There are no Eichmanns in modern day terrorism wherein, let us say, there exists a reified and strongly held Islamism or the invented past the world over, including Sri Lanka of the not-too-distant past. I want to bear in mind that the term "Evil" in the strong sense from our analytical point of view is for the most part not a discourse *of the Other* but rather a discourse *on the Other*. The moment we attribute Evil to someone, that someone has to respond to us in similar terms, its ghastly or ghostly reciprocity. For example, if we affirm that the Islamic State is Evil in its strong sense, we will have to reckon with the fact that they would similarly impute that very evil to us. The discourse on Evil cuts both ways. I now want to briefly examine how this discourse emerged in Western thought, focusing on whether Evil in this strong sense might have some relevance for Buddhism.

In his important paper on "Theological Thoughts about Evil," Donald Taylor discusses the more formal notions of evil in the Western traditions of Judaism and in Catholic and Protestant theology. Nevertheless, it seems to me that Evil as an alienation from God is central to all three traditions, irrespective of the theological ups and downs of the idea. Taylor refers to a strong version of evil exemplified in Milton's *Paradise Lost*, which "in fact did much to mark the word 'evil' as being that which is radically opposed to God in the English language" (Taylor 1985). On the popular level, Satan is the being who represents evil as "radical evil." It seems to me that while many Christians might believe in Milton's form of radical evil, the idea of evil as a malevolent force can also be found in popular Christianity, especially in its more fundamentalist form and, one might add, even in atheistic denials of God. This is not surprising because Christian thought is intrinsic to those who would in a formal sense reject it. I would say that most Euro-Americans would find no difficulty in identifying Hitler and fascism in general as constituting "radical evil," even though they might not use the word evil. For example, one can speak of a mass murderer, of the sort we are now familiar with here in the US or elsewhere, as a terrible person, a malevolent being, and use all sorts of adjectives to characterize that being; but if one were to ask whether that person is "evil," he or she would surely expect a nearly unanimous response that the mass murderer embodies radical evil. I am sure there are people who would be able to imagine whole nations as "evil," as in "evil empire." Whether self-consciously articulated or not, both Christian and atheist could, when pushed to the wall, designate certain individuals or classes of people as Evil, either explicitly or implicitly.

It is owing to its "universality" that one of the great radical thinkers of our times, Friedrich Nietzsche, could famously write *Beyond Good and Evil*, because to deny these terms or to critique them is to accept their reality in Christian thought (Nietzsche 1966). To deny evil might well involve a recognition of its existence! As far as I know, it is Nietzsche's bête noire Emmanuel Kant who first introduced the term "radical evil" in his major work on "Religion" as an innate disposition, yet contained within the sphere of Reason. Evil is radical because it is innate and, though innate, it is rational insofar as human beings can confront it and subject it to the rigorous Kantian Moral Law (1996). I do not want to get into the details of Kant's thesis, except it is hard to believe that, in spite of his denials, "radical evil" in his sense is not just another version of "original sin" and the popular Protestant notion of the innate depravity of human beings but now given systemic and moral justification in abstract Kantian (Kant 1996) ethics. Nevertheless, for our purposes here, I will use the term "radical evil" for the strong sense of evil, whether based on the original Christian sense of the irremediable alienation from God, or the rational evil of Kantian ethics, or the evil of fundamentalist usage, or an implicit recognition that such a phenomenon exists in the sense of extreme malevolence. It is not easy to slip out of notions of good and evil if you are living in a Christian society, but if you are in a Buddhist world, you might have another vision of "radical evil." In this regard, I assume with others that identity of meaning is nowhere found except in claims made in dictionaries. Instead, one has to be satisfied with what Wittgenstein, strongly influenced by Nietzsche, labeled "forms of life" based on "family resemblances."[2] But unfortunately, unlike mathematical and scientific statements, family resemblances have to be identified in a particular context—in this case, its strong forms as unmitigated malevolence or radical evil. Radical evil must be distinguished from the many forms of life that resemble evil in its multiple senses without being saddled with identity of meaning.

Buddhism's Evil

Buddhist thought or soteriology is reexpressed nowadays very much in the mold of classical Western philosophical thought whether one is writing about Theravada or Mahayana. In my view, such a move is part of our modernity, and educated Buddhists have to be given a distillation of Buddhist knowledge that brings it in relation to the Western modernity. In this sense, contemporary Buddhism is the child of the "radical enlightenment" (Israel 2002) following Spinoza in particular, where emphasis is placed on mathematical and scientific knowledge and the developing empiricism. Christianity as well as Western philosophical thought in general had to be reconciled to the movements within radical enlightenment, which in turn has anticipated our contemporary modernism. In spite of my reservations, I recognize Buddhist modernism's need to be consonant with the analytical discourses of the contemporary world. It is therefore not surprising when we find that, prior to our own times, Buddhism could not possibly have been represented in this manner. Consider the very heart of the doctrinal tradition: the *suttas* (*sutras*) that begin, not with some form of a categorical imperative, but with the words "thus have I heard," namely the voice or voices of a key disciple, rather than the actual words of the Buddha. Buddhist texts are dialogical in form, very much like Plato's, and nonauthoritarian, and we miss much of their context when we present their distilled essence to present day audiences. I am not against the modernist move in which we all participate, but only suggest that we miss the ways in which Buddhist and Platonic thought were once expressed through their dialogues and story telling traditions. It is easy to demonstrate that later Buddhist thinkers, such as Ashvaghosha, never once wrote in the style of our current Buddhist modernity (for a wonderful example, see Ashvaghosha 2008). Hence, the unanswered question is: How does one catch the spirit of these dialogues and their representations in later thinkers and at the same time attempt to present Buddhism in terms of our modernity? In my own prejudicial thinking, the phrase "thus have I heard" constituted the multiple and sometimes contradictory and maddeningly obscure voices of the Elders who, had they been aware of it, would have scorned the "radical Enlightenment" as not quite the ways of the "Buddhist Enlightenment." Or should I say the "Buddhist Awakening"?

I have no answer to such questions except to restore dialogue and storytelling, which was the way Buddhism was taught and heard in sermons by Buddhists. I remember in the early 1960s, I used to visit an important Buddhist pilgrimage center on special holy days and listen to old people reciting from Sinhala books dating from the thirteenth and fourteenth centuries stories derived from the *Jātaka*s on the Buddha's heroisms and self-sacrifice. Stories were the ways in which the more abstract and difficult doctrinal *sutta*s were concretized and filtered into the imagination of ordinary Buddhists.[3] To this day, these are the stories narrated by monks on special occasions, such as on alms-giving ceremonials. This was the stuff of popular narrative and it exemplified the ethical norms of Buddhism and ideas of transience and impermanence so important to Buddhism, whether popular or doctrinal, Mahayana or Theravada. Therefore, let us lay our books aside and listen to two stories that exhibit family resemblances to the Western notions of radical evil.

The first case I refer to is that of an upper caste nobleman who took to killing people and cutting a finger from each victim, then hanging them in a necklace or garland, hence his name Angulimāla, meaning "finger-garland"—a being known to most Buddhists and often referred to in monk sermons. In one popular version among Buddhist lay-folk, Angulimāla killed 999 people and wanted one more to complete his garland, when decided to kill his own mother. When the Buddha heard of this, he traveled many a mile, accosted the brigand, and, with the flow of his compassion, he converted this terrible and terrifying figure into a force for good such that Angulimāla eventually became a monk and an arahant, a figure who had realized nirvana. The version in the Pali dialogues is much longer and has fascinating details, some of which I shall now relate (Ñānomoli and Bodhi 1995).

The horrible bandit belonged to the kingdom of Kosala whose king was Pasenadi; but the king's forces failed to capture the brigand (the number of fingers are not found in the classical Pali text). The Buddha sensed the problem through his superior insight "and taking his bowl and outer robe, set out on the road leading towards Angulimāla," ignoring the warnings of people of the bandit's presence. Activating his supernormal powers (*iddhi*), the Buddha met Angulimāla and walked his normal pace; whereas the bandit, fully armed and walking briskly, could not catch up with him, try as he might. Then follows a dialogue in verse form between the puzzled bandit and the Buddha, because while the Buddha had stopped his walk (or seemed to have done so), Angulimāla still could not keep pace with him.

> While you were walking, recluse, you tell me you have stopped.
> But now, when I have stopped, you say I have not stopped.
> I ask you now, O recluse, about the meaning:
> How is it that you have stopped and I have not?

Most readers would know that "stop" has a double meaning, never explicitly stated in the text—namely, the stoppage of violence, evident now in the Buddha's response:

> Angulimāla I have stopped forever,
> I abstain from violence towards living beings;
> But you have no restraint towards things that live:
> That is why I have stopped and you have not.

Thus, needless to say, Angulimāla became a convert to Buddhism. This conversion is not on the order of the passionate St. Paul on the road to Damascus, but entails slow walking that brings about a stoppage of violence through the Buddha's paranormal gifts in combination with the flow of his healing compassion.

The brigand has now become a wandering monk. In one episode, King Pasanedi of Kosala had come to pay homage to the Buddha and actually warned the sage of the brigand Angulimāla who cuts people's fingers off and has devastated his own kingdom. On that occasion, Angulimāla happened to be seated near the Buddha who now spoke to Pasanedi: "Great King this is Angulimāla." The king was taken aback, frightened, but soon realized that his fears were not well founded and became so pleased with Angulimāla that he wanted to offer the erstwhile bandit many robes, alms in plenty, and good resting places. But the text tells us why Angulimāla did not accept these gifts. "Now *at that time* the venerable Angulimāla was a forest dweller, and alms food eater, a refuse rag wearer, and restricted himself to three robes. He replied: 'Enough, great king, my triple robe is complete'" (Ñānamoli and Bodhi 1995—emphasis mine). There is a deliberate ambiguity here. In theory, a monk is allowed to wear three robes, but Angulimāla wears only the three parts of a single robe: the first outer robe, the second more formal one, and the inner robe for bathing or washing. The emphasis in the text indicates that *at this time*, the monk was engaged in extreme ascetic practices, documented in the great meditation manual, *Visuddhimagga* ("Path of Purification") and entailing, among other things, the following: living in the open without a roof (*abbhō kasika*); living in a cemetery (*sōsānika*); foregoing seats as well as blankets and sheets (*yathāsantatika*); remaining seated without sleep (*nesajjika*). The conclusion is irresistible: Aṅgulimāla was practicing penances to expiate his guilt and punishing his body in acts of self-mortification, and also, like the guilt stricken Macbeth, he has "murdered sleep." Some of the doctrinal versions tell us that when people heard of the redeemed bandit, they accosted him and hurt him, but the Buddha did not stop that punishment and neither, I assume, did Aṅgulimāla resist it because, it is implied, he was lucky to escape the myriad punishments in endless births and rebirths for his terrible crime. Aṅgulimāla eventually becomes an arahant, but his is not an easy way out. He has to expiate his bad karma through repentance and self-mortification and suffer the punishment of those who have been wronged by him. But that, I shall soon show, is an inconclusive ending.

One form of his expiation for his early crimes, which we might want to label as his "guilt," comes next. On one occasion on his alms-round, he saw a woman with a deformed child. Aṅgulimāla was overwhelmed with sadness and was not sure what to do and, following the example of other disciples, sought the Buddha's advice. Based on that advice, he accosted the distraught woman and spoke to her thus: "Sister, since I was born [twice born] with the noble birth, I do not recall that I have ever intentionally deprived a living being of life. By this truth may you be well and may your infant be well." And of course they became well and were restored to wholeness, such being the power of the truth (*saccakriyā, satyakriyā*). This part of the text has gone into popular usage as a *paritta* (*pirit*), a recitation by pregnant mothers whereby, owing to the "power of the truth," they may expect a safe delivery. It is a recitation or wish performed by Buddhist mothers to this very day, even in the government maternity wards where all Sri Lankan mothers go nowadays to deliver their babies. Women are healed by compassion and kindness that flowed from the Buddha into Aṅgulimāla and from Aṅgulimāla to pregnant women through the power of the truth. That assumptive set is never explicitly formulated but contains an implicit understanding through the message of the text. It is analogous to the way in which Evil in the strong sense is implicit in discourses of malevolence in the Christian tradition, even though that word may not spontaneously occur, unless reminded of its relevance. What is remarkable in the Buddhist tradition is compassion-kindness (*maitri/karunā*) that originally flowed from the Buddha into Aṅgulimāla can flow now from Aṅgulimāla as a force that can heal expectant mothers through the recital of the archetypal words. I find it fascinating that a figure that embodies extreme malevolence can be transformed by the flow of compassion or love, be it in its Buddhist or Christian senses. I am sure it is the case with most atheists who would have secularized words such as love or compassion.

I shall now return to Nietzsche and borrow his term *ressentiment* to represent an extreme expression of malevolence or radical evil. Nietzsche used this term in contrast to the noble man who is never afflicted by *ressentiment*. I want to divorce this term from Nietzsche's context and have it refer to extreme malevolence or the extreme of radical evil whether or not it stands in contrast to its opposite in the noble man. I think Nietzsche himself sees the man of *ressentiment* as "the Evil One" (Nietzsche 1969, 39). I do not think the contrast between the noble man and the man of *ressentiment* is going to take us far, and I reject that oppositional dialectic, which, I might perversely add, is un-Nietzschean! Who, then, is the man of *ressentiment* of my revaluation? Let Nietzsche provide the answer when he says that it is the person who carries a deep grudge or a sense of irremediable wrong done to him, without rhyme or reason, a person with a "venomous eye." I would add that it is the eye of Iago or Richard III. In contrast to his hypothetical noble man, says Nietzsche, "the man of *ressentiment* is neither upright nor naïve nor honest and straightforward with himself. His soul *squints*; his spirit loves hiding places, secret paths and back doors, everything covert entices him as *his* world, *his* security, *his* refreshment; he understands how to keep silent, how not to forget, how to wait, how to be provisionally self-deprecating and humble" (Nietzsche 1969). I would add that the man of *ressentiment* needs the "noble man" with all his foibles and follies, just as Iago needs Othello. Unfortunately, Nietzsche did not realize that those who harbor *ressentiment* were only too common in his own times and, of course, are more so in our world today. The Buddha did recognize their existence and noted that compassion or love can turn *ressentiment* around; and this turn-around can also apply to those given to what Christians might call "radical evil." I think it is not so much the opposition between the man of *ressentiment* and the noble person that is at issue. Rather, the noble person—be it Jesus or the Buddha or figures of our time such as the Dalai Lama or even Gandhi or Desmond Tutu—and many lesser beings among us can in a smaller way turn *ressentiment* around through the flow of compassion and kindness and, if like the Buddha we can give it public expression, we can help reverse the crude notion of an evil empire that swallows large entities as representations of "radical evil." It is Buddhist compassion and kindness that can go beyond "good and evil"; and I would say that in practice if not in theology, this capacity to go beyond good and evil is also true of Christian love, caritas.

The Conscience of the Parricide

I do not want to shove under the carpet the moral question of how Angulimāla, the brigand, could realize the Being of an arahant after committing horrendous acts of violence. I will take up the troubling issue of Angulimāla's conscience after we examine the conscience of another killer—not a mass killer such as Angulimāla, but one who had committed a horrendous act of parricide. To begin with, I want to translate the term "conscience" in terms that would make sense to Buddhists—namely, the manner in which morality and ethics are internalized (introjected) in the minds and consciousness of people, whether or not a term such as "conscience" is employed. In that sense, one could say that conscience is not a uniquely Buddhist or Christian problem, but one found in many religions where moral values are introjected or internalized in one's mind or consciousness, albeit expressed in conceptual terms in the Christian tradition or as a story in the Buddhist. However, we would be naïve if we did not also recognize the omnipresence of a "false conscience," the negativity of conscience that the Buddha and Christ rejected, such as hate, lust, envy, and so forth, oft times enshrined, if you will forgive that word, in the public consciousness, as we know from many examples in our contemporary world, such that one's conscience can be polluted by them. These values, expressive of the negativity of conscience, are especially significant in Buddhism owing to its emphasis on *tanhā*, attachment or greed, as the root of human suffering and impermanence. Consequently, its huge conceptual vocabulary of what I have labeled "false conscience" (not to be confused with "false consciousness") coexists with the tradition of storytelling, just as is the case with caritas or love in Christianity. To put it differently: if there is a conceptual silence in Buddhism in relation to terms such as "radical evil" or conscience or, for that matter, guilt or remorse of conscience ("agenbite of inwit") so prominent in Christian discourse, that conceptual imperative is now reexpressed in the discourse on the negativity of conscience with its proliferation of negative or denigrating terms based on the Buddhist imperative of attachment/impermanence, *tanhā*, greed. Storytelling, however, occurs in both traditions, whether or not conceptual terms are explicitly used, warning us not to be seduced by concepts and imagining that we can enter into the worlds of meaning by focusing on conceptual imperatives alone.

Let me now narrate the story of parricide, which expresses on another level the paramountcy of the Buddhist ethics of compassion (*karuṇā*) and loving kindness (*mettā/maitri*) and their devalued opposites (which we have observed in Aṅgulimāla), located in one of the most powerful texts in the Buddhist storytelling tradition: that of Ajātasattu. Although I have dealt with this story in my book *The Work of Culture* (1990), the event is worth recounting here in a more shortened form. There are multiple versions of this popular story, and the one I chose is from the thirteenth century Sinhala text, *Pūjāvaliya*, "the garlands of the faith" (Nanavimala 1965). In this instance, the popular traditions of the parricide king are much more powerful and known to ordinary people than the doctrinal view of this king expressed in the great text on renunciation, *Sāmaññaphala Sutta* on the "fruits of the homeless life."[4] I will refer the reader to my extended discussion of Ajātasattu ("enemy before he was born"), a parricide by destiny who ended up killing his father Bimbisāra, the disciple of the Buddha on the instigation of Devadatta, the Judas of the Buddhist tradition. Here is the outline of the story.

I will delete those parts of the story relating to the pregnancy cravings of Ajātasattu's mother, her fears that according to prophecy her son would kill his father, her attempts to destroy her fetus, and her husband's admonitions to desist from killing their future son. I will deal instead with Ajātasattu as a grown prince and Devadatta's attempts to usurp the Buddha's authority, whose hatred of the Buddha existed from many previous births and rebirths, a carry-over of hatred through endless lives. Devadatta, himself a monk, wanted to take over the kingdom of the Buddha's teaching and enticed Ajātasattu by frightening him with his own miraculous powers. He took the guise of an "infant divinity" and created seven cobras over his body and head and right shoulder, imitating, as it were, the Brahmanic thread of the twice born. Draped in snakes, he appeared before the frightened Ajātasattu, but Devadatta calmed his fears, saying that he has not come to harm him but to win his heart. Ajātasattu then fell under Devadatta's spell and treated him well and donated a monastery to him and his five hundred followers. The evil Devadatta wanted to be the king of the Dhamma just like the Buddha, but with that horrendous thought, Devadatta lost his supernormal powers (*iddhi*).

Unsatisfied by his failure to kill the Buddha-king, Devadatta now enticed his acolyte Ajātasattu to kill his own father, the ruling monarch, urging him to take over his father's kingdom so that he,

Devadatta, could reign over the kingdom of the Buddha. Ajātasattu, with a dagger tied to his thigh, waited in fear and trembling to kill his father. He was soon discovered with his (phallic) dagger by the king's attendants and hauled before the monarch. Under questioning, he admitted his desire for the kingdom for himself enticed by "the desire (greed) of kingship." The king said if that was what his son wanted, he would abdicate his throne in his son's favor, which he did. But the unsatisfied Devadatta informed Ajātasattu that this was a ploy and urged him to kill his father. The prince then informed Devadatta that he could not possibly kill his father in any direct manner, to which Devadatta suggested a solution—namely, to imprison him and ensure his slow starvation to death. I will not discuss here the ruses adopted by the queen to bring food to her husband, but all her efforts ultimately failed, and hapless, at last, she informed the king: "Lord, you did not want to kill him in his infancy [as the queen had instructed], you have nurtured your own enemy." And following Devadatta's advice, Ajātasattu had his father killed in slow stages in the most gruesome manner. I will skip much of the tale and simply refer the birth of Ajātasattu's son, which sprang within him the feeling of "son-love," an elemental force that compelled him to think that his own father must have loved him just as he loved his own newborn son. He urged his courtiers to go rescue his father, but it was too late because the king had already died. When his mother informed Ajātasattu of the manner in which his father had loved and nurtured him, Ajātasattu wept, stricken by a terrible grief. Meanwhile, another drama was taking place as Devadatta hoped, futilely, to kill the Buddha; but when he attempted to do so, a huge chasm opened up and Devadatta was dragged into hell.

That day, people were joyous that Devadatta, the very incarnation of "evil," was no more. Ajātasattu, however, was seated with his ministers in his throne. Why, asks the text, was he in his throne at this time of the night? In order to avoid sleep and because he was fearful to be left alone. From the time he killed his father, whenever the king shut his eyes, it felt as if his head were being hit by sledgehammers and his body being cut up with a thousand weapons. He could not sleep owing to the horrible pains he felt, but he refused to inform his courtiers. Instead, he inquired in roundabout fashion: What kind of monk or Brahmin should one seek to obtain solace? The upshot of the request was the decision to seek the Buddha, who was a friend of his father Bimbisara (and, one might add, a surrogate father). But Ajātasattu was afraid to confront the Buddha, and so he sought the help of Jīvaka, a famed physician and friend of the Buddha, to accompany him to the Buddha so he could hide behind his back! Why so, asks the text? Because of the harm he had done in killing his father, a devotee of the Buddha. The Buddha, sensing the fears of the approaching parricide, projected his great compassion toward him, and such was the Buddha radiance that Ajātasattu felt like a child seated on someone's lap and felt as if his hair were being stroked. He was still fearful of meeting the Buddha, and he held the hands of Jīvaka, the healer. Ultimately, at Jīvaka's urging, he went up to see the sage. The assembled monks looked serene and calm, like a forest of lotuses in a windless place, and the king then wished that his son, Prince Udaya, would enjoy the freedom of a similar serenity. Meanwhile, the Buddha, sensing the king's thoughts and fears, decided to dispel them by a resounding "Brahma-sound" that I assume is a sound that is heard and yet conveyed in silence. "Great king, like the rain that falls over a rock and collects in a hollow down below, the waters of love that sprang within you as a result of my dispensation have now gone toward your own son, haven't they?" Now Ajātasattu had enough courage to confess his faults and "like a man who leaving the burning sun has gone into a cool pond," he greeted the monks from afar with clasped hands. Meanwhile, the Buddha administered various exhortations to the parricide and then recited the great discourse that extols the virtues of renunciation, the *Sāmaññaphala Sutta*. It is assumed that the sense of the text affected the conscience of the king. Consequently, the Buddha went on to say that if Ajātasattu had not committed the sin of parricide, he could even have entered the second of the three stages of the nirvana path. "That king Ajātasattu could not sleep day or night from the time he killed the king, his father, yet having heard the sermons of the Buddha he could now sleep peacefully."

But not in the long run. The Buddha can calm the parricide but cannot really absolve him of his crime. It is not just any sin, but a huge one. According to Buddhism, parricide is one of those five heinous crimes having immediate effect (*ānantarika kamma* [*karma*]), these being patricide, matricide, killing an arahant, wounding a Buddha (with intent to kill), and creating dissensions in the Buddhist order. Ajātasattu will have to pay for his sin (*pāpa karma*). However, having heard the sermons of the Buddha, "the river of compassion," he has become a changed person. Although Ajātasattu asks for the Buddha's forgiveness (*samāva*), the Buddha cannot give it, such being the nature of the crime of parricide. He will be born in the dreaded *avici* hell and then to the lower level of that hell where he will live in suffering for another thirty thousand years; and then to the bottom of that hell for yet another thirty thousand, and then he will ascend to the top of that hell. Because of the good acts he has performed, he will live for one hundred thousand eons enjoying the pleasures of heaven and earth, and ultimately, he will be redeemed from the cycle of existence (saṃsāra) when he will be born as a minor Buddha named Vijitasena. Owing to the Buddhist view of continual rebirths, there cannot be notion of eternal damnation, and the person guilty of one of the worst crimes in Buddhist terms will, after millennia of suffering, end up being a Buddha, albeit a minor one. Ajātasattu's crime in the Buddhist scheme of things will eventually be expiated and the erstwhile parricide will be "redeemed" in Buddhist terms as a minor Buddha.

I do not intend to analyze this text in any detail, because my readership will be able to grasp the significance of the parricide king who has murdered sleep and is calmed by the cool compassion of the Buddha as Angulimāla was calmed. I will take up the soteriological implications of these two texts later; but for the moment, note that the Buddhist doctrinal tradition that we nowadays reify in abstract terms is also about stories that percolate into the popular traditions such that in the days of my childhood, it would be a rare person unacquainted with the story of Angulimāla and Ajātasattu, in addition to hundreds of tales from the *Jātakas* and the Buddha legend. These stories are often painted on Buddhist temple (vihāra) walls as frescoes such that any person visiting them will be made aware of these stories, triggering mnemonic recollections from the one form of life to the other, from stories to paintings and the other way around. The doctrinal texts themselves we noted have a kind of Platonic quality; they are dialogues and contain arguments, debates, and the taking of positions. Sometimes, these dialogues are embedded in short illustrative stories; sometimes, long ones. Either way, I think we ought to replace, at least imaginatively, the Buddhist abstractions that we have given prominence in our current intellectual lives with the contexts of dialogues from which our abstractions are derived such that we get a double reward from the concretizations of abstract thought in terms of the rich stories about lived existence.

The moment we focus exclusively on our newly invented abstract philosophical texts, we begin to wonder: Where is the space for notions such as guilt, remorse, repentance, and, of course, conscience? These are words from the Western lexicon, and we cannot find their conceptual representations in our Buddhist texts. Of course, we could use dictionaries, but at the best of times, they can rarely give us reasonably accurate meanings of difficult concepts as we translate them from one language to another, engaging in play with language games. When playing these games, we are in the realm of stories, and those ideas such as guilt and repentance that we mentioned in the Christian tradition begin to make sense. For example, I would say that the story of Ajātasattu when he expresses his terrible sorrow for killing his father is about "guilt," although that word is not found in the Buddhist lexicon. So with his "repentance" and "remorse," and I would also add Ajātasattu's workings of his "conscience," but without conscience there is no way that Ajātasattu, of our text, could possibly have visited the Buddha in order to ask of the Buddha for forgiveness (*sāmava*). The fears afflicting his conscience are there at the very beginning when, tying his dagger on his thigh, he is fearful of being found out. Or when he thinks of his father when his son is born. I would therefore say that far from being troubled by the absence of words associated with guilt and remorse in our Buddhist lexicon, we should be thrilled to know that in spite of huge epistemological differences between the two traditions, we can still relate to each other through storytelling and Buddhists and Christians can be brothers and sisters to each other, at least for some of the time, if we can fumble around and get rid of our ingrained prejudices. Some of the words in the two lexicons can be remarkably similar; for example, the word *samāva* can easily be translated as "forgiveness." But even so, we cannot talk of identity of meaning, such a beast does not exist, but we can talk of "forms of life" and "family resemblances," stealing Wittgenstein's terms. In the cases of Ajātasattu and the displaced castration complex of our finger-cutting brigand, we are dealing with such things as guilt and remorse, words from the Christian tradition, and seeing their family resemblances to our Buddhist stories in spite of the fact that we are bridging two seeming heterogeneous elements together—namely, a concept or idea with a story or a narrative. But the reverse is also true. We Buddhists often talk of two principal ethical notions, *karunā* and *mettā/maitri*, compassion and loving kindness (I would simply say Kindness). I sense their family resemblance to the Christian tradition whenever I read the wonderful lines from 1 Corinthians 13, which is on love or caritas (even *agape*) but is very close to the Buddhist *mettā* and *karunā* combined, that is, compassion and kindness fused together. And time and change that happen to us all, as Ecclesiastes 9:11 tells us, is very much in the spirit of the Buddhist ideas of impermanence and is so recognized by sensitive souls everywhere, whatever their formal religious affiliations. Freud, a kind of Buddhist without knowing it, used the term *Thanatos* to describe the phenomenon of impermanence, according to which death is around the corner, however much we deny it and reify Eros as the central imago of our lives, as most Euro-Americans do. On the other hand, there are plenty of Buddhist concepts that have no conceptual parallel in Christian texts, but I am sure there are stories there too that can pick up family resemblances to those stories we find in the Buddhist traditions. To sum up: we should shun for the most part identity of meaning and look for family resemblances; when we do this, we might see our own species being reflected in the language games of the Other.

I now want to tell the somewhat disquieting news that these wonderful stories are rarely known or embraced by the Buddhist public in Sri Lanka, trapped by the temptation of greed of our troubling modernity. What is even more disturbing is that parents rarely recite these stories to their children and, although they are found in the official school syllabuses for Buddhist children, they are taught without much understanding of the ethics underlying them. For storytelling to work, obviously, one has to have agents who would related them to a public, especially for school children. I am not sure that stories that are used for cramming at exams can take the place of storytelling by older persons, monks, and parents. Certainly, TV stories might take their place, but they cannot replace the voices of mothers relating stories to children. In Buddhist Sunday schools, young children, overwhelmingly girls, attend Dhamma (Dharma) classes tutored by monks or lay-folk, but I am not sure how much of their syllabuses pertain to storytelling. I once met a young student, and when we talked about his school education, he said that although he was a Buddhist, he could not believe in rebirth as an animal because such a condition is quite impossible. He could empathize with the idea that the Buddha was born as a noble creature like an elephant or lion, but not as a lowly animal such as a fox or a wild sow or a monkey or a hare, and he of course had problems with the dozens of stories in the *Jātaka* tales where humans could be born as lowlier creatures such as dogs or crows. I pointed out to the young man that even if he did not *literally* believe in rebirth as animals, one should be able to imagine their profound *symbolic* significance as parables, namely, that we human beings are part of a larger cosmic order that we share with the lowest of the low. I am sure Darwin would have appreciated it had he known a little bit of Buddhism; but, alas, he did not. I also know that many Buddhist children, given their current pseudo-modern education, find the stories of the Buddha sacrificing his life to save a herd of elephants or monkeys hard to accept. But we can take a hint from the Protestant theologian Rudolf Bultmann and learn to "demythologize" Buddhist stories, not in Christian terms but in terms of a Buddhist modernity, a Buddhist form of demythologization, a recognition that these stories express a symbolic truth about life and death and of the world we inhabit in the here and the now. Then those who are skeptical about treating these stories as real events that occurred in history can at least accept their profound meanings as symbolic truths in a story, and as such, they might still have significance for the molding of our consciences.

The stories of the life of the great Buddhist hero were sung in collective rituals about gods and demons and their exorcisms, pejoratively labeled by missionaries as "devil dancing." The ritual dramas of village society also enacted the themes of the stories about the Buddha. And local and foreign gods, incorporated into the Buddhist tradition through time-embodied Buddhist values, while demons, those terrifying beings that inhabit the village landscape, represented their devalued opposites such as hate, greed, violence, and the absence of ethical restraint—or, to put it differently, radical evil. The abstract ethics and the abstruse concepts of the doctrinal tradition were given immediacy, concreteness, and an ethical salience in everyday society through storytelling. Since they were for the most part stories, whether enacted or recited, parents could relate them to their children very early. Children, of course, have no problem listening to stories. Through parental identification and the introjection of parental values, children could incorporate the sense of these stories as part of their own conscience.

Interrogations: Buddhist Practice and *Ressentiment*

In my rethinking of *ressentiment*, I have suggested that the term expresses the kind of motiveless evil embodied in figures such as Iago (his "motiveless malignity" as Coleridge expressed it) or Richard III and could reasonably be contrasted with the noble person, even though I would not accept the larger implications of Nietzsche's two terms. The question I now pose is as follows: How is it that a person who has committed such evil as Aṅgulimāla can be absolved from his crime simply by the flow of the Buddha's compassion, powerful though it is; or by his penances entailing extreme asceticism; or by the punishment by neighbors and so forth? The only way one could resolve this problem is to affirm that there are areas in Buddhism and Christianity where family resemblances cease to occur, and we have to recognize and maybe even empathize with the significance of difference. If one speaks in soteriological terms, the two religions can be worlds apart. That difference permits us to question Aṅgulimāla in our imagination and ask how the erstwhile mass killer can get away with it and become a redeemed being, even if he is blessed with the flow of the Buddha's compassion. The attempt to resolve that issue brings us to Buddhist rebirth, where a human being is born and reborn in countless existences, during which time he has committed good deeds and bad, acts of evil in the multiple senses of that term and acts of goodness. Thus, in the case of Aṅgulimāla, one can say that he got off so lightly owing to the cumulative effect of his good actions in the past. Through his long karmic sojourn, he would have expiated his bad actions and hence his terrible acts do not loom as terrible in the long run. The effect of the Buddha's compassion does not exist by itself, but in the larger context of the karmic past of Aṅgulimāla. That flow of compassion, whether by the Buddha or by monks at sermons or by us in our own lives, carries with it a load of meanings that are sometimes explicitly articulated in Buddhist stories and sometimes implicitly, simply because there is no need to spell out the soteriological significance of past actions in relation to present realities. Gerard Manley Hopkins asks of God in anguish:

> Why do sinners' ways prosper and why must
> Disappointment all I endeavor end? (Hopkins 1979, 106)

There is no Christian theodicy in the Buddhist answer: sinners' ways prosper because of their karmic past that is unknown but has to be inferred from present realities. I will admit, however, that for me as a Buddhist of sorts, neither Hopkins's case nor that of Aṅgulimāla provides a satisfactory answer. I doubt without being a doubting ethnographer. But I do brush my objections aside and let us now examine how radical evil, in the sense of unmitigated *ressentiment*, is expressed in ordinary Buddhist lives in our contemporary world.

There are many among our Buddhist politicians who steal, cheat, bribe, and rape and yet seem to thrive, at least in accumulating wealth and power, and seem untroubled by the flagrant un-Buddhist nature of their actions. There are people without conscience in our contemporary political modernity. Theirs is a magnification of kings in the past who had to kill their enemies and sometimes their friends and then had to resolve their crimes by gift-giving to monks and other consumptions of conspicuous piety. Sometimes their consciences are assuaged, and sometimes not. Contemporary politicians are a different kind of fish, one might even say a shark, in the extremes to which corruption, venality, even violence and murder are committed without much concern for their karmic effects, except in old age or at the death-bed when these concerns begin to surface. My question is: How does a Buddhist monk officiate at a funeral and handle those who have committed radical evil or have engaged in unmitigated acts of *ressentiment?*

In general, monks do not appear at funerals. That is left for the grieving friends and kinfolk. But they do enter the household of the deceased prior to the actual funeral in a key practice known as the *pānsakūla*. Contemporary Buddhists have forgotten its older meanings, which I will now resurrect. *Pānsakūla* is the offering of a cloth, often nowadays a white cloth, placed near the coffin and then offered to the monks after their sermon and benediction for the dead. If you are a true bourgeois Buddhist, the *pānsakūla* is nicely gift-wrapped and donated to monks. *Pānsakūla* has been transposed into a clean act of Buddhist bourgeois piety. Etymologically, however, *pānsakūla* refers to the discarded rags from corpses, and *pānsakūlikas* are those extremist Buddhist monks who have expressed their dissatisfaction with the world by wearing the cast off cloths of the dead. Angulimāla, for example, tells the king that he does not need a monastery, and he has only three robes (two inner robes and one outer robe that are worn on public occasions, which is the monk garment even today.) Angulimāla engages in a deliberate ambiguity or a pun. A monk is, in theory, expected to possess no more than three full robes, but Angulimāla puns on that idea by saying that his three robes are really the three parts of a single robe. It is not likely that Angulimāla actually wears a discarded robe from the charnel ground, but that is what he does as a kind of parable. Thus, until very recently, in some of the remoter villages, I know people gifted to the monks the actual clothes worn by the dead person and wrapped round the corpse before the cloth is removed for burial or cremation. If you are poor, the actual shroud, or if you are rich, a new white cloth is placed on or against the corpse. The monk, by profession, is immune to corpse pollution, and as someone much possessed by death and the transience of lived existence, he can absorb the corpse pollution and free the devotees from it. *Pansakula* renders the corpse pollution-free. In three or seven days after the funeral, there is a remembrance rite where monks are invited to a noon-day *dāna* or almsgiving (nowadays a huge feast), a *mataka dāna* or remembrance almsgiving for monks where friends and relations reassemble to receive the monk's blessings. I will not go into its details except to say that the merit acquired by the almsgiving and other pious acts of the living enhance the future favorable rebirth of the deceased. What is quite remarkable is that irrespective of whether the deceased exemplified an enormity of cruelty or malevolence, the monk recalls the good done by the deceased (imagined or real), and then wishes the dead person the eventual "bliss of nirvana." Even the person who has committed radical evil or *ressentiment* is assured of the great Buddhist realization of salvation, nirvana, but in the long travail of almost immensurable time spans. The catch is clear: a person who has committed Evil is *not* acquitted of his crimes; he *has* to repay, but in the long, long karmic run, although not as long as our parricidal friend Ajātasattu had to undergo. But then he too eventually *stops* in the style of Angulimāla. In general, a person will expiate his past sins, and the monk's sermon hopes that the deceased, after unknown births and rebirths, eventually realize nirvana. It is no paradox or contradiction for the monk to offer nirvana for the deceased evil person, but not quite yet. Or if I may be permitted to parody the Christian Saint and affirm: grant me chastity O Lord, but not yet. Stop.

Gananath Obeyesekere, Emeritus Professor, Princeton University

Notes

1. The classic study is, of course, Hannah Arendt, 2006, *Eichmann in Jerusalem*. In the introduction to Arendt, Amos Elon says, "That in retrospect, she was sorry she had used [that phrase]. It had led her into an ambush." The ambush was her Jewish critics who said that the phrase seemed to exonerate Eichmann's Evil. In my view, Arendt was bold enough to affirm the important fact of the normality of evil among seemingly ordinary people. We see plenty of Eichmann types in our world today in the bourgeois normality of everyday terror. Nevertheless, what is striking about Eichmann is his almost willingness to be captured and his firm conviction that he would be executed such that, as Arendt says, it "even enabled him to look upon death with remarkable equanimity." He had declared at the beginning of his long police investigation: "I know the death sentence is in store for me" (Arendt 2006, 243). I find this a very disturbing book both for what is said and what is unsaid. There is, however, no sense of guilt or even a plea for forgiveness from a person who self-righteously believed he did no harm to others. There is, however, an unmistakable equanimity in the manner in which he went to his death, and I am not sure Arendt understood the reason why. It is unfortunate that she was thoroughly hostile to psychoanalysis.
2. The idea of "language game" and "forms of life" is found only in nine occurrences, with five of them in *Philosophical Investigations*, according to Finch (1995, 50). These terms are not easy to pin down in Wittgenstein's aphoristic discourse in *Philosophical Investigations* (1958). As I rephrase it, "language games" are found everywhere, but a "form of life" is more

specific and contained within the larger language game. "To imagine a language game means to imagine a form of life" (8e, 19.) Or in 11e, 23: "Here the term 'language-*game*' is meant to bring into prominence that fact that the *speaking* of language is part of an activity or of a form of life." In my view, we have to adapt these important terms for social analysis and must, I think, incorporate into Wittgenstein's idea of "family resemblances," a term I employ to critique the idea of identity of meaning. I have discussed these terms at length in my book *The Work of Culture*. As for his aphoristic thinking, see my book *The Awakened Ones*, 59, 61–62, and for what I call "aphoristic thinking" in general, see 45–62.

3. The *Jātaka* are 547 stories but generally designated with the round number 550. They are part of the canon known as the *Khuddaka Nikāya*, or the "minor anthologies" of the Pali Canon. The *Jātaka* deals with the past lives of the Buddha, but modern scholarship rightly assumes they are late inventions of the canon. However, some of these stories are immensely popular among ordinary folk and many have been rendered into popular Sinhala poetry in the post sixteenth century period, although the stories themselves are mentioned in the literature of the fourteenth century and after.

4. References to Ajātasattu are found in several doctrinal texts, perhaps the most important being *Samaññaphala Sutta* ("fruits of the homeless life") of the *Dīgha Nikāya* in Walshe (1995, 91–109). Perhaps the most connected account of the life of Ajātasattu is in the massive Sinhala work *Pūjavaliya*, 634–42. While the *Samaññaphala Sutta* is a brilliant discussion of the fruitfulness of the homeless life, its discussion of Ajātasattu is nowhere near as powerful as the popular Sinhala version. That version is the one known to most Sinhala Buddhists. The doctrinal version plays down the myth of Ajātasattu's parricide. Malalasekera rightly says that this text makes no mention of Ajātasattu's impiety. "Instead, when Ajātasattu expresses his repentance at the end of the discourse, the Buddha accepts his confession and lets him off almost too lightly" (Malalasekera 1983, 32. This is in complete contrast to the Sinhala tradition of the *Pūjavaliya*. It is as if there had been another text on the parricide king that had been elided or forgotten in the doctrinal tradition but is in full force in the *Pūjāvaliya*.

For my earlier study, see my discussion of "The parricide in Buddhist history," in *The Work of Culture*, especially 148–56.

References

Arendt, Hannah. 2006. *Eichmann in Jerusalem: A Report on the Banality of Evil*. New York: Penguin.
Ashvaghosha, A. 2008. *Life of the Buddha*. Translated by Patrick Olivelle. New York: JJC Foundation.
Finch, Henry Le Roy. 1995. *Wittgenstein*. Rockport, MA: Element.

Hopkins, G. M. 1979. *The Poems of Gerard Manley Hopkins*. Oxford: Oxford University Press.
Israel, Jonathan. 2002. *Radical Enlightenment: Philosophy and the Making of Modernity, 1660–1750*. Oxford: Oxford University Press.
Kant, Immanuel. 1966. *Religion within the Boundaries of Mere Reason*. Cambridge, UK: Cambridge University Press.
Malalasekera, G. P. 1983. *Dictionary of Pali Proper Names*. Delhi: Munshiram Manoharlal.
Ñānamoli, Bhikku, and Bhikkhu Bodhi. 1995. *The Middle Length Discourses of the Buddha: A Translation of the Majjhima Nikāya*. Kandy: Buddhist Publication Society.
Nietzsche, Friedrich. 1966. *Beyond Good and Evil*. New York: Vintage Books.
———. 1969. *On the Genealogy of Morals*. Translated by Walter Kaufmann and R. J. Hollingdale. New York: Vintage Books.
Obeyesekere, Gananath. 1990. *The Work of Culture*. Chicago: University of Chicago Press.
———. 2012. *The Awakened Ones: Phenomenology of Visionary Experience*. New York: Columbia University Press.
Taylor, Donald. 1985. "Theological Thoughts about Evil." In *Anthropology of Evil*. Edited by David Parkin, 26–41. Oxford: Basil.
Walshe, Maurice. 1995. *The Long Discourses of the Buddha*. Boston, MA: Wisdom Publications.
Wittgenstin, Ludwig. 1958. *Philosophical Investigations*. Translated by G. E. Anscombe. New York: Macmillan.

Chapter 8

ARE SPIRITS SATANIC?

THE AMBIGUITY OF EVIL IN NIGER

Adeline Masquelier

Spirits, Islam, and the Problem of Evil

David Parkin (1985, 9) notes in *The Anthropology of Evil* that scholars typically describe moralities as either "monistic" or "Manichean," depending on the extent to which evil can be distinguished from good. In the monistic tradition, evil is conceived as contiguous to good and the two often coexist in a single cosmological agent. In Manichean traditions, on the other hand, the forces of goodness are unmistakably distinct from the power of evil. In the Hausa-speaking and overwhelmingly Muslim town of Dogondoutchi, Niger, where many of the spiritual forces (*iskoki*; plural of *iska*, which also means "wind") that intersect with human trajectories were traditionally conceived as both the sources of and the remedies to human suffering, it could be argued that morality belongs to the monistic register. With the recent intensification of practices aimed at purifying Islam from "animism," however, existing moral ambiguities are dissolving, giving way to a more absolute notion of evil that is fully distinct from good. Muslim preachers describe spirits in their sermons as malevolent creatures whose sole aim is to tempt humans into straying from the right path. Spirits, the preachers claim, are Satan's servants, against whom Muslims must guard themselves by relying on the power of prayer. When they attack people, they must be exorcized rather than be allowed to use humans as hosts in the context of ritualized possession performances. And in no circumstances should they be placated through offerings of any kinds, for they are the personification of evil. Having dealings with them is said to lead straight to hell.

In this chapter, I explore how the demonization of spirits by Muslim religious leaders has transformed local conceptions of evil and how it has changed the way that both Muslims and non-Muslims deal with these "new" manifestations of evil. As nonhuman and (mostly) non-Muslim, spirits are the ultimate other—the expression of a wild yet powerful alterity that can seldom be contained within the ordered parameters of social life. Whereas spirit devotees communicate with spirits to channel their powers productively, Muslims, on the other hand, must avoid all interactions with these ethereal creatures—even when it is the spirits that initiate contact. Yet, by redefining spirits as satanic creatures bent on destroying what is good on earth, Muslims have not relegated them to irrelevance. Instead, they have reconfigured the spiritual landscape so as to incorporate spirits into the larger battle between the forces of God and Satan (or Shaytan, depending on the vernacular). Meanwhile, for spirit devotees, the loss of heritage (*gado*) and the abandonment of indigenous practices aimed at protecting people from bothersome and threatening spirits have resulted in an increase of spirit attacks, against which Islam is often said to be powerless.

To illustrate how both Muslim and spirit devotees make sense of these transformations in moral and cosmological terms, I consider two distinct manifestations of evil that take the form of spiritual attacks. The first one concerns the mass possession of schoolgirls by vindictive and occasionally lecherous spirits—a problem that has been reported throughout the country. The rise of spiritual attacks in schools is largely attributed to a lack of modesty on the part of schoolgirls, as well as inadequate Islamic education. Put differently, it is because schoolgirls are behaving as improper Muslims that they cannot resist the devil's snares. The second case of evil involves a category of spirits with whom people make Faustian pacts to acquire riches. These spirits are often described as the personification of evil because in exchange for amassing wealth for their masters, they kill people to satisfy their thirst for human blood. Yet, the suffering people experience is not entirely attributable to an outside force since the proliferation of these bloodthirsty spirits is understood to be a direct consequence of human greed and selfishness. In sum, moral responsibility cannot be entirely deferred to the spirits. Such recognition, in turn, shapes the mechanisms through which this sort of evil is controlled and contained.

By addressing Dogondoutchi residents' preoccupation with malevolent spirits, I highlight the changing role that responsibility, intentionality, and moral judgment play in local conceptions of evil (*mugunta*). As we shall see, on the one hand, the vernacularization of Islamic morality and the demonization of local spirits appear to have spawned a more Manichean model of good and evil. On the other, the fact that spirit attacks and suspicious deaths, even when attributed to ruthless spirits, mobilize traditional forms of treatment and adjudication aimed at assigning human responsibility suggests how diffuse local understandings of evil remain. Far from being subsumed neatly under an Islamic register that attributes all bad deeds to the working of Satan—the antithesis of good—people's conceptions of evil are still refracted by a broad repertoire of spirits whose ambiguous persona stand in mimetic relations to human society. Dogondoutchi, the setting for this chapter, is a provincial town situated close to the Nigerian border. Its residents largely rely on subsistence farming.

Hausa Conceptualizations of Evil

In Hausa, the term *mugunta* translates as both badness and evil, while the related adjective *mugu* (*mugunya*, feminine; *mugaye*, plural) is used to describe that which is bad (or mean) as well as that which is evil. Now, bad actions (such as theft or immorality) and evil deeds are not the same. Anyone can behave badly at one point or another, but it is worth noting that being bad generally implies a temporary state from which one eventually emerges. In contrast, evil points to a more permanent condition. By the same token, evil people are inherently bad. The fact that these two dimensions of "wickedness" are commingled in a single term despite occupying distinct positions on the spectrum of malfeasance complicates any attempts to locate the categorical boundaries of evil and consider the role of agency and intentionality in the performance of evil acts. Moreover, the specific meaning assigned to "*mugunta*" (or "*mugu*") can vary widely depending on the context, the speaker's status, and his relation to his intended audience as well as his tone of voice, as the following vignette illustrates.

A neighbor of mine once recounted an encounter between Noma, a man in his fifties who was subsequently accused and convicted of being a witch, and a youth from the same village. The young man, who was returning home from a day of hunting, had reportedly been disrespectful to the elder. Upon being asked whether he had shot the two guinea hens he was carrying, he told Noma it was "none of his business." "Young man, be careful," an offended Noma allegedly countered. "*Yaro ba shi wa mugunta zahi* [the child is too young to become mean]!" Despite the young man's protestations that he had said nothing wrong, Noma left the scene of the encounter swearing angrily that he was the last person the young man would ever insult. By the time the young man returned home, his head was reportedly twisted in such a way it faced backward. A few hours later, he was dead.

Since at the time everyone already suspected Noma of being a witch, there was no ambiguity as to who the evil person was in this story for those who heard it. The fact that the innocent victim—not the witch—was accused of engaging in *mugunta* exemplifies how flexible the Hausa concept is and how this flexibility can be used to create a multilayered effect. Far from referring to the intrinsic evil Noma himself allegedly personified, *mugunta* here evokes the kind of badness (or insolence) that elders associate with the younger generation. In this highly hierarchical society, every relationship is defined by rank: the five-year-old is expected to show respect to the ten-year-old, the ten-year-old to the fourteen-year-old, and so on. Given how seniority dictates appropriate behavior between people, youths who do not defer to their elders in all things are seen as headstrong, insubordinate, and wayward. In a word: rude.

Noma's warning to the young man that he was "too young to be mean" was also a reminder that, while he could boast all he wanted about his successful hunt, as a youth, he occupied the bottom rung in the local hierarchy. In other words, his experience (measured in terms of meanness or "potency") was not comparable to that of a grown man like Noma. People in Niger often say that the greatest chiefs are the greatest witches—capable of not only caring for commoners and dependents but also harming them (see Geschiere 2013). *Mugunta*, therefore, does not refer merely to the idea of evil (or badness); it also encompasses notions of agency, power, and effectiveness, highlighting once more the contiguity of good and evil.

Spirits, Human Suffering, and the Ambiguity of Power

When I was conducting research in Dogondoutchi in the late 1980s, non-Muslim residents described spirits (*iskoki*) as mysterious creatures who belonged to the wild and could never be fully domesticated—hence their name, *mutanen daji*, or "people of the bush." Enigmatic and, at times, unpredictable, spirits were nevertheless said to share many qualities and attributes with humans. Like humans, spirits were born into families, married, produced children, and became grandparents. They also stole from each other, committed adultery, and had illegitimate offspring. Some were known for their propensity to cheat, others for their avarice or bad temper. A few of them were reputedly generous and forgiving, others less so. Like their human counterparts, they felt pleasure, pain, and anger, and they sometimes experienced irritation or jealousy. And just as humans did, they befriended or protected one another, or, conversely, fought and competed among themselves. What this means is that spirits are neither inherently evil nor 100 percent benevolent. Save for a distinct minority known for their uncompromising cruelty (and who are best left alone), spirits can be reasoned with and even enlisted to provide protection against a variety of calamities.

This is especially true of the *bori* spirits, a category of spirits that possess human hosts to make their wishes known and provide advice to those who need it. Unlike their wilder peers who are condemned to invisibility (but occasionally take on a human appearance to "trick" people), *bori* spirits momentarily become "fleshy" beings, endowed with substance and voice when they take hold of their hosts' bodies (Masquelier 2001). Take the fierce Zarma spirits who are responsible for rain, lightning, and thunder. While they are known to strike people, animals, and homes with lightning, at times causing great suffering, they only target those who have incurred their wrath. And when, during a *wasa* (possession ceremony), they throw an ax on the ground, it is to warn people of the general direction in which they will throw lightning during the next rainy season. Although these spirits take revenge seriously, they are not irretrievably bent on evil, and people have no reason to fear them as long as they respect them and follow their commands.

People who suspect that their problems are spirit-caused are encouraged by non-Muslim healers to seek forgiveness from the spirits and, if necessary, to become their lifelong devotees by joining *bori*, a cluster of practices centered on spirit possession. Spirits are held responsible for a wide variety of misfortunes ranging from drought to disease to a general failure to thrive. However, their interventions are described as afflictions (or misfortunes) rather than an expression of evil—though some of these interventions are more evil than others. They are not a symptom of the spirits' inherent badness and propensity to inflict suffering. Instead, they signal to the victim that she has been selected by the spirits to serve as their human host or that she has offended them. Either way, offerings must be provided and amends must be made before the victim's health (or her situation) can improve. Spirits can sometimes be demanding, but one learns, of necessity, to negotiate with them (Masquelier 2001).

Spirits do not inflict infertility, paralysis, or skin rashes because they are mean but as a retribution for being ignored or offended by people (or they may wish to attract their attention). Although a victim may not have known she was committing an offense, she is nevertheless at fault and must express contrition while promising to care for the spirit in the future. While she shares responsibility for her own suffering, she is simultaneously given an opportunity to solve her problems and obtain spiritual protection from a host of other issues. Even when a spirit known to be particularly vicious is blamed for a person's ill health, or even her death, one cannot describe him or her as patently evil as the following story suggests.

During a *wasa*, a woman reportedly made fun of Magaji, a long-time *bori* adept and host for a Zarma spirit named Harakwey. The next day, Magaji told friends he had dreamed during the night that his spirit had speared someone. Soon after, he learned that the woman who had mocked him had died. The deep wound the body allegedly bore was evidence that the woman had been struck mortally by a spear. If it confirmed that Harakwey was not a spirit one could afford to disrespect, no one gave any indication that they saw the spirit as unequivocally evil. Put plainly, there was nothing arbitrary about Harakwey's violence. Spirits, *bori* devotees often reminded me, can be very prickly, and (advertently or inadvertently) incurring their wrath can be costly. Tragic as it was, the woman's death nevertheless did not surprise those, like Magaji, who were familiar with Harakwey's mercilessness. Morality must therefore be understood as contextual and contingent. Because spirits themselves react idiosyncratically to rudeness, immorality, selfishness, or inappropriate behavior, it is not a stretch to suggest that goodness (as moral integrity) is constantly renegotiated in the context of people's encounters with spirits. In fact, one could argue that by keeping people alert as to the consequences of their blunders, spirits are actively policing the boundaries of the moral.

Spirit Possession and Spoiled Girlhood

The past decade has witnessed an efflorescence of spirit possession in secondary schools all over the country. During these incidents, schoolgirls (and more rarely university students) are seemingly overtaken by wild and violent spirits. Some of them exhibit the classic signs of possession. They start shivering and shaking and their gaze loses focus. Some become increasingly agitated, screaming and thrashing around while frothing at the mouth and rolling their eyes. Others run wildly in a number of directions or jump in the air. Yet others become catatonic or exhibit bouts of paralysis. Confronting the crisis has often meant shutting down schools and inviting Muslim and non-Muslim religious specialists to rid the places of evil influences before classes can resume (Masquelier 2016).

The disturbing symptoms exhibited by entranced schoolgirls have been attributed to stress or diagnosed as epilepsy (or hysteria) by local health officials reluctant to concede the reality of spirit possession. Many people, nevertheless, take the furious contortions or death-like apathy of schoolgirls to be signs of spirit possession. They often cite the immodest conduct of young women—particularly, the fact that they do not veil—as the probable reason for the recrudescence of spirit attacks. Far, then, from operating randomly, the possessing spirits aim for young females whose lack (or loss) of virtue mark them as "improper" Muslims in need of moral regulation. In 2010, rumors had it that a spirit targeted *budurwoyi* (young unmarried women) by disguising himself as a taxi driver looking for clients. He earned the nickname of *génie tchatcheur* ("chatty demon") because of his ability to seduce young women with words. When school let out, he reportedly picked up female students at the wheel of a luxurious vehicle. In Niamey, Niger's capital, the *génie tchatcheur* ravished girls who evaded parental permission and left their homes at night. He was reportedly fond of young women with "intact hymens" (Anonymous 2009; *Libération* 2004). Although the spirit's modus operandi varied, the profile of his targets did not: the *génie* preyed exclusively on girls and young women, most of them students. The encounter allegedly left the victims traumatized.

In Niger, Islamic morality has traditionally translated into a set of rules that prescribe male and female dress and demeanor. Since the 1990s, a number of Islamic organizations, including the Society for the Removal of Innovation and Reinstatement of the Sunna (known colloquially as "Izala"), have focused their attention on women and the creation of "docile bodies" (Foucault 1977) in an effort to return to what they take to be authentic Islam, devoid of cultural accretions (Kane 2003; Loimeier 1997; Masquelier 2009). They share with other reformist Islamic movements the world over a vision of femininity and domesticity that is not easily reconciled with secular liberal notions of gender, autonomy, and agency (Mahmood 2005). As they see it, women's impious and dissolute conduct epitomizes the evils of Western secularism—and the loss of moral values (Sounaye 2009)—and, therefore, "re-moralizing" society implies, among other things, containing female sexuality. In the 1990s, members of Izala campaigned to shroud female bodies and turn them into vessels of piety. Preachers took to the radio to provide vestimentary advice and urge women and girls to cover their heads. One of them warned his female audiences they committed a sin by braiding their hair and that they should not wear heels because it was a form of deception. Dress thus became a pivotal medium for circumscribing women into Islamically scripted roles. Today, many women and young girls express their religious devotion by wearing the hijab, a tailored veil of varying length and coverage. Because the hijab marks its wearer as inherently virtuous, many of them have often adopted it regardless of the extent of their religious commitment (Masquelier 2013). The intimate connection between veiling and morality is critical to the interpretations that arise to account for the *génie tchatcheur*'s pattern of predation.

Just as *karuwai* (prostitutes, sex workers) have been (and occasionally still are) systematically chased out of their villages and neighborhoods during periods of droughts under the pretext that they are responsible for the absence of rain, so schoolgirls abused by the *génie* and other creatures of this ilk are thought to contribute to their own misfortune. Conventional wisdom has it that the victims of these spiritual attacks do not veil. Indeed, their improper body coverage is what supposedly attracts the spirits to them in the first place (Masquelier 2016). Despite the fact that veiling practices in Niger are neither uniform nor stable and that "modest dress" means different things to different people, including adolescent girls, many people assume that schoolgirls who walk around bareheaded and wear tight-fitting clothes are less pious and more likely to be targeted by spirits than their veiled counterparts.

The hijab here performs a double function. First, it projects an image of piety that matches social expectations of what virtuous women look like, therefore deflecting unwanted (human) male attention. Second, by neutralizing the wearer's sexuality, it makes her less attractive to male spirits looking for adventure with eye-catching schoolgirls. Add to this the fact that spirits are said to enter through the head, and it becomes clear why the hijab is hailed by Muslim preachers and pundits alike as women's best remedy against spiritual attacks: it literally shields women against spiritual violation. For young women who must fend off multiple threats to their virtue, the hijab's moral capital is thus heightened by its use as a tangible safeguard.

In Niger, *budurwoyi* who disregard prescriptive rules regulating female dress and conduct are considered "bad" Muslims by many. Their revealing, body-hugging clothes mark them as bearers of Western contamination. Yet even as they flout the rules of modesty, *budurwoyi* feel the pressure to present themselves as pious Muslims. Because their comings and goings are carefully monitored, they occasionally resort to subterfuges (such as wearing the hijab) to escape parental scrutiny. Muslim preachers of all persuasions vilify them in their sermons for embodying "moral disorder" (*fitna*). Some young women have suffered physical attacks at the hands of men for wearing short skirts. In the eyes of their attackers, female immodesty—a troubling sign of depravity—must not be tolerated (Cooper 2006). In this context, the possession of scantily clad young girls by supposedly lustful spirits speaks to the impact of moralizing discourses about modesty and propriety on female audiences. It suggests that the normativization of public piety affects all women, even those who pretend not to be swayed by it. It also signals schoolgirls' deep ambivalence toward education at a time when so many Muslims criticize the presence of post-pubescent girls in the classroom and advocate early marriage as a remedy to sexual promiscuity. Career aspirations notwithstanding, the pressure to present oneself as a modest (and therefore respectable) Muslim woman often overrides any dreams of social success and financial independence (Masquelier 2016).

By uncovering their bodies to cultivate a certain fashion forwardness, schoolgirls enhance their permeability to spirits while also metonymically symbolizing a breach to the moral order. Women, people say, are more vulnerable to spiritual attacks than men. Schoolgirls whose modish appearance and brash comportment turns them into objects of male desire thus provide a point of entry for Satan's servants, thereby compromising the moral integrity of Nigerien society.

Inadvertent (that is, unintended *and* unwanted) possession at the hands of a wild spirit is, by all accounts, a harrowing experience for the victim and a source of anxiety and embarrassment for her family. Many girls who suffer a spiritual attack drop out of school and give up their dreams of being "modern." In the end, the spectacle of schoolgirls helplessly flailing and shrieking on the classroom floor or jumping over desks offers a moral inversion of humanity. For some people, it is a reminder of the Muslim community's susceptibility to the workings of Satan when the principles of moral containment enunciated by the Qur'an are no longer followed or when the ritual mechanisms that prevent evil forces from gaining a foothold in people's lives are no longer performed. Yet, as we shall see, how families choose to confront the attacking spirits owe as much, if not more, to pre-Islamic practice as to Islamic therapeutics.

Expelling Spirits or Negotiating with Them?

The frequent outbreaks of group possession among schoolgirls have raised questions about the suitability of gender-mixed settings for post-pubescent girls and the need for more stringent forms of control over female sexuality. Yet there is also a widely shared sense that the attacks have to do with people's inability to keep the past from periodically irrupting into the present. Spirits, I have often been told, once resided on the very sites where schools now stand. The construction of new classrooms to accommodate growing cohorts of students is what led to their displacement. Moreover, in past decades, people have massively turned to Islam and forgotten about the spirits. The displaced spirits are now causing trouble to remind people of their existence. As a pundit once put it:

> In the good old times, the presence of spirits was linked to the bush or the cemetery. Today everywhere from Arlit to Birni N'Koni to Niamey, spirits who rape schoolgirls are the talk of the town. Thanks to these rumors Niamey has become a veritable forest of genies and other evil spirits. (Le Républicain 2004, 6)

Caricatures of the urban landscape aside, the perceived proliferation of spirits in the age of Islam is a classic example of Foucault's (1990) repressive hypothesis. Far from disappearing under the combined onslaught of modernity and Islamization, the "people of the bush" (and the narratives that circulate about them) haunt classrooms. This is somewhat ironic given that classrooms are symbols of rationality and seats of knowledge, and as such, the very places that should exemplify the erasure of these and other "superstitions." In certain districts, reports of the creatures' phantasmic presence—they supposedly take over some schools in their entirety when students leave at the end of the academic year—feed the rumor mills and fill the pages of newspapers. Scenes of mass possession in the classroom have been featured on television. On the radio, *malamai* (Muslim religious specialists) rant against society's growing immorality while instructing people on what verses of the Qur'an best protect against spiritual intrusions.

It is worth noting that Muslims do not question the existence of spirits. Well-known verses of the Qur'an make references to *aljanu* (from the Arabic *djinnī*), bodiless beings made of smokeless fire who can shape-shift and move across space at great speed. Over time, the creatures that spirit devotees refer to as *iskoki* have been assimilated to the Qur'an's *aljanu*. To ward off their harmful powers, many Muslims purchase *layu* (amulets) and other protective medicines from Qur'anic scholars. In the past few decades, reformist Muslims have condemned such practices as un-Islamic, however. They caution against wearing amulets and drinking *rubutu* (liquid Qur'anic verses) to prevent spiritual interference in human lives and tell people to rely solely on the power of supplicatory prayer (*addu'a*) when seeking protection against evil forces. Honey can be prescribed as well, since the Prophet is known to have relied on it for curative purposes. By casting spirits as the servants of Satan and identifying prayer as the only means of fighting them, Muslim reformists demonstrate the strength of good over evil.

Although Muslims concede that spirits are part of God's creatures, many of them view spirit-centered practices—notably possession by *aljanu*—with considerable suspicion. They have been warned that associating with spirits is a grave infraction and that spirit altars must be destroyed. Rituals traditionally held by spirit practitioners to purge communities from evil and pestilence have been progressively abandoned. In Dogondoutchi, possession now indexes poverty and social marginalization. Muslim women who visit *bori* healers to remedy problems of infertility, shield themselves from jealous cowives, or preserve the stability of their marriages do so discreetly so as not to attract attention. Meanwhile, their husbands claim they want nothing to do with *bori* and deny any involvements with spirits, even if some of them occasionally rely on *bori* therapies to confront crises—such as a daughter's descent into "hysteria" (Masquelier 2001).

The mass possession of schoolgirls is the kind of crisis that demands immediate action. It is not unusual for *malamai* to be invited by school authorities to perform exorcisms (*ruqiyya*) and cleanse the schools of evil influences. On occasion, even the services of a *bori* healer may be requested to ensure that no alien presence remains in the school before classes resume. Meanwhile, many parents—deaf to Muslim reformists' warnings that *ruqiyya* is inspired by "animist" traditions and therefore unacceptable as a type of treatment—take their daughters to *malamai* to have the spirits driven from them.

Ruqiyya requires the *malami* (singular of *malamai*) in charge to converse with the spirit until he can convince the creature to let go of her victim. As such, it mirrors *bori* exorcism procedures whose aim is not to domesticate the spirit (considered dangerous and untamable) but to expel her permanently from the human victim. *Bori* healers and *malamai* thus "negotiate with spirits in very similar ways and assume the necessity of long-term management of recurring spirit problems" (O'Brien 2001, 237). Because their techniques often rely on instructional texts from Saudi Arabia and Egypt and involve the recitation of Qur'anic verses (O'Brien 2001), *malamai* insist that their modus operandi is legitimate and distinct from *bori* procedures. Yet, the fact that both *malamai* and *bori* healers treat the invading spirits as interlocutors that can be reasoned with suggests that the problem for Muslims wishing to differentiate themselves from spirit worshipers is "essentially moral, not cosmological" (Launay 1992, 105). Some parents whose daughters were "caught" by spirits at school stayed away from *bori* healers because, despite the healers' reputations as accomplished exorcists, they wanted to distance themselves from what they perceived to be backward practices.

Ruqiyya is a potentially risky procedure that can only be performed by a skilled practitioner. It is also a lucrative source of income for *malamai* known for their efficient "handling" of undesirable spirits. Note that the expulsion of the spirit is only the first step. Critical to the treatment's overall success is the adoption of a set of measures that will deter the spirit from reentering the victim's body. Afflicted women are enjoined to recite certain Qur'an verses, cover their heads at all time, and refrain from watching risqué videos (see O'Brien 2001). According to some *malamai*, young women's failure to invoke God's protection—before going to sleep, entering latrines, and so on—is what makes them particularly vulnerable to spiritual attacks.

Other Muslim scholars go further, explicitly linking the recrudescence of spirits to the younger generation's ignorance of Islam. Claiming that parents no longer teach their children how to use the Qur'an as a protective tool against meddling *aljanu*, they stress the importance of learning the verses that provide spiritual protection. A Muslim preacher once recalled falling prey to a spirit attack. As a Qur'anic student, he was writing a Qur'an verse on his board when he felt something tugging at his wrist. He recited a verse of the Qur'an and soon after felt better. He knew then that the weight on his wrist had been Satan sending a spirit to tempt him into abandoning his lesson. Satan, he stressed, was always on the lookout to lead people astray.

Despite attempts to purify Islam from what educated Nigeriens call animism, the "people of the bush" are well entrenched in Muslim spaces. By dramatizing young women's susceptibility to spirits, the narratives of mass possession in the classroom illuminate the ambiguity of evil and the difficulty of consigning moral responsibility to external forces, independent of human agency. In fact, the popularity of Islamic techniques of exorcism inspired by *bori* methodologies suggests that while Muslims draw from the Qur'anic script that has cast *aljanu* as Satanic creatures, they nevertheless remain wedded to conceptualizations of evil in which humans, following their erasure of the spiritscape, share the blame for the violence that is currently visited upon some members of the younger generation.

Doguwa Spirits and the Immorality of Wealth

When it comes to evil, no creature in Dogondoutchi and the surrounding region measures up to the Doguwa, a wide-ranging category of ruthless spirits believed to feed on human blood. "Doguwa spirits, once they get going, do not stop until they have killed everyone," is how a *bori* devotee once put it. Merciless as these Doguwa spirits are rumored to be, what is significant about them is that they are not considered to be inherently evil. Nor, I should add, do all Doguwa spirits feed on human blood. Once their destructive powers are unleashed by human appetite for riches, however, the Doguwa are not easily neutralized. Understanding this particular manifestation of evil thus requires that we scrutinize the location of agency and intentionality in people's narratives.

Doguwa spirits were once the custodians of the land. It is they who permitted people to settle in the region and farm if, in exchange, people made sacrificial offerings. Originally venerated for their role in warfare and agriculture, some of them became progressively domesticated as tutelary spirits who were propitiated on behalf of specific subgroups or lineages. With time, the organization of the sacred further evolved to include spirits who had individualized relations with hosts, whom they periodically possessed in the context of *bori* rituals. Not all Doguwa spirits have come to engage in reciprocal relations with humans, however. Many of them have remained hidden away in the bush. Only when (deliberately or inadvertently) approached by people do they end up interfering in human lives. What this means is that unless they are displaced or offended by people (or, as we shall see, invited to select victims), spirits rarely attack people. They occasionally visit markets, driven by curiosity or attracted by the beauty of people, their homes, and their things, but, save for rare exceptions, they are not considered to be inherently wicked.

What has transformed spirits, and specifically Doguwa spirits, into dangerous, bloodsucking creatures ready to pounce on the nearest person they come across is human greed. In their increasing desire for wealth, people strike Faustian bargains with Doguwa spirits. Once a deal is struck, Doguwa is made to do the bidding of her human master if, in exchange for the riches she produces, she is fed human blood. The spirit creates wealth for her guardian as long as her craving for blood is satisfied. Narratives of spirits toiling for their owners who amass enormous assets attest to the perversion of the original covenant between spirits and people. Far from being enjoyed communally, wealth is now secretly generated and benefits but a few. Moreover, this immoral production exacts an enormous price in human lives. At a time when the pressing need for cash is met with a rising inability to procure it, stories of bloodthirsty Doguwa build on the notion that wealth is not so much the result of honest labor as it is a windfall conferred by dark and dangerous forces that, once awakened, cannot be easily kept in check.

Requesting the services of a Doguwa spirit is relatively simple. All one has to do is go to the bush and leave a calabash of milk (or, alternatively, honey) at the foot of a tree. The Doguwa will ask the gift-giver what he wishes in return. Alternatively, a knock on the tree will signal to the spirit someone is looking for her. In some cases, repeated offerings must be made before the spirit can be swayed. Once the spirit agrees to follow someone to his home, however, there is no going back. The Doguwa feeds on chickens at first, but she soon develops a craving for human blood. The master initially designates victims from among cohorts of strangers, but when he "runs out" of prey, he has no choice but to select neighbors and, after that, his own kin. Once she has sucked a person dry, the spirit moves on to her next victim. Therefore, her master must continually search for new prey. In the end, he has no choice but to offer his own children to satisfy the ravenous spirit. The Faustian pact one makes with a Doguwa strikes at the heart of reproduction, thereby sacrificing "the very possibility of a future" (Smith 2004, 268).

Because this kind of deal involves the extraction of vital human fluids to fuel the nefarious production of riches, it is identified as a form of witchcraft (*maita*). A classic example of "the use of preternatural power by one person to damage others" (Austen 1993, 90), *maita* here subverts the conventional meaning of sacrifice in which the life of an animal is substituted for the life of a person and offered to a spirit in exchange for protection and prosperity. Rather than enjoying a spirit's protection, the victim of *maita* is depleted of her vital substance to sustain that spirit. The individual whose excessive greed awakened the destructive potential of a bloodthirsty Doguwa is called a *maye* (witch, masculine form) or *maya* (witch, feminine form). If enough evidence is provided to substantiate the accusations against them (before killing her victims, the Doguwa possesses them and identifies her master), alleged witches are forced to submit to an ordeal that will determine whether they are guilty or not. The ordeal neutralizes their power over the malevolent Doguwa but does not get rid of the spirit. "One cannot get rid of a Doguwa. She stays forever in the family," is how a *bori* healer put it, to stress how insidious and irrevocable this form of witchcraft is.

Human Agency and the Problem of Evil

As is evidenced by extensive anthropological literature on the malcontents of modernity, people in Africa and elsewhere routinely link the social transformations conventionally defined as modernization with narratives of perverted and predatory consumption. From the mines and cane fields of South America (Taussig 1980) to the markets of Nigeria (Bastian 1998) to the coastal towns of East Africa (McIntosh 2009), the contradictions of global capital are apprehended through a "poetics of predation" (Comaroff and Comaroff 1993, xxvi; see also Geschiere 1997) that equates wealth production with the illicit extraction of human labor or human vital substances. In Niger, narratives of witchcraft, demons, and vampiric creatures concretize the perils of social inequality and the cost of possessive individualism while encoding a moral critique of Islamic mercantilism. In the eyes of many residents for whom hard work never seems to translate into prosperity, the wealth of some people, most of whom are Muslim, invites suspicion that these individuals are harboring a Doguwa. Their glaring good fortune does not appear to obey the laws that govern the production of ordinary people's income. This can only mean that it originated in a corrupt deal with a spirit.

Aside from helping make sense of the hidden logic of wealth production, the rhetoric of witchcraft also sheds lights on what Muslims supposedly hide behind their monotheism. Joseph Greenberg, writing about Hausa morality in northern Nigeria over half a century ago, observed that keeping an evil spirit in one's home meant that one sacrificed to bush spirits "inside the compound instead of at the appropriate place in the bush" (1946, 47). Those who "[were] not bent on evil," but who wished to sacrifice to the bush spirits did so outside their compounds to avoid raising suspicion (1946, 47). In Dogondoutchi, I often heard spirit devotees accuse prosperous Muslim businessmen of sacrificing to the spirits to ensure their and their households' prosperity, and some of these individuals were eventually accused of *maita*.

Bori devotees too can be accused of keeping a Doguwa spirit for nefarious purposes, especially if they are seen as antisocial individuals. In 2008, a female *bori* devotee was accused of having sent her spirit on a dozen individuals, mostly young people, who had died rather suddenly. She was forced to undergo a *ritual* to help undo the hold that her spirit had on her last victim after the spirit, during a particularly violent possession episode, had revealed the ugly truth. Rumors circulated that Niamey-based financiers and politicians had recruited her to avail themselves of the services of her spirit. These individuals wished to eliminate competitors or embezzle funds without being caught, which is why they had sought the protection of a Doguwa spirit. If witchcraft accusations are occasionally leveled at *bori* devotees, economically successful Muslims perceived to be selfish, uncaring, and close-fisted are nevertheless likely targets of *maita* accusations.

Ironically, Muslims do not criminalize wealth production—far from it. They take prosperity to be an undeniable sign of God's goodwill. In Dogondoutchi, as in the rest of Niger, Islam is now equated with status, power, and *arziki* (prosperity, well-being)—so much so that one cannot succeed in business or politics if one does not identify as Muslim. And since *alhazai* (persons who have gone on the pilgrimage to Mecca) are often well-to-do individuals, the term itself has become synonymous with wealthy businessmen. The status of these individuals as pilgrims provides further evidence that wealth and piety presuppose one another. Yet, as previously noted, the tight association between prosperity and Islamic piety does not protect wealthy Muslim entrepreneurs from accusations of *maita*.

Far from disappearing with the resolute progress of Islam, notions of witchcraft have remained central to the ways that many ordinary Dogondoutchi residents objectify evil and explain social inequality. As a "relational calculus of resentment, fear, and envy" (Apter 1993, 124), witchcraft here works to demystify Islam by shedding light on its covert workings and its "mysterious currencies, its political pieties, its threat to the viability of known social worlds" (Comaroff 1997, 10). Aside from evidencing that Muslim elites dabble with the occult, the identification of Muslim witches effectively sets the boundaries of morality while assigning responsibility for much of the current evils to uncontrollable human desire for material wealth.

Let me stress once more that Doguwa spirits only turn malevolent at the prompting of individuals who use them to serve their own selfish ends. Spirits, people say, "are like children." Like them, they will do what they are asked to do. What this means is that, like children who are taught wrongly, Doguwa spirits learn from their unscrupulous masters how to perform immoral tasks. In other words, they become the unwitting instruments of human covetousness. As a *bori* devotee explained: "When you take a Doguwa, she takes on the personality of her master. If he is mean, she becomes mean." From this perspective, it is exposure to human greed and selfishness that transforms Doguwa spirits into thoroughly wicked creatures that stop at nothing to satisfy their own (newly developed) craving for human blood. Doguwa may be feared for their ruthless predation on human beings, but it is ultimately the masters for whom they work who are perceived to be the source of wickedness, and it is they who are punished for the victimization and suffering that are perpetrated under their command.

Conclusion

In this chapter, I have suggested that for Dogondoutchi residents, the demonization of spirits by Islam has not resulted in an unequivocal opposition between good and evil. Despite *malamai*'s attempts to cast spirits indiscriminately as Satan's subordinates, spirits remain morally ambiguous creatures that cannot be defined as inherently bad. Even though Muslim preachers try to paint them with a broad brush as unequivocal expressions of evil in the world, they exhibit complex moral dispositions that are not easily reducible to one-dimensional qualities. More often than not, the misfortunes, sickness, and deaths they cause are read by many people as warnings or retributions for past human deeds.

When schoolgirls are targeted by lewd spirits, they are often blamed for having brought these torments on themselves through their inappropriate dress and conduct. Put simply, young women who dress in skimpy clothing or walk around bareheaded invite the spirits to take advantage of their vulnerability. By focusing on the young victims' lack of modesty, the discourses that emerge to account for the spirit attacks highlight how the markers of morality have fallen heavily on women's shoulders. Although everyone agrees that the spirits who attack schoolgirls are evil, the burden for this immorality is partially displaced on the victims themselves who—wittingly or unwittingly— attract the spirits with their charms. By exposing themselves to the spirits, *malamai* claim, schoolgirls hand Satan a victory, for it is he who tempted them to "sin" in the first place. Ultimately, however, the methods employed to deal with the possessing spirits suggest that the boundary between good and evil is not clear-cut.

Narratives of bloodthirsty Doguwa spirits hidden away in their masters' homes similarly exemplify the decentering of culpability onto human actors. The *maye*'s lack of empathy for other people and his willingness to sacrifice human lives for the sake of personal wealth are what turns an ordinary spirit into a merciless killer. Whereas schoolgirls who "seduce" lecherous spirits are merely "weak," people who harbor spirits for nefarious gains are willing perpetrators of evil. They bear a large measure of responsibility for the deaths of their spirits' victims and cannot be easily exonerated for the suffering they have caused. The harsh punishment they are inflicted (they are stripped of their clothes and a stick covered in hot pepper is inserted in their rectum) highlights the contingent nature of the evil they embody: it is they and not the spirits who are punished.

Max Weber (2005 [1930]) is known for forcefully arguing that the adoption of the Protestant ethos would inevitably lead to the disenchantment of modern society. Yet he was well aware that in practice, things are more complicated. "The path to monotheism," Weber observed, "has been traversed with varying degrees of consistency, but nowhere was the existence of spirits and demons permanently eliminated" (1993 [1922], 20). The decisive consideration, Weber further writes,

> was and remains: who is deemed to exert the stronger influence on the individual in his everyday life, the theoretically supreme god or the lower spirits and demons? If the spirits, then the religion of everyday life is decisively determined by them, regardless of the official god-concept of the ostensibly rationalized religion. (1993 [1922], 20)

In Dogondoutchi, Islam's ostensibly monotheistic orientation is routinely undercut by the critical role attributed to spirits in everyday life. As I have pointed out in this chapter, this has important consequences for the way that people conceptualize and confront evil. By demarcating the "edge of Islam" (McIntosh 2009) and offering an alternative moral order in which human and spiritual lives are complexly entangled, *aljanu* routinely complicate Islam's Manichean division between good and evil.

Adeline Masquelier, Tulane University

References

Anonymous. 2009. "Un génie séducteur s'invite aux épreuves du baccalauréat sportif à Konni, au Niger." *Agence de Presse Africaine* (20 May).

Apter, Andrew. 1993. "Atinga Revisited: Yoruba Witchcraft and the Cocoa Economy, 1950–1951." In *Modernity and Its Malcontents: Ritual and Power in Postcolonial Africa*. Edited by Jean Comaroff and John Comaroff, 111–28. Chicago: University of Chicago Press.

Austen, Ralph. 1993. "The Moral Economy of Witchcraft: An Essay in Comparative History." In *Modernity and Its Malcontents: Ritual and Power in Postcolonial Africa*. Edited by Jean Comaroff and John Comaroff, 89–110. Chicago: University of Chicago Press.

Bastian, Misty. 1998. "Fires, Tricksters and Poisoned Medicines: Popular Cultures of Rumor in Onitsha, Nigeria, and Its Markets." *Etnofoor* 11(2): 11–32.

Comaroff, Jean. 1997. "Consuming Passions: Child Abuse, Fetishism and the 'New World Order.'" *Culture* 17: 7–19.

Comaroff, Jean, and John Comaroff. 1993. "Introduction." In *Modernity and Its Malcontents: Ritual and Power in Postcolonial Africa*. Edited by Jean Comaroff and John Comaroff, xi–xxxvii. Chicago: University of Chicago Press.

Cooper, Barbara. 2006. *Evangelical Christians in the Muslim Sahel*. Bloomington: Indiana University Press.

Foucault, Michel. 1977. *Discipline and Punish: The Birth of the Prison*. Translated by Alan Sheridan. New York: Vintage Books.

———. 1990. *The History of Sexuality, Vol. I: An Introduction*. Translated by Robert Hurley. New York: Vintage Books.

Geschiere, Peter. 1997. *The Modernity of Witchcraft: Politics and the Occult in West Africa*. Charlottesville: University of Virginia Press.

———. 2013. *Witchcraft, Intimacy, and Trust: Africa in Comparison*. Chicago: University of Chicago Press.

Greenberg, Joseph H. 1946. *The Influence of Islam on a Sudanese Religion*. New York: J. J. Augustin Publisher.

Kane, Ousmane. 2003. *Muslim Modernity in Postcolonial Nigeria: A Study of the Society for the Renewal of Innovation and the Reinstatement of Tradition*. Leiden: Brill.

Launay, Robert. 1992. *Beyond the Stream: Islam and Society in a West African Town*. Berkeley: University of California Press.

Le Républicain. 2004. "Des génies partout." 13 May: 621.

Libération. 2004. "Psychose du génie 'tchatcheur.'" 13 May: 4. http://www.planeteafrique.com/liberation/AfficheInfos.asp?affiche=0072/6.asp.

Loimeier, Roman. 1997. *Islamic Reform and Political Change in Northern Nigeria*. Evanston, IL: Northwestern University Press.

Mahmood, Saba. 2005. *Politics of Piety: The Islamic Revival and the Feminist Subject*. Princeton, NJ: Princeton University Press.

Masquelier, Adeline. 2001. *Prayer Has Spoiled Everything: Possession, Power, and Identity in an Islamic Town of Niger*. Durham, NC: Duke University Press.

———. 2009. *Women and Islamic Revival in a West African Town*. Bloomington: Indiana University Press.

———. 2013. "Modest Bodies, Stylish Selves: Fashioning Virtue in Niger." In *Veiling/Counter-Veiling in Africa*. Edited by Elisha Renne, 110–36. Bloomington: Indiana University Press.

———. 2018. "Schooling, Spirit Possession, and the 'Modern Girl' in Niger." In *Femmes d'Afrique et émancipation: Entre normes sociales contraignantes et nouveaux possibles*. Edited by Muriel Gomez-Perez. Paris: Karthala.

McIntosh, Janet. 2009. *The Edge of Islam: Power, Personhood, and Ethno-Religious Boundaries on the Kenya Coast*. Durham, NC: Duke University Press.

O'Brien, Susan. 2001. "Spirit Discipline: Gender, Islam, and Hierarchies of Treatment in Post-Colonial Northern Nigeria." *Interventions: The International Journal of Post-Colonial Studies* 3(2): 222–41.

Parkin, David. 1985. "Introduction." In *The Anthropology of Evil*. Edited by David Parkin. Cambridge, UK: Blackwell.

Smith, James H. 2004. "Of Spirit Possession and Structural Adjustment Programs: Government Downsizing, Education, and Their Enchantments in Neoliberal Kenya." In *Producing African Futures: Ritual and Reproduction in a Neoliberal Age*. Edited by Brad Weiss, 262–93. Boston, MA: Brill.

Sounaye, Abdoulaye. 2009. "Islam, État et société: À la recherche d'une éthique publique au Niger." In *Islam, État et société en Afrique*. Edited by René Otayek and Benjamin Soares, 327–52. Paris: Karthala.

Taussig, Michael. 1980. *The Devil and Commodity Fetishism in South America*. Chapel Hill: University of North Carolina Press.

Weber, Max. 1993 [1922]. *The Sociology of Religion*. Translated by Ephraim Fischoff. Boston, MA: Beacon Press.

———. 2005 [1930]. "The Protestant Ethic and the Spirit of Capitalism." Translated by Talcott Parsons. Routledge: New York.

PART III

Evil and Violence

Chapter 9

ENGAGING EVIL AND EXCESS IN PALESTINE/ISRAEL

Julie Peteet

Evil, a term both perplexing and expansive, and often assumed to be a universal, is a transcendent category and a hotbed of ambiguity. Rhetorically, we are familiar with the "axis of evil," the "evil empire," and quotidian comparisons to those icons of sadistic evil: Hitler, Charles Mason, the Khmer Rouge and Pol Pot, Saddam Hussein, the Iranian regime, al-Qaeda, communists, and more recently ISIS, among others. TV crime shows relentlessly traffic in profiles of the evil lurking among us typically in the form of the grotesque: brutal rapes, murders, child abuse, and torture. With our heightened sense of American exceptionalism, we prefer "to picture the evil that was *there*" (Sontag 2003, 88) rather than that closer to home, unless it unfolds at the individual level (hence the TV mania for dramatizing evil). As Susan Sontag astutely notes, there is a Holocaust Museum in Washington, DC, but not a museum of slavery.

This chapter probes how evil becomes legitimized and normalized and thus attains a level of acceptability. In the contemporary era, invocations of "security," "self-defense," and "terrorism" are recast as legitimate acts that might otherwise be considered evil. In the case of Palestinians, their imputed evil actions are justification for the evil done to them, echoing former Vice-President Dick Cheney's "dark side" where imputed evil allows for disproportionate responses. Slavery and genocide are widely accepted as evil practices. Evil may encompass acts of extraordinary violence but can equally be constituted by the mundane quotidian acts of subjugation, degradation, and petty violence that characterize life under Israeli occupation and colonialism, or, closer to home, Jim Crow and its contemporary iteration in the "new Jim Crow" (Alexander 2012).

As a polysemic term, what David Parkin has called an "odd-job word" (1985, 1), evil can take on a multiplicity of meanings. In this chapter, using ethnographic material from Palestine, I will position it as cruel and rationally calculated excess beyond the boundaries of particular moral and ethical codes of conduct. It is the intentional, calibrated infliction of suffering and pain, often accompanied by self-congratulation, celebration, and a well-honed apparatus of denial.

Israel can be classified as a settler-colonialism state and society of the sort once common in South Africa and Algeria, among others. In honing in on daily life under a settler-colonial occupation, this chapter takes heed of Malinowski's self-critique of his Trobriand Islands ethnographies that he was "lured by the dramatic, exceptional and sensational" to the neglect of the "every day, inconspicuous, drab and small-scale" (2002 [1935], 462). With this in mind, from ethnographic research in Palestine over the course of the past decade, I explore how evil, or violent excess, is calculated and built into the structures and patterns of everyday life under occupation from the micro or daily small-scale indignities to the macro-scale of military assault.

This chapter explores evil as calibrated excess through the overlapping registers of military assault, suffering and indifference to it, visibility and the violent spectacle, and abandonment and expulsion in Palestine/Israel. The infliction of suffering is a means to end Palestinian national aspirations and compel obedience. I probe the calculated-ness of excess using science and technology by the state and the Palestinian experience of dwelling in such an environment as daily fare. The violence experienced by Palestinians under occupation operates on a spectrum: from the structural bureaucratic-administrative violence of the permit system and the segregated road system to the physical violence of torture, imprisonment, random beatings, and murder, to siege and military assaults. Where structural violence seems to prevail, it is always backed by the visible threat of violence in the armed colonist or the ubiquitous military/police or private security personnel.

What actions have come to fall under the category of evil? The Iraqi Ba'athist regime deploying chemical weapons against Kurds in Halabja is commonly accepted as an evil act, but less so the US assaults on Iraq that resulted in a death toll in the hundreds of thousands (Atwan 2015, 33), or intermittent and deadly Israeli assaults on an already besieged and sanctioned Gaza. Apartheid in South Africa was widely understood as a form of evil, yet apartheid in Palestine, within the parameters of the accepted definition of apartheid, is vigorously denied (Peteet 2016a). Here and there, us and them, now and then point to a differentiated conception of evil and malefactors. In other words, it is the violence of others that is malevolent. The term began to appear in political rhetoric with US President Ronald Reagan and the Iranian Ayatollah Khomeini—with the axis of evil and the great Satan respectively—and the worldwide rise of religion as an animating political force in the mid-to-late twentieth century. As the Cold War ended, Islamists have supplanted Communists as the face of the evil other.

With roots in religion, ethics,[1] moral codes, and folk traditions, attributions of evil have renewed currency in the late twentieth and early twenty-first centuries and, in many instances, they have been largely secularized. Evil's religious underpinnings and continuing reverberations can make it appear a retrograde concept, one social scientists can find discomforting. Over time, evil has come to refer less to the supernatural and more to both individual psychological states and the pathologies of specific political and economic regimes that routinely inflict pain, violence, and suffering; these often intersect—hence the framing of some individuals or regimes, usually non-Western, as the epitome of evil.

An indeterminate somewhat opaque category of actions, evil's ambiguity and incertitude rather than stability of meaning, however, does open a wide berth in which to explore it. The term "evil" may be a way of capturing conduct and actions for which speech and legal categories fail us. As an appellation, evil creates meaning, however expansive, where other sorts of language fail to capture the magnitude of cruelty, suffering, and pain. Those who rather routinely impute evil to others, particularly in the "War on Terror" (WoT), use it with a Manichean certitude to package action: military incursions and assaults, torture, sanctions, and the suspension of the laws governing warfare. The "clash of civilization" and WoT discourses provided a rhetorical framework for casting some violence as evil and others as a necessity and hence the "lesser of evils" (Weizman 2011). As a term of reference, evil, like terrorism—those twinned rhetorical devices—is not a self-appellation and its imputation lends itself to the suspension of normative codes of conduct, which may themselves rank as evil. Both terms are seductive as their invocation justifies violence in the name of security, another magical and murky term. The WoT slotted whole communities into binaries of good/evil, terrorists/innocents, and Islamists and the West. In armed conflict, spaces can become morally ranked, such as Iraq, Afghanistan, and Palestine. In these battlespaces, life can be taken with near impunity. In these spaces of ostensible evil, where people are outside the boundaries of the fully human, the dead are not grievable (see Butler 1997).

Does the term "evil" help move us beyond the more concrete term "unethical"? Steve Caton (2010, 166–67) makes this point in his discussion of the abuses committed at the Abu Ghraib prison in Iraq and offers an alternative to locating the concept in either the domain of the universal or that of cultural relativism. He proposes "situational evil" or "evil of singularity" (2010, 175), a conceptual framework that allows use of the concept in contingent circumstance. This leads to questions of the systemic. What if excess is built into a particular structure of governance, an excess that is often improvised and culturally acceptable? Think Gaza. What if inhumane acts are not merely or always the obeying of orders but are willfully and cheerfully engaged in in an atmosphere of a colonial occupation, racialized difference, routine petty cruelty and violation of rights, punctuated by intermittent full-scale military assaults that inflict massive damage and incur a substantial death toll, and impunity for perpetrators? The question becomes: What is excess and what is standard, acceptable behavior during conflict?

Cultural relativism has been trumped to some extent by mid-twentieth century human rights law and discourse. International Humanitarian Law (IHL), which regulates conduct in war, established a framework for understanding evil as excess beyond internationally accepted norms of behavior in armed conflict; in essence, IHL legitimizes conflict by defining the boundaries of unacceptable and acceptable behavior. "Disproportionality" and "war crimes" came to stand in for what had once been considered evil. Excess is a key term in IHL and a key tenet of proportionality, what Israeli architect Eyal Weizman notes is a "manifestation of the lesser evil principle" (2011, 11). Proportionality is "not about clear lines of prohibitions but rather about calculation and determining balances and degrees." Thus, calculation and quantification stand out. What distinguish state violence are its assumed legality and its style—its war machinery, the discursive apparatus accompanying it, and the degree of suffering inflicted and on whom. Abu Ghraib and Bagram prisons come to mind, as does Gaza, a fenced ghetto, besieged for over a decade, and periodically assaulted by Israel. Imputations of evil may be associated with the exceeding of the doctrine of proportionality and when perpetrators are absolved of responsibility. Equally, evil may reside in the day-to-day willfully inflicted microcruelties.

As enacted in the colonization of Palestine, Zionism, a nationalist settler-colonial movement and ideology with messianic overtones, works within territory it considers sovereign space to delineate boundaries between Arab and Jew, between those who belong and those who are excluded from the polity. The categories of them and us have been spatialized, institutionalized in law, are well patrolled for transgression, and endowed with a rhetorical and discursive life. The categories have a rhetorical and experiential valence—of superiority and full humanity on the one hand and a lesser sort of humanity on the other.[2]

Israelis and Palestinians attribute evil to each other. Juxtaposing acts of violence need not imply symmetry—indeed, to the contrary, it can highlight disparity. Palestinians throw stones and once engaged in suicide bombings, those iconic acts of "terrorism"; the Israeli state launches massive military assaults, expropriates Palestinian resources, and Jewish-Israeli colonists in the West Bank engage in attacks on the indigenous Palestinian population and their property with impunity. Death ratios, those blunt, cold quantifications of violence and suffering, part of the "economy of violence" (Weizman 2011, 4), are barometers of the capacity to act on one side and a register of vulnerability and diminished military capacity on the other; they are also a means of assessing proportionality. A subtext to death tolls in armed conflict is "proportionality." Israel's Dahiya Doctrine (named after the southern suburbs of Beirut), details *disproportionality as a strategy* and raises serious questions about excess, the rule of law, and impunity. The Dahiya doctrine refers to the overwhelming use of air power to destroy infrastructure (electricity, water and sanitation, telecommunications, roads, and transportation hubs, etc.) and compel Palestinians (and Lebanese) to refocus energies and resources on immediate survival and endless reconstruction. Implemented extensively in the 2006 Israeli invasion of Lebanon, it has been pursued in Gaza several times since, most notably in 2008–09, 2012, 2014, and 2018. In the occupied West Bank, immiseration characterizes daily life. Immiseration works beyond the use of overwhelming military force; structural violence is always backed by the threat of military/police assault. The imposition of policies (closure)[3] and structures (the separation wall and checkpoints) are designed to immiserate through immobilization, confinement, and a steady diet of humiliation in which the ordinariness of daily life—from children going to school, to adults seeking to reach work, to Palestinians simply desirous of visiting family and friends—is the target. Intermittent military assaults punctuate the daily-ness of immiseration.

Language

The interaction between utterance and action, language and behavior, is a point of departure for a conversation on evil. As Judith Butler contends, "We do things with language, produce effects with language" (1997, 8). Language serves as both an early warning system of impending violence and a diagnostic tool for grappling with conceptualizations of the other. Linguistic anthropology understands "speech not only within the context of action but *as* action" (Lambek 2010, 5). The ability to act on imputations of evil and perceived threat is distributed unevenly, as evidenced when state officials voice racist invective and possess the means to act on it. Talal Asad encapsulated the distinction between the liberal democratic state and terrorist violence as one of "capability" (2007, 4) and unpacked the "ingenuity of liberal discourse in rendering inhumane acts human. This is certainly something that savage discourse cannot achieve" (2007, 38). That is why ISIS's murderous and inhumane actions arouse the epithet "evil," but the vastly larger death toll and destruction from the US invasion and occupation of Iraq are not similarly cast; the excess of one is evil but not the other. Attribution of evil hinders exploration of the context in which it occurs; it becomes its own explanation, unique and incomparable. Casting state violence as a response to the imputed irrational violence of evilness facilitates the disavowal of responsibility by blaming the victim. Unarmed Gazans are shot dead because they demonstrated near the fence that imprisons them. They are the demon other. In this worldview, Palestinian behavior compels the Israeli response. A sort of "they made me do it," the ruse of domestic abusers, can be detected. Casting the fence as a "necessary evil" (Luntz 2009, 70) works in a similar fashion. The most illustrative example of this sort of victim blaming occurred when Israeli Prime Minister Netanyahu, now widely circulated and commented upon, stated during the 2014 assault on Gaza that dead Palestinians were telegenically dead (Erekat 2014; Feldman 2014; Peteet 2016b; Puar 2015). Referring to Hamas, he said, "They want to pile up as many civilian dead as they can. They use telegenically dead Palestinians for their cause. They want the dead, the more the better" (Winer 2014). In other words, Palestinians themselves, as a collective body, compel the suffering Israeli inflicts on them and exploit piles of dead bodies as a telegenic moment. Israel is therefore relieved of accountability.

Can a sequencing of language, action, and impunity be discerned? A mantra-like reiteration of certain terms or phrases constructs the scaffolding upon which is built a narrative and imagery of Palestinians as hate-filled, irrational aggressors (Peteet 2016b) and Israel as acting in self-defense. For example, the verb "to rain," in reference to rockets fired from Gaza, is repeated *ad naseum* in the media. Rain implies an infinite number of things, conjuring up an innumerable quantity and conveying the impression of a massive military assault. "Thousands of missiles have already rained down on our cities," Israeli PM Netanyahu claimed in a September 23, 2013, speech to the UN. Rain implies a steady deluge of unlimited and uncountable things, hardly appropriate descriptions of this small number of technologically crude rockets. Palestinian rockets are consistently quantified: "Hamas launched [insert number] rockets today." Quantification is assumed to speak for itself. The starkness of numbers overstates Hamas' military capacity, putting it on a par with that of a state. In this unevenly matched arena, Israeli air and artillery strikes are rarely subject to quantification in the media. Disproportionate actions, then, are swallowed up by the security mantra and claims of existential threat.

The threat of unbounded violence, its looming potential, has become part of the state's arsenal. Israeli Knesset member Ayelet Shaked posted a threat on Facebook during the 2014 war on Gaza reminiscent of the Rwandan Interhamwe's pronouncements about Tutsis as cockroaches in the run-up to the 1994 genocide:

> Behind every terrorist stand dozens of men and women, without whom he could not engage in terrorism. They are all enemy combatants, and their blood shall be on all their heads. Now this also includes the mothers of the martyrs. . . . They should follow their sons, nothing would be more just. They should go, as should the physical homes in which they raised the snakes. Otherwise, more little snakes will be raised there. ("'Mothers of all'" 2014)

On the academic side, Professor Mordechai Kedar of Ben Gurion University seemed to advocate rape as a deterrent to Palestinian violence, such as the 2014 kidnapping and killing of three settler youths, when he baldly stated: "The only thing that can deter terrorists, like those who kidnapped the children and killed them, is the knowledge that their sister or their mother will be raped. It sounds very bad, but that's the Middle East."[4]

While the US Embassy was moving to Jerusalem on 14 May 2018, amid joyous celebrations with US President Trump's daughter Ivanka Trump and her husband Jared Kushner in attendance, Israeli forces were mowing down and maiming unarmed Palestinian demonstrators in Gaza. As is usually the case, Likud Party foreign affairs director Eli Hazan uttered that "all 30,000 [protestors] are legitimate targets" (quoted in Makdisi 2018). Words and actions are important here. Israel refers to its intermittent assaults on Gaza as "mowing the lawn." Mowing is a form of maintenance; what is being maintained here is Palestinian subjugation and suffering and Israel's dominance. On this day, Israeli forces killed fifty-eight and injured twenty-four hundred Palestinians; the simultaneity with the opening of the US Embassy was not lost on most observers. Amnesty International noted: "Victims were shot in the upper body, including the head and chest—some from behind . . . many were deliberately killed or injured while posing no immediate threat."As Puar (2015, 2017) argues, Israel has arrogated to itself the right not just to kill but also to maim, which debilitates the population and diminishes the capacity to resist.

An elaborate linguistic strategy of obfuscation and denial operates alongside outright violence against Palestinians. In reference to Nazism, Hannah Arendt (1963) called "language rules" a "code name" to refer to "what in ordinary language would be called a lie." The effect "was not to keep these people ignorant of what they [Nazis] were doing, but to prevent them from equating it with their old, 'normal' knowledge of murder and lies." Modern Hebrew "employs word laundering to mask an arrogant, violent and even racist attitude toward the Arab enemy," which "allows a state to wash itself clean of any responsibility" for violent actions (Burg 2008, 59, 61). "Language rules" now have public relations personnel, such as well-known Republican strategist Frank Luntz, to draft documents such as *The Israel Project's 2009 Global Language Dictionary*, which at 116 pages is chock-full of talking points for responding to any question about Israel and Palestine from what works to what does not. Israel's dualistic "us and them" view of the world, with deep roots in a history of European persecution and anti-Semitism, is apparent in its discourse on the "Arab" or the "Palestinian." In this worldview, Israeli writer and former Knesset member Avraham Burg writes: "When every enemy is absolute evil and every conflict is a war to the death, all is justified in our eyes. We do not distinguish between levels of hostility nor do we view our enemies as rivals with possibly legitimate needs: they are all against us all the time, and all we can do is defend ourselves" (2008, 56). The concept of "moral panic" captures the atmosphere when a particular group (Iran and Palestinians) is "negatively framed and labeled as the enemy of society's cosmological order of things and as threat to its interests" (Ram 2009, 17).

By transposing evilness to Arabs/Muslims/Palestinians, Zionism depoliticizes and dehistoricizes conflict and Palestinian grievances and suggests that Palestinian actions are irrational, pathological, and beyond the pale of lawful response. Thus, its own actions, often exceeding the doctrine of proportionality, are seen as legitimate responses to the evil and violence nearby. Paired with irrationality, this attribution of evil suggests dwelling in an alternate temporal zone—the premodern, in contrast to the alleged modern rationality of the Zionist state. Palestinians tend to argue based on international law and the depravations of colonialism in keeping with their understanding of Zionism as a political ideology and colonial endeavor. Evil lies not just in the colonial system but also in its deeply rooted ideological apparatus of denial of Palestinian grievances and colonial culpability.

Indifference and Calibrated Deprivation

I met Munira, a twenty-seven year old Palestinian nurse, a few days after a distressing checkpoint experience. Over coffee in her office, she bitterly expressed her understanding of the occupation's interventions into everyday life with a consciously calculated infliction of suffering and a generalized indifference to the suffering of others:

> They have what I call a "misery committee." I envision a group of Israelis sitting around and devising well-organized forms of misery to inflict on us. We are either killed or we rise above the misery. The situation is so bad, I don't know how we don't all go crazy. For example, I have to pass through the Bethlehem checkpoint every day to go to work. Last week they wanted to strip search me, and I refused. Do you know, they made me wait at that checkpoint for twelve hours without food or drink or anyone knowing where I was. They were waiting for me to submit to a strip search. They finally let me go after twelve hours. The genius of the misery committee is to operate through the smallest details that then obscure the larger picture. It is amazing the way they think up ways to humiliate us and make our daily lives miserable.

Munira's envisioned "misery committee" is actually a multistranded, but fairly cohesive, set of Israeli civilian and military units wielding power over Palestinians and imposing suffering: the IDF, border police, the General Security Services (Shin Bet), the Civilian Administration, private security personnel, and over half a million Jewish colonists. The "misery committee" articulates with a description of a "state of violence that is managed according to ... [an] economy of calculation" (Weizman 2011, 3). The occupation and settler-colonialism, with its displacing imperative, craft policies and engage in actions to maximize suffering and foster an environment that cultivates violent excess and impunity. The occupation and the policy of closure are pronounced spatial expressions of bio-power that target the fabric and rhythms of daily life; the "smallest details," calculated for intent and effect, impose unpredictable delays and inflict irreparable harm, suffering, and humiliation.

The five hundred or so checkpoints strategically scattered across the landscape of Palestine, and the siege of Gaza, shed light on excess and disproportionality. In intent and effect, calculated indifference exceeds depraved indifference; however, both indicate a wanton disregard for life. Depraved indifference usually refers to the risk or danger to which indifference subjects its victims. However, calculated indifference actually creates, through quantification, the conditions of risk and danger, and mathematically anticipates harm and suffering, and their subjugating impact. "Intent" is a key term in the UN Convention on Genocide.[5] It is the *intent* to inflict excessive violence and suffering, beyond that allowed by IHL.

The "misery committee" operates in the domain of security and military technology and scientific knowledge. Janus-faced, science and technology have been mobilized to dominate, punish, and compel submission. Daily caloric in-take (DCI), along with electricity, water, and medicine, is one such sort of knowledge subject to calibration and quantification. Quantification of items necessary for life in the most elemental sense guides determinations of aid in humanitarian emergencies and provides a standard for human nutritional health and well-being. Yet food and DCI requirements have become part of military arsenals, or in the recent vernacular, weaponized. Israeli-imposed food restrictions on Gaza provide a catalogue of excessively calibrated punishment and deprivation (Gisha 2012). It is a violation of IHL to use basic goods to apply pressure on or punish a civilian population. In 2006, Dov Weisglass, an adviser to then Israeli Prime Minister Ehud Olmert, quipped in reference to the siege of Gaza, "The idea is to put the Palestinians on a diet, but not to make them die of hunger."[6] In besieged Gaza, Israeli-imposed sanctions form a craftily spun web of restrictions that keep Palestinians alive, but on a highly restricted diet. The calculation of 2,290 calories per person requires 170 daily trucks of food, but often only a third of that number have been allowed in, reducing DCI to 1,388. In other words, Palestinians are suspended in a precarious web of minutely calibrated life.

What might render a calculated reduction of the caloric in-take of a whole population to a bare minimum as a form of evil is its precise calibration in terms of quantity, signaling the intent to manufacture nutritional deprivation. Such deprivation has harmful effects on reproductive potential and child development that have well-known long-term impacts on an aggregate population. Most significantly, maintaining a population just below bare life keeps them alive but not thriving and, it is anticipated, diminishes their potential for political life. Excess and disproportionality are evident here and justified by claims that siege and assault are self-defense tactics to compel the population to disavow Hamas' leadership in Gaza and protect Israel from threat.

When Palestinians respond to the mundane inquiry, "How are you?" with "I am breathing but not alive," they speak in the register of the living dead—"breathing" but not thriving. Rather than resembling bio-politics and a clear-cut politics of life or death, the siege holds life in calibrated and precarious suspension between life and death, a state of being more aptly characterized as a remotely controlled, violently managed life. A regime that works assiduously to calculate the lives of a besieged, essentially captive population down to the minimum DCI, and inflicts debilitating injuries in the thousands by purposely shooting unarmed Palestinians protestors in the legs to maim, represents a politics of calibrated misery and excess beyond international law and ethics. Puar (2015, 2–3) argues that Israel has claimed a right to maim and debilitate Palestinian bodies and their environment (i.e., infra-structure); furthermore, she argues that this is a productive policy that is part of a rehabilitative economy. This resonates with Bauman and Donskis's seminal work on liquid evil in which "in terms of military campaigns, tends to disrupt the economy and life in certain territories or societies by bringing there as much chaos, fear, uncertainty, unsafety and insecurity as possible" (2016, 7). Israel, I would argue, sits on the cusp of evil under conditions of solid modernity, where power and the means of violence is concentrated in the state, and liquid evil, which seeps or oozes through the everyday lives of individuals under colonial occupation.

In Palestine, mobility, order, and a sense of security for one population are maintained through the imposition of a punishing immobility, anxiety-inducing unpredictability, and confinement on the other (Peteet 2017). At the large Qalandia checkpoint, which controls Palestinian movement into Jerusalem and between north and south in the West Bank, the capriciousness of control as well as petty cruelty are well established. When paramedics Nabil and Maher, on the front lines of the world of emergency medical care for over a decade, were driving an ambulance with a patient seeking cancer treatment:

> Two soldiers come to check the identity card of the patient and they made him get out of the ambulance. Luckily, it was sunny day, not too cold. I hear the older say to the younger one, "Give them their cards

and let them pass." But the young one puts them in his pocket. So we phoned the ICRC. They called the checkpoint but still this guy would not give us the identity cards. So, we waited with an ill patient for a couple of hours for no apparent reason other than this guy wants to show who is the boss.

At checkpoints, the occupation authorities determine who and what can move and at what speed; Israeli-issued permits, a laborious process to acquire, determine the scope of Palestinian mobility. Medical issues illustrate the cruel and excessive nature of the controlling apparatus of closure. Palestinian conversations are laced with stories of the ill and incapacitated trying to get through checkpoints. With the land confiscation and the building of Jewish colonies, the wall, checkpoints, the permit system, and the segregated road network, Palestinians reside in shrinking spaces resembling an archipelago of small islands or enclaves. Now patients face long and arduous trips often over bumpy back roads to reach medical facilities in towns. Many villages are served by small primary health care clinics and residents are routinely denied unimpeded and uncertain access to other larger towns. If the wall divides a town and the hospital is on other side, Palestinians may have to drive for hours through multiple checkpoints to reach a hospital that is otherwise a few miles away. There are well-over 150 documented cases of denial of access to medical care at checkpoints leading to death, including infants. Moreover, Jerusalem's six specialized hospitals are off-limits to West Bank Palestinians without a permit to enter the city. Palestinians requiring treatment in a Jerusalem medical facility must obtain a permit that requires detailing their medical condition and ascertaining that they have an appointment at a particular hospital and can only receive the appropriate treatment at that hospital.

Palestinian ambulances are not allowed to enter Jerusalem so at Qalandia, patients must be transferred to an ambulance with Israel license plates; at other checkpoints, patients must leave the ambulance and walk across crowded checkpoints with the usual lengthy waits (see "West Bank" 2011). Nabil elaborated on passing through a checkpoint in an ambulance ferrying the ill and injured:

> First, we wait, always waiting. The soldiers open the doors—front and back. They check everyone's identities, including the patient's. They look at the equipment. At Qalandia—it is hard. They delay you no matter what the condition of the patient and they call the District Coordinating Office. There is a woman there, [an Israeli] Rachel— everyone knows her. Sometime she refuses to let you pass. Once she did not let me pass because the patient, although critically injured, did not have a permit.

Soldiers, nonmedically trained, step into ambulances and check the wounded, often causing delays; they may compel patients to walk or be carried through the checkpoint to take another ambulance on the other side, or prevent access altogether. Sometimes, soldiers will declare a patient not ill enough to pass; Nabil said the "younger soldiers are the worst—the older ones are readier to let them pass. Once a young soldier asked a patient, 'How do you feel when I am searching this ambulance?' Another time at a checkpoint, a soldier told a patient traveling for treatment, 'Get your treatment somewhere else!'" and denied him passage.

It is hard to miss the cruelty, indifference, and callous disregard for Palestinian lives. In other words, willful debilitation and humiliation have become routine occurrences. Nabil related an instance, one among many he noted, when, in his opinion, someone died as a result of denial of passage at a checkpoint. The ambulance went to a checkpoint to pick up an elderly man with heart problems. "When we arrived at the checkpoint, they made us wait ten minutes. I kept telling them it was urgent. The soldier said he would check. I could see the older man across the checkpoint with a younger man supporting him. When they eventually let us cross to take him—nearly forty-five minutes later—he was dead."

Some stories circulate widely in this terrain where interventions on the Palestinian body are intimate, constantly mutating, and publicly displayed. In 2008, I heard this calamitous checkpoint story from several people; it remained remarkably consistent in the telling. Munira, the nurse who waited at the checkpoint to meet the patient, related:

> A woman in a wheel chair accompanied by a female relative arrived at Eretz checkpoint. Once the two exited the main part of the checkpoint, they reached a set of cement blocks in the road—these are about three feet high—you see them everywhere. These were arranged in parallel rows with about three feet between them. So, this woman had to rise up out of the wheel chair and hoist herself on top of the cement barrier. When she crossed to the second barrier, a couple of young men tried to help her. To gently help her down, they put their hands under her armpits. She has just had a double mastectomy—an incredibly painful surgery that included the removal of glands under the arms. She was screaming in pain. Her companion was wearing a long dress. When she went to cross the double barrier, she slipped and fell between the two cement blocks. She panicked—she was stuck—like a turtle on its back that cannot turn over. The Eretz checkpoint is a masterpiece of what I call the "misery committee"! They are so cruel. Can you imagine making someone in her condition go through this?

Such stories embody themes of pain, suffering, empathy, and the pragmatics of daily life under settler-colonial siege conditions.

In a protracted settler-colonial setting, the local civilian population faces frequent exposure to stressful situations. Home itself is a battle front subject to military incursion. House demolition is a prime example. Between 1967 and 2012, over twenty-eight thousand Palestinian structures were demolished (Schaeffer and Halpern 2012, 1). Body counts and home demolitions graphically express how violence dramatically suffuses ordinary life, but it is also the unquantifiable quotidian, seemingly mundane details of every day existence, particularly chronic humiliating encounters, that are unnecessarily excessive and incredibly stressful as well (Barber et al. 2013).

Colonial endeavors and their privileging projects prompt questions about subjectivity and what it means to be a human in face of overwhelming control over daily life's contours, temporal rhythms, and spatial parameters. Arwa, a young employee with a local NGO, dreads checkpoints.

> I have a feeling of panic as I approach them as though I can't breathe and all my muscles tense up. . . . I feel a loss of control, a complete loss of control. I feel as if I am not a human being. I am without dignity or respect—as though I am a big bug, as if I am stripped of human existence. Once I am out of the checkpoint, I relax. I feel physically different.

The anxious anticipation of the impending encounter, then the liminal state of being temporarily "stripped" of human status, followed by a state of relaxation conforms loosely to the elements of a rite of passage although there is no celebration of a new status, simply passage from one space to another. My neighbor, middle-aged Sami, occasionally requests a permit to visit relatives in Jerusalem, just ten kilometers away, and pray at the Church of the Holy Sepulcher: "I am so humiliated by the process of asking for a permit." Relating his experiences once at the checkpoint, he said: "I felt so humiliated. I hold up my permit to the plexi-glass window and this eighteen-year-old bitch flicks her wrist at me to go as if I am a fly, as if I am nothing. I waited so long for a permit that she barely glanced at."

One detects a self positioned in a sub-human zoomorphic zone. These sentiments, reflections, and analyses by Nabil, Munira, and Sami reference a heightened awareness of subjugating structures; their engagement in constant critical analyses underscores being inside and outside simultaneously. Palestinians experience and observe others being subjected to cruel and petty indignities as well as violence. This double positioning situates Palestinians in a complex range of subject positions in a vortex of excessive, humiliating, and debilitating control: observers and participants, performing subjugation while witnessing and remaining critical commentators and analysts.

Visibility, the Spectacle, and Entertainment

Selma, a Bir Zeit University student, elaborated upon being compelled to watch the subjugation of others and her feelings of helplessness and empathy:

> I hate it when I see someone treated badly. Once at Qalandia there were many people—one soldier ordered: "Line up one by one." There was a line for men and a line for women. There was a young man—twenty-one or twenty-two years old. When he did not respond quickly enough, this soldier runs up, grabs him, throws him to the ground, and starts kicking him. Imagine this! I hate these things. I don't like to see them happen to others.

This section engages with the spectacle that compels Palestinian visibility and draws audiences for gratuitous acts of humiliation and violence as entertainment, the "education" of Palestinians, and their disciplining and punishment. The war in Gaza and Israeli checkpoints illuminate the entanglement of evil with spectacle. There are two immediate, on-the-ground interpretive audiences to Palestinian visuality and the spectacle: Israelis and other Palestinians. For both, they reiterate and reaffirm the occupiers' sense of control and domination, compel subordination, and provide examples of punishment and lessons in appropriate behavior. Participation in spectacles as an audience can be compelled, as when simply being there is to witness cruelty as Selma did, or voluntarily, as when Israelis set up viewing areas to watch Palestinians in Gaza being pummeled by Israeli military forces. In both instances, destruction and pain became spectacle. During Israel's Operation Cast Lead targeting Gaza in summer 2014, residents of the nearby Israeli town of Sderot were gathering with plastic chairs, sofas, hookahs, and soft drinks, beer, and popcorn to view the bombardment and carnage. Unparalleled air power, and a severely lop-sided military capacity, resulting in over two thousand Palestinian deaths, allowed for this sort of proximate viewing. The "Sderot cinema," or reality theater, imparted a festive atmosphere to the war as spectators cheered the military as the bombs fell on Gaza. The gaze is on the victims, whether in Gaza or on Iraqi prisoners in Abu Ghraib. In the photos of the latter, or from the view in Sderot, they are seen rather than seeing. The camera is replaced by the live eye watching what, for viewers, is an entertaining spectacle. In this case, the evil resides in the enjoyment of the infliction of daily death, pain, destruction, and humiliation as entertainment.[7] The pain of others as entertainment meshes the pervasiveness and passion for reality TV with an unfolding in real time, on-the-ground, and proximate macabre of extreme violence and suffering. The evil examined here does not cohere well with Arendt's classic "banality of evil" where the perpetrator is a "cog" in a bureaucratic wheel. What is striking here is the suffusion of evil into the most mundane aspects of life and its calibration and yet its improvisation and a willfulness that flourish in an atmosphere of entertainment and unaccountability and impunity from social or legal censure.

Photography can be a means of regarding "other people's pain" at a distance (Sontag 2003, 13). In Sderot, military superiority allowed Israelis to watch and revel in the pain of others. With front-row seats, this was a low-tech visualization. Whereas war photographs, from Spain's brutal civil war to the devastation in Vietnam for example, were meant to inspire horror at war and empathy with victims, the view from Sderot was entertainment and the atmosphere celebratory.

A few words are in order about Sderot. In 2014, it was much in the news because of the numerous rockets launched at it from Gaza. Crudely fashioned from materials smuggled through tunnels and unguided, these rockets cause few casualties. Seldom mentioned in this extensive media coverage is Sderot's history (and that of other Israeli settlements in the area around Gaza) and upon what it is built. Established in 1951 on the land of the Palestinian village Najd (Khalidi 1992, 128), its inhabitants were expelled by the Palmach Negev Brigade on 13 May 1948 (Morris 1987, 128); the villagers and their descendants remain refugees in Gaza. The Israeli colonists who took over the village lands were largely poor North African and Arab Jews. Sderot/Najd's (in Arabic: elevated area) hilltop provided a panoramic view of the assault on the refugees, most of whom are from villages in the area. Over sixty years after expulsion from the area, the pain and suffering of these refugees and their descendants were a source of entertainment for the colonists and their descendants who replaced the former. Separated by decades, they remain irrevocably linked in a chain of cruel displacement and continuing attacks. Evil in this instance is a long-drawn out and continuing process punctuated by outbursts of horrific violence to keep Palestinians, whose very existence disrupts the Zionist narrative of a right to Palestine, at bay.

Checkpoints constitute another encounter space where visibility and the spectacle unfold. Checkpoints ensure that Palestinians are visible to the state's surveillance apparatus. They impart daily physicality to heterophobia and the impulse to separate, as does the separation wall built deep into the West Bank and the segregated road network crisscrossing the occupied West Bank. An Israeli narrative casts checkpoints as security measures to deter violence by monitoring, managing, and blocking Palestinian movement. Microcosms of the colonial constellation of power, these ritualized encounter-spaces are one of the principal spaces and moments of Palestinian-Israeli interaction where the Palestinian body is ordered and slowed, surveyed, interrogated, tracked, and disciplined. At checkpoints, lessons in subordination are imparted and subjectivity takes shape. Most significantly, the boundaries of the body are violated as the Palestinian is subject to scrutiny and visualization and can at any moment be stripped, exposed, humiliated, physically abused, and detained. In these small confined spaces, it is an intimate encounter. Each reads the other for signs: one seeks to detect signs of the military/police/private security's daily orders and individual mood, all subject to frequent change, the other to detect risk. Israeli soldiers' attribution to Palestinians of an inner state of a potential violence animates their constant search for its signs. Overall, checkpoints accomplish two things: they organize and display the spectacular nature of occupation, closure, and domination and they screen, filter, and funnel Palestinian mobility, exercising control over its scope and speed. Soldiers' own military training and discipline are replicated in their treatment of Palestinians when they refer to them as the "youngsters of the youngsters" (Ben Ari et. al. 2005, 31) or aim to "educate" them and "teach them a lesson" (Grassiani 2009). An ethnography of Israeli soldiers reaffirms conceptualizations of checkpoints as punitive and didactic mechanisms where, as soldiers say, they mete out "corrective punishment" to make sure the Palestinians know "who is in charge" and where they are "taught a lesson" (Grassiani 2009, 126). These lessons are public, as evident in this recollection by an elderly Palestinian woman of passage at a large checkpoint:

> Once, there was a little girl and the Israeli soldier wanted her to take her clothes off—she was a little girl—about five or six years old. She would not take them off. She started crying and screaming and so on. She made her take off her clothes and stay waiting until all the people after her in the line finished, and then she told her to go. It was like a punishment for the little girl. She made her stand naked while she examined all the other people. Everyone saw the little girl but they could not say

anything. They do what they want to do. Nobody tells them not to. You see, there is nobody to stop them. They are without any feelings, any feelings for other people.

At checkpoints, little is hidden from sight as people observe and hear what happens to those around them. Checkpoints can compel publicly repetitive, often intimate, gendered performances of hierarchy in which Palestinians are both actor and audience. Randa's description of passage at Gaza's Eretz checkpoint highlights the combination of sophisticated technology with harassment and a gendered, voyeuristic field of view:

> Eretz checkpoint is the worst, and it is the most technologically advanced. They use a scanning machine that sees through clothes, so it is a problem for women. You are in this machine but there is no person—you have no contact with another human being. Suddenly, a voice will shout from above, "That bra you are wearing—does it have underwire?" This is so humiliating! Most women, including myself, are terrified of this sort of bodily invasion.

This sort of dehumanizing spectacle reiterates an ethnicized sociospatial order and the power of visualization with gendered contours. Sometimes gender is built into the physical structure. For example, some checkpoints initially had separate lines for women and men, making for a different experience—women's lines moved faster and involved less waiting and intensive searches. Sometimes the category is further broken down, as in the following encounter in which ideal types of feminine beauty were overlaid with racialized aesthetics. Over lunch with Lana, a science professor at Palestine's Bir Zeit University, she related the following story about nearby Surda checkpoint:

> I use to go through it every day, twice a day, coming and going from the University. Once the soldiers asked us women to form two lines—one line for ugly women and one line for pretty women. We were stunned and of course outraged. This was too much and so insulting. There was a woman who was confused by this order. She stood in the "pretty line." The soldier shouted at her: "Go to the ugly line!"

These spectacles of subordination and hierarchy infantilize and humiliate to the point of despair. Sami complained bitterly about the young female soldier who humiliated him at a checkpoint: "Who is she to treat me this way—making me stand there like a child!?" I ran into a visibly agitated Jumana, a university student, on the street. She had just visited her distraught father and related this story: "My father was with his friend—these are men in their fifties. They forced my father's friend to take off his pants and shirt and go through the checkpoint in his underwear. He pleaded with them, but they insisted that he remove his clothes; he is a bit overweight and was so embarrassed. My father came home and cried!" Lana had witnessed a similar episode on her way to the University:

> In line at Surda checkpoint, I see one of my male graduate students. The soldiers stopped him and ordered him to remove his clothing down to his underwear. Everyone watched in horror as this scene unfolded. I was still in line when he turned and saw me. He could not look me in the eye until nearly the end of the semester. This was terribly humiliating for him and for me.

Forced undressing in public, with others compelled to watch by virtue of being there, is not infrequent and stories circulated in both hushed tones and with a sense of moral outrage. Whatever the tone, in making public an intimate, private act, or in impromptu dividing by the imposed categories of ugly and pretty, the meaning is the same: assaults on cultural notions of self and propriety and the gendered social order and, most of all, on one's dignity. These quotidian disciplinary routines, reiterating defeat, humiliation, and powerlessness, may be designed to produce a gendered subject of compliance.

Expulsion and Abandonment

With Israeli settlers ensconced in their colonies, linked to each other and Israel by the segregated road system, and Palestinians sequestered behind the wall, the latter are visible at a distance to most Israelis. With colonies built on high ground, they loom over Palestinian villages that they can keep under surveillance. In other words, Palestinians are simultaneously visible and yet out-of-proximity. Aisha, an engaging young woman with three small children, and I struck up a conversation while waiting several hours at a checkpoint. We sat on the hard ground in the cold and wind as she tried to calm her restless and increasingly hungry children. With measured deliberation, she explained: "Closure is not about security. It is about numbers—of them and us. They are going to lock us in these walled prisons and then they will not care how many children we have. We will be behind walls and left to our own devices. Nobody will care what becomes of us." Zionism is a form of settler-colonialism in which land and water resources are expropriated for the exclusive use of the colonial population, and the indigenous are slated for removal and replacement, or at the least, containment rather than incorporation as a labor force. In this vision of an exclusivist Jewish state, there is no ideological imperative to bring the colonized into the Zionist ideological orbit. Indeed, it is this specifically predatory and displacing political economy that distinguishes Zionism as a form of settler-colonialism.

When and under what conditions does disposability occur, and what are the processes that expel people from social order? The historical record is full of disposable people and spaces of exclusion and abandonment, with varying degrees of distance, penetrability, and fixity, including asylums, refugee camps, detention centers, prisons, reservations, concentration camps, and so on. We live in an era where surplus people proliferate and, through "elementary brutalities" (Harvey 2005; Sassen 2014), are consigned to the sociospatial margins. Minimal protection and vulnerabilities suffuse these spaces of expulsion and abandonment whether refugee camps, enclaves (Peteet 2016c), or prisons. Here, abandonment is conceptualized as excision from the sociospatial order. However, for those under occupation, it unfolds in the space of home. With Palestinians confined to shrinking enclaves carved out by the closure's mechanisms, the question of responsibility looms large. Israel absolves itself of its responsibility by rejecting the classification of their rule as an occupation, and argues instead that the Palestinian Authority and the international donor community should bear responsibility for the local population.

What are the early warning signs of abandonment? What policies, actions, discursive formations, and ideologies are its precursors? Confinement is suggestive of bare life, as are refugee rations and talk of putting Palestinians on a diet. Disposability and abandonment are operative at checkpoints when women have been compelled to give birth and ambulances with critically ill patients are kept waiting or when soldiers or private security guards confiscate groceries from Palestinians, telling them they are not allowed to carry that much food. The nonrecognition of their physical presence, rights, or humanity and yet the hyper-vigilance over their movements captures the paradox of abandonment and excessive cruelty with an elaborate set of mechanisms to survey and control.

More recently, key policies of the new congressional "Israel Victory Caucus," launched on 27 April 2017 and cochaired by Rep. Bill Johnson (R-OH) and Rep. Ron DeSantis (R-FL), include an end to US funding of the Palestinian Authority and UNRWA, the agency that has provided assistance (rations, healthcare, education, and emergency assistance) and employment to thousands of Palestinian refugees since the early 1950s. As anticipated, the US did cut its contribution to UNRWA from $364 million in 2017 to $60 million in 2018. Speaking at the Caucus's first meeting, Daniel Pipes, head of the Middle East Forum and well-known anti-Muslim extremist, argued that Israel should "convince the Palestinians that they have lost." "Victory means imposing your will on your enemy so that he no longer wants to fight, and I think that's the essence here," Pipes said. He then added, "Winning doesn't mean slaughtering your enemy, but it means imposing your will on your enemy." It also appears to mean depriving an already besieged community of healthcare, education, and emergency assistance and demanding complete acquiescence to the US–Israel agenda (Deger 2017). It is the intentional, calculated infliction of suffering and pain in order to immiserate, debilitate, and subjugate, with the anticipated consequence of a victory that promises access to and dominion over Palestinian resources, that permits an assessment of this behavior as evil.

In Joao Biehl's poignant ethnography of Vita, a Brazilian site housing the mentally ill, the drug addicted, and sufferers of AIDs, an informant described it as a "dump site of human beings" (2005, 1). Biehl describes it as "the end-station . . . where people go when they are no longer considered people" (2005, 1). Does denying the rights of a fully human status to those designated as outside the social order constitute a form of evil? In spaces of abandonment, inhabitants lose some of their human status; Biehl writes of the "ex-human" and the "social death" that precedes "biological death" (2005, 52). The "term 'ex-human' helped me to make relative the claims of a generic humanness and to think about the contingency and pervasiveness of the forms of human life I found in Vita."

In a settler-colonial setting, abandonment crystallizes as a sort of collateral damage. Rather than points on a spectrum of more of one and less of the other, discipline, control, and abandonment are triangulated. Humanness exists on a gradient with some lives highly authorized, with a full complement of rights, with others relegated to the margins. A cable from the US Embassy in Tel Aviv succinctly summarized calibrated abandonment: "Israel officials have confirmed . . . on multiple occasions that they intend to keep the Gazan economy on the brink of collapse without quite pushing it over the edge" (quoted in Khalili 2013, 183). Palestinians hover at the margins of abandonment, on "a diet" but not completely "over the edge." Theirs are managed and calibrated lives of misery, wobbling precariously on the remotely controlled, quantified, and calibrated cusp of life and death.

Conclusion

Fuzziness and indeterminancy undergird evil's wide latitude of meaning. In Palestine/Israel, an assemblage of petty, day-to-day, routine acts of microaggressions, tremendous physical violence, severe restrictions on mobility, and humiliation, in all their constancy, constitute predictable evil. What we can say for sure is that attributions of evil, that inscrutable concept, are easily cast and allocated differently. Once located primarily in the realm of religion, evil's more secularized presence (albeit with undertones of religion) has a solid presence in political discourse and popular media.

Attributions of evil, murky at best—designed to appeal to the lowest possible base—depoliticize and dehistoricize conflicts and injustices. The clearest example of this may be Iran, which for several decades has been cast as evil incarnate. Evil is present in another realm, that of the US military in Iraq and Afghanistan and in the Israeli colonial occupation. Attributions of evil are integral to the "moral panic" that has characterized Israeli attitudes toward Iran (Ram 2009) and Palestinians. Perhaps evil is excesses for which we have yet to develop a lexicon appropriate to the ever-mutating forms of violence that characterize the current era. Evil may be a default category for the unfathomable, the irrational, and the unnecessary acts of cruelty that violate international law and human sensibilities. Most significantly, with calibration relying on science and technology, evil includes and relies on the "lesser evils" discourse and logic that are now thoroughly operationalized as part of conducting war and counterinsurgency and maintaining an occupied population in a state of prolonged subjugation.

The excess generated by the irrepressible desire for Palestinian land and water resources, for expansion and domination by a powerful state that insists on separation from its environs and its right to inflict extreme as well as "lesser" forms of violence to maintain power seems to belong to the realm of evil. This is hardly the evil of the magical realm of the supernatural or the religious. Indeed, it is the very stuff of the modern project of colonial dominance and subjugation. Let us hope that Bauman and Donskis are prescient when they opine that optimism "is a belief that evil is transitory and does not vanquish humanness . . . [it] means that hope and alternatives do indeed always exist."

Julie Peteet, University of Louisville

Notes

1. See Lambek (2010) for an in-depth discussion of ordinary ethics.
2. In the Hebrew–Israeli tradition, the Amalekites are historic enemies of the Jews, followed by the Crusaders, the Spanish Inquisition, and Nazi Germany. Reference to the Amalekites invokes an "existential threat'" and has become popularly associated with Arabs and Muslims. When asked to gauge PM Benjamin Netanyahu's anxiety about Iran, one of his advisors replied: "Think Amalek" (Goldberg 2009, 14).
3. Launched in the mid-1990s, closure is a policy designed to seal off the occupied West Bank and Gaza through measures such as the twenty-four-foot high cement wall snaking deeply into the West Bank and the fence around Gaza, and the five hundred plus checkpoints and the permit system that control Palestinian mobility. Closure forbids Palestinian entrance to Jerusalem and Israel without a permit. Most significantly, it severely regulates mobility between Gaza and the West Bank and within the West Bank itself.
4. Or Kashti, 2014, *Haaretz*, 22 July.
5. The United Nations Convention on the Prevention and Punishment of the Crime of Genocide, adopted on 9 December 1948, lists a series of actions that constitute genocide if they are "committed with intent to destroy, in whole or in part, a national, ethnic, racial or religious group . . . ."
6. The 'diet' was supposed to dry up support for Hamas. (Urquhart 2006.) Allegedly stated in a private meeting, Weisglass denied making the statement. "The political sources who took part in the meeting quoted Weisglass: 'We must cause the Palestinians to become thinner, but not die'" (Sofer 2006). Israeli has reportedly "relied on mathematic formulas which computed minimum nutritional requirements . . . . Based on these formulas, the state determined the amount and volume of goods that were permitted to enter the Strip" (Hass 2011).
7. Other such instances include the photos of Iraqi prisoners in Abu Ghraib that circulated as war mementos but also as a form of entertainment; they remind of the early twentieth-century postcards of the lynchings of African Americans sent to friends and family.

References

Alexander, Michelle. 2012. *The New Jim Crow: Mass Incarceration in the Age of Color Blindness*. New York: The New Press.

Amnesty International UK. 2018. "Why Palestinians risk their lives for their rights." 16 May 2018. Retrieved 20 May 2018 from www.amnesty.org.uk/blogs/ether/why-palestinians-risk-their-lives-their-rights.

Arendt, Hannah. 1963. *Eichmann in Jerusalem*. New York: The Viking Press.

Asad, Talal. 2007. *On Suicide Bombing.* New York: Columbia University Press.
Atwan, Abdel Bari. 2015. *Islamic State. The Digital Caliphate.* Berkeley: University of California Press.
Barber, Brian, Clea McNeely, Joseph Olsen, Carolyn Spellings, and Robert Belli. 2013. "Effect of Chronic Exposure to Humiliation on Wellbeing in the Occupied Palestinian Territory: An Event-History Analysis." *The Lancet* 382, special issue S7 (December 5).
Bauman, Zygmunt, and Leonidas Donskis. 2016. *Liquid Evil: Living with TINA.* Cambridge, MA: Polity Press.
Ben Ari, Eyal, Meirave Maymon, Nir Gazit, and Ron Shatzberg. 2005. *From Checkpoints to Flowpoints: Sites of Friction between the Israel Defense Forces and Palestinians.* Jerusalem: Harry S. Truman Research Institute for the Advancement of Peace, Hebrew University.
Biehl, Joao. 2005. *Vita: Life in a Social Zone of Abandonment.* Berkeley: University of California Press.
Burg, Avraham. 2008. *The Holocaust Is Over, We Must Rise from the Ashes.* New York: St. Martin's Press.
Butler, Judith. 1997. *Excitable Speech: A Politics of the Performative.* New York: Routledge.
Caton, Steven. 2010. "Abu Ghraib and the Problem of Evil" In *Ordinary Ethics. Anthropology, Language, and Action.* Edited by Michael Lambek, 165–84. New York: Fordham University Press.
Deger, Allison. 2017. "A Republican Plan for Peacekeeping: 'Break the Will' of the Palestinians and Force them to 'Accept Defeat.'" *Mondoweiss.* 8 May. Retrieved 20 July 2018 from http://mondoweiss.net/2017/05/republican-palestinians-defeat/.
Erekat, Noura. 2014. "Five Israeli Talking Points on Gaza – Debunked." *The Nation.* Retrieved 15 December 2016 from http://www.thenation.com/article/180783/five-israeli-talking-points-gaza-debunked.
Feldman, Allen. 2014. "Genocidal Desistance in Gaza." *Social Text* (ST Collective). Retrieved 26 May 2017 from https://socialtextjournal.org/genocidal-desistance-in-gaza/.
Gisha. 2012. "Reader. Food Consumption in the Gaza Strip – Red Lines." Tel Aviv-Jaffa: Gisha.
Legal Center for Freedom of Movement. Retrieved 26 November 2018 from http://www.gisha.org/UserFiles/File/publications/redlines/redlines-position-paper-eng.pdf.
Goldberg, Jeffrey. 2009. "Israel's Fear, Amalek's Arsenal." *New York Times.* 16 May. Retrieved 26 May 2018 from http://www.nytimes.com/2009/05/17/opinion/17goldberg.html?_r=0.
Grassiani, Erella. 2009. "Soldiering under Occupation: Processes of Moral Numbing among Israeli Conscripts during the Al-Aksa Intifada." PhD dissertation, University of Amsterdam.
Harvey, David. 2005. *A Brief History of Neoliberalism.* New York: Oxford University Press.

Hass, Amira. 2011. "Defense Ministry Ordered to Release Internal Documents on Gaza Policies." *Haaretz*. 30 March. Retrieved 26 May 2017 from https://www.haaretz.com/1.5143999.

Hinton, Alexander. 2002. "Introduction: Anthropology and Genocide" In *Genocide: An Anthropological Reader*. Edited by A. Hinton. Malden, MA: Blackwell Publishers.

Khalidi, Walid. 1992. *All That Remains: The Palestinian Villages Occupied and Depopulated by Israel in 1948*. Washington, DC: Institute for Palestine Studies.

Khalili, Laleh. 2013. *Time in the Shadows: Confinement in Counterinsurgencies*. Palo Alto, CA: Stanford University Press.

Lambek, Michael, ed. 2010. *Ordinary Ethics: Anthropology, Language, and Action*. New York: Fordham University Press.

Lazaroff, Tovah. 2018. "'There are no innocents in Gaza,' says Israeli Defense Minister." *The Jerusalem Post*. April 8. Retrieved 26 November 2018 from https://www.jpost.com/Arab-Israeli-Conflict/There-are-no-innocents-in-Gaza-says-Israeli-defense-minister-549173.

Luntz, Frank. 2009. *The Israel Project's 2009 Global Language Dictionary*. Washington, DC: The Israel Project.

Makdisi, Saree. 2018. "The bare facts about the Gaza demonstrators are correct, but the rest of the story is missing." *Los Angeles Times*. April 6. Retrieved 26 May 2018 from http://www.latimes.com/opinion/op-ed/la-oe-makdisi-media-palestinian-gaza-massacre-20180406-story.html.

Malinowski, Bronislaw. 2002 [1935]. *Malinowski: Collected Works. Vol. VII: Coral Gardens and Their Magic. Part One*. London: Routledge.

Morris, Benny. 1987. *The Birth of the Palestinian Refugee Problem, 1947–1949*. Cambridge, UK: Cambridge University Press.

"'Mothers of all Palestinians Should Also Be Killed,' Says Israeli Politician." 2014. *Daily Sabah*. 14 July. Retrieved 26 May 2018 from http://www.dailysabah.com/mideast/2014/07/14/mothers-of-all-palestinians-should-also-be-killed-says-israeli-politician.

Parkin, David, ed. 1985. *The Anthropology of Evil*. New York: Basil Blackwell Inc.

Peteet, Julie. 2016a. "The Work of Comparison: Israel/Palestine and Apartheid." *Anthropological Quarterly* 89(1): 225–60.

———. 2016b. "Language Matters." *Journal of Palestine Studies* XLV(2): 1–17.

———. 2016c. "Camps and Enclaves: Palestine in the Time of Closure." *Journal of Refugee Studies* 29(2): 208–28. DOI: 10.1093/jrs/fevo14.

———. 2017. *Space and Mobility in Palestine*. Bloomington: University of Indiana Press.

Puar, Jasbir. 2015. "The 'Right' to Maim: Dismemberment and Inhumanist Biopolitics in Palestine." *borderlands* 14(1): 1–27.

———. 2017. *The Right to Maim: Debility, Capacity and Disability*. Durham, NC: Duke University Press.

Ram, Haggai. 2009. *Iranophobia: The Logic of an Israeli Obsession*. Palo Alto, CA: Stanford University Press.

Sassen, Saskia. 2014. *Expulsions: Brutality and Complexity in the Global Economy*. Cambridge, MA: Harvard University Press.

Schaeffer, Emily, and Jeff Halper. 2012. "Israel's Policy of Demolishing Palestinian Homes Must End: A Submission to the UN Human Rights Council by the Israeli Committee Against House Demolitions (ICHAD)." Retrieved 26 May 2018 from http://www.icahd.org/node/458#sthash.ILp3bvKk.dpuf.

Sofer, Ronny. 2006. "Hamas Sworn In: Israel to Cut Off Funds." *Y Net News*. 15 February. Retrieved 26 May 2016 from http://www.ynetnews.com/articles/0,7340,L-3216790,00.html.

Sontag, Susan. 2003. *Regarding the Pain of Others*. New York: Farrar, Straus and Giroux.

Urquhart, Conel. 2006. "Gaza on the Brink of Implosion as Aid Cut-off Starts to Bite." *The Observer*. 15 April. Retrieved 26 May 2018 from http://www.guardian.co.uk/world/2006/apr/16/israel.

Weizman, Eyal. 2011. *The Least of All Possible Evils: Humanitarian Violence from Arendt to Gaza*. London: Verso Press.

"West Bank Movement and Access Update." 2011. Special Focus August 2011 OCHA. United Nations Office for the Coordination of Humanitarian Affairs in the occupied Palestinian Territory. Retrieved 26 May 2018 from http://unispal.un.org/UNISPAL.NSF/0.

Winer, Stuart. 2014. "Netanyahu: Hamas Wants 'Telegenically Dead Palestinians.'" *The Times of Israel*. 20 July. Retrieved 26 May 2018 from http://www.timesofisrael.com/netanyahu-hamas-wants-telegenically-dead-palestinians/.

Chapter 10

THE VIOLENCE OF EVIL

A BIOCULTURAL APPROACH TO VIOLENCE, MEMORY, AND PAIN

Ventura R. Pérez

States like these and their terrorist allies constitute an axis of evil, arming to threaten the peace of the world.
—George W. Bush (29 January 2002)

Abdul-Rahman was taken from us in an act of pure evil by a terrorist group that the world rightly associates with inhumanity.
—Barack Obama (16 November 2014)

He brutally murdered more than 50 people, and wounded hundreds more. It was an act of pure evil.
—Donald J. Trump (2 October 2017)

There are moments that define you, that force you to bring into focus the fears of life—like standing and staring into the abyss. This chapter and this book were that moment for me. Writing this chapter required me to consider the concept of evil as a human reality from the perspective of a scientist. I have seen things in my work that continue to shadow me every single day. I study violence from the micro level to the macro level with the body as my canvas. The moments of instant rage or a lifetime of suffering are captured on this fleeting vessel that carries our conscience through our earthly existence. Identifying these physiological markers of violence is not complicated, but relating the story behind them is. This is further complicated when we attribute the violence to the acts of evil men and women.

The concept of evil has been well studied by theologians and philosophers, so why would a biocultural anthropologist who was trained as a bioarchaeologist want to take on the concept of evil as an ideological construction of a moral imperative? In part, it is because the field of bioarchaeology (the study of human remains in an archaeological context) has been undertheorized for years. It was a descriptive discipline simply documenting the presence or absence of pathologies and creating biohistories (age at death, health, sex, stature, etc.) with no real interest in social theory. The use of social theory and violence theory, particularly in bioarchaeology, has become increasing more popular (Martin and Harrod 2015; Martin, Harrod, and Pérez 2012; Pérez 2012; Pérez, Nelson, and Martin 2008; Klaus 2012; Agarwal and Glencross 2011; Sofaer 2006; Walker 2001). However, too often, violence theory is used as an adjective to describe a *type* of violence rather than as a mechanism for exploring the concept of violence that is bound to the place and time of a specific event. Ideas like genocide, structural violence, symbolic violence, and cultural violence are tacitly used to identify anomalies in the archaeological past and the ethnographic present, such as trauma or health disparities. Too often, bioarchaeologists and archaeologists rush to infuse violence theory into their work without understanding the nexus of these social theories. Reading Johan Galtung (1969) and citing Paul Farmer (2004) falls woefully short of understanding structural violence as a mechanism for deciphering trauma pattern recognition, disease distributions within a population, or maternal mortality rates. Klaus cautioned "careful and critical use of structural violence in bioarchaeological analysis" (2012, 35).

In recent years, I have begun to critique the use of violence theory in bioarchaeology (see Pérez 2016). I do not mean "critique" in the sense of passing judgment or criticizing, but, rather, to embrace the Ancient Greek κριτική (kritikē), meaning to cut, rift, separate, discriminate, or decide (Hanssen 2000). Thus, my goal is to critique the use of violence theory as it applies to bioarchaeology through exploring the poetics of violence. By this, I mean the logic of violence and its reproductive characteristics as they relate to a specific time and place. "Critique invariably involves rigorous legislation of the field over which it holds court, the setting up of a tribunal but also vigilant border patrol" (Hanssen 2000, 4).

This chapter both explores the concept of evil as an obscuring mechanism to acts of violence and contrasts that to the necessity of recognizing and situating the use of violence within often-contested conceptual borders like force and power (which are almost always imbedded in regulated feedback systems) (Hanssen 2000). It also challenges the idea that evil makes sense of senseless acts. Evil is used as the explanatory model for the unexplainable because the scale of the horror is beyond our comprehension. Yet, is it a useful concept to explain acts of violence? Should we rely on an explanatory model that is often seen as having its origin in nonhuman forces such as the devil, Satan, or Mephistopheles (Staub 1999)? To label violence as evil obstructs human reasoning and responsibility by creating a good–bad binary that expunges us from the responsibility of the actions. Bad things are done by bad people because they are evil.

Much of the work I do is profoundly disturbing and is often seen as an episodic event carried out by sociopaths who are often deemed evil. The problem with this is that the concept of evil, when held up for examination, offers no explanation at all for acts of violence being committed. My work is an effort to problematize and challenge prominent discourses on violence by using a transtemporal analysis of performative violence. This work is a multiscalar investigation of violence using the body as a starting point while considering treatment of corpses and the materiality of death as it operates as a kind of unconscious historiography of a perceived brutality of the social experience. The meaning associated with the corpse has a great deal to do with the condition in which and location at which it is found (Verdery 1999). If the goal is creating what Taussig (1984) has appropriately termed a "culture of terror," then mutilation, destruction, and/or disappearance of this powerful symbol are effective mechanisms in achieving the desired effect. Central to the understanding of how and why acts of violence are committed is the notion that acts of violence can be manifestations of cultural performances or spectacles.

Biocultural Approaches to the Study of Violence

Violence is a key feature in human interactions. Its presence has a long and profoundly complicated history with our species (Bocquentin and Bar-Yosef 2004; Kelly 2000; Martin and Harrod 2015; Schmidt and Schröder 2001). It has been discussed in terms of our evolutionary make up (Ahlström and Molnar 2012; Wrangham and Glowackie 2012), as an extension of primate aggression. I see this as problematic in that violence is culturally specific. It is maintained through linguistic, cultural, psychological, political, economic, and social forces, whereas aggression is not bound to these parameters. As Knauft (1991) noted, "This raises an important larger question: what is the overall trajectory of violence and sociality in human evolution?" This is a question that I cannot answer now considering the size limitation of this chapter. Primate aggression and the study of evolutionary genetics has a place in informing a conversation on violence, but it is not interchangeable with, nor does it drive the concept of, human violence. Rather, aggression and violence should be seen as a construct of a layered discourse from the molecular to the metaphysical (Stewart and Strathern 2002).

Throughout human history, periods of relative peace have been marred by eruptions of interpersonal or institutional violence. A biocultural approach to analysis of human remains offers an extremely useful method to the classification and interpretation of traumatic injuries that are often indicative of conflict and violence. Bioarchaeology, when done through the lens of a biocultural paradigm, accomplishes this by bridging the chasm between biology and the social and environmental dimensions of the populations being engaged. When interpreting skeletal evidence of violent trauma, the challenge lies in trying to decipher the complexity, variability, and ambiguities of the total picture of the population's mortuary behavior and its relationship to abandonment, migration, conflict, resource scarcity, ethnic identity, settlement patterns, and other factors that could lead to the social conditions necessary for violence and warfare to occur.

Human Remains: A Biohistory of Past Populations

Skeletal tissue represents unswerving confirmation of the biohistory of past populations (Sofaer 2006; Geller 2009; Agarwal and Glencross 2011). Advances in understanding taphonomic processes have helped illuminate both the subtle alterations that can occur on human skeletal remains and their meanings. The complexities surrounding the reconstruction of past lifeways of archaeological skeletal material is often exasperated by the confusion that can arise in determining the cause of skeletal changes. Recent advances in bioarchaeology and taphonomic and forensic sciences have added a significant level of required precision in the evaluation of data used in drawing inferences regarding human behavior from skeletal material (Martin and Frayer 1997; Larsen 2001; Walker 2001; Wedel and Galloway 2013; Martin and Anderson 2014).

Over the past thirty years, the analysis of human skeletal remains from archaeological sites has shifted from a solely descriptive endeavor to a scientific subfield that embraces hypothesis testing in the context of anthropological archaeology (Sofaer 2006; Geller 2009; Agarwal and Glencross 2011; Martin, Harrod, and Pérez 2013). The difference between skeletal analysis and bioarchaeology is that the latter employs an interdisciplinary and cross-cultural research tool that can aid in the analysis of a wide range of data on violence. The goal of bioarchaeology is to interpret the biological data in relationship to social and ecological contexts such as changes in diet, increases in population size and density, shifts in power and stratification, and differential access to resources.

The Effects of Violence on the Body

Illness and death are the end result of an accumulated set of biological, behavioral, and cultural processes, so it makes sense that to understand how people come to be infirmed or to die will be a complex linking of an interrelated set of variables. Age, sex, clan, occupation, marital status, political affiliation, socioeconomic status, and access to social support, health care, resources, and power compose a constellation of interacting factors that temper and affect how dangerous or deadly acts of violence are. The mortuary component of an archaeological site provides an abundance of data, but the interpretation of that data is an arduous task. From the "where, how, and why" of corpse treatment, a range of culturally appropriate activities may take place. Human bodies can be buried, left unburied, reburied, displayed, hidden, sacrificed, articulated, disarticulated, defleshed, dismembered, painted with ochre, hung from rafters, stored in containers, and utilized in ceremonies.

Because we were not there, all our reconstructions of illness, dying, and death are "third party interpretations." Mummendey and Otten (1993) have noted that third party interpretations of violence are almost impossible to make without knowing the mindsets of the perpetrators and the victims. Violence has specific and often unique cultural meanings associated with it and should never be reduced to its physicality when trying to understand its use (Scheper-Hughes and Bourgois 2004). This is because violent acts often exemplify intricate social and cultural dimensions and are frequently defined by these same social contexts. Disease and death are never random in a population. The distribution of nongenetic diseases are almost always an outcome of inequalities among members of a group in terms of food and medicine, shelter and housing, potable water, protection from physical insults (in the form of microbes or abuse), and hygiene and environmental stressors (Cohen 1989). Episodes of violence and warfare have also been linked to inequality, political economic stratification, and differential access to resources that can become heightened in periods of unpredictability and environmental degradation (Ember and Ember 1997; Ferguson 1997; Knauft 1991; Sluka 1992). Deciphering the physical alteration left on the human corpse along with the death space and place it occupies offers similar changes. The presence of offerings and type of preparation of the body can be related to politics, gender, power, and ritual, but the real meaning may be difficult to interpret by outsiders to the culture.

I have argued (2016) that a useful diagram for understanding the use of violence theory within a biocultural/bioarchaeological context is a stacked Venn diagram (figure 10.1). This diagram illustrates the importance of each of the concepts in identifying and understanding violence in both the ethnographic present and archaeological past. In this configuration, you see the importance of each of the categories in building the base required to inform the core idea. The understanding of violence we see on the body gets stronger as we move through each level toward the core. Each idea is only as strong as the evidence that comes before it.

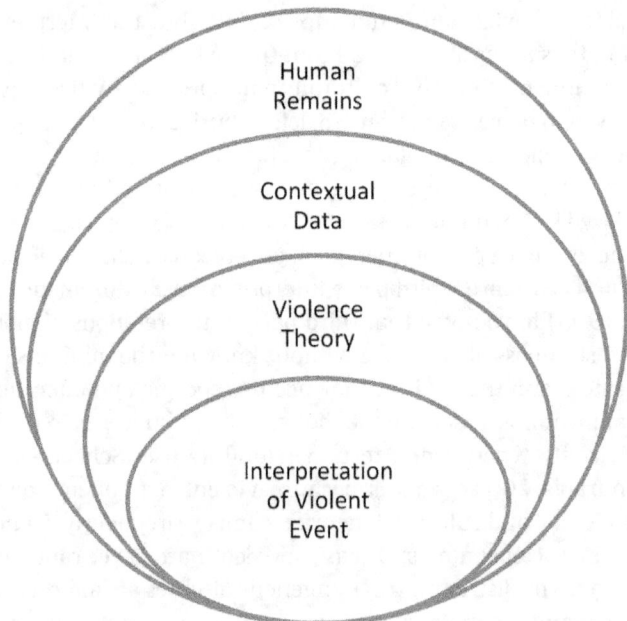

Figure 10.1 Diagram of a biocultural analysis of violence. Figure created by the author.

Thus, the use of violence theory as an interpretive tool is only as strong as the analysis of the human remains and contextual data. Violence theory is further complicated by the necessity to embed it within a system of poetics. Structural violence cannot be understood as violence unless we understand it in terms of systemic violence. Who occupies the structures, how were they formed and maintained, and how are they part of a recognizable system that is excessive, expressive, and symbolic (Pawlett 2013)? Finally, what are the conditions under which the structures in systemic violence are permitted to move to direct/physical violence? Rarely does systemic violence reach the level of physical violence without it being concealed within ideological justifications, like warfare and sacrifice.

Evil as an Epistemological Framework

When I think about the word "evil," I begin with this quote: "Is he willing to prevent evil but not able? Then is he impotent. Is he able but not willing? Then is he malevolent. Is he both able and willing? Whence then is evil?" (Hitchens 2007, 268). Here, Hitchens is referring to God, of course, and this is my starting point for thinking about the concept of evil. Truth be told, I do not like the word "evil." It obscures and confounds truly horrific acts of violence by creating a categorical "out" by assigning the behavior to a theological or genetic explanation. Demonic influence or possession becomes the ideological explanation for behaviors that are profoundly outside of a community's norms and values. It is far easier to assign such behavior to some evil being that is imposing its will on these people than to explore the cultural norms that could foster such acts of mindless violence. Another rationale is genetic. Our scientific stand-in for a "demonic" explanation in the twenty-first century is "genes." As with demons exerting their unholy will on humankind, genetics offers a scientific explanation for evil behavior. When extreme acts of violence are committed for which society has no rational explanation, it is the person's genetic code or biological affinity that is used to explain the behaviors that do not fit neatly into the cultural values of a society. Both explanatory models create the ultimate mythical other as a way of rationalizing extreme deviant behavior.

With that said, the challenge lies in understanding how, on occasion, "ordinary" people have committed extreme acts of grotesque violence without relying on the idea of evil. What are the philosophical, sociological, and culturally normative elements found in humanity throughout space and time that can allow for individuals to engage in extreme acts of grotesque violence, and what are the common mechanisms of social interaction that allow for people to become perpetrators? That many of the perpetrators of evil were not exceptional people is not, of course, a new discovery. This has been well covered in theological and philosophical texts. In these two disciplines, the origin of evil is an insoluble mystery. Evil cannot be subsequent or parallel to human will, because then there would be no explanation of the universality of sin. But, evil cannot precede human will either, since it must either be part of our nature or outside our nature. If evil is part of our nature, then the moral law no longer applies to us, and evil could not still be evil. If evil is not part of our nature, then the evil we do is the result of this alien intrusion, and we are not responsible. Perhaps John Steinbeck said it best: "All the goodness and the heroisms will rise up again, then be cut down again and rise up. It isn't that the evil thing wins—it never will—but that it doesn't die" (1975, 221).

However, I am not concerned with proving or disproving the existence of evil as a motivator for human behavior. Instead, I want to explore how the concept of evil obstructs the analysis of violence, trauma, and warfare by the fact that violent acts often exemplify intricate social and cultural dimensions. These acts and practices are encoded with meanings and are part of a cultural, social, and political logic. Evil provides many with an epistemological framework to make sense of senseless acts, but at the exclusion of how memories of violence are negotiated through cultural frameworks and mediated by the collective consciousness of a community. The concept of evil is bound to the ideological construction of a moral imperative. In Latin America, this moral imperative is understood through a meta-narrative of colonialism and the Catholic Church. For thousands of years, the Mesoamerican identity of much of Latin America has not strayed far from traditions of celebrating lost souls and the cycle of life and death. However, the Spanish-Catholic conquest and colonization of Latin America introduced the concepts of "hell" and "evil" into cultures in which they did not exist. Today, this landscape of evil encompasses a public space of violent performance in the form of rape, torture, murder, and systemic forms of quiet violence, malnutrition, and poverty, alongside the silencing of dissension (Rabasa 2000).

Violence Theory

The literature on violence and warfare has become so large that a truly comprehensive overview is no longer feasible. Some of it is theory-driven, but most of it is written to address social problems rather than building general models and research paradigms. Numerous studies have been written discussing specific kinds of violence (e.g., Bourgois 2003; Brownmiller 1975; Bulhan 1985; Burnt 1980; Durkheim and Denis 1915; Erikson 1966; Fanon 1963; Fromm 1973; Gerson 1986; Givens and Nettleship 1976; Hoefnagels 1977; Klaus 2012; Kwitny 1984; Lifton and Falk 1982; Martin and Harrod 2015; Martin, Harrod, and Pérez 2012; Pearce 1982; Pérez 2012; Pérez 2016; Pérez, Nelson, and Martin 2008; Renzetti 1997; Rieder 1984; Sanders 1983; Scheper-Hughes 1992; Scheper-Hughes and Lock 1987; Schwendinger and Schwendinger 1983; Stockwell 1978; Taylor 1999; West 1993; Wright 1983 [1942]). However, there have been few systematic efforts at cross-cultural comparisons exploring underlying themes or patterns (Turpin and Kurtz 1997; Scheper-Hughes and Bourgois 2004; Schmidt and Schröder 2001; Whitehead 2004). Perspectives on violence have been too narrowly conceived, and it is time for theoretical paradigms to be broadened. Therefore, it is essential that we understand and explain the cultural mediation of real world conditions that foster the use of violence. Arguably, the most influential current definition of violence is from Riches's *The Anthropology of Violence*, which classifies violence as "an act of physical hurt deemed legitimate by the performer and illegitimate by (some) witness" (1986, 8). Although not everyone who studies violence agrees with this definition, most believe it to be a good starting point. Most contemporary violence researchers (Aijmer and Abbink 2000; Harvey and Gow 1994; Riches 1986; Turpin and Kurtz 1997; Scheper-Hughes and Bourgois 2004; Schmidt and Schröder 2001; Sluka 1992; Whitehead 2004), myself included, agree on the following: "that violence is pervasive, ancient, infinitely various, and a central fact of human life, but also that it is poorly understood in general" (Whitehead 2004, 55).

When thinking about the application of violence theory to the interpretation of archaeological remains, I am reminded of the problem with defining and conceptualizing violence in the social sciences in general, which has been very aptly commented on by Zygmunt Bauman:

> Virtually all writers attempting to come to grips with the phenomenon of violence find the concept either under-, or over-defined, or both. They also report in other writers (if they not display it themselves) an amazing reluctance, or ineptitude, to resolve the confusion and put things straight. Above all, they find in the texts they read plenty of understatements and half-truths, a lot of embarrassed silence, and other signs of shamefacedness. (1995, 139)

The challenge of infusing social theory in general and violence theory specifically to bioarchaeological models of analysis lies in part in the paradox of violence. In his introduction to *Aspects of Violence: A Critical Theory*, Schinkel (2010) lists ten of these apparent paradoxes regarding violence:

1. Violence breaks down social order—violence is constitutive of social order.
2. Violence is a social problem—violence is a standard solution to social order.
3. Violence is a purely destructive form of sociality—violence is a positive form of sociality bringing people together.
4. Violence is a way of dealing with contingency—violence is a prominent form and source of contingency.
5. Violence is norm breaking—violence is norm-strengthening.
6. Violence is a visible situation—violence is a hidden process.
7. The violence of the state is reactive towards illegitimate violence—the violence of the state is already active in the very distinction between legitimate and illegitimate violence.
8. Violence is a meaningful social process, which has a meaning in referring to an external referent—violence is a social process characterized exclusively by self-reference.
9. Violence is a repellent—violence is a magnet.
10. Violence is a means to an end—violence is an end to a means.

With these apparent contradictions, how are we to identify and explain violent behavior? To begin with, it is important to clarify which explanatory model you are using and why it is relevant to the analysis at hand. There are times that a researcher is less concerned with the causes and consequences of violence than with the logic of violence. By that, I mean social scientists often concern themselves with the analysis of violence while philosophers are more concerned with the concept of violence. As I noted at the beginning of this chapter, these ideas are not mutually exclusive but are important for researchers to define at the onset of their analysis.

Even within the analysis of a first-order level of inquiry (scientific analysis) of violence, there are multiple starting points that can easily become blurred or obscured if not clarified at the outset. Due to the length constraints of this volume, I am going to provide only a very truncated example of one idea, that of "power." The concept of power is central to the idea of direct and indirect violence as defined by Galtung:

> We shall refer to the type of violence where there is an actor that commits the violence as *personal* or *direct*, and to the violence where there is no such actor as *structural* or *indirect*. . . . whereas in the first case [the] consequences can be traced back to concrete persons or actors, in the second case this is no longer meaningful. (1969, 170–71)

Our next step is to define what is meant by power. Foucault's definition, which is heavily referenced in the social sciences and anthropology in particular, is worth citing here in its entirety:

> [Power] must be understood in the first instance as the multiplicity of force relations immanent in the sphere in which they operate and which constitute their own organization; as the process which, through ceaseless struggles and confrontations, transforms, strengthens, or reverses them; as the support which these force relations find in one another, thus forming a chain or a system, or on the contrary, the disjunctions and contradictions which isolate them from one another; and lastly, as the strategies in which they take effect, whose general design or institutional crystallization is embodied in the state apparatus, in the formulation of the law, in the various social hegemonies. (1973, 91–92)

Foucault's definition of power now serves to guide the reader of the researcher's use of structural violence in terms of systemic violence. This idea of systemic violence can further be placed into particular paradigms such as creative, moral, and destructive power as discussed in Vahabi's *The Political Economy of Destructive Power* (2004).

The final step in building our explanatory model for the violence being interpreted is to consider it within a system of poetics. What I mean by that is the violence being explained must be considered within the time and place of their actions.

> Ethnic cleansing in Bosnia that emphasized rape and execution with mallets and hammers, civil war in Sierra Leone that took the hands and feet of prisoners, anal impalement that invokes key cultural categories in Rwanda, kneecapping in Northern Ireland, and so on—all these specific forms of violence are not produced by the febrile excess of savage or pathological minds but are cultural performances whose poetics derive from the history and sociocultural relationships of the locale. (Whitehead 2004, 73–74)

So, we take our complex and nuanced definition of violence that we have laid out for the reader and apply it to the historical and wider sociological forces present. Thus, these "generative schemes" (Bourdieu 1977) are given meaning through what Whitehead (2004, 60) refers to as historically entrenched configurations of symbolic and social behavior that inform individual agency through symbols and icons. The term "poetics" serves to focus our understanding of violence as a core cultural expression of an essential and complex component of a society (Whitehead 2004, 68).

Performance Violence—A Complicated Aesthetic—Mexican Case Studies

The diversity of the assemblages with which I work demonstrates the challenges in trying to decipher the complexity, variability, and ambiguities of performative violence. In most of these cases, the dead take on an afterlife that supersedes their mortal life and their individuality. Thus, the body becomes simultaneously "visible" (but only through a prismatic system of political and ideological systems) and "invisible" (as their humanity and life history becomes less important than the performance of their death). These acts of violence and the cultural space in which they take place result in the border between the living and dead being reworked. The symbolic aspects of this performative violence help to form the foundation of the collective memory of the groups who have experienced it. Memory becomes the bridge between the collective remembering of violence and the formation of political, social, and cultural channels, which creates a (re)ordering of societal ethos, thus contributing to the group's social identity.

Much of my work explores how politicians, activists, and survivors explain and exploit violent events within and outside of Mexico by reproducing the "language" of violence in written and oral forms. Bodies evidencing trauma become the parchment upon which the literal writing of violence codifies meaning and structure to the objective world they occupy. How someone died becomes infinitely more important than the fact that he is dead. Individuals lose their identity but continue to circulate through the language of violence in the media and politics. This circulation has a profound impact on US–Mexico security policy (Pérez and Sherry 2013). Drawing on archival research, participant observation, and interviews, I build on my own family's experience with death and violence along *la frontera* to produce what Waterson (2013) and others have termed an "intimate ethnography." It illustrates how various forms of violence are not only implicated in individual stories, but also help to create and maintain hyped up security policies and agendas along the US southern border.

Mexico's current humanitarian crisis has been exacerbated by more than a decade of ineffective anticartel and US–Mexico security policies, which resulted in unprecedented murder rates and remade power relations among political elite, drug cartels, and local communities. The official *guerra contra el narcotráfico* [the war against drug trafficking] began in Michoacán, Mexico, in 2006 (Shirk 2011). Since this seminal moment and throughout the three preceding decades, scholars have documented policy trends and drug violence within Mexico. Major news sources have documented public outrage at the perceived spillover violence into the US from communities situated along almost two thousand miles of international border. This research views spillover violence as a tool for the creation of rigid security policy that fails to address the root causes of violence, rather than as a predominately lived experience.

As a subset of violence, security policy engages the collective identities of victim, perpetrator, witness, and community. Violence escapes concrete definition because it is not a finished, self-contained behavior. Similar to violence, policy is always in process. This research asks: What are the poetics of violence that create a synergistic bond between the security policy process and violence? In answering this question, suggestions emerge to eradicate the violence that plagues society through the redistribution of security resources and understanding of spillover violence as part of a policy process. The term "poetics" charges researchers to understand violence and death with regard to biology and social function and as a form of profound cultural expression (Whitehead 2004). Policy can open up possibilities to change the social structures—deplorable education, unemployment, and extreme poverty—that produce violence in Mexico. Conversely, policy can reify institutionalized inequalities that unevenly direct the flow of power and resources. Tracing the formation of US–Mexico security policy through case studies provides a comparative analytic opportunity to interrogate the bonds between legal process and violence to make evident key factors in violent cultural expression that bring about ineffective policy.

Since 2009, I have documented the ways in which US policymakers mobilize and propagate images of extraordinary acts of violence, such as corporeal mutilation, to produce hyped up security policies and agendas along the southern border. Most recently, I have been studying these issues through homicide databases, security policy documents, and ethnographic case studies. Extraordinary acts of violence—some true, some based on circulating rumors—serve primarily as a point of departure to consider the social structures that institutionalize inequality. Structures produce more insidious forms of violence, which launch an unrelenting attack that erodes people's ability to survive and transform their lives. I hypothesize, based on preliminary research data, that US security policy along its southern border has been reactive to extraordinary acts of violence and ineffective in combating structural forms of violence. Anthropologists are well positioned to break through the reactionist framework and explore the bonds between legal processes and forms of violence, which embody the history and culture of the societies that generate them.

Since 2007, crime has been the number one public concern in Latin America. Surveys typically show public trust in police is low, ranking below the military, business, and banks. Complaints include corruption, impunity, and unequal treatment. The level of trust in police was 46.9 percent, compared to 61.7 percent for the army, according to one report (Meyer 2014). Mexico's police were federally organized like those in the US, where the authority of law enforcement comes from Article II of the Constitution, which establishes the executive branch. However, in contrast to the US practice, in which the police function with broad authority at the municipal level and are relatively respected public servants that we call on during times of need, the reverse is true in Mexico. Additionally, in the US, local police have jurisdiction to investigate all crimes that are not under federal or tribal jurisdiction. During seven decades of single-party rule under the PRI in Mexico, the municipal police were ineffective, poorly trained and paid, prone to seeking bribes, and subservient to local politicians. The armed forces ensured order at the national level until the 1970s, when they were withdrawn from that role after participating in the violent repression of student protesters (Meyer 2014).

The widespread abuse of citizens is not the only problem that plagues Mexican police forces. Forces at all levels are riddled with corruption and are seen as ineffective in enforcing the law or even as enabling crime. Mexican government officials publicly acknowledge the endemic weaknesses of the country's police; after leaving office, President Calderón stated that corruption was an "endemic evil" in Mexico and that there were "towns and cities where the police was totally consumed by corruption" (Meyer 2014).

I witnessed this corruption in 2014 while having lunch at the Restaurant La Gloria in Mexico City. Around 2:00 p.m., a white sedan pulled up near this open-air café. I heard a young teenaged girl—probably no more than fifteen—screaming. A crowd formed around the car and tried to keep it from moving. The girl was being pulled into the car by men who claimed to be officers executing an arrest warrant. While the teenaged girl was fighting to free herself, her younger sister and friend kept screaming, "What order?! What order?!" A police van arrived, and for a moment I believed everything would be okay. But men with automatic weapons emerged from the van. The crowd moved away from the car and the kidnappers sped off followed by the police van. I have no photos of this event because as I went to pull my camera from my bag, the café waitress looked at me and shook her head no.

Later, a senior official of the Federal police was canvassing the area with other officers. He proclaimed loudly several times so other bystanders and I could hear that a man had fallen down a manhole in the street and they were here to investigate that accident. When I spoke to the front desk staff of the building I was staying at, I was told that police wanted to make sure everyone "knew" what happened. Indeed, everyone did know what happened, but nobody would speak about it. A young woman had been abducted off the street in broad daylight with the help of the police and now that same police force was conducting an investigation.

The 2017 National Victimization Survey, conducted by Mexico's National Institute for Statistics and Geography, estimates there were 31.1 million crimes committed in the country that year, of which only 9.7 percent were reported; and of those reported, authorities opened official cases in only 65 percent of instances. According to the survey, 34.2 percent of Mexican households were victims of crime in 2016, and more than 90 percent of crimes go unreported. The reasons people do not report crime include a lack of confidence in authorities (16 percent) and others consider it a waste of time (16 percent).

As stories of crime and violence play out in the headlines, Mexico is in the midst of a major transformation of its judicial sector. Mexico has been gradually implementing reforms that advocate hope and will dramatically improve public security and the administration of justice over the next decade. Central to the process of judicial reform in Mexico is a package of ambitious legislative changes and constitutional amendments passed by the Mexican Congress in 2008 with planned implementation by 2016. Together, these reforms touch most aspects of the judicial sector, including police, prosecutors, public defenders, the courts, and the penitentiary system. The reforms include significant changes in Mexican criminal procedure, new measures to promote greater access to justice (for both criminal defendants and crime victims), new functions for law enforcement and public security agencies in the administration of justice, and tougher measures for combating organized crime. Advocates of the reforms hope they will help Mexico to achieve a more democratic rule of law by introducing greater transparency, accountability, and due process to Mexico's judicial sector. However, critics note the reforms attempt to achieve too much in too little time, contain blatantly contradictory features, and fail to address persistent problems of institutionalized corruption.

In the past few years, I have become increasingly aware of and driven to contribute to broader debates on how policies transform lives around the globe. Policies are being forged around the world to address critical topics from health pandemics, economic development, undocumented immigration, race-driven murders, and outpourings of refugees from conflict-ridden regions. Policies often emerge as a response to visible acts of violence, but how does violence work? And, more specifically, how does violence work in policy making?

Death, poverty, drugs, and human trafficking—when confronting Ciudad Juárez, we seem truly to stand before a "death zone" in which the politics of civility and democratic conflict have been erased and the public space has become a realm of violent performance, a place in which public acts take the form of rape, torture, and murder. Ciudad Juárez has become synonymous with Narco violence and a cultural space where death is being reshaped, and its borders reworked, in part by the many beheadings and mutilations that have occurred. These acts have included public displays of battered human heads, some thrown into plazas or placed on car rooftops, some thrown outside schools; mutilated torsos hanging from meat hooks; threats and taunts to rival cartels written on walls with the blood of butchered adversaries; and video-postings of torture and beheadings on YouTube. These acts of performance violence regulate a sphere of embodied memory that warrants special attention, for this type of violence has created a collective memory of cultural trauma or a tear in the social fabric of Juárez.

Mexico's economy is strongly dependent on economic conditions in the United States, because more than 80 percent of its exports are destined for the US market, and the United States is its primary source of tourism revenues and foreign investment (Villarreal 2018). Mexico is also a major producer and supplier to the US markets for heroin, methamphetamine, and marijuana and the major transit country for as much as 90 percent of the cocaine sold in the United States. Indeed, although neither the North American Free Trade Agreement

(NAFTA) nor its partial replacement (the US–Mexico Trade Agreement) officially include drug exports, they are an integral part of Mexico's comparative advantage in an expanding regional trade relationship. It is critical that any analysis of cartel violence examines the social and political consequences resulting from the economic transformations that depress standards of living and destroy the social fabric of communities. The murders, the environmental degradation, and the poverty of Ciudad Juárez cannot be written off as "a grotesque exception," but perhaps instead should be viewed as the "window" that looks out on the havoc that economic globalization can wreak.

There has been an alarming spike in violence in Mexico in recent years, most of which is associated with the trafficking in the aforementioned illegal drugs and the efforts of the Mexican government to shut down that trade. The extent of violence was already at a troubling level as early as 2002. Since then, though, the situation has dramatically worsened, and the carnage is increasingly impacting communities throughout Mexico. *El Universal* reports that out of the 8,327 officers who passed their entrance exams between 2007 and 2010, over 6,000 of them have since become inactive. Approximately 400 were killed, while 5,890 quit. The number of officers who quit between 2007 and 2009 tripled, rising from 662 to 2,170.

Although there are nearly a dozen drug trafficking organizations in Mexico, including seven significant cartels, two groups are especially powerful. One is the Federation (sometimes called the Pacific cartel), an association that emerged from a 2006 accord between the Sinaloa cartel and several secondary trafficking syndicates in and around Mexico's Pacific state of Sinaloa. The Federation's principal rival is the Gulf cartel, based in the city of Matamoros in the Mexican state of Tamaulipas along the eastern portion of the border with Texas. It has another major base farther west in the city of Nuevo Laredo (Lee and Renwick 2017). Both groups are extremely violent, with the Gulf cartel having an especially potent team of enforcers—the Zetas—who are highly trained antidrug military personnel who defected to the traffickers. A third faction, the Tijuana cartel (once perhaps the most powerful organization), has declined somewhat in recent years as several top leaders have been arrested or killed. Indeed, over the past six or seven years, the Tijuana cartel has been the frequent target of high-profile police and military operations (Beittel 2018; Grayson 2014).

The Juárez cartel is headed by Vicente Carrillo Fuentes and is based in Ciudad Juárez, across the border from El Paso, Texas. The Juárez cartel was dominant in the 1990s but became less dominant following the death of leader Amado Carrillo Fuentes. Although the cartel was weakened, it has a presence throughout much of Mexico and is considered one of the four major cartels. In January 2008, the Sinaloa Cartel, led by Joaquin "Chapo" Guzman, went to war with Vicente Carrillo Fuentes and its old partners in the Juárez Cartel for control of the city. To fight this war, the Juárez mob recruited a street and prison gang called the Barrio Azteca while the Sinaloa Cartel recruited a rival gang called the Artist Assassins, or Double A's (Beittel 2018).

For most Mexicans, rich and poor alike, a psychological leap into a state of generalized fear and a perception of acute vulnerability coincided with an increase in gruesome displays of barbarism since the spring of 2006. I propose to understand these killings as a performance, a political performance, and to regard the killers as political actors *par excellence*. As a bioarchaeologist imbedded within a biocultural paradigm, I am uniquely suited to examine the cultural taphonomic indicators indicative of violent trauma. This was accomplished by placing the corpses into the larger cultural and environmental dynamics that can produce and maintain violence within populations. Analysis of this type of trauma was used to examine how the symbolic aspects of violence have the potential to create order and disorder depending on the specific social context within which the violence is expressed.

An example of this violence comes from an analysis of the torture, murder, and mutilation of Alejandro Estrada. At 9:10 p.m. on June 6, 2010, the fifty-one-year-old man's body was found dumped on a street in Juárez. Estrada worked for a local television station, and his mutilated body was part of a threat made to his employer. His fingers and toes had been severed, along with his arms, legs, feet, hands, and head. His nose had been cut off and placed in his anus, and his penis and genitals were placed in his mouth with his head facing his buttocks. His voter ID card was nailed to his forehead, and his eyes were placed in a plastic bag and taped to his chest. This type of performative violence has spawned a new vocabulary to explain and exploit these events. The brutal public killings that began about five years ago have worsened as Mexican drug cartels try to outdo each other in their quest to scare off rivals, authorities, and would-be informers—and still stun Mexicans increasingly numbed to the gory spectacles.

Deciphering the precise and highly ritualized repetition of these performance murders—the sequence of abduction, torture, beheading, and disposal of the body in a public place—is to be found in almost every account of the crimes. As a result, the community is constantly reshaping its borders. In consequence, inclusions and exclusions are being clearly and explicitly delineated, and a political message is sent. Each killing seems to "cite" the previous one and in itself constitutes a mere rendering of the next. Thus, the murders, a form of direct violence, are being shaped and *are shaping* the cultural and structural violence implicit within the system.

An example of this is a story I came across on the Internet of a young girl who was beheaded in Florida by members of a Mexican cartel who were engaged in human trafficking. The story flew across the Internet after Bill Stewart, the Deputy Chief of Staff for the Florida Attorney General Bill McCollum, provided public testimony on House Bill 287(g) regarding immigration legislation on 8 April 2008. The 287(g) program is one of Immigration and Customs Enforcement's top partnership initiatives, allowing state and local law enforcement to enter into a partnership with US Immigration and Customs Enforcement (ICE), under a joint Memorandum of Agreement, in order to receive delegated authority for immigration enforcement within their jurisdictions. The program has come under severe criticism from civil rights, community, and immigrant rights organizations because local law enforcement agencies that have been granted 287(g) powers are using the program to target communities of color. This has compromised public safety while doing nothing to solve the immigration crisis. What follows is an excerpt of Stewart's (2008) testimony:

> It is impossible to separate national security issues from illegal immigration, and one of the most important illegal immigration issues in Florida is the issue of human trafficking. I will just leave you with a recent story that occurred in the panhandle. There were several girls that were trafficked into the panhandle from Mexico. These girls were raped repeatedly over a week's period of time, and one of them actually resisted while she was being raped. So the smugglers grabbed all of these girls, chained them in chairs, and put them in a room. They brought in the girl who refused to be raped, and they beheaded her, in front of all of the other girls that were in that room. And they left them there, with her body, and those little girls, for several hours. . . . This is the reality, of dangerous criminal aliens, in our state, and what happens.

The problem with Stewart's public testimony is that the event never happened. The morning of his testimony, Stewart received a threat assessment report from the Florida Fusion Center (FFC), a post-9/11 intelligence agency. That report cited a story that was published by the *Bradenton Herald* on 11 March 2008 entitled "Task Force to Fight Human Trafficking" in which the reporter provides the aforementioned story of the beheading. What the FFC failed to notice was that on 19 March 2008, the *Bradenton Herald* printed a retraction, because its reporter fabricated the story. When I confronted Stewart, he admitted that a mistake had been made, but his office made no public retraction of his testimony. As such, the story continued to gain traction and received a new dose of validity in 2010 when it was referenced in Bunker et al.'s paper "Torture, Beheadings, and Narcocultos," which was published in the peer-reviewed journal *Small Wars and Insurgencies*.

Unfortunately, this is not the only instance of the appropriation of the collective traumatic memory of the performance violence being endured by the people of Juárez. On 29 June 2010, Arizona Governor Jan Brewer claimed, "Our law enforcement agencies have found bodies in the desert either buried or just lying out there that have been beheaded," suggesting that the beheadings were part of the so-called "spill over violence" along the US–Mexico border (Barr 2010). I contacted every US county medical examiner's office from San Diego, California, to Brownsville, Texas, and learned there has only been one confirmed case of beheading or mutilation that is possibly related to cartel violence on US soil. This took place in Chandler, Arizona, when the body of Martin Alejandro Cota-Monroy was found on 10 October 2010 in an apartment with his severed head placed a few feet from his stabbed body. It is thought that Mr. Cota-Monroy stole four hundred pounds of marijuana from one of the cartels ("Police" 2011). However, it should be noted that so far, the beheading has not been linked to a specific cartel. There is little doubt that this was a drug-related murder, but it does not by default mean Cota-Monroy's beheading was ordered by one of the Mexican cartels. It seems more likely that his beheading was meant to mimic a cartel hit given that it was carried out on the American side of the border.

Biological anthropologists have long used the human body in its corporeal state as a lens through which to examine cultural processes. How dead bodies are discussed, hidden, and displayed can be used as a point of departure for examining the forms of violence that produced their deaths. We can observe the way the deaths are perceived and further used as people try to make sense of violent acts. Dead bodies are far more than just decaying matter. As Mary Douglas (1966) noted, (1966) "The body is a model which can stand for any kind of bound system." To do even minimal justice to the symbolic complexity of the human body requires consideration of political symbolism; cultural death rituals; analysis of the type of corpse manipulation within the wider regional cultural dynamics; and how the manipulation of the corpse will impact local histories and create spatial memory.

The meaning associated with the corpse has a great deal to do with the condition and location in which it is found. If the goal is creating what Taussig has appropriately termed a "culture of terror," then mutilation, destruction, and/or disappearance of this powerful symbol are effective mechanisms in achieving the desired effect. Central to the understanding of how and why acts of violence are committed is the notion that acts of violence can be manifestations of cultural performances or spectacles. Large-scale violence and massive trauma destroy the fabric of the sociocultural bonds and trust that make human life possible.

Through the use of a biocultural model, the performative nature of the beheadings and mutilations taking place in Cuidad Juárez can be understood not as a bifurcated analysis of literal versus metaphorical violence but rather as a complicated aesthetic. As I noted earlier, bodies evidencing such trauma become the parchment upon which the literal writing of violence codifies meaning and structure to the objective world they occupy. The new syntax of this "language" of violence is then reproduced in written and oral forms that are used by a variety of individuals (politicians, activists, survivors) to explain and exploit these events. Thus, the performance and memory of these murders are being shaped and are shaping the cultural and structural violence implicit within the system. As Matt Matsuda (1996) has written, "memory is not a generic term of analysis, but itself an object appropriated and politicized."

On 8 September 2008, *Time* magazine ran a story entitled "Behind Mexico's Wave of Beheadings" in which the author quoted Archaeologist Ernesto Vargas as saying that "the tactic of the cartel beheadings could even reflect the pre-Columbian use of beheadings, a common tactic of the Mayan people who dominated southern Mexico and Guatemala before the Spanish conquest." Even if it was not Vargas's intention, he emphasized the practice of beheadings as a quintessential Mexican practice for potentially thousands of readers. The practice of writing about violence comprises the representation of the event (torture, mutilations, or beheadings) as well as the categories and concepts informing those events. The performance violence being practiced by the Mexican cartels is an example not just of the physical violence endured by the victim but also of the symbolic violence of recorded history. That is to say that writings of the US and Mexican presses, social scientists, and governmental agencies all have performative powers to establish laws and normalize the cultural and structural violence being espoused regarding US immigration policy.

The meaning associated with the corpse has a great deal to do with the condition and location in which it is found. If the goal is creating a "culture of terror," then mutilation, destruction, and/or disappearance of this powerful symbol are effective mechanisms in achieving the desired effect. Central to the understanding of how and why acts of violence are committed is the notion that acts of violence can be manifestations of cultural performances or spectacles. These extreme acts of grotesque violence can be understood only through a multiscalar investigation of the violence, using the body as a starting point while considering treatment of corpses and the materiality of death as it operates as a kind of unconscious historiography of a perceived brutality of the Mexican social experience.

Pulling Back the Curtain of Evil

We experience our present world in a context that is causally connected with past events and objects. Because memory is not simply an unmediated representation of the past but rather a recreation dependent on social contexts that are often influenced by the hegemonic narrative of the dominate culture, it is imperative that anthropologists recognize how violent events of the past impact the landscapes of the present. Understanding the circulation of violence and trauma through the collective memory of the victims, perpetrators, and societies in which it occurs provides us with a framework to understand how hyped up security policies and agendas along the US southern border is created, legislated, and implemented by both the US and Mexico.

US–Mexico border enforcement costs $18 billion a year, which exceeds all other federal criminal law-enforcement agencies combined, according to the Migration Policy Institute figures cited by *The Economist* (2013). Nevertheless, Mexico's struggling economy and violent crime force migrants to undertake an increasingly violent journey to cross the border.

The concept of evil obstructs the analysis of major policy priorities and obscures the more insidious language of policies, which slowly strips immigrants, organized crime members, and victims of their humanity and deemphasizes the deplorable social conditions that produce and justify violence. Evil provides many with a convenient framework with which to make sense of senseless acts, but at the exclusion of how memories of violence are negotiated through cultural frameworks and mediated by the collective consciousness of a community. The concept of evil is bound to the ideological construction of a moral imperative. As Ervin Staub noted, "The word *evil* is emotionally expressive for people: It communicates horror over some deed" (1999, 180). This creates a simplistic explanation for the violence that is happening in Mexico (or anywhere for that matter), for the violence is often seen as an episodic event conducted by evil doers and tied to the universal assumption that the victim must be "dirty" and got what he had coming to him. Focusing on physical violence as an act of evil ignores the complexity of structural systems, culture, and history of the communities in which these acts are produced.

Conclusion

As a Mexican American bioarchaeologist who primary works in Mexico and studies violence in both the archaeological past and the ethnographic present, I struggle constantly with tensions that come from explaining the theoretical framework of the violence I am studying without creating a narrative of its inevitability, an innate evil. Yet, I am a product of Mexican violence along *la frontera*. The death of my paternal grandfather for whom I am named illustrates the usefulness of Waterston's intimate ethnography. My grandfather was born in Guerrero, Mexico, in 1925. Because of the turmoil caused by the Mexican Revolution, my family, like many others during this period, left for the United States. Unfortunately, the Great Depression, along with the Dust Bowl, led to the US policy of forced repatriation of over 2 million Mexicans and Mexican Americans during the 1930s (many of whom were US citizens) (Reyes 2016). This forced repatriation set in motion a series of events that led to my grandfather's murder in 1951 in the pueblo of Santa Apolonia near the town of Rio Bravo in Tamaulipas, Mexico. Hacked to death by a man wielding a machete, he was the victim of a revenge murder. His death led to my grandmother (who was born in Texas) moving her two young sons back to the United States. The multigenerational effects of interpersonal and institutional forms of violence have profound consequences for the victims, the perpetrators, and the communities in which they are produced. Each of the aforementioned groups will have a selective re-creation of the memory of the violence, as well as the landscapes of the contested sites of pain the violence produced. It is a concept many of the people of Mexico and I know all too well. To explain my grandfather's death as the act of an evil man fails to account for the intersections of global capitalism, Mexican political and economic aspirations, and US–Mexico security policies that continue to produce structural, cultural, and direct systems of violence to this day.

Experiences of violence often are part of the social conditions of policy formation and part of the policies themselves, marginalizing those most affected by the legislation and its production. The violence behind policy formation is obscured by government discourse on reforms spanning infrastructure, joblessness, and the need to secure a country's spot on the global economic stage. Anthropologists are well placed to break through reductionist frameworks and explore policy as a cultural concept and set of processes that "encapsulate the entire history and culture of the society that generated them" (Wedel et. al 2005). No other approach has allowed me to better grasp the unremitting ebb and flow of policy and violence. It is within the frameworks of structural, symbolic, everyday, and quiet violence that I conceive ethnographic studies are most fruitful, relying on personal stories and experiences with social opposition, state repression, and marginalization to reveal models for perpetuating inequalities and models for disrupting them.

Ventura R. Pérez, University of Massachusetts

References

Agarwal, Sabrina C., and Bonnie A. Glencross. 2011. *Social Bioarchaeology*. Malden, MA: Wiley-Blackwell.

Ahlstrom, Torbjörn, and Petra Molnar. 2012. "The Placement of the Feathers: Violence Among Sub-Boreal Foragers from Gotland, Central Baltic Sea." In *Sticks, Stones, and Broken Bones: Neolithic Violence in a European Perspective*. Edited by Rick J. Schulting and Linda Fibiger, 17–33. Oxford: Oxford University Press.

Aijmer, Görn, and John Abbink, eds. 2000. *The Meaning of Violence: A Cross-Cultural Perspective*. New York: Berg Publishers.

Barr, Andy. 2010. "Brewer's Beheading Claim Questioned." *Politico*. 30 June. Retrieved 4 January 2019 from https://www.politico.com/story/2010/06/brewers-beheading-claim-questioned-039240.

Bauman, Zygmunt. 1995. "Making and Unmaking of Strangers." *Thesis Eleven* 43(1): 1–16.

Beittel, June S. 2018. *Mexico: Organized Crime and Drug Trafficking Organizations* (CRS Report No. 41576). Congressional Research Service. Retrieved 4 January 2019 from https://fas.org/sgp/crs/row/R41576.pdf.

Bocquentin, Fanny, and Ofer Bar-Yosef. 2004. "Early Natufian Remains: Evidence for Physical Conflict from Mt. Carmel, Israel." *Journal of Human Evolution* 47(1–2): 19–23.

Bourdieu, Pierre. 1977. *Outline of a Theory of Practice*. Cambridge, UK: Cambridge University Press.

Bourgois, Philippe. 2003. "Crack and the Political Economy of Social Suffering." *Addiction Research and Theory* 11(1): 31–37.

Brownmiller, Susan. 1975. *Against Our Will: Men, Women, and Rape*. New York: Bantam Books.

Bulhan, Hussein A. 1985. *Frantz Fanon and the Psychology of Oppression*. New York: Plenum Press.

Burt, Martha R. 1980. "Cultural Myths and Supports for Rape." *Journal of Personality and Social Psychology* 38: 217–30.

Bush, George W. 2002. "Text of President Bush's 2002 State of the Union Address." *Washington Post*. 29 January. Retrieved 4 January 2019 from http://www.washingtonpost.com/wp-srv/onpolitics/transcripts/sou012902.htm.

Cohen, M. N. 1989. "Population Differences in Dental Morphology View in Terms of High and Low Heritability." *American Journal of Physical Anthropology* 41: 473.

Douglas, Mary. 1966. *Purity and Danger: An Analysis of the Concepts of Pollution and Taboo*. New York: Routledge.

Durkheim, Émile, and Ernest Denis. 1915. *Who Wanted War? The Origins of the War According to Diplomatic Documents*. Paris: Armand Colin.

The Economist. 2013. "The US-Mexico Border: Secure Enough." 22 June. Retrieved 4 January 2019 from http://www.economist.com/news/united-states/21579828-spending-billions-more-fences-and-drones-will-do-more-harm-good-secure-enough.

Ember, Carol R., and Melvin Ember. 1997. "Violence in the Ethnographic Record: Results of Cross-Cultural Research on War and Aggression." In *Troubled Times: Violence and Warfare in the Past*. Edited by Debra L. Martin and D. W. Frayer, 1–20. Amsterdam: Gordon and Breach.

Erikson, K. 1966. *Wayward Puritans: A Study in the Sociology of Deviance*. New York: Wiley.

Fanon, Frantz. 1963. *The Wretched of the Earth*. New York: Grove Press.

Farmer, Paul. 2004. "An Anthropology of Structural Violence." *Current Anthropology* 45(3): 305–25.

Ferguson, R. B. 1997. "Violence and War in Prehistory." In *Troubled Times: Violence and Warfare in the Past*. Edited by Debra L. Martin and D. W. Frayer, 321–55. Amsterdam: Gordon and Breach.

Foucault, Michel. 1973. *The Birth of the Clinic: An Archaeology of Medical Perception*. New York: Routledge.

Fromm, E. 1973. *The Anatomy of Human Destructiveness*. New York: Holt, Rinehart & Winston.

Galtung, Johan. 1969. "A Structural Theory of Integration." *Journal of Peace Research* 5(4): 167–91.

Geller, Pamela L. 2009. "Identity and Difference: Complicating Gender in Archaeology." *Annual Review of Anthropology* 38: 65–81.

Gerson, Joseph, ed. 1986. *The Deadly Connection: Nuclear War and U.S. Intervention.* Philadelphia, PA: New Society Publishers.

Givens, R. Dale, and Martin A. Nettleship. 1976. *Discussion on War and Human Aggression.* The Hague: Mouton & Co.

Grayson, George W. 2014. *The Evolution of Los Zetas in Mexico and Central America: Sadism as an Instrument of Cartel Warfare.* Carlisle, PA: U.S. Army War College Press.

Grillo, Ioan. 2008. "Behind Mexico's Wave of Beheadings." *Time.* 8 September.

Hanssen, Beatrice. 2000. *Critique of Violence: Between Poststructuralism and Critical Theory.* New York: Routledge.

Harvey, Penelope, and Peter Gow, eds. 1994. *Sex and Violence: Issues in Representation and Experience.* New York: Psychology Press.

Hitchens, Christopher. 2007. *God Is Not Great: How Religion Poisons Everything.* New York: Twelve.

Hoefnagels, Marjo, ed. 1977. *Repression and Repressive Violence.* Amsterdam: Swets and Zeitlinger.

Kelly, Raymond C. 2000. *Warless Societies and the Origins of War.* Ann Arbor: University of Michigan Press.

Klaus, Haagen D. 2012. "The Bioarchaeology of Structural Violence: A Theoretical Model and a Case Study." In *The Bioarchaeology of Violence.* Edited by Debra L. Martin, Ryan P. Harrod, and Ventura R. Pérez, 29–62. Gainesville: University Press of Florida.

Knauft, Bruce M. 1991. "Violence and Sociality in Human Evolution." *Current Anthropology* 32(4): 391–428.

Kwitny, Jonathan. 1984. *Endless Enemies: The Making of an Unfriendly World.* New York: Congdon and Weed.

Larsen, Clark Spencer. 1997. *Bioarchaeology: Interpreting Behavior from the Human Skeleton.* Cambridge, UK: Cambridge University Press.

———. 2001. "Frontiers of Contact: Bioarchaeology of Spanish Florida." *Journal of World Prehistory* 15(1): 69–123.

Lee, Brianna, and Danielle Renwick. 2017. "Mexico's Drug War." *Council on Foreign Relations.* 25 May.

Lifton, Robert J., and Richard Falk. 1982. *Indefensible Weapons: The Political and Psychological Case against Nuclearism.* New York: Basic Books.

Martin, Debra L., and Cheryl P. Anderson, eds. 2014. *Bioarchaeological and Forensic Perspectives on Violence: How Violent Death is Interpreted from Skeletal Remains.* Cambridge, UK: Cambridge University Press.

Martin, Debra L., and David W. Frayer. 1997. *Troubled Times: Violence and Warfare in the Past.* Amsterdam: Gordon and Breach Publishers.

Martin, Debra L., and Ryan P. Harrod. 2015. "Bioarchaeological Contributions to the Study of Violence." *Yearbook of Physical Anthropology* 156: 116–45.

Martin, Debra L., Ryan P. Harrod, and Ventura R. Pérez, eds. 2012. *The Bioarchaeology of Violence*. Gainesville: University Press of Florida.
———. 2013. *Bioarchaeology: An Integrated Approach to Working with Human Remains*. New York: Springer.
Matsuda, Matt K. 1996. *The Memory of the Modern*. Oxford: Oxford University Press.
Meyer, Maureen. 2014. *Mexico's Police WOLA: Many Reforms, Little Progress*. Washington, DC: Washington Office on Latin America.
Mummendey, Amelie, and Sabine Otten. 1993. "Aggression: Interaction between Individuals and Social Groups." In *Aggression and Violence: Social Interactionist Perspectives*. Edited by R. B. Felson and J. T. Tedeschi, 145–67. Washington, DC: American Psychological Association.
Obama, Barack. 2014. "White House Confirms Latest ISIS Beheading." 16 November. Retrieved 4 January 2019 from http://time.com/3587678/isis-peter-kassig/.
Pawlett, William. 2013. *Violence, Society and Radical Theory: Bataille, Baudrillard and Contemporary Society*. Farnham, Surrey: Ashgate.
Pearce, Jenny. 1982. *Under the Eagle: U.S. Intervention in Central America and the Caribbean*. Boston: South End Press.
Pérez, Ventura R. 2012. "The Politicization of the Dead." In *The Bioarchaeology of Violence*. Edited by Debra L. Martin, Ryan P. Harrod, and Ventura R. Pérez, 13–28. Gainesville: University Press of Florida.
———. 2016. "The Poetics of Violence in Bioarchaeology: Integrating Social Theory with Trauma Analysis." In *New Directions in Biocultural Anthropology*. Edited by Molly Zuckerman and Debra L. Martin, 453–69. Hoboken: Wiley & Sons, Inc.
Pérez, Ventura R., and Ashley Sherry. 2013. "A Humanitarian Crisis: Violence, Secrecy, and Hope in Mexico." *Anthropology News*, Special Issue on Crisis, June 2013.
Pérez, Ventura R., Ben Nelson, and Debra L. Martin. 2008. "Veneration or Violence: A Study of Variations in Patterns of Bone Modification at La Quemada." In *Violence in the Prehispanic Southwest*. Edited by Patricia Crown and Debra Nichols, 123–42. Tucson: University of Arizona Press.
"Police: Arizona Beheading Tied to Mexican Drug Cartel." 2011. *Albuquerque Journal*. 3 March. Retrieved 4 January 2019 from https://www.abqjournal.com/7489/police-arizona-beheading-tied-to-mexican-drug-cartel.html.
Rabasa, José. 2000. *Writing Violence on the Northern Frontier: The Historiography of Sixteenth-century New Mexico and the Legacy of Conquest*. Durham, NC: Duke University Press.
Renzetti, Claire. 1997. "Violence in Lesbian and Gay Relationships." In *Gender Violence: Interdisciplinary Perspectives*. Edited by L. O'Toole and J. Schiffman, 285–93. New York: New York University Press.
Reyes, R. R. 2016. "Hasta la Vista: Mexican Repatriation in Depression Era Tejas." *Journal of South Texas*, 29(2): 34–51.

Riches, David, ed. 1986. *The Anthropology of Violence*. New York: Blackwell
Rieder, Jonathan. 1984. "The Social Organization of Vengeance." In *Toward a General Theory of Social Control*. Edited by D. Black, 131–62. Orlando: Academic Press.
Sanders, Jerry Wayne. 1983. "Empire at Bay: Containment Strategies and American Politics at the Crossroads." *World Policy Institute* paper, no. 25.
Scheper-Hughes, Nancy. 1992. *Death without Weeping: The Violence of Everyday Life in Brazil*. Berkeley: University of California Press.
Scheper-Hughes, Nancy, and M. M. Lock. 1987. "The Mindful Body: A Prolegomenon to Future Work in Medical Anthropology." *Medical Anthropology Quarterly* 1(1): 6–41.
Scheper-Hughes, Nancy, and Phillipe Bourgois. 2004. "Introduction: Making Sense of Violence." In *Violence in War and Peace: An Anthology*. Edited by Nancy Scheper-Hughes and Phillipe Bourgois, 1–32. Malden, MA: Blackwell Publishing.
Schinkel, Willem. 2010. *Aspects of Violence: A Critical Theory*. London: Palgrave Macmillan.
Schmidt, Bettina, and Ingo Schröder. 2001. *Anthropology of Violence and Conflict*. Abingdon, UK: Routledge.
Schwendinger, Julia R., and Herman Schwendinger. 1983. *Rape and Inequality*. Beverly Hills, CA: Sage.
Shirk, David A. 2011. "The Drug War in Mexico: Confronting a Shared Threat." The Council on Foreign Relations, Inc. Council Special Report No. 60. March 2011.
Sluka, J. A. 1992. "The Anthropology of Conflict." In *The Paths to Domination, Resistance, and Terror*. Edited by C. Nordstrom and J. Martin, 18–36. Berkeley: University of California Press.
Sofaer, Joanna R. 2006. *The Body as Material Culture: A Theoretical Osteoarchaeology*. Cambridge, UK: Cambridge University Press.
Staub, Ervin. 1999. "The Roots of Evil: Social Conditions, Culture, Personality, and Basic Human Needs." In *Personality and Social Psychology Review* 3, no. 3: 179–92. doi:10.1207/s15327957pspr0303_2.
Steinbeck, John. 1975. *Steinbeck: A Life in Letters*. New York: Viking Press.
Stewart, Pamela J., and Andrew Strathern. 2002. *Violence: Theory and Ethnography*. New York: Continuum Publishing.
Stewart, B. 2008. Public testimony on House Bill 287g—Immigration legislation—Florida House of Representatives—State Affairs Committee—8 April 2008.
Stockwell, John. 1978. *In Search of Enemies: A CIA Story*. New York: Norton.
Taussig, Michael. 1984. "Culture of Terror, Space of Death: Roger Casement's Putumayo Report and the Explanation of Torture." *Comparative Studies in Society and History* 26, no. 3: 467–97.
Taylor, Christopher C. 1999. *Sacrifice as Terror: The Rwandan Genocide of 1994*. Oxford: Berg Press.

Trump, Donald J. 2017. "What we know so far about the Las Vegas shooting." *The Guardian*. 3 October. Retrieved 4 January 2019 from https://www.theguardian.com/us-news/2017/oct/02/las-vegas-shooting-what-we-know-so-far.

Turpin, Jennifer, and Lester R. Kurtz, eds. 1997. *The Web of Violence: From Interpersonal to Global*. Urbana: University of Illinois Press.

Vahabi, Mehrdad. 2004. *The Political Economy of Destructive Power*. London: Edward Elgar Publishing.

Verdery, Katherine. 1999. *The Political Lives of Dead Bodies: Reburial and Postsocialist Change*. New York: Columbia University Press.

Villarreal, M. Angeles. 2018. *U.S.-Mexico Economic Relations: Trends, Issues, and Implications* (CRS Report No. 32934). Congressional Research Service. Retrieved 4 January 2019 from https://fas.org/sgp/crs/row/RL32934.pdf.

Walker, Phillip L. 2001. "A Bioarchaeological Perspective on the History of Violence." *Annual Review of Anthropology* 30(1): 573–96.

Waterston, A. 2013. *My Father's Wars: Migration, Memory, and the Violence of a Century*. New York: Routledge.

Wedel, Vicki L., and Alison Galloway. 2013. *Broken Bones: Anthropological Analysis of Blunt Force Trauma*. Springfield, IL: Charles C. Thomas Publisher.

Wedel, Janie R., Cris Shore, Gregory Feldman, and Stacy Lathrop. 2005. "Toward an Anthropology of Public Policy." *Annals of the American Academy of Political and Social Science* 600: 30–51.

West, Cornel. 1993. *Race Matters*. Boston, MA: Beacon Press.

Whitehead, Neil L. 2004. "On the Poetics of Violence." In *Violence*. Edited by Neil L. Whitehead, 55–77. Santa Fe, NM: School of American Research Press.

Wrangham, Richard W., and Luke Glowacki. 2012. "Intergroup Aggression in Chimpanzees and War in Nomadic Hunter-Gatherers: Evaluating the Chimpanzee Model." *Human Nature* 23: 5–29.

Wright, Quincy. 1983 [1942]. *A Study of War*. 2nd edition. Chicago: University of Chicago Press.

Chapter 11

THE INTENTION OF EVIL

ASRAM IN ASANTE

William C. Olsen

Death of children requires explanation. Everywhere. Infant death presents a moral paradox of youth versus injustice, innocence versus incomprehensibility. How was the young life compromised? Can disease and death be explained with models beyond biomedicine?

Human suffering and evil in Asante come from abject existential events. These circumstances are known to all; and many experience them personally. These include cruelty, natural disasters, and childlessness (Obeng 1996, 205). Infertility and the absence of children are both regrettable and unbearable conditions. As chronic symptoms, they become matters for medical intervention. Childlessness due to premature death of an infant, or *mpatuwuo*, brings about suspicions of malevolent powers and of witchcraft, or *bayee* (Obeng 1996, 90). Such an assault upon children and families is evil, or *bɔne*. Disease or death of this kind must be disclosed by divination.

As Macfarlane notes, the essence of evil brings together an array of qualifying pejorative attributes of life: shadowy, mysterious, and hidden. By themselves, he argues, these features do not sufficiently provoke suspicions of malicious people or things. Evil must contain an aggressive and active force. Witches consume live human flesh. A witch with strong powers may even bring about death of infants. Because it is unprovoked and unjust, this attack is evil. Because of intentions of suffering, the perpetrator is evil. "These attacks are not justified; either they are motiveless, or the motives are perverted" (Macfarlane 1985, 57). This fact is summarized by an Akan healer:

"Evil thoughts and intentions, whether you are aware of them or not, make yourself and other persons ill" (Fink 1989, 199). For Asante, few areas in life present greater suffering and torment than the lack of children and family. As is commonly noted, "There is the expectation that every married couple will be able to have children and will give birth to children." Suffering arises in Asante when this premise to family life is challenged. "A child has the potential of having a good life and many blessings and much happiness. Attacking the child is an assault to those things which can come in the life of a child." Bringing harm upon children "creates a reality of suffering for both parent and child." It is a way of "causing the family pain and a way of making the lineage and family have no future." "Causing suffering via *asram* is not just a physical and medical reality. It is also a financial reality which brings about financial suffering. It is a way of altering the future of the family."

Such remarks are handedly made in discussions about childhood death. This chapter deals with evil intentions to destroy the family, especially in relation to the death of infants. Child deaths are acts of mystical hostility often initiated from persons close to the household. "It is jealousy from within that breeds occult aggression" (Geschiere 2013, 93); and it is resentment of new status or prosperity that triggers the "decisive turn, exploding the coherence of the triangle of witchcraft, intimacy, and (dis)trust" (2013, 90). Bringing disease and harm to any infant is a reprehensible. It is evil.

In this chapter, I write about the sudden death of infants from symptoms identified as a form of sent-sickness, or *ɔma yaree*. The affliction is known as *asram*. How do infants die suddenly from sickness? Do other persons bear some responsibility? How can infants with *asram* be treated? I investigate the premise of evil in such events. Asante notions of evil will be outlined; and it will be shown how Asante apply the ideas of evil to the moral circumstances of disease and death of infants. Also relevant to this case is how Asante view evil as an expropriation of health, vitality, identity, and the future. The article reviews what is done both medically (through biomedicine) and mystically (through divination) to rectify the health of a child and to remedy the immediate social environment of the family and neighborhood that make up the living environment of the child.

The town is Ashanti-Mampong, which is found in Sekyere West district, one hour northeast of Kumasi in western, central Ghana. I analyze *asram* as intentional malice on the part of those who may bring the disease to the infant and its family. It is a mode of evil, or *bɔne*, according to Asante precepts of morality. I pursue the notion that *asram* indicates one of the most sinister forms of *bɔne* among Asante. I analyze the cultural foundations of therapy, which include medical pluralism of Western medicines, herbal remedies, and spiritualist medical interventions within divinatory ritual.

Asram Example #1: 5 May 2012

> While attending divination in the village of Penteng, a grandmother requested me to return to her compound and witness the symptoms currently afflicting the woman's granddaughter. The infant's symptoms were a disease syndrome which commonly attacks the internal organs and also the skin, complexion, and head size of infants. Over weeks, I observed the symptoms diminish as the child's mother made repeat appearances at the diviner's shrine and hospital. The mother sought the healing powers of the spirits, or *abosom*, as they are manifest among humans through a diviner and healer known locally as *ɔkɔmfɔ*. The grandmother pursued medication from Mampong Government Hospital. Drugs given included Metronidazole, an antibiotic used to address anaerobic infections and also for certain dermatological conditions; and Floxa, a broad spectrum antibiotic. Both are suitable for treating infections and fever in small children. Through the diviner, the *abosom* interceded in the child's body and its malfunctions. The grandmother also recognized the complex of symptoms identifiable as *asram*. The seriousness of *asram* symptoms are well understood as being potentially fatal. The diviner concurred in this diagnosis; and the relevant course of action then shifted toward understanding the cause of the disease and setting out to find a cure.

Both women concluded pharmaceuticals took effect on the baby, whose symptoms subsided after the correct drug regimen. Even so, they also concluded that there was very little room for error. They thus believed that the desired course of therapy should be the quickest route to finding an alternative mode of treatment. That day, the child was brought to the diviner at Penteng. One week later, the child's health gradually improved. By the family's account, doctors' intervention, drugs, herbs, and divination protected and cured the child. The infant as victim is similar to hundreds of other illness narratives caused by witchcraft. I have written before on this subject of child death: "Children and the unborn were the most common victims of witchcraft. Asante children perpetuated the future of the matrilineage. In no other areas of Asante life was witchcraft more pronounced than in the incapacities of women to bear children" (Olsen 2002, 539).

Asram in Asante

Asram is a folk illness identified with the diseases of young children under the age of twelve months. Its symptoms are physical, yet it has metaphysical origins. *Asram* is classified locally as a kind of dangerous disease, or *yaree a ehu*, because the potential result of disease symptoms may be death or long-term impairment. A local healer notes, "There is no cure for the disease or the person may die very soon when they have these diseases." Or, "they know soon they will leave this planet." Symptoms of *asram* include rash, reduced weight, enlarged head, high fever, distended stomach at birth, low red-cell blood count so the child becomes ashen or white, forehead is pushed back, small holes in the head which allow child to breathe through those holes, small white bumps on the upper back and stomach, enlarged veins especially around the stomach, different colored veins, and the face becomes multicolored—usually green or sometimes the color of a mashed, fried egg. There is also *asram mpampo*, when a large boil develops around the neck area; and there is *asram bodibwo*, where the infant develops wrinkles on the upper body making him "resemble an old person." Babies who suffer from *asram* "lose weight, cannot nurse from the mother, cannot lay down comfortably, will have sores on or around the mouth, may have a line on the head or a 'divided head,' or visible veins on the forehead, or an extended stomach. One or more of these symptoms provides adequate evidence for suspecting *asram*."

A child is rarely born with symptoms of *asram*; but *asram* may happen when someone sends sickness to the fetus through the mother's womb. There are minimal opinions as to its origins. Some say *asram* may have a biomedical causal basis. An infant exposed to these symptoms elsewhere may contract *asram* symptoms, for example. Differing perspectives on the cause of *asram* included anemia, "general dirtiness" or unclean surroundings, or bad hygiene of the family. It is also recognized as cerebral malaria. Poverty is also said to be a cause. Most argue that *asram* is brought about by the unspoken desires of a close neighbor or family member who seeks to harm the family by bringing suffering and death to the household. *Asram* is usually introduced within the first weeks of life, and is generally "passed by someone with malicious intent who visits the family to see the child during the first weeks or months after the birth." Both sources of *asram* are critical since both neighbors and kin represent the kind of intimacy of witchcraft spoken in Africa, where a witch's "most threatening attack is still supposed to come from inside" (Geschiere 2013,

16). This "leitmotif" represents a combining of the danger and aggression of the outside world in an "interface of intimate relations within the house" (Geschiere 2013, 16). It is the combining of closeness with assault that brings such horror to the act.

Asram Example #2: 12 June 2014

> Howa's younger sister gave birth in 2013. A woman herbalist, who passed by the house each day, heard the newborn cry. The herbalist used *asram* on the baby, and so the baby developed lock-jaw and was unable to breastfeed and eat. It began losing weight. The herbalist offered to treat the child for a fee. The family agreed; and after two days the child became asymptomatic and gained weight. The herbalist was suspected because this happened several times in the village. But she was never confronted.

Asram is a set of disease symptoms caused primarily by mystical agency found exclusively in infants under the age of six to twelve months. The child is inflicted with one or more of the aforementioned symptoms. These fester in the infant for two or three months. The child may gradually lose weight and die. *Asram* may become manifest in symptoms that are familiar to medical doctors. Every mother who spoke to me about *asram* in their child had been to the Mampong Government Hospital to treat the child for the manifest symptoms. *Asram* is also known to be the result of a virus or bacteria, but because it is considered to be spiritual, it is resistant to Western biomedicines. Biomedical remedies are used; but biomedicine alone is ultimately incapable of bringing about a cure for individual *asram* cases. "It is passed by wicked people: those who are very rich, or those who cheat, or there may be wicked who will give the child its *sunsum yaree*." At its core, *asram* assaults the basic principles of the family, marriage, and procreation. It is also believed to attack the personal destiny of the afflicted child. T. E. Kyei spoke of how common the disease was in the early twentieth century:

> A child might have the disease at birth or be attacked later. The head bones of the victim were said to be so soft that pulsation was distinctly visible on the crown of the little child. Its breath was in the form of snoring. It looked feeble and was lacking in the normal body movements. The disease was said to be deadly in those days, claiming the lives of many newly-born babies. . . . Immediately on delivery she put the child under the care of the *asram* specialist. (2001, 95)

Healing of *asram* comes most likely through intervention by the *abosom* as they work through a particular diviner. Left untreated, *asram*'s influence may impact the wider lineage and thereby spoil or threaten a line of descent, a condition (McCaskie 2000, 93) known historically as *abusua yade*. Witch-finding and aggressive modes of witchcraft in Asante spread in the region in the late nineteenth and early twentieth centuries as wealth increased, generally due to rubber, gold, and cocoa; and these were no longer controlled by the *asantehene* (McCaskie 1986). Sudden wealth often gave rise to suspicions of mystical powers; and the new bearers of wealth also protected their resources through witchcraft. M. J. Field wrote of one entrepreneur, "My kinsmen envy me and have sent me a sickness" (1960, 115). Quarrels over debt and financing provided a foundation for greater suspicion. Loans went unpaid. Money was squandered. New wealth became a form of private riches. Because there was little distribution by a wealthy kinsman, someone may "give him a river," meaning they had "implored the river-god to destroy him" (Field 1960, 115). Busia argues that cocoa was so lucrative that it introduced elements of instability into the matrilineage. Tensions strained relationships between a man's wives and his sisters (Busia 1951, 127). Fortes observed this firsthand in 1945: "In Ashanti, money is everything. If you have none you are nobody; if you have *sika* (wealth) you are a man, and you can be proud" (ASSM 1945a). In times past, and in the Asante present, witchcraft took the heaviest toll on children. Women were made sterile, their wombs turned upside down by a witch. A woman may also become "*awo ma wu*, one who brings forth children for death, meaning the children all die prematurely in infancy" (Debrunner 1961, 43). Witches were known to steal the womb itself, or render the family devoid of any posterity. Women were known to bring forth dead children, and thereby confess they had eaten the child within the womb (Olsen 1998).

As in the past, diviners and herbalists also use herbal remedies to treat *asram*. It is estimated by many in Mampong that of children who die before the age of one, about 70 percent die from symptoms associated with *asram*. Herbalists state they treat *asram* with shea butter cream, which is used to massage the joints, the veins, and the head until the skull bones are maneuvered back into place. The infant may also be given an herbal concoction that helps it to digest properly. The ɔkɔmfɔ is also likely to administer similar herbal remedies for the dermatological symptoms associated with *asram*. These actions invoke the magnificent healing powers and abilities of the *abosom*, who will favor to heal the child if divination is performed correctly and if sacrifice from the client, or the child's family, is well received. The diviner at Penteng declared:

More serious symptoms mean greater need for mystical intervention by the *abosom*. When *asram* is making a child die, the *abosom* intervene on behalf of the child. They are instrumental in alleviating the disease symptoms of the infant and restoring the child to good health. Because of the intervention of the *abosom*, there must be some sacrifice. This is usually a chicken.

Asante divination involves a healer and his staff who are associated with named deities known as *abosom*. Spirit possession by ritual is used to inhabit the body of the diviner. Patrons attend shrine performances seeking such powers. Only the diviner has access to particular *abosom*. "Through possession, I can see and hear whatever the *abosom* want to tell me or let me know." *Abosom* wish to fulfill requests for healing, financial blessing, and sometimes romantic desires. The diviner's claims of authority in healing matters assert a position of power with the *abosom*. "The *abosom* chose me. They want to help people through me." He also declared, the "whole of my body becomes possessed. I am the agent to communicate" the messages and powers of the deities. Thus, "I am able to tell people who come here this is what the *abosom* are saying" about their particular issues. As with other diviners, the healer at Penteng was chosen by the *abosom*. He continues to learn how to heal, including the use of herbal remedies. Local healing, including herbal meds, is associated with the vast powers of the forest and with history.

> The *abosom* taught our fore-fathers about everything: how to marry, about families, how to run the state and be king, how to form the kingdom. But they also taught us about medicines and healing— through herbal drugs. Herbs are directly from our ancestors and the *abosom*.

As one senior man described local Asante medicines, "Black man's medicine is better than white man's medicine. The people who cure *sunsum yaree* today are in the villages. You go to the village because it is near the bush; and the bush is more powerful to treat *sunsum yaree*."

Asram Example #3: 19 March 2009

An eighteen-month-old male was diagnosed in the hospital with cerebral malaria. Doctors treated the child with an antibiotic, and *Di Quinin*, an antimalarial drug. Child's condition did improve steadily. Parents wanted different treatments; so they promised to take the baby for analysis at Komfo Anokye Teaching Hospital in Kumasi. When the child was brought by his mother and grandfather and initially admitted to Mampong Government Hospital, he was unconscious and had been in a coma for four days. The father stayed in the village. After diagnosis of malaria, the mother spoke with her husband by phone. They became convinced the child was partially paralyzed and had *asram*. In the village, the panicked husband consulted with a Christian pastor and a diviner. The pastor declared that the disease was *sunsum yaree*, and that only he could help the child through prayer and ritual. Meanwhile, even though the child gradually improved in the hospital and was now eating, the family remained convinced of the diagnosis of *sunsum yaree*. The child received hospital meds for one week. He improved, was crying and eating on his own. The parents discharged the child; and the head nurse believed they returned to the village to treat the child through spiritual healing.

To understand *asram*, it is important to comprehend how the body is perceived, including the component of each individual known as *sunsum*. I will also briefly describe various elements of the body and spirit.

Human Bodies

At birth, an Asante child bears both physiological and social dimensions. These forms serve to help it become recognized as a human person whose being is constituted of the various features of Asante human physical existence and cultural life. These include body (*honam*), soul (*ɔkra*), spirit (*sunsum*), breath (*honhom*), blood (*mogya* or *bogya*), and a sense of destiny (*nkrabea*) (Gyekye 1987; Wiredu 1980). The *ɔkra* is the "humanizing principle;" and as such, it helps differentiate human persons from animals or plants or inanimate objects. "*ɔkra* is in the body; it gives you your life. Without *ɔkra*, you are dead. Sight, speech, hearing, and touch are all controlled by *ɔkra*." And it is the "presence of *mogya* that makes the child a human being" in Asante. (Twumasi 1975, 21).

A child is born with the *mogya* of the mother and so he or she is a member of his mother's extended family, the matrilineage, or *abusua*. The *abusua* is considered a group of kin who are living and also those who are dead, a "kin group across the boundary of death" (de Witte 2001, 28). Scholarship of gender and of labor provide deeper meanings to *mogya* and *abusua*. Allman and Tashjian write about new trends for women, work, and money as growing economies emerged in the late nineteenth and early twentieth centuries. Parenting remained an important feature of women's status and of familial identities. "Childlessness was the worst of all possible female fates" (Allman and Tashjian 2000, 48). Focus on reproduction and the *abusua* was paramount as children were more kin to their maternal than they were to the father's family. The future was so bound up in children that infertility was often grounds for divorce, as was "death of most or all of the children from a particular marriage" (Allman and Tashjian 2000, 47). Thus, marriage and children provided identity and fiscal stability to women. "It was through marriage that a woman expected to bear children; it was through marriage that she hoped to increase the numbers in her own family and insure her security and well-being in old age; it was through marriage that she sought spiritual and economic protection for both herself and her children" (Allman and Tashjian 2000, 49–50). Gracia Clark also confirms that identity with one's matrilineage is a moral principle and emotional component of women: "Asantes may try to evade specific lineage obligations, but they cannot deny them in principle without denying the blood in their veins" (Clark 1994, 97). Asantes may refer to marriage relations as transitory; but ties to members of one's own blood (*mogya*) are ever-enduring through life. These relations serve as a means of mutually financial assistance, independence, and social welfare. "A woman without an income is not a real woman, but like a child or, more precisely, an idiot" (Clark 1994, 107). Disruptions or assaults to realities of kinship, such as infertility or premature death, are viewed with suspicion, contempt, and horror.

A critical dimension of the human person is one's *sunsum*. *Sunsum* is spirit, often known to be a qualifying dimension of "soul." "*Sunsum* is the pivot of the whole body. It doesn't like the body to offend or to sin. It keeps the body alive." *Sunsum* is inherited from the father; and insulting or offending one's father may bring about illness and death to the offender. "We have people whose *sunsum* is sick and they are unable to eat or sleep well for many years." McCaskie has well elaborated on *sunsum* in Asante history. These are the facts even today:

> A *sunsum* could leave the body during sleep, was involved in dreaming, and was susceptible to the spiritual malady of witchcraft. But a "heavy" *sunsum* was regarded—quite predictably—as the best defense against witchcraft (*wo sunsum ye duru ɔbayifoɔ ntumi wo*: "if your *sunsum* is 'heavy' the witch cannot overpower you"). A *sunsum* could become agitated and harbor malice; this might presage illness in the individual, and malaise in society. (1995, 168)

"*Sunsum* should be in control; then the person's health is good." Such statements of health and the human spirit are widely offered in general conversations about medicine and disease. Fortes noted a child cannot thrive if he has become alienated from the *sunsum* of the father (1950, 266). Archbishop Peter Sarpong said in personal interview, someone "with a strong *sunsum* who does not weaken his personality by bad behavior is more resistant to *bayee*." One cannot be healthy with a weak or ineffective *sunsum*. Some may attempt to destroy another's health by attacking an individual's *sunsum*. When the *sunsum* is assaulted, disease symptoms are recognized as spiritual sickness, *sunsum yaree*. "If someone is doing something to you by your *sunsum*, you can't see it; but your body will feel it. *Sunsum* can affect the body by making it sick." This is the case of *asram*, as noted by the diviner at Penteng: "Doctor and pharmaceutical procedures improve health; but they cannot cure *asram*. *Sunsum* can affect the body by making it sick." In rare cases, a father or mother may not want a child who has physical or mental defects to survive. They may, he said, "give the child a bad *sunsum* and change its *nkrabea*. This will change its appearance or will cause it to become ill and die." This is known to happen only in unlikely events of disability or mental impairment.

A vital feature of the self is *nkrabea*, or one's destiny. The concept is outlined elsewhere by Meyer Fortes (1983). All living beings possess a particular set of defining aspects of their own life and future, or what they may become and are meant to be. God, who is *onyame*, is the final arbiter of existence and of *nkrabea*. This is prior to mortality; and *nkrabea* is placed within the person before the individual's birth. Destiny and disposition of a child are also formed by the child's father (Fortes 1950, 266). Obeng describes *nrabea* in present-day Asante: "Successes and failures of people, and time, place, and manner of death, fall within the category of the 'givens' an individual possesses." The foundation of those "givens" was established "as the individual was departing the presence of God to be born into an *abusua*" (Obeng 1996, 89). Altering one's *nkrabea* is similar to mocking God's judgement. Alex, age thirty-eight and a life resident of Mampong, speaks of *nkrabea* of the child in a family who may be targeted for *asram* because of their gifts and abilities:

> It is believed that in every Asante family, there may be one child who rises up above present economic and material conditions of that family. Attacking the child with *asram* is one way of potentially eliminating that living, healthy child who may improve the family. The perpetrator is sometimes able to see the future of a child; and it is that future which is also being attacked.

Thus, the medical sickness of *asram* becomes an arena of a wider moral conflict of individuals, families, and economic and financial well-being.

Choosing to defer children, or avoid them altogether, is unheard of. Two young nurses corroborated this fact: "This may happen in Europe or America; we see that kind of thing take place in movies and on TV. But it would not happen here." An honorable life is being in a family, living as husband or as wife, and having children. "There is the expectation that every married couple will be able to have children and will give birth to children." It is "presumed" that every "female will give birth to children at some point." Within the family, diseases such as *asram* are seen not simply as biomedical realities. Rather, they must be considered as an assault on the viability and the future of the *abusua*. Such an assault on the individual becomes a collective affront on the household. According to the diviner at Penteng, because of its degradation of individual potentiality, *asram* also confounds the moral foundation of the person:

> A child has the potential of having a good life and many blessings and much happiness. Attacking the child is an assault to those things which can come in the life of a child. Attacking a child creates a reality of suffering for both mother and child. If the mother has offended someone or caused pain, then attacking the new born with *asram* will cause suffering through vengeance. Limiting or negating the future of the *abusia* is another way of altering the *nkrabea* of the family and also of altering its future. Both of these are considered *bɔne*. The suffering of the child has a reality beyond that of the immediate body of the child.

Evil

Evil, or *bɔne*, in Asante is most often defined by actions manifesting nefarious character. Intention to do *bɔne* was narrated to Fortes (ASSMa) in 1945: "There are some bad men in the world. Some of them inherit wickedness from their fathers. Some bad men are not men. They may be bad spirits (*sunsum mmɔnce*) who came to be born by women." Degrees of punishment, public and private, become appropriate responses. Being a thief is *bɔne* (Olsen 2015). For any population to classify evil is to establish a mode of power, the power to bring about suffering. Associating expressions of evil with a medical system is similar to that of any other sectors of life that form people's being, their identities, and their futures. When powers are mystical, and when they are meant to harm, anyone of any age or gender is prepared to frame them within moral parameters of the reality of evil.

Identifying *bɔne* in Asante, especially in cases of *asram*, requires a greater comprehension of three aspects of Asante morals. Actions and thought that are *bɔne* are deemed unacceptable and deplorable.

Asante identify three features associated with actions or persons that are bɔne. These are *ahinta* (hidden), *mepeese* (intention/desire), and *emorosoɔ* (excess). Thoughts and actions that are bɔne include at least one of these characteristics. Within the Asante moral ethos, various kinds of behaviors have been designated by numerous people in Mampong as having explicit elements of bɔne, and as thereby being reprehensible and undesirable modes of public or private conduct. *Ahinta* means hidden or purposely concealed; and it refers to things especially reviled and hidden such as *bayee*.

Theft becomes the means to potentially disrupt social and commercial flows of money and property; and these are often utilized as tools of social welfare, business affairs, and commercial enterprise. Theft is more than the taking of an object. It is taking of livelihood. Responses condemned it as an assault upon present and future family and commercial connections. Asante recognize theft as evil not just because of the expropriation of another's goods or money; theft of objects also undoes individual plans, social networks of exchange, and the cooperation of communities to provide for future interests. Theft destroys the future (Olsen 2015). Theft of livelihood, of household tranquility, and of health are modes of bɔne.

ɔma yaree: Sent Sickness

Sent sickness, or *ɔma yaree*, includes dangerous symptoms due to the use of mystical tools that bring disease and sometimes death to a victim. In cases of infant children, these include sudden and unexplainable disease symptoms. Children are especially vulnerable to *ɔma yaree* because they have weak *sunsum*. On suspicion of *asram*, families encounter infant illness within a moral framework of intentionality. Illness symptoms in Asante are most often identified as the result of viruses, pathogens, trauma, genetics, and other features of a biomedical model. Nevertheless, human and spiritual agents are known to bring suffering and disease. *Asram* is "passed by very wicked people" who willingly harm children because of their greed and desire to harm, according to the grandmother example above. Their mystical tools are widely known to be a form of *bayee*. "This sickness is usually introduced within the first weeks of life, and it is generally passed by someone with malicious intent who visits the family to see the child during the first weeks or months of life." For this reason, new parents often restrict nearly all visitors who wish to see the new infant at home. The witch sends symptoms upon the child because he or she is having some issue of jealousy or anger with the child's mother or immediate family member, or because they envy the otherwise healthy infant. "Attacking a child creates a reality of suffering for both mother and child. If the mother has offended or brought pain in a moral sense, then attacking the new born baby via *asram* will cause suffering on the mother" in retaliation or out of jealousy for that mother.

Asram Example #4: 15 June 2014

> A new mother at twenty-nine, Grace, was told by her own mother not to take the child outside the house or compound for three or four months, as any stranger could project *asram* on the infant. At two months, her baby developed *asram*. Symptoms included hydrocephaly, greenish skin on the chest, and stunted growth. She resisted going to the hospital. Her first mode of therapy was a herbalist, who bathed the child in medicinal forest herbs three times daily for three weeks. Herbs were also mixed in a concoction for the baby to drink. After one week, rashes on the body indicated "*asram* coming out of the body." After three weeks, the baby was asymptomatic. Grace did not know who or why someone sent this sickness to her baby. But she said, "Someone can see you have a child or are having a baby; and they want to harm the child. That is the kind of person they are." In other cases, babies brought to the hospital have been treated with western pharmaceuticals.

Young children, infants, and unborn fetuses—including those not yet conceived—are icons of the battleground between mystical forces of good and evil. "Not all eyes are good. Some are very, very bad. And all these people must do is look at the child, and this person may pass along *asram*." When the health of a child or family member is compromised, especially in unexpected and sudden cases, a cursing agent may be suspected. When somebody is cursed, the perpetrator "curses you and everything around you or about you. In the case of resulting sickness, then the *abosom* who was invoked in the curse will bring the sickness on the entire family: mother, child, and infant." Effects of witchcraft cursing are serious, and sometimes fatal. The life of an infant or even a fetus may be at stake in a kind of war between good and evil. The witness of the diviner at Penteng was clear. In some cases, witchcraft is used prior to conception and may result in a sterile womb.

> In some cases when the witch has taken a woman's ovaries, the witch may be reluctant to give them back. As the *abosom* comes to retrieve them in divination, the witch may refuse—thus causing a war between

the two forces. The *abosom* does not always win that conflict. In some cases, the *abosom* does not win or cannot help. Then the diviner cannot help; and the patient cannot be treated—or the child may die. The diviner can only do what the *abosom* will allow him to do or are willing to do for the patient.

In this battle:

> the *abosom* have their own weapons of war: swords, cutlass, guns, and even airplanes. Because of this arsenal of weapons, the *abosom* usually prevail; and the woman's ovaries are reinstated. But in some cases, the *abosom* does not prevail. The witch prevails; and the ovaries of the woman are not recaptured and returned. She will then remain infertile. All this battle takes place in the spiritual realm.

Because of Ghana's National Health Scheme, most women and children have access to hospitals and clinics, three pharmacies, and ten chemical stores in town. Prescription and over-the-counter pharmaceuticals manufactured in the UK, Germany, United States, and China are sold. Most people self-medicate in conditions of yellow fever, typhoid, hypertension, malaria, and anemia. Nevertheless, disease symptoms found in young children are very often suspected as being the result of some human agent who has sent the illness in order to manifest envy over the life and health of the child; or they may be manifesting greed over the wealth of the parents, as noted previously. Perspectives on *asram* vary. It is considered by many as the most likely form of disease-causation when illness symptoms occur among infants and small children. Visitors to the household of the newborn may be suspected of bringing the illness. There was also certainty that, though unusual, *asram* could be sent by mobile phones or via the Internet. *Asram* may be passed by simply glancing at the child, or by hearing its voice. It may be passed by someone taking a piece of baby clothing and infecting the item with disease. Gifts or food brought for the infant are also suspect. *Asram* may even be passed to the fetus in the womb; and this may result in complicated pregnancy and birth, stillbirth, or a child that is prone to sickness. Local healers see many such cases; and one healer described the possible scenarios this way:

> Some people develop the medicine on the back part of their hand. If they are sharing an eating bowl with you or something, if the hand touches you, you will get it. If you touch the hand, or maybe if a pregnant lady is by the pipe getting water, someone could offer to carry her water and easily give it to her. (Matos 2005, 15)

Infant death may be discovered to be the result of a struggle between family members and the parents. Rapidly ascending illness symptoms in an infant and the sudden death of young children are possibly suspect of sent sickness from extended family or household visitors. Tension resides within marriage and a household. In 2005, I witnessed a day-long divinatory cleansing of two cowives who had become so jealous and embittered of one another that each woman made dangerous mystical curses toward the other. Some cursing was directed toward children. Each woman's curse invoked powers of named *abosom* who dwell on the powerful Antoa River. The intent was to bring death of the cowife and her children. As sickness came upon the older wife, the younger revealed her animosity and deception. Both sought the assistance of a senior diviner in order to reverse the mystical actions.

> If the child becomes sick or dies, the sickness and death may be the result of the *bɔne* of the birth mother or father. In that case, it may be the mother was unfaithful or it may be that the child is the result of infidelity. Or, someone who has cursed you for some reason—this may fall on and effect the health of the child. When somebody curses you, they curse you and everything around you or about you.

People describe the act as so malicious that once the guilt of the sender is established, there may be beatings and even brutal death to anyone who perpetrates this upon a child. Because the guilt of the sender often cannot be firmly established, people don't take the law into their own hands with such a serious punishment. Instead, since the illness is mystically caused, the victim must see the diviner (*ɔkɔmfɔ*). The perpetrator, also, must stand before the healer, confess his or her wrongs, and agree to abide by any instructions and guidance given during the cleansing rite. More commonly, a mother and child will bathe in water flush with herbal remedies designed to protect; or the mother will cover a very small child with a blanket while out in the market since "covering the baby makes it harder for someone to send the child *asram*" (Matos 2005, 16).

Factors of *asram* may be present in infant bodies but they are active only when an agent causes them to be so through cursing or witchcraft. Symptoms of any disease may be the result of *ɔma yaree*. Understanding those symptoms and the root causes becomes part of a medical continuum in which patients seek out a plurality of remedies that combine local forms of healing, self-medication by way of a half dozen pharmacies in town or traditional herbal medicines, and medical intervention from the Mampong Government Hospital. Medical therapy may likewise be sought out since the patient now recognizes that the symptoms are responsive only to a healer who will have power over them.

Evil and *Asram*

Why consider human intentions when children become gravely ill and die? Why send the sickness upon the child? By the late 1930s, earnestness by British colonial courts to prosecute for medicines via witch-finding had waned. Shrine owners adapted requests that allowed them to identify their witch-finding practices as medical clinics. Diviners began a new era of practicing witch-finding by becoming legalized and licensed. The Manhyia Palace Archives in Kumasi have many applications for medical practice by shrine priests. They are very similar to the following: "The usefulness and services of this fetish is most abundant—viz, it wards off all manner of diseases, facilitate fertility in both sexes of mankind, guards against any wicked intentions and means of injuring to human beings" (MPA 1/1/102).

New laws in the 1930s abrogated any medical and social concerns. Treatment to ritually reverse physiological barrenness in mothers and fathers began in earnest. Today, realities of infertility are reversed from the situation of the 1930s. Anxious parents often seek biomedical help for infertility. Western doctors and local herbalists have become the method of choice for concerns of fertility. Instead, eradication of children through supernatural assault now happens most often after the birth. Mystically realized killing of children is more common than the sterilization of an earlier era. There are three reasons for this development.

First, sending sickness is a mode of contempt. Someone despises members of the victim's family for some reason yet to be discerned. This perspective of contempt was supposed in each of the four *asram* examples. The mother of the infant may have done "something disrespectful to a family member, extended family or neighbor." A mother whose child suffered *asram* suspected her husband's sister as the perpetrator. Years of bitter feelings and resentment resulted in the attack. The act itself may be entirely personal between two members of an extended family, or neighbors, or even cowives. The outraged party then retaliates for the offense by "harming the most vulnerable feature of the mother's life: that is her child." Because Asantes are matrilineal, it is well known that offenses by the father are less objectionable. The tension is most notable with the *abusua* (Fortes 1950, 275).

Second, envy for the beauty or appeal and serenity of the child and happiness of the parents exist within the extended family. Likewise, destroying the future and livelihood of the extended family by harming the child are also known. Fink has noted this for the Akan: "Sickness puts a person into a painful situation by preventing one from fulfilling all one's social duties." In that case, commonly regarded actions of the perpetrator "are entirely unprovoked. Instead, they are acting out of evil intention and malice" (1989, 223). *Asram* may also be a way to make a family suffer through the expenses of hospital time. The medical sickness of *asram* becomes an arena of a wider moral conflict of individuals, families, and economic and financial futures. "For that sickness, the parents would suffer a lot. The parents would be frightened; and they would spend a lot on any child who goes to the hospital." Because of weak *sunsum*, infants have a lessened ability to resist the attacks of sent sickness.

Third, motivations, including suffering, are revealed. "The intended victim may never be said to be a single human being. The suffering of the child has a reality beyond that of the immediate body of the child." In all cases, an ɔkɔmfɔ determines the intentional meanings of the *sunsum yaree*. Such persons historically were "acknowledged to be a deadly subversion of community" (McCaskie 2000, 101). These malevolent individuals, notes Alex (age thirty-eight):

> may be infertile; may be single and childless; may be unable to conceive for some reason. That person thus sees the mother's life as mocking or ridiculing her/him for what she/he does not have. *Asram* will bring pain to the lives of the mother and father. Sending *asram* may also be a conscious effort to destroy the future of the victim's family.

This scenario is consistent with the description of African witchcraft and its ties to intimacy. "Everyone knows that when an 'innocent' . . . is attacked, she or he will die slowly" (Geschiere 2013, 13). The witch imposes a "treacherous opening in the closure of the family, draining the community of its life force" (2013, 130). "What is valuable for you is what they want to take from you." Their offending actions mean they are not simply "the very negation of community" (McCaskie 2000, 101). But there are also connections between *asram* and destroying the extended family.

The reality of medical treatment also brings a financial burden upon families and the broader lineage. Some cases of *asram* are severe and quite serious. This may result in prolonged doctor or hospital visits, including in-patient care and medications. As stated, *asram* may also bring death. In both circumstances, the family is forced to spend many hundreds, even thousands, of *cedis* in order to medically treat the child and also to bury the child in case of death.

But the life of a child represents more than a biomedical assessment. As described to me by senior men speaking from a lifetime of understanding, "It is believed that in every Asante family or household, there may be one child who rises up above the present economic and material conditions of that family. Attacking the child with *asram* may be one way of potentially eliminating that living, healthy child which could be the person to improve the family's wealth." More than any other form of *sunsum yaree*, a child with *asram* brings to a household the grief and uncertainty of not only child loss but also a mystical assault on the wider kinship system. The perpetrator may be "capable of seeing the future of that child; and it is that future which is also being attacked." Thus, the diviner Gyasi claims the medical symptoms of *asram* become an arena of wider "moral conflict of individuals, families, and economic and financial futures."

> Witches know the future of persons. They can see into the future. They can see if one person will become a doctor, or if another person will be president, or someone else will grow and do wonderful and helpful things for his family. It is this future that the witch desires to place in peril. The witch wants to destroy, to harm, to disable, and to even kill. If the witch can cause serious sickness—or even death—via *asram*, then the witch has become successful at damaging the lives not just of infant child but also of the larger family network.

Thus, *asram* is much more than its debilitating symptoms. The infant's body is a living symbol of active destructive and negative mystical forces. The child's body is used for purposes of *bɔne*. The body is then a dynamic receptacle of human envy and of the purposes of misery. Such forces may even be successful at bring about the death of a child. The body becomes a recipient of *bɔne* in a way that is directly opposed to the body of the *ɔkɔmfɔ* in attempts to vanquish evil. The child's body becomes a vessel for the *abosom* to work their powers of healing. Sickness and death, in this case, may be seen as immediate manifestations of an abundance of *bɔne* active in the natural world.

Rhetoric of evil and child death has captured the imagination of self-ordained evangelical pastors.

Conclusion

Evil in Asante involves the intention to cause suffering. "A child has the potential of having a good life and many blessings and much happiness. Attacking the child is an assault to those things which can come in the life of a child." Asante hold great value and expectations for the parents and extended family. Mystical assault on the youngest member of the lineage because of their vulnerability becomes a way of causing great pain. Suffering via *asram* is not just a physical and medical reality. There are also financial costs in those cases involving hospital and doctor visits. Death is also a tremendous emotional, as well as financial, burden. *Asram* also becomes a way of altering or diminishing the future of the family and lineage. "Asante believe it is Nyame who is taking care of them by giving them a child to one day care for the parents." Sent sickness may change the future of the individual. It may alter the course of family needs or extended kin relations. "The sender of *asram* will see it as a conscious effort to destroy the future of the victim's family. That person may have some witch powers; and he/she may want to use those powers to change the future of that family." By eliminating life or by degrading the body and capacity of a child to become an adult, one who brings *asram* becomes recognized as a person with a "conscious effort to destroy." By assaulting the life of an infant, that person is known to be deconstructing "the ways of deity." The child's sick body becomes an active emblem of evil.

> The sick child is identified by the forces of *bɔne* which intend to do it harm, and may even be successful at bringing about the child's death. Sickness and death, in this case, may be seen as immediate manifestations of an abundance of *bɔne* which is active in the natural world.

Viewed in this manner, *asram* may also be regarded as an offense toward deity, since it is Nyame who created the *nkrabea* of the individual infant or child that may bring about those improvements. In a moral sense, this is *bɔne* since the malfeasance is directed toward the family; but ultimately, it is also an offense against divinity. Attacks of *asram* enter a wider moral conflict of individuals, families, and economic and financial futures. Death of a particular child eliminates that child's capacity to care for and to bring possible financial relief to parents in their aging years.

Misappropriations of life, health, property or wealth, and social resources like friendship and family commitments in Asante represent acts of *bɔne*. Like thieves, witches take things wantonly and out of greed. They take no heed for any suffering of victims, and are attentive only to their interests to harm or to acquire. They show disregard for a peaceful flow of life. A child's diseased body thus becomes an emblem of a larger moral struggle about evil. Sickness and death of children, in this case, may be seen as immediate manifestations of an abundance of *bɔne* active in the natural and social world.

William C. Olsen, Georgetown University

Primary Sources

ASSM: Asante Social Survey, Cambridge. "Thirteen Texts in Ashanti and English from Interviews"
ASSMa: "A *Sono Suman*—Talisman War by Sick Child."
MPA: Manhyia Palace Archives, Kumasi.
NAG: National Archives of Ghana.

References

Allman, Jean, and Victoria Tashjian. 2000. *I Will Not Eat Stone*. Portsmouth, NH: Heinemann.
Busia, K. A. 1951. *The Position of the Chief in the Modern Political System of Ashanti*. Oxford: Oxford University Press.
Clark, Gracia. 1994. *Onions Are My Husband*. Chicago: University of Chicago Press.
Debrunner, Hans. 1961. *Witchcraft in Ghana*. Accra: Prebyterian Book Depot.
De Witte, Marleen. 2001. *Long Live the Dead!* Amsterdam: Aksant.
Field, M. J. 1960. *The Search for Security*. Evanston, IL: Northwestern University Press.
Fink, Helga. 1989. *Religion, Disease and Healing in Ghana*. Munich: Trickster Wissenschaft.
Fortes, Meyer. 1950. "Kinship and Marriage among the Ashanti." In *African Systems of Kinship and Marriage*. Edited by A. R. Radcliffe-Brown and Daryl Forde, 252–82. Oxford: Oxford University Press.
———. 1983. *Oedipus and Job in West African Religion*. New York: Cambridge University Press.
Geschiere, Peter. 2013. *Witchcraft, Intimacy and Trust*. Chicago: University of Chicago Press.
Gyekye, Kwame. 1987. *An Essay on African Philosophical Thought*. New York: Cambridge University Press.
Kyei, T. E. 2001. *Our Days Dwindle*. Portsmouth, NH: Heinemann.
MacFarlane, Alan. 1985. "The Root of All Evil." In *The Anthropology of Evil*. Edited by David Parkin, 57–76. Oxford: Basil Blackwell.
Matos, Adriana. 2005. "Maternal Grief and the Vulnerable Infant in Asante, Ghana." BA thesis, Brigham Young University.
McCaskie, T. C. 1986. "Accumulation, Wealth and Belief in Asante History II." *Africa* 56: 3023.
———. 1995. *State and Society in Pre-Colonial Asante*. Cambridge, UK: Cambridge University Press.
———. 2000. *Asante Identities*. Edinburgh: Edinburgh University Press.
Obeng, Pashington. 1996. *Asante Catholicism*. Leiden: E. J. Brill.

Olsen, William C. 1998. "Healing, Personhood and Power: A History of Witch-Finding in Asante." PhD dissertation.

———. 2002. "Children For Death: Money, Wealth, and Witchcraft Suspicion in Colonial Asante." *Cahiers d'Etudes Africaines* 167: 521–50.

———. 2015. "Theft and Evil in Asante." In *Evil in Africa*. Edited by William C. Olsen and Walter van Beek, 302–25. Bloomington: Indiana University Press.

Twumasi, P. A. 1975. *Medical Systems in Ghana*. Tema: Ghana Publishing Corporation.

Wiredu, Kwasi. 1980. *Philosophy and an African Culture*. New York: Cambridge University Press.

Chapter 12

MONSTERS, SADISTS, AND THE UNSPECTACULAR TORTURE EXPERIENCE

Nerina Weiss

> Auschwitz was not hell, it was a German concentration camp.
> —Martin Walser, *Heimatkunde*

> Welcome to paradise. Here is neither a god nor a prophet. It is us who decide.
> —Inscription on wall of Mamak prison, Ankara in the 1980s

This chapter critically engages with the notion of torture as evil. My explorations are grounded in a decade-long engagement with Kurdish activists in Turkey and in Scandinavia, where many sought refuge and treatment. I draw on interviews with torture survivors and the therapists treating them in a Danish rehabilitation center as well as on an analysis of the medical files of Kurdish and Turkish torture survivors, which I gathered from the Danish rehabilitation center.[1] Throughout my engagement with the Kurdish activists and Danish therapists, notions of evil seldom featured in our conversations and discussions about torture. There seemed to be no need to raise the issue of evilness. We knew all too well about the politically motivated systematic torture in Turkey. We knew of the torture methods used, the deaths in prison, and the scars on the body and mind that were a testament to the torture endured. We were all engaged in fighting against the use of torture. None of us, therefore, had to be convinced that torture was bad or even evil—we already implicitly knew.

A shared, though mostly unarticulated, understanding of torture as bad was also very visible when reading the medical files. The mere fact that the therapists and torture survivors—mostly called the client, patient, or simply by their name—needed to meet was proof enough that torture was bad and had to be eradicated. Most interactions and efforts at the center focused on alleviating the sequelae of torture, fighting for justice for torture survivors, and, at an even a higher level, lobbying for the abolishment of torture as such. There was no further need to discuss the evilness of torture.

The system of torture was thus seldom described as evil, either in conversations between the activists and therapists or in the medical files. That being said, symbols of evilness, such as connotations to hell and paradise and to demons and monsters, existed, especially in the Turkish context. Torture survivors retold how they, as prisoners, were greeted with slogans such as "Welcome to paradise. Here is neither a god nor a prophet. It is us who decide." The period when most of these tortures took place, specifically in the 1980s following the coup d'état of 1980, is commonly called "the period of barbarity" (Zeydanlioglu 2009), and the most notorious prisons where much of the torture took place have been described as hell (Zana 1997). Also in the medical files, one can find a ranking of torture; whereby some practices and events were considered more evil than others. In this ranking, torture seemed worse when conducted by sadists; and torture seemed more evil when spectacular and carried out in excess.

Elaborating on Martin Walser's quote—"Auschwitz was not hell, it was a concentration camp" (1968)—I want to explore what it means to conceptualize torture as evil, the torturers as sadistic monsters, and prison as hell. Is there not a danger, as Fiala (2006) puts it, that by focusing on the exceptional cases, we normalize the violence and readjust the moral lines that guide the use of violence? Are we not at risk of only focusing on the exceptional cases, losing sight of the bigger system of state violence and oppression? Are we not also ignoring the complexity of torture experiences?

As I will argue, the reality of people's experiences—such as what haunts them years after they have been released from prison—very often does not correspond to the common categorization and hierachization of torture as frequently found in the therapeutic sessions, among Kurdish and Turkish activists, and in the international political and academic discourse. If only excess and sadism qualify torture as an act of evilness, what are the consequences for the torture survivors, the therapy sessions, and, not least, for how torture is perceived by a wider (more or less informed) public?

Torture as a Collective Experience

Politicians and academics have long disagreed on whether torture is actually evil or not. This debate gained new vigor in the wake of the "War Against Terror" (Castresana 2007; Fiala 2006; Greenberg 2006). At the crux of the argument is the question: Is torture an absolute evil, which has to be abolished, or are there different types of torture, some of which are evil, while others are not? Whereas most would agree that terroristic torture (i.e., "torture which is excessive violence and cruelty used to send a message to a population" [Fiala 2008, 102]) is morally bad, people disagree on the permissibility of interrogative torture. This type of torture is "intended to produce information or some other form of compliance" and "is supposed to be directed only at the guilty" (Fiala 2008, 102). Defendants of this kind of torture, such as Dershowitz (2002) and Casebeer (2005), argue that torture is a lesser evil than, for example, terror, and thus is permissible in a controlled way. Others argue that there is no such thing as "interrogative torture," and thus all torture is terroristic and evil (see, for example, Castresana 2007; Dorfman 2007; Fiala 2006).

Part of this debate is also about the definition of torture. What defines torture, what is classed as inhuman treatment, and what is summarized as "rough" interrogation? Here, violence is graded into practices that are to be avoided (torture), condemned (inhumane treatment), or permitted given certain circumstances (rough treatment). Which practices fall into the different categories may even change depending on the political context. With the increased securitization of the Western world, laws have even been changed in some countries to allow certain torture methods (such as water boarding, sleep deprivation, and isolation) for the greater good of fighting terror. In some cases, like in the US, the definition of torture has been reduced "to be synonymous with death rather than torment—organ failure, rather than cruel and inhumane treatment" (Taylor 2007).[2]

A gradual understanding of torture was also conveyed in documents related to the legal procedures set up following World War II to prosecute war criminals, particularly in the Auschwitz trials. The prosecutors had initially planned to put the entire "Auschwitz Complex" on trial, but, it could be said, they ended up legitimizing Nazi standards of criminality: "The majority of defendants received only mild sentences because they did not show individual initiative. ... The Court had only come down on the 'monsters,' who had created their own instruments of torture, lived out their evil fantasies, and committed crimes so heinous that even the Nazis had investigated them for their excess" (Wittman 2007, 10).

According to Martin Walser (1968), who had followed the Auschwitz trials that were held in Frankfurt, Germany, between 1963 and 1965, the Auschwitz trials failed to judge the system that had created these monsters and devils that were on trial. Auschwitz remained hell. In his critique of the Auschwitz trials, Walser engages with the language of evil used to describe the defendants and their horrendous deeds. Defendants were called "devils" and "beasts," and in descriptions of the concentration camp, observers alluded to *Dante's Inferno*. Auschwitz had become hell simply because people were unable or unwilling to relate to the horrors and suffering, and therefore were unable to imagine the offenders as humans (Walser 1968). The spectacular of the few convicted monsters manifested the camp's evilness, while references to an otherworldly "Inferno" placed the audience at a secure distance from it. However, as Walser repeatedly reminded us:

> The conditions that allowed for this brutality are far too colourless, too completely situated in the realm of the historical, the political, the social, so they fade away in the face of the juicy embodiment of an SS man whom we stylize as a devil. We care just as little about the conditions when we read Dante. . . . Auschwitz is not something fantastic, but rather an institution that the German state created, with great care and planning, for the exploitation and extermination of human beings. (Walser 2008, 10)

Auschwitz was therefore nothing outside our world, but inherently part of reality.

Walser's critique of the demonization of the perpetrators is highly relevant also for the rest of this chapter; however, for a slightly different reason. Unlike Auschwitz in the postwar trials, which the majority of Germans could only observe from a distance, torture in Turkey is securely placed "within a collectivity" (de Saussure 1966 [1919]), indeed a contemporary collectivity. Torture in Turkey was systematically used against most detainees. After the military coup d'état of 1980, security forces cracked down on the (peaceful and militant) left as well as on the emerging Kurdish nationalist movement. In the 1980s alone, more than 1 million people were reportedly tortured in Turkish police stations and detention centers (TIHV 1992). During that time, political activists knew that their arrest and torture was only a question of *when*, not *if*. To quote from the medical files of a Turkish leftist revolutionary: "During these years, every Turkish man with self-respect has been arrested and tortured" (November 1982).

Whereas state violence was mostly directed against political activists in the west of Turkey, violence in the eastern, and Kurdish-dominated, parts of the country affected the entire population. Given the decades-long conflict between the Kurdish Worker's Party (PKK) and the Turkish state forces, the introduction of new antiterrorism laws, and the military presence in the Kurdish regions, the majority of the Kurdish population had at some point been subjected to torture and physical and psychological abuse by state security forces. In particular during the 1980s and 1990s, considered as the "hot years" of the Kurdish–Turkish conflict, torture was practiced in place of detention as well as during house searches and village raids (TIHV 1995). Relatives of political activists and PKK guerrilla fighters were repeatedly beaten and tortured in order to get information from them and not least to put off others becoming politically active (Begikhani, Hamelink, and Weiss 2018). Torture was thus very much part of people's reality. Zeydanlioglu even argues that the torture of the 1980s had a

> highly important place in the Kurdish social memory and in the discourse of Kurdish nationalism . . . it can easily be asserted that the practices in Diyarbakir, the unofficial capital of the Kurdish region, played a crucial role in the crystallization of nationalist secessionist ideas and the radicalization of a generation of Kurds, large numbers of which went on to join the ranks of the militant Kurdistan Worker's Party PKK. (Zeydanlioglu 2009)

Among Kurdish and leftist activists in Turkey and in the diaspora, experiences of torture were linked to status and collective identity. Torture was given a pivotal place in the political hierarchy of suffering, and political prisoners and torture survivors were and still are celebrated as heroes (Weiss 2012).

Torture Discussed in Therapy

Most therapists and torture survivors remain convinced that the aim of the torture was not the gathering of information, which academics would call interrogative torture (Fiala 2006). The systematic practice of torture, especially in the Kurdish regions, was terroristic in the sense that it was used to insert terror into the torture victim and into the entire population. The aim was to break people, to attack their dignity, and to destroy them forever.

Activists knew that torture was almost inevitable if they were caught. Therefore, most political training of leftist and Kurdish activists in Turkey also encompassed the preparation to endure torture. This preparation was twofold, consisting of knowledge and ideological preparation. Activists needed to know as much as possible about torture; therefore, organizations collected survivor reports about torture carried out under different regimes. The following quote from a patient file explains how the torture survivor was able to endure his torture:

> Sedat[3] explains that, prior to his arrest he already had good knowledge of both physical and psychological torture. He and his friends had studied [different types of torture] by reading about the Vietnam War as well as the Second World War under Hitler. He further explains that until the military coup d'état, he had been part of a group that played street theatre in slums and in the countryside to teach the population about state oppression. They once played the theatre during working hours, and their audience consisted thus mostly of women and children. They tried to involve the audience in the play. He played a random person on the street who had been arrested and tortured. The play was so real that the audience started to throw stones at them. (Medical file of a Kurdish leftist revolutionary man, April 1987)

Ideological training was the other component in activists' preparation. Knowing what they were fighting (and ultimately suffering) for was important for most political activists in Turkey. Only with strong political conviction and a firm ideology would it be possible to make sense of their atrocious treatment and thus survive the torture without disclosing (too much) information. And only with a strong ideological conviction would they stand a chance of remaining reasonably sane upon release. As one of the torture survivors I interviewed in Turkey summarized it: "Those who had a weak ideology had their brains eaten"; in other words, "they went mad."

Therapists know that some form of mental preparation is important to endure torture (Basoglu et al. 1997). However, the Danish therapists mostly met torture survivors who had some sort of physical and/or mental sequelae of the torture experience. Therefore, many doubted the importance of ideology for a survivor's post-torture life. In several comments in the patient files, the therapists criticized the survivors for lingering on political talk instead of opening up emotionally. As one therapist put it, "Torture had taken hold of the survivor, who has been contaminated by evil." The idea here seems to be that the evil of torture had been internalized and had to be fought off. Ideology had clearly failed to do the job, and it was the therapist's role to heal and clean the torture survivor. It was only through therapy, or by giving testimony, that the evil of torture could be externalized again (see also Agger and Jensen 1990). It was thus important to talk about the torture experience and to connect it to memory, emotion, and the body. The therapists thus operated with a clear victim–perpetrator dichotomy. Victimhood was an essential quality of the torture survivors. The torturers, on the other hand, were the morally bad perpetrators or executioners [bøddel].[4] As I will show in the example of Mehmet later on, problems arose when torture survivors refused to narrate their experience within this dichotomy of victim versus perpetrator, and rather blamed the power establishment and the system for their suffering. Such intellectualization and politicization was not seen as part of the survivor's ideological training and essential for his or her emotional and mental survival. Such "intellectual ideologization" was rather seen as a hindrance to the survivors' healing and reconnection of their body, mind, and soul.

Torture in Excess

As mentioned earlier, the use of torture in the early 1980s was considered one of the worst in Turkish modern history. The years after the coup d'état of 1980 are commonly called the *period of barbarity* [vahşet dönemi], and some prisons gained a special notoriety during that time, such as the Diyarbakir Military Prison. In the *Hell of Diyarbakir* [Diyarbakır cehennemi], prisoners "were exposed to horrific acts of systematic torture" (Zeydanlioglu 2009). The systematic torture was so severe that some researchers compared the Diyarbakir Military Prison with a concentration camp (Paker 2003). During this period, torture, in Diyarbakir and other prisons, was "primarily aimed at breaking down and humiliating the prisoners" (Zeydanlioglu 2009). Zeydanlioglu argues that the use of torture in Turkey was "rarely solely about obtaining information or the work of an 'evil' person acting on his/her 'sadistic urges.' Instead torture is best understood as not arbitrary but [as a] systematic practice of state sponsored violence against internal/external enemies" (Zeydanlioglu 2009). While researchers such as Zeydanlioglu (2009) and Parker (2003) acknowledge and stress the structural and all-encompassing violence of the torture regime, they seem to fall into the same trap as the prosecutors of the Auschwitz trials. The plan had been to lay bare the entire system of state violence and oppression. However, the only perpetrator who was mentioned by name in, for example, Zeydanlioglu's article is the sadistic Captain Esat Oktay Yildiran. Yildiran and his German Shepherd dog Jo, who both gained notorious fame among political prisoners, and feature in several accounts of that time. In a way, Yildiran, with his sadistic torture methods, has become the personification of the hell of Diyarbakir. Like in the Auschwitz trials, also in the Turkish oral and written literature on torture, sadistic monsters have become the image and representation of the torture experience.

> When a new prisoner arrived at the prison, Captain Yildiran met him at the entrance and then turned to a guard and said, "prepare him a bath; then take him to the dormitory." This was a ritual. So, almost twenty guards accompanied the prisoner. He received a good welcoming thrashing, and then he was dragged, unconscious, to the "bath," a bathtub full of shit in which they left him for a few hours. Sometimes they told him "eat it now." Other times they put the new arrived naked on a stool above the excrement and left him there for two days in that pestilent and acidic odor. (Zana 1997)

The focus on the spectacular, which we can find in the description of Yildiran's torture methods, could also be found in the medical files I analyzed. As I mentioned earlier, references to evilness seldom appeared in the files—not necessarily because therapists did not regard torture as evil, but rather because the evilness of torture was one of the premises upon which the therapy took place. The evilness was only mentioned in the files when the torture experience was particular or spectacular.

Let me take an example from one of the patient files I analyzed. The case concerns Yusuf (which of course is not his real name), who had been politically active in the late 1970s and early 1980s. Against the norm of that time, he had been living with his politically active fiancé and their son, who was born out of wedlock. After the coup d'état in 1980, Yusuf knew that his arrest was imminent, and so he went underground, carrying false identity papers and staying in different places. He still managed to provide for his family. A fisherman by trade, he secretly fished in low waters and close to the coast in order to avoid the coastal service.

Yusuf was apprehended in 1982. Soon, the Gendarmerie established his real identity, and Yusuf was transferred to a military prison. There, he was tortured for two months. Compared to the average torture length and torture severity of that period, Yusuf could be classed as being tortured severely. He was systematically beaten, hanged from his hands, exposed to electronic torture, and several of his teeth were pulled out. He was humiliated; had to do military exercises; was deprived of food, water, and sleep; had to undergo mock executions; and was continuously threatened. According to the medical files, Yusuf's worst experience in prison was, however, when his fiercest torturer informed him of his wife's alleged suicide that had also killed their son. The day before he got that dreadful news, he and other prisoners had refused to sing fascist songs. As a punishment, they were given bad food, which means they were served a soup far too salty. When Yusuf refused to eat the soup (anticipating that they would not be given water for the rest of the day), he was additionally punished and not given food or water for the rest of the day.

> Then came the captain—a captain who many times had taunted, humiliated, and tortured him. He came with his usual, slightly smiling, irritating face and asked Yusuf to tell him his name and where he lived. Yusuf did so, and the captain said: "Well, so is it your wife and son who have burned to death in your house that has been burned down. And it looks like it was suicide, but of course it could also be sabotage." Yusuf thought that the captain wanted to provoke him, as he had done many times before and accused him thereof. The captain, however, produced a newspaper, opened it on a specific page and let Yusuf read it. In a very short article it was written that a woman, who had an illegitimate child (this is Turkey, they weren't married and so hadn't received a birth certificate for the child), could not bear the neighbours' gossip and rejection, and had therefore allegedly committed suicide by burning herself, the child, and the house. It was also mentioned that the child's name was . . . . (Medical file of a Turkish male political activist, November 1985)

Upon receiving the news, Yusuf was shocked. He lost all self-control and fell into a deep depression. His mind was split. On the one hand, he was convinced that his fiancé, who also had been politically active, would never commit suicide, and would never harm their child. On the other hand, he could not get rid of the doubt that she might, for some reason, have committed suicide after all. Yusuf cried and cried. Before this all happened, he had paid someone to provide him with a picture of his fiancé and son. It was this picture, the only picture he had, that he held on to and cried.

> One of the torturers of lower rank than the captain took the picture from him, and told him it was forbidden to have something like this in prison. He tried to get the picture back again, but the soldier slipped out of the cell and locked the door. He showed his face and the picture in the little window of the prison door, and burned the picture in front of Yusuf's eyes. It was as if Yusuf relived the loss and the burning of his family once more.

The loss of the only picture of his fiancé and son led to Yusuf's total breakdown. He became neurotic and so severely ill that he did not respond to the torture anymore. His torturers, and particularly the aforementioned captain, first accused him of yet another form of resistance and increased the intensity and severity of the torture. But as Yusuf still showed no signs of reaction, the torturers eventually had to give up and then transferred him to hospital and then to a civilian prison.

This sequence of Yusuf's torture experience was the topic of a number of his therapy sessions and therefore featured often in the medical files. Each time, the therapists used particular—and rather unusual—terms, such as "in a particularly vicious manner" [på en særdeles onskabsfuld måde], "with an evil smile" [med et ondt smil], "horrendous" [redselsfuld], or "horrible" [forferdelig], to describe Yusuf's torturers (Medical file of a Turkish male political activist, October 1985).

The Complexity of Evil

The unnamed captain in Yusuf's story and the sadistic Captain Yildiran of the Diyarbakir Military Prison have seemingly become the "poster boys" of the period of barbarism in the 1980s. They were the most sadistic villains, and most closely resembled the monsters sentenced to death in the Auschwitz trials. But neither the unnamed captain nor Captain Yildiran had acted on their own. In fact, quite the contrary. In the shadow of Yildiran's spectacular sadism, for example, are stories of countless other prison guards. In his memoirs, Mehti Zana, former mayor of the city of Diyarbakir and later inmate at the Diyarbakir Military Prison, mentions at least twenty guards who accompanied a prisoner during his first day "in paradise." Also in Yusuf's account, it was not the captain, but a low rank soldier who had burned the picture of Yusuf's fiancé and child. In most other torture accounts I have read and heard, the torturers have neither a face nor name.

This raised the question of who these nameless perpetrators were. How were they conceptualized by their victims? As I had never talked explicitly about evil when conducting interviews with torture survivors in Turkey, I turned to a Turkish friend of mine in Norway for some clarification. A leftist revolutionary in the 1970s, he had experienced the "barbaric" time of torture in the 1980s—in his case, in the Metris military prison in Istanbul. My friend contemplated for a while my question of evilness and then explained: "Of course the prison guards were not only monsters, or evil machines. . . . They were also fathers and husbands, who took care of their family." In order to make his point, he told me about the prison conditions during his time there. He told of the incredible amount of filth and vermin in the prisons. A newcomer would, even after just a few hours in the cells, be covered with fleas and bugs. The prison guards who accompanied them to the interrogation or torture were always careful not to touch the prisoners. The blindfolded prisoners had to hold on to a two-meter long stick so that the prison guards could lead them around the prison. "With two meters between us, they led us around. Why? Well, they did not want to be covered by fleas and bugs. Some even told me that they had their wives and children to think of. They could not just infect their home with that vermin! So, you see, they were no monsters. They took care of their family!" (Interview in Oslo, Norway, May 2016). Although my friend stressed their caring for their families as proof of their humanity, this in itself, I believe, does not necessarily make them less monstrous or sadistic. More interesting is the everyday interaction between prison guards and prisoners. In my Turkish friend's account, the prison guards communicated with their prisoners. And even explained—in between the torture—why they did not want to touch them. My friend's story pointed to a highly ambivalent social interaction between prisoners and guards, which also featured in a few of the medical files. However, not all the therapists seemed interested in the prison guards and torturers or in their relationship to the survivors and vice versa. But in a few files, the torture survivors themselves brought up the issue, and each time, such mentioning complicated the therapists' dichotomy between victim and villain. This became clear also in the following quote from one therapy session:

> Mehmet, [a torture survivor of Kurdish origin] relates an event in prison, where he had been punished for not obeying orders. He had to hold his arms out of the hatch in the door and was beaten on his palms. A few hours later, the same soldier who had previously punished him, called him by his name—which was quite unusual in the prison setting. Prisoners were also not allowed to look the prison guards in the eyes, but this time, the guard kindly asked him to do so. He recognized the guard as the smaller brother of his good friend from his village, a person he had had frequent contact with back then. While the prison guard had made Mehmet aware that they knew each other, he continued to hit him. Later on, he smuggled letters out to Mehmet's parents and ensured the latter that Mehmet was fine (that is, he lied, and said that he was much better than he was in reality). Mehmet explains that each time Mehmet and the prison guard talked, the latter hit him on his palms. (Medical file of a Kurdish leftist revolutionary man, August 1987)

The story continues and the therapist learns that this same prison guard visited Mehmet and his family shortly after Mehmet's release. His parents, as well as several other family members, were present. In the middle of the festivities, Mehmet suddenly said with a smile that this prison guard had also beaten him in prison Those present took this information apparently with humor and laughed.

Again, the therapist has difficulties understanding this, and presses Mehmet to reflect on that scene. How could his family laugh when being informed that they had a torturer in their midst? Mehmet did not see the problem; but as the therapist pushes further, he finally comes up with an "intellectual" explanation. His family had been oppressed by the entire system. Had they not been so, they would have kicked the prison guard out of their house. In a later entry, the therapist seems finally to have made sense of it all: "I finally understand. The prison guard was forced to do so [hit Mehmet on the palms] to cover his back."

Mehmet's interaction with the prison guard, the fact, that the two knew each other from before, and the fact that the guard could act as a friend and could simultaneously torture Mehmet, seemed incomprehensible to the therapist. Finally, the therapist was able to place the prison guard. The prison guard was not evil, but had to hit Mehmet in order to cover their friendly interaction. While the therapist had now placed the prison guard, though, this did not solve the entire problem. According to the therapist, the natural feeling of a victim toward the perpetrator is anger, hatred, and wanting revenge. Mehmet refused to have such feelings, and so the therapist accused Mehmet of coming to the sessions "with his intellectual ideological viewpoints stating that the ones in power and the system should be combated" (Medical file of a Kurdish leftist revolutionary man, August 1987). Mehmet refused to feel hatred for the prison guards. For him, torture was an entire system in which the torturers and the prisoners were equally victimized. The therapist, on the other hand, seemed to hold on to the dichotomous notion of the evil torturer versus the good (though relatively passive) victim. Whereas Mehmet seemed to use his ideological conviction to give meaning to his struggle before, during, and after the torture experience, the therapist concluded that Mehmet's intellectualizations were only symptoms of his problems with emotional relations. As the aim of the therapy was to convince Mehmet to break the emotional barriers, and to get back in contact with his feelings, the therapist therefore returned several times to Mehmet's ambivalent relation to the prison guard and to his emotional numbness.

> We talk again about his emotional relations to the torturers [bøddel]. He confirms that he, because of the torture and the prospect of having to stay imprisoned and being tortured for many years, numbed his feelings, so that he could endure. When he was tortured by the torturers,

he smiled at them instead of reacting spontaneously with anger or grief. Mehmet confirms also, that this emotional numbness bothered him later on, after he had been released from prison. What concerns his emotional relations to the torturers today, he is again highly intellectualizing. He all the time puts all the blame and responsibility on those in power behind the torturers—and thus tries to avoid any direct confrontation with the feelings he has, or had toward those people who had abused him. (Medical file of a Kurdish leftist revolutionary man, October 1987)

Mehmet refused to hate his torturers. He also refused to accept that his emotional numbness, which was a necessity to survive the torture, had anything to do with his lack of hatred toward the prison guards. If anything, they were to be pitied. It was the system and those in power who were responsible for his suffering. Many of the politically trained torture survivors agreed in terms of focusing on the system instead of the low rank torturers.

Mehmet saw the torturers like dogs with rabies, which he earlier had taken part in hunting down and killing. The dog was not to blame for being ill, but it had to be killed anyhow. It was quite similar with the torturers. Even if they had a reason to do what they did, they still had to be shot. His hatred, however, was not personal anymore and not directed against the individual torturers. His hatred was more directed against what they did, and against the system. When I asked him directly, he said that he felt pity for the torturers. (Medical file of a Turkish leftist revolutionary man, August 1988)

"Auschwitz was not hell, it was a concentration camp." The Turkish prisons of the 1980s were likewise not actually hell; they were places of detention where systematic torture was practiced against political opponents. The prison guards, whom the therapists seemed to see as the violent villains, were pitiful victims of that same system. Elon highlights this point in his introduction to Hannah Arendt's book *Eichmann in Jerusalem*: "[Eichmann] personified neither hatred or madness nor an insatiable thirst for blood, but something far worse, the faceless nature of Nazi evil itself, within a closed system run by pathological gangsters, aimed at dismantling the human personality of its victims" (Elon 2006). Elon still refers to the pathological gangsters—a move Arendt herself does not make. However, setting the reference to the pathological gangsters aside, Elon repeats Mehmet's and Walser's point about the importance of not losing sight of the system.

Without focusing on the system of torture as a holistic phenomenon, I would add, we are unable to see that torture is experienced along a continuum with complex relations and even more complex experiences. If we focus on the monsters, the morally corrupt torturers, we not only validate the torture experiences and their sequelae on the basis of assessing the level of the torture in terms of spectacular and monstrous; we also end up reproducing simple dichotomies, such as between the victim and perpetrator, whether it is really torture or not torture, and whether it is truly evil or morally acceptable (if not good), which have very little to do with the experiences of (some of) the torture survivors.

Torture as a Potentiality

To make my point, I finish this chapter with two "unspectacular," but nevertheless important, cases. These tell of events that probably would not qualify for any of the particular status and respect that are so commonly given to torture survivors. They do not tell of any spectacular torture or monstrous excess—and their experiences of violence would not even be defined as torture in most countries. In the two cases, seemingly unspectacular events, sometimes even just a few words, had the most severe effect on the victim. The body may not have been broken, but the victim's mind and dignity were severely disturbed. In effect, the unspectacular left the deepest marks.

The first of these two cases is that of Fatima. Fatima was one of the few women from Turkey who was treated as a primary victim at the Danish rehabilitation center. First, she was registered as the wife of a torture survivor: her husband, who had been politically active and consequently severely tortured during his detention, had been a patient at the center for some time, and Fatima joined some of the sessions as his wife. After only a few months, it became clear that Fatima had her own experiences of torture. While her husband had gone underground and later fled to Denmark, she and her mother-in-law had been arrested and interrogated. Fatima was tortured to reveal the whereabouts of her husband. Fatima, however, had early on in prison decided that she would rather die than talk. She described her torture, which was recorded as follows:

> The torture was as follows. The ordinary guards blindfolded her when it was her turn to go to the torture chamber. She was led from the cellar to the 5th floor. She does not know who tortured her, but she could deduce by the many voices that there must have been more than five people present. She was tortured almost daily. They started by saying terrible things to her, humiliating perfidies, and sexually humiliating things. After the verbal humiliation, they started to cross-examine her, asked many questions and if she did not reply she was hit everywhere,

especially on her hands. They whipped her palms so that there were large blisters and open sores. She was slapped in the face, and got three teeth broken. (Medical file of a Kurdish woman, July 1985)

The physical torture left marks on her body. However, in the therapy session, Fatima focused on the psychological torture and, here especially, on the threats:

The worst threat she can remember came at the time when she should be released. They had not really found any basis upon which to keep her imprisoned and her brother had paid a bribe to speed up the process leading to her release.

The threats she suffered before she was released haunt her even today (two years later). The threats were as follows: If she ever said anything other than that she had had a great time in prison, the police would immediately imprison the entire family, both her family and the family of her husband, including small children. They would all be subjected to torture, and the first thing they would do, was to take the dialysis machine from her brother (who suffered from renal insufficiency, and needed chronic dialysis treatment). These threats are something she is living with today, and which she is dreaming of. The woman ends up saying that this was just too awful, so indescribably horrible, and that it is something she will never ever forget. (Medical file of a Kurdish woman, July 1985)

Soldiers had also threatened her with rape and other forms of sexual violence. Fatima was prepared to kill herself if the prison guards actually attempted to do so. From a fellow prisoner, she knew about a window in the interrogation room. If the guards tried to rape her, she was prepared to rip off the blindfold, run to the window, and jump. Fatima described the sexual threats as dreadful, but it was the threats to her family that haunted her and that caused the most severe problems in her everyday life in Denmark:

She has severe sleeping disorder, often wakes up after only a few hours and doesn't dare to go back to sleep again. The reason is that she is afraid of the horrible nightmares she has. These nightmares have earlier been about her own torture, but now she dreams about something related to her torture, but which concerns her own family. She imagines that the threats the authorities had come with during her torture, had become real. This means that the family will be arrested and tortured like she had been. (Medical file of a Kurdish woman, July 1985)

The effect of threats and the potentiality of torture are even more visible in the case of Mustafa. Mustafa, a Kurd, who had lived in Scandinavia since childhood, described himself prior to his torture experience as "actually not really the active guy, average politically oriented." He had travelled to Turkey for family reasons. Upon arrival at the airport, he was apprehended, accused of being a member of the PKK, and tortured during interrogation. His torture lasted around a week. He was unsystematically beaten and kicked. He was exposed to both cold and heat, locked up in cramped surroundings with insufficient and inedible food, was deprived of sleep, and lived under severely deteriorated general hygienic conditions (Medical file of a Danish torture survivor, October 1996). In addition, he was exposed to psychological torture—both direct threats and mock executions. During his interrogation, Mustafa was repeatedly asked to admit his links to the PKK. As he refused to accept any false statements, "He felt a metal object against his right temple, there was a click, as if a gun was triggered, and he got frightened, cold-sweating and feared for his life." Mustafa still refused to accept their accusations and was threatened further. "We will give you one last chance. If you don't accept that, you will be thrown out from a building, and your relatives will be told that you have committed suicide." At that point, Mustafa confessed to whatever they wanted him to. The same day, he signed a number of papers, which he could not read as he was blindfolded. However, "at that time, he did not care at all about what he was signing, as his only wish was to avoid more torture."

Mustafa spent one week in prison awaiting trial. He first shared a cell with two other men, whom he assumed to be "normal" criminals, and was then transferred to an overcrowded cell of political prisoners. Most of them were Kurds. Mustafa learned of their prison conditions, the severe torture they had experienced, and their total lack of medical treatment. Mustafa struggled to place his own experiences of torture into the collective experience of torture. Had he any right at all to feel traumatized, given that the political prisoners he shared his cell with had experienced so much worse? His time in prison was, relatively speaking, far shorter than that of the other Kurdish political prisoners, and his torture was, as he acknowledges himself, far less violent and brutal. Mustafa is also open to the fact that he confessed after only twenty-four hours. Whereas Mustafa was also treated for physical sequelae stemming from his beatings, it is especially his conviction that his life had been in danger several times that feature in the psychological therapy session.

In particular, one episode haunts Mustafa. During the therapy session, this episode was introduced as follows:

> He explains that he doesn't want to abuse those people who have experienced worse torture. He tries to forget, but also knows that this is not possible. At the same time, he can understand that he had been lucky that he had not been exposed to more severe torture methods, despite

the fact that he had undergone severe psychological torture. (Medical file of a Danish torture survivor, January 1997)

The episode goes on:

After the court session, he was driven back to the prison together with the other prisoners. A couple of hours later, he was told that he was to be released, upon which he took leave of the other inmates. He was then taken to the prison governor, and a civilian police officer came to fetch him. At first, the civilian policeman refused to sign a receipt for having fetched Mustafa, but when the governor insisted, the receipt was signed. The civilian officer took him out through a back door, where Mustafa's relatives, his lawyer, and the representative of the Danish Embassy were waiting at the main entrance. Then two civilian police officers drove him out through a back entrance of the prison, drove around for about an hour in a part of the town that Mustafa did not know. On the way, he heard them talk about that the press was not to see them, and that they had a friend in the neighbourhood whom they might visit. After some time, the police officers were ordered back to the police headquarters via their walkie-talkie, and they went back to the parking lot in the basement to where Mustafa had been taken after his arrest. He got very nervous and thought that he was going to be tortured again. (Medical file of a Danish torture survivor, October 1996)

Mustafa was taken up several sets of stairs in the building and brought to a police officer who verbally abused him. Mustafa spent another night in custody, this time in the immigration section of the police, and the following day was escorted to the airport and flown back to Denmark.

In the first retelling of his experiences, this last car drive remained uncommented on. In later sessions however, it turned out, that Mustafa regarded this car drive as the one of the most frightening situations during his time in prison. Seen from the outside, there was nothing spectacular or brutal about the car drive. He was driven around an unknown area for a few hours, and then returned to the prison. No physical harm, no verbal threats—no torture, by the legal definition. Mustafa, however, had been convinced that he would be disappeared, or that the civilian police officers would stage his suicide. He had good prior knowledge of the torture system in Turkey, and had recently gained even more insight into how Kurdish political prisoners were usually treated. The fact that he had no idea where the car was heading to, combined with the silence of the civilian police officers and the fact that he actually should have been released that same day, all played into Mustafa's fears. His knowledge about torture and disappearances, and his recently gained insight into the treatment of prisoners only increased his fears. Mustafa's torture experience was not so much linked to actual torture, but rather to the *potentiality* (Risør 2010) of torture, which he—as part of the collective—was painfully aware of.

Conclusion

This chapter critically engaged with torture presented as evil. The aim was not to engage in a political debate about the evil or lesser evil of torture, or whether some forms of torture may be considered permissible. I remain firm in my belief that torture in all its forms has to be abolished. My concern in engaging with the notion of evil was rather informed by Martin Walser's quote "Auschwitz was not hell, it was a concentration camp" (1968). I argued that a focus on the spectacular evilness of torture leads our focus away from analyzing torture as a holistic and all-encompassing system, where torture methods and the torture survivor's experience are to be found along a continuum.

Taking the case of torture in Turkey, I argued that torture was a collective experience. Especially among Turkish leftists and the Kurdish population, torture and the potentiality thereof was an integral part of their social and political lives. Against a backdrop of such normalized violence, it was the exceptional cases, the spectacular and the excess, that gained recognition and, as a consequence, status and respect for the torture survivor. Among the many unnamed torturers, the infamous Captain Esat Yildiran and his dog Jo have become the embodiment of the *hell* of Diyarbakir. The Diyarbakir Military Prison of the 1980s, on the other hand, has become the icon of the collective experience. In fact, for one torture survivor and former inmate of the prison (named here as Yusuf), his experiences describer earlier fit well into this spectacular view on torture. Yusuf, who thought he had not only lost his family in a fire, but also his only picture of the two, which was burned in front of his eyes, reacted by turning mad and numb against his ever increasing torture. Yusuf's case could be classed as severe. Other experiences, unspectacular moments that are not even strictly defined as torture as they only contain the potentiality thereof, are ignored or normalized: these include events such as Mustafa's car drive—where nothing actually happened, but where the prisoner believed he was to be disappeared—and the sexualized threats against Fatima and the threats against her family. Although threats are part of the list of torture and maltreatment, threats in themselves are seldom considered in the same intensity of evil as the sadistic destructiveness experienced by Yusuf. Still, the long-term effect can be quite similar.

A similar logic could also be found in the medical files of a Danish rehabilitation center. Torture was the norm, upon which therapists at the center tried to place different torture experiences. Although the therapists acknowledged the suffering of Yusuf and Fatima, they also seemed at times to scale the intensity and evilness of the torture. The focus on the exceptional, the monstrous, and the heroic also easily leads to a dichotomist presentation of torture, where torture or not torture, absolute evil or not, operate in a binary manner, which loses sight of the complexity and ambivalence of the torture experience. Primarily, the binary opposition of the torture survivor as a victim and the prison guards as villains (if not monsters), under which the rehabilitation center operated, turned out to be problematic. As several of the files showed, the prison guards were not just bad, but could also be highly respected by and even helpful to the prisoners. The ambivalent social relations that some prison guards and prisoners had were often incomprehensible to the therapist. As the case of Mehmet indicates, only when the therapist manages to rationalize and not victimize the perpetrator (he had to beat him in order to communicate, and thus help him, or else he himself would have ended up in trouble) can such stories be placed in a narrative of victimhood. The torture survivors' refusal to show feelings like anger, hatred, or revenge toward their torturers and their insistence on directing these emotions against the authorities, the establishment, or the system as such was therefore not taken at face value. Whereas the revolutionary torture survivor built their identity around their resistance against the system, and had used their ideological conviction to survive the torture, the therapists pathologized that such a patient had yet to connect their body, mind, and soul.

Beyond the spectacular of the monstrous and sadistic torturers lies a continuum of experience. Not all of these experiences fit into the community of the collective (be it now the therapists, the anti-torture activists, or the political community), and torture was quite often experienced as individualizing, directed at the victim's mind and dignity. In such cases, it was not the spectacular torture methods and the most horrific torture that broke and haunted the torture survivors. Like in the cases of Mehmet and Fatima, it was the torture, which in most countries would not even be defined as torture—not the brutal spectacular torture—that had the most severe effect on the victim and left the deepest marks.

Nerina Weiss, Fafo Research Foundation, Oslo

Notes

1. I analyzed 140 files, between five and one hundred pages long, that reflect the multidisciplinary treatment the torture survivors received at the Danish rehabilitation centre. Upon referral, the potential patient is called in for a first consultation, where the background of the survivor, his or her torture experience, and the torture sequelae are documented, and consequently the survivor's eligibility for treatment is assessed. If accepted for treatment, the torture survivor will then have access to medical treatment, physiotherapy, psychotherapy, and a social worker, who assists in practical matters. The files contain the therapists' notes and reflections after each session, as well as the correspondences, medical reports, and applications filled out on behalf of the torture survivor.

   The files do not contain any transcriptions of what has been said during the sessions, but present a condensed, more-or-less detailed summary. Nearly all the treatments of the Turkish and Kurdish torture survivors took place with the participation of a translator. The files are thus twice translated: first from Turkish to Danish in the session, and then from an often incoherent narrative, to a coherent summary by the therapist.
2. Taylor refers to the new definition by the US government, which defined torture as having to be "equivalent in intensity to the pain accompanying serious physical injury, such as organ failure, impairment of bodily function, or even death" (Gonzales 2005 in Taylor 2007).
3. All names in this chapter are pseudonyms.
4. The association of torture survivors as pure victims has been strong since the establishment of the rehabilitation center in the early 1980s. Then, therapists were encouraged not to explore the torture survivors' own experiences as perpetrators. This is especially interesting in the Turkish case: many (but by far not all) of the Turkish and Kurdish torture survivors had engaged in violent acts prior to their imprisonment, either as members of violent revolutionary groups on the far left, or as guerilla fighters in the nascent Kurdish nationalist movement. Also during my stay in early 2010, the center refused to treat Danish soldiers who had returned traumatized from their mission in Afghanistan.

References

Agger, Inger, and Søren Buus Jensen. 1990. "Testimony as Ritual and Evidence in Psychotherapy for Political Refugees." *Journal of Traumatic Stress* 3(1): 115–30.

Basoglu, M., et al. 1997. "Psychological Preparedness for Trauma as a Protective Factor in Survivors of Torture." *Psychological Medicine* 27: 1421–33.

Begikhani, Nazand, Wendy Hamelink, and Nerina Weiss. 2018. "Theorizing Women and War in Kurdistan: A Feminist and Critical Perspective." *Kurdish Studies* 6(1): 5–30.

Casebeer, William. 2005. "Torture Interrogation of Terrorists: A Theory of Exceptions (with Notes, Cautions and Warnings)." In *Philosophy 9/11*. Edited by T. Shanahan, 261–272. New York: Open Court.

Castresana, Carlos Gonzalez. 2007. "Torture as a Greater Evil." *South Central Review* 24(1): 119–30.

Dershowitz, Alan. 2002. *Shouting Fire: Civil Liberties in a Turbulent Age*. New York: Little Brown.

De Saussure, Ferdinand. 1966 [1919]. *Course in General Linguistics*. New York: McGraw-Hill.

Dorfman, Ariel. 2007. "Are There Times When We Have to Accept Torture? / Are We Really So Fearful?" *South Central Review* 24(1): 95–100.

Elon, Amos. 2006. "Introduction: The Excommunication of Hannah Arendt." In *Eichmann in Jerusalem: A Report on the Banality of Evil*. Edited by H. Arendt. New York: Penguin Classics.

Fiala, Andrew. 2006. "A Critique of Exceptions: Torture, Terrorism, and the Lesser Evil Argument." *International Journal of Applied Philosophy* 20(1): 127–42.

———. 2008. *The Just War Myth: The Moral Illusions of War*. Lanham: Rowman & Littlefield Publishers, Inc.

Greenberg, Karen J., ed. 2006. *The Torture Debate in America*. Cambridge, UK: Cambridge University Press.

Paker, Murat. 2003. "Boğazımızdaki Yumru: Türkiye'de İşkence." *Birikim* 172: 10–22.

Risør, Helene. 2010. "Twenty Hanging Dolls and a Lynching: Defacing Dangerousness and Enacting Citizenship in El Alto, Boliviea." *Public Culture* 22(3): 465–85.

Taylor, Diana. 2007. Double-Blind: The Torture Case. *Critical Inquiry* 33(4): 710–33.

TIHV. 1992. "İşkence görenler tedavi merkezleri raporu 1990–1992." *Türkiye İnsan Hakları Vakfı*. Ankara.

———. 1995. "Tedavi ve Rehabilitasyon Merkezi Reporu 1995." *Türkiye İnsan Hakları Vakfı*. Ankara.

Walser, Martin. 1968. *Heimatkunde: Aufsätze und Reden*. Frankfurt am Main: Suhrkamp Verlag.

———. 2008. "Our Auschwitz." In *The Burden of the Past: Martin Walser on Modern German Identity*. Edited by T. A. Kovach and M. Walser, 7–18. New York: Camden House.

Weiss, Nerina. 2012. *Ambivalent Victims: Conflict, Gender and Expressions among Kurdish Activists in Eastern Turkey*. Department of Social Anthropology, University of Oslo.

Wittmann, Rebecca. 2007. "Torture on Trial: Prosecuting Sadists and the Obfuscation of Systemic Crime." *South Central Review* 24(1): 8–17.

Zana, Mehti. 1997. *Hölle Nr.5: Tagebuch aus einem türkischen Gefängnis*. Göttingen: Die Werkstatt.

Zeydanlioglu, Welat. 2009. "Torture and Turkification in the Diyarbakir Military Prison." In *Rights, Citizenship and Torture: Perspectives on Evil, Law and the State*. Edited by W. Zeydanlioglu and J. T. Parry, 73–92. Oxford: Inter-Disciplinary Press.

AFTERWORD

David Parkin

Evil: A Tangled Skein

It is testimony to the wide-ranging and in-depth quality of the contributions to this volume that direct or indirect attempts to define evil vary so much. Indeed, it might be thought that the concept is beyond consistent formal definition. And yet, as is also clear from the cases presented, all societies experience times when the unspeakable horror of destructive human behavior, natural events, and metaphysical intervention defies understanding and acceptable explanation. A minimal definition of evil is "malevolent destructiveness" (Csordas). This suggests some common human recognition of the phenomenon, turning as it does on the semantic cluster of "malevolence" as wishing evil on someone, malediction as speaking evil of or cursing someone, and malignity as the sometimes hidden evil intention to injure. The evil will to harm may indeed range from an openly explicit intention—"just you wait and see"—to a smoldering, silently hidden drive to destroy, sometimes not signaled as such to the prospective victim who may be left only suspecting it. The shading of evil intention from expressed ("when will s/he strike?") to unexpressed ("is s/he disposed to harm me?") gives rise to its fearful uncertainty. The semantic cluster is thus more than a collection of near-synonyms; it can cover a span of emotions of anticipation and fear and so defines some of what we call evil in the English language. But language is not good at capturing the constantly shifting suspicions and experiences of evil, and varying cross-cultural translations make it even more elusive. Perhaps analytically useful here is Ardener's (1978) semantic notion of a "language shadow," which refers to a common and collective sense of a happening, which, however, words cannot convey easily, consistently, or at all. It can be applied to the negative as well as positive or neutral dimensions of morality and so seems very well suited to such seemingly ungraspable concepts as evil.

When we write in English, however, are we entitled to use as our analytical starting-point the very term, "evil," in an exploration of a particular moral system (see Good)? And can labeling acts and actors as "evil" paradoxically obscure understanding by explaining them away as being beyond rational analysis (see Pérez)? On the one hand, there is the danger that the Abrahamic religious associations of the verbal concept in English prejudge the moral loading of suspected examples and obscure rather than enlighten our understanding cross-culturally. On the other hand, if we agree that all humanity, in whatever sociocultural guise, experiences the incomprehensible horror of behavior and events that we translate as evil, then we remain challenged as to how to identify our starting-point for social groups lacking comparable terminology. We surely cannot say that there are human societies whose majority of members never feel the horror of unspeakable happenings; so to that extent, "evil" is universally experienced (see Obeyesekere). Yet, while some peoples do have a term that seems broadly translatable as the English term "evil," such as the Asante term *b]ne* (Olsen), sinister occurrences exciting horror are often neither consistently identified verbally nor assume the same forms among all peoples. Among the Hausa of Niger, as among many peoples, the two English senses of "bad" and "evil" are combined in the same term. But people do also distinguish between permanently bad people, (i.e., who are inherently evil) and temporary badness from which people recover, such as theft, and which is less than evil. The semantic load of terms thus alters by context, speaker, audience, and voice tone (Masquelier).

The editors of this volume (Olsen and Csordas), in fact, adopt the notion of "situational evil" to refer to the many socioculturally diverse expressions of events translated by the term. Like "context of situation" or "situational selection," such analytical concepts have a long tradition of use in anthropology. While, in a sense, they are an admission of inadequate knowledge of a phenomenon (e.g., "this issue can only be understood in context") or as only the beginning of investigation, such concepts do provisionally, at least, try to capture the variability and overlapping relatedness of phenomena and behavior. They can be applied to actual examples and do not retreat into such abstractions as the distinction between universality and relativity, which raises more questions than it answers. Nor can we assume that a notion of "evil" as distinct from simply "bad" exists everywhere as part of the human condition, whether or not lexically identified, and that peoples commonly identify them differently from each other. Perhaps all we can say here is that peoples have relative notions of "badness," with some acts and events more horrific than other calamities in their experience. The real issue, however, is the process by which people try to explain events that are at first inexplicable and viscerally charged by the horror of what is happening. And here the notion of situational evil seems to be the most valid starting-point of analysis since it is empirically evident in the flexible shifting between word and nonword by which people try to identify and understand allegedly horrific events and persons.

The idea of situational selection is, in fact, a nice entry into questions of practical morality, for it presupposes decisions that have to be made and dilemmas encountered. Pérez raises the inevitable question of the extent to which actions identified as human evil may be regarded as part of that person's "nature" (e.g., his/her genetic makeup) and are thus outside the control of social morality (akin to the Hausa idea noted by Masquelier that some people are permanently bad). We can take as a complementary view that which sees human evil as resulting from external circumstances imposed on the allegedly evil person, meaning that morality is here also regarded as lying outside the perpetrator and resting somewhere else, such as in society, the environment, nature, or gods/spirits.

This perspective places us firmly within the question of human culpability in relation to metaphysical (i.e., gods/spirits) and so-called natural evil (earthquakes, floods, epidemics, etc.). And what we find is that even when gods/spirits are blamed for natural evils, there is often a point at which the misfortunes are seen as divine retribution for human perpetrators, who are therefore regarded as ultimately responsible through their own evil intentions, dispositions, and negligence. For instance, taking the case of natural evil, Gellner points out that so-called natural disasters may in fact be attributed from a traditionalist viewpoint to human malice or error. Or, from a modernist perspective, they may be seen as resulting from human ignorance and educational inadequacy. Either way, human failings are to blame. Indeed, given the widespread view that both natural and metaphysical suffering may in the end be regarded as due to human failing, this is tantamount to saying that "evil," however approached, is most likely to be seen as the grotesque consequences of extreme human fault, whether called sin, violation of prohibitions, unjustifiable negligence, limitless greed, envy, or, most horrific of all, guiltless, wanton, malevolent destructiveness and the infliction of suffering and death for pleasure or gain. Among the Asante of Ghana, the disease *asram* kills children and is sent by witches to destroy family and lineage growth, which is the worst evil imaginable among Asante (Olsen) and indeed many other African societies. Witches are driven by envy and malice certainly. But the question remains: What is the origin of this or some other human fault? And does discovering and thence explaining the human fault (e.g., the witch him/herself lacks children and so is understandably envious) relocate evil within rather than outside acceptable human understanding, so lessening its horror? This is part of what Csordas calls "the enigma of evil." In Obeyesekere's account of Buddhist mythology, the bloodthirsty brigand who maliciously cut off 999 human fingers is transformed by the Buddha's compassion into a model of piety. The initial horror of the story's audience is turned into their understanding of the transformative benefits of compassion. Its occurrence in myth signals the possibility of such transformation in everyday life.

Sociocultural outsider and insider interpretations may moreover be contradictory. The outsider may perceive and identify human existential dilemmas that cannot be resolved and regard them as contained within a believed "necessary evil." This idea is well explored in one of the chapters on traditional feud-like headhunting (Beatty): I must kill you for the glory it confers on me, as you must kill me, a cultural circle that cannot be broken but which places us both in a state of constant fear and horror. But if insiders see this culturally ordained killing as "necessary," is the outsider entitled to call it evil? And do insiders themselves never question the rightness of this culturally defined mutual agreement to kill?

It might at first be thought that such culturally compulsory "evil" acts of a cyclical nature (e.g., the obligatory taking of heads in feuding) are indeed beyond human control. And yet humans do take measures to modify, if not escape, them. The example given by Beatty is of shedding one's normal humanity and guilt and assuming the status of predator rather than victim in order to kill with moral impunity. In Trinidad (Littlewood), a symbolic inversion occurs in which the "good" Mother Earth becomes characterized as an evil manifestation of the Devil, while her son, previously identified with evil whites, becomes divine. It is an escapist technique found in many parts of

Africa, as in, for instance, the custom of naming a child negatively (e.g., "Trouble" or "Rubbish") in order to ward off the evil intentions of harmful spirits. As Littlewood notes, symbolic inversions of this type help people create irony and nuances in the otherwise rigid grip of hegemonic cosmology and, by extension, of racism and colonialism.

A related technique is to transform one's selfhood in order to escape the evil taint of a previous existence. Acquiring "new life" through Christian conversion, especially so-called Pentecostal, involves rejection of a former self and earlier (im)morality. Entities and actions belonging to the past become evil while those of the new present are virtuous. But the deployment of evil as judgment then becomes flexible. The negative and positive labeling of past and present as evil and virtuous respectively is not just a rejection of old for new. Newly formed, the converts may go further by "situationally" asserting moral claims over their sociocultural and religious environment, renaming some "good" aspects as evil and some formerly "evil" as "good" (Coleman).

The concept of situational evil tends to rest on moral questions of choice and decision-making and to focus on such stereotyped perpetrators as the witch. However, as is evident in the many graphic descriptions of warfare and its consequences, our understanding of what constitutes evil needs to also consider events and powers that are, after all, regarded by ordinary people, the victims, as beyond their control. Insidious rumor compensating for this lack of explanatory control may flourish, with political rivals sometimes blaming opponents for secret acts of evil malpractice as well as conventional warfare. This is the view that many humanly perpetrated evils emanate from more widely encapsulating forces than the agency of ordinary individuals. In other words, a greater evil encapsulates derivative evil. Such wider forces include globally induced wars and postwar disease, the floods and famines resulting from climate change, the poverty and inequality brought on by the relentless insatiability of corporatism, and the social marginalization of peoples unable to be part of the world's accelerating technological expansionism. This is to locate understandings of purported evil over the long duration rather than in the singular event. As Pérez illustrates with regard to his study in Mexico, an individual act such as murder may require layers of historical explanation, which the concept of evil, focused on the individual act alone, may obscure and proves inadequate.

This shifts the focus on evil from the micro to the macro (i.e., from the individual person and event to a more widely encompassing blight afflicting a population). Peteet documents the shift over time between evil as supernatural, as arising from individual pathologies or as caused by the pathologies of particular political regimes. This wider purview is associated with political talk and the popular use of ethnic, minority, or national stereotypes. President Reagan's characterization of the Soviet Union as an "evil empire," later echoed by President Bush, is an example. Peteet further notes how, at the time of writing, "Islamists" have for many western politicians of the current generation supplanted "Communists" in this characterization. Taking this further, the macro perspective on the micro is evident in evil as barbaric spectacle when, for example, a large gathering watches, enjoys, and even celebrates the violent suffering of an individual or minority: "Torture seems more evil, when spectacular and in excess" (Weiss). Related to this is the idea that causing extreme individual suffering, an act which would ordinarily be viewed as evil, can be justified by a political state, for example, as a necessary punitive defense of its wider interests if the victim is regarded as a threat. Two moves may be involved here. First, the suffering inflicted on the individual is regarded as the necessary but "lesser" evil compared with the "greater" evil of state sabotage that the individual (and possible collaborators) is suspected of planning. Second, justifying this lesser evil makes it "virtuous" to the state as perpetrator and therefore no longer evil. The implication in this comparison is that there are different levels or scales of evil. It recalls the popular sentiment that it is possible to talk of "strong" as against "weak" senses of evil (see Gellner and Obeyesekere). But the line between such levels of evil shifts situationally and according to changing moral judgments. This hinders attempts to codify and stabilize morality. While constantly shifting morality may sometimes be welcomed as the lifting of rigid behavioral restrictions, it may also provide moral gaps through which malevolent destructiveness can flourish unchecked.

Language can be used to identify these gaps by giving a name to the heinous acts of evil that pass through them. Thus, when evil is identified verbally through accusations, as at the Auschwitz trials, the language of evil that is used (e.g., demonizing the perpetrators as "monsters" or "devils") may gradually become a language of discussion and then even of partial understanding as reasons are found to explain perpetrators' behaviors even while condemning them (Weiss). Or discussion of evil can in due course locate its causes in the sociopolitical conditions that helped give rise to it (Good).

Language, thus, has the potential to draw an unedifying conceptual shadow into tenuous debate in search of its meaning. This is to move from the visceral and unspeakable horror of evil acts to their speakability. Explanatory ambivalence here takes the place of unverbalized horror: as when the Auschwitz evil-doers are deemed to have acted under the orders of their seniors; or when the witch, who, it is publicly agreed, should not have carried out his/her evil deeds, is in due course regarded as motivated by envy, even justifiable envy, like the rest of us. The terrifying edge of evil may even be blunted by the rationale of alternative explanations, as in Csordas's contrast between the psychoanalytic view of "evil" as regression and the Catholic priest's understanding of it as possession.

Perhaps, in fact, we should reserve the term "evil" for acts or events producing the viscerally charged horror that people experience when they first witness or hear of certain acts that are so gruesomely destructive as to be beyond verbal expression—at first, there simply are no words for the horror. The same acts repeated thereafter (e.g., the recurrent spectacle of wartime atrocities) may begin to take on the beginnings of a kind of routinization as people need to confront and explain them and become, if only slightly, inured to them.

This suggests a distinction between, on the one hand, a sense of evil that is experienced as if for the first time and for which utter horror is the total and only possible response, and, on the other hand, that which is recognized as having happened before and for which the horror is made less by a need to understand. We might even go further and suggest that "evil" that does not evoke total horror is not evil, but has moved into the domain of morality by becoming an object of moral judgment through the need to understand. It moves from outside to within morality. Evil is thus process: first involving preverbal and premoral horror, and then progressing to something that can be analyzed and brought within the realm of moral judgment.

This conceptualization of a horrific act or event as at first beyond human understanding and later as invoking the will to comprehend it in moral terms, may shed light on its emotional, cognitive, moral, and verbal origins. Thus, let us speculate that early human horror of phenomena does not at first draw on moral precepts but originates in disgust of the offending phenomenon. For example, rotting flesh and the stench of a corpse not only violently repel people, they involve them in the horror of death and of what brought it about. It is an experience that retains a shuddering first-time effect and, until gods or practical reason are invoked for explanation, is unlikely to be tempered by time nor satisfactorily explained in terms of a moral code. Is this not the primal archetype of evil? So how does premoral and preverbal disgust/repulsion leading to horror eventually become verbalized and brought within moral explanation?

We have suggested before that this materialist archetype is that of visceral revulsion (Parkin 1985). It may take the form of gross excess as, to take an ethnographic instance, when a child is born with more than the normal number of limbs and other bodily features, prompting some people to have to destroy what is perceived to be an omen of evil consequences. Or it may come as the opposite, in the form of ugly decay, emaciation, and bodily incompleteness, again prompting its destruction. But such manifestations of this primal archetype get taken up over time by successive cultural elaborations. People struggle to reconcile their natural love of their children, for example, or their empathy for fellow humans with the social imposition of beliefs and practices that see physical abnormalities as threatening society. Profligate excess or withering decay are thus two sides of the same cultural coin and may eventually both become explained as evils attributed to gods or as the "mystical" result of human fault. Over time, they may, thankfully in some cases, also be redefined as only malevolent in appearance but not in essence and so deserving of humanitarian attention. But such development is not automatic and, like many historical movements seeking to turn revulsion and prejudice against physical difference into tolerant acceptance, has to be worked at consciously.

This is not just to posit a linear development of the benefits of sociocultural evolution and of societies aspiring to a "higher" morality. On the contrary, it is rather to acknowledge that people may see moral changes for better or worse as occurring in different areas of experience if not in all. Coleman says that his informants' "awareness of evil is the latter's ubiquity combined with its flexibility, its ability to inhabit every nook and cranny of people's lives, and indeed to emerge in contexts where variations of excess, imperfection, and incompleteness are uncovered." Acts and actors identified as evil sometimes disappear from the public imagination and sometimes emerge in different situations, as well as varying globally and historically. We may here also ask with Gellner how much differences of "secularization" or, alternatively, "enchantment" among societies affect local perceptions of evil as being, for instance, either strong, weak, or constant. Whatever its variable expression, the archetype lurks in the present as it did in the past, altering its mask and site but not its cognitive–emotional essence and impact.

At the time of writing, a noticeable western media trend in some quarters is to move away from absolutist depictions of "murderous" terrorists as utterly and incomprehensibly evil. They may certainly be regarded as having committed evil acts, but as being of unbalanced mental condition, or young and socioethnically marginalized, and as therefore susceptible to ideological brainwashing. It reverses the still-widespread view of them as almost entirely ideologically driven but as sane and not especially socially disadvantaged.

Notwithstanding the discursive hesitations that these conflicting "liberal" and "reactionary" viewpoints create, the archetypal concept of evil does not disappear. Its enunciation changes, as does the moral framework within which it is identified and, sometimes, explained. Moreover, prior to its enunciation and moral identification, the preverbal horror of evil is of ugly abnormality. More than one contributor to this volume invokes Ricoeur (1967) on evil. Of particular note is Ricoeur's notion of evil as "defilement" and as pre-ethical in the sense that it is not yet taken up in the language of morality and theology. Defilement is a notion that Beatty equates with Douglas's (1966) gloss on pollution as "matter out of place" or simply "dirt." It may be further seen as an aspect of the archetypal experience of either gross excess or wasting depletion as described above, both of which may trigger an emotional response of disgust and horror, and in due course, may indicate "evil" as the named culprit.

The idea of an underlying archetype of evil may seem to be a long way from the cases of purported evil presented in this volume. And it is true that this notion constitutes a speculative excursion into cognition, emotion, evolutionary development, and existential dilemmas of the human condition. It is true also, as has been argued, that in the last instance, global and local inequalities, exploitation, war-like violent depredation, deprivation, and helplessness in the face of natural disaster and loss are the ultimate conditions for the emergence of resentments fuelling the human hatreds that spawn acts deemed evil. However, hatreds resulting from ultimate deprivations do not take predictable forms. Their variable expression as perceived acts of evil are always interpreted and reinterpreted psychologically as well as socially.

There is thus a case to be made for linking cognition, emotion, and evolution to the sociocultural expression of what is experienced everywhere and sometimes identified as evil. The epistemological gap between the evolutionary, psychological, social, and semantic areas of investigation is undoubtedly wide, but perhaps not insurmountable. Reverting to the idea of evil as process, we can regard the archetype as long-term, and particular sociocultural expressions of it as situational. Evil as process thus moves from the unverbalized horror of an act to its identification through words as being outside human morality. This marks a red line between acceptable and unacceptable dimensions of morality and can lead to attempts at explaining the evil as "immoral" or "amoral." The process can be evolutionarily long-term or a short social episode. The long-term is the recurrent visceral archetype that at first resists verbal or other identification, while the short-term is described or explained through existing sociocultural bricolage. Situational evil is the latter, which draws on the archetype.

If this gloss leads to greater understanding of how certain acts and events instill unspeakable horror, become interpreted as evil, and in due cause qualify for explanations leading to attempts at remedying the underlying inequalities and depredations fuelling the precipitating resentments and hatreds, this would be a significant addition to the already many writings on the subject, including the current excellent collection of essays.

David Parkin, Emeritus Professor, University of Oxford

References

Ardener, E. 1978. "Some Outstanding Problems in the Analysis of Events." In *The Yearbook of Symbolic Anthropology I*. Edited by E. Schwimmer. London: C. Hurst.

Douglas, M. 1966. *Purity and Danger: An Analysis of the Concepts of Pollution and Taboo*. London and New York: Routledge and Kegan Paul.

Parkin, D. J., ed. 1985. "Introduction." *The Anthropology of Evil*. Oxford: Basil Blackwell.

Ricoeur, P. 1967. *The Symbolism of Evil*. Boston, MA: Beacon Press.

AUTHORS AND INSTITUTIONS

William C. Olsen, *African Studies, Georgetown University*

Thomas J. Csordas, *Anthropology, UC San Diego*

Byron J. Good, *Department of Social Medicine, Harvard University*

Andrew Beatty, *Anthropology, Brunel University*

Roland Littlewood, *Anthropology, UC University of London*

Simon Coleman, *Department of Religion, University of Toronto*

David N. Gellner, *Anthropology, Oxford University*

Gananath Obeyesekere, *Emeritus Anthropology, Princeton University*

Adeline Masquelier, *Anthropology, Tulane University*

Julie Peteet, *Anthropology, University of Louisville*

Ventura R. Perez, Anthropology, University of Massachusetts

Nerina Weiss, *Senior Researcher, Fafo Institute of International Studies*

David Parkin, *Emeritus Anthropology, Oxford University*

INDEX

A
abandonment, 200, 217–19
abosom, 260, 268
Abrahamic associations, 298
abusua, 261–62
Aceh (Indonesia), 52–54
affliction, 181
Angulimala, 160–73
anthropology and evil, 4–7, 35–42
Arendt, Hannah, 6, 576
   Eichmann in Jerusalem, 174, 287
   on language, 206, 214
Asad, Talal, 204
Asante, 254–72
asram, 254–71
Augustine, 56, 71
Auschwitz
   Auschwitz Trials, 277–78, 281

B
Badiou, Alain, 39
Banyuwangi, 82, 87
Bathara Kala, 81–84
Beal, Timothy, 90
Bible, 76–78
biocultural, 228
blood, 178, 189, 190, 193
bori, 181, 187
   healers, 187, 188
   rituals, 189
Buddhism, 157–74
Burg, Avraham, 206
Butler, Judith, 55, 61–63
   on language, 204

C
calibration, 200, 208, 209, 214, 220
   deprivation, 207
caste, 139–40, 145–46
Caton, Steve, 202
checkpoints, 203, 207, 208, 210, 211, 212, 215, 216, 217
   Eretz checkpoint, 211, 216
children and death, 254, 259
China, 145
Christian conversion, 76–81, 90
Christianity, 139, 147
Ciudad Juárcz, 240–41
closure, 203, 210, 221
colonization, 75, 78, 86
communism, 86, 88
corpse, 245, 246
crime, 238
crimes against humanity, 13
Csordas, Thomas J., 111, 115, 131

D
daily caloric in-take (DCI), 208, 209
diet, 218, 219
dark side (Amélie Rorty), 55, 56, 59
death drive, 61
death space, 230
death squads, 13
demonic, 231
demons, 17–21
Derrida, Jacques, 35–36, 64
destiny (*nkrabea*), 263
development, 138, 144
Devil, 98
diaspora, 111, 116, 120, 121, 125, 128

Dinka, 14
disproportionality, 199, 202, 205, 207, 208
  Dahiya Doctrine, 203
divination, 256, 260
divinity, 15, 15–21
Dogondoutchi, 177, 180, 187, 189, 192, 194
Douglas, Mary, 82
drugs, 241–42
Dutch East Indies, 75

E
education, 133–34, 136, 146
entertainment, 213, 214
eschatology, 71–72, 81
ethical restraint, 171
evil
  and anthropology, 4–7, 35–42
  and cosmology, 76, 81, 89–90
  and emotion, 80, 90–91
  and political violence, 85–86, 88, 89
  and power, 82–83
  and the self, 74–75, 77, 79–81, 82, 90
  and torture, 275–94
  and violence, 225–28
  and visceral horror, 298–300, 302–03, 305–06
  anthropology, 35–42, 48–49
  archetype, 303–5
  as conceptually elusive, 297
  as paradox, 298
  as process, 299, 303, 305
  Christianity, 38–39
  complexity of, 284–88
  discovery of, 76, 77, 81, 90
  elementary structure of, 41–42
  enactment of, 79, 84
  explaining away, 298
  historical diversity of the concept, 56
  in Asante, 254–72
  in translation, 72–73, 76–77
  levels of, 302
  location of, 71–73, 80, 89, 91
  morality, 36–39
  personification of, 81
  philosophy, 36–37
  problem of, 71–73, 81, 90–91
  radical, 158, 160, 164, 173
  spectacular evil, 276, 278, 282, 284, 288, 292–93
  situational, 298–99, 301, 303, 305
  strong vs. weak, 135–37, 144, 148
  symbolic inversions of, 300
  witchcraft as epitome of, 134, 139–40, 148
  working definition of, 35, 41
excess, 111, 112, 113, 115, 200, 202
exorcism, 12, 13, 81–84, 88, 89, 90, 134, 142, 144, 171, 177
  ruqiyya, 187, 188
  Roman Catholic, 42–48

F
Fall, 71–72
Fischer, Michael M. J, 57, 65
forgiveness (Christian), 169
Free Aceh Movement (Geraken Aceh Merdeka, GAM), 53
Freud, Sigmund, 61, 64, 80, 91

G
Gaza, 201–6, 208, 209, 213, 214, 216, 219
Geertz, Clifford, 11, 40
gender, 146, 216, 217
genocide, 2, 15
gold, 75, 76
Good, Mary-Jo DelVecchio, 52, 54, 65, 66
Gordon, Avery, 64
Grayman, Jesse, 53

H
haunting, hauntology, 63–64
hauntological ethics, 64
Hausa (language), 179
headhunting, 73–74, 90

Index 311

Headley, Stephen, 81
healing, 139, 142–43, 147
hell
   and Dante, 278
   and prison (*see* prisons)
   Diyarbakir prison, 282
Hell Valley, 95
Herriman, Nicholas, 86–87
hijab, 184, 185
homodicy, 40
Hopkins, Gerard Manley, 172
hot/cold bipolarity, 104
human trafficking, 240, 243

I
Indonesia, 90
intent, 208
intention, 13–14, 269–71
International Humanitarian Law, 202
International Organization for Migration (IOM), 53
Islam, 177, 178, 183, 186, 188, 192, 193
   layu (amulets), 187
   prayer (*addu'a*), 187
   rubutu (Qur'anic verses), 187
Israel Victory Caucus, 218–19

J
jahat (Indonesian evil), 54
Java, 75, 82
Jim Crow, 200
Job, 73, 78

K
Kaguru, 10, 15
Kant, Emmanuel, 158
Kedar, Mordechai, 205
Kleinman, Arthur, 59
Kurds, 275–76, 278–80, 285–87, 289–92, 294
Kyei, T. E., 258

L
Laidlaw, James, 8
language, 204–7

language shadow, 297
Lemelson, Robert, 59
liquid evil, 209
London, 114, 116, 117, 118, 119, 120, 121, 124, 125, 127, 128, 129, 130
Lord of the Flies, 42–45, 48
Luntz, Frank
   on language, 204

M
malamai (Muslim religious specialists), 86, 187, 188, 193, 194
malediction, 45–48, 49
malevolent destructiveness, 35, 41, 49
Malinowski, Bronislaw, 200
Mampong Government Hospital, 258
medicine, 134, 147
Mexico, 236–45
Migration, 138–39
misfortune, 133–37, 149
missionaries, 75, 77, 78, 79, 100
mobility, 209, 220
modernity, 138, 149,
monsters, 89, 90–91
moon, 105–6
moral geography, 115, 120, 121, 122
morality, 7–12, 36–39, 177, 179, 182, 183, 184, 191, 192, 193, 255
   Manichean, 177, 179, 194
   monistic, 177
Mother Evil, 95, 97
mugunta (evil), 179, 180
   Faustian pacts, 178, 190

N
NAFTA, 240–41
Navajo, 14
Netanyahu, Benjamin, 204, 205, 221
Nias, 73, 90

Nietzsche, Friedrich, 38, 39, 56, 59, 156, 158–63
Niger, 177, 180, 184, 185, 191, 192
Nigeria, 114, 115, 116, 117, 118, 119, 120, 121, 122, 124, 125, 126, 127, 129, 130
ninjas, 85

O

Obeyesekere, Gananath, 38
obscenity, 97
occult, 112, 113, 114
occupation, 200, 207, 210, 215, 218
Olmert, Ehud, 208
ontology, 48–49, 134, 149
Oppenheimer, Josh, 59
otherness, 74

P

Palestine/Israel, 199–224
Parkin, David, 39, 40, 111, 112, 113, 124, 177
parricide, 164
Pentecostalism, 111, 112, 113, 114, 115, 119, 120, 121, 122, 123, 126, 127, 128
performative violence, 236
phenomenology, 45
philosophy and evil, 5–7
poetics, 231
political prisoner, 279, 281, 290, 291
political violence, 51, 55, 59
pollution, 82, 83
possession, 44–45, 48, 134, 137, 139–40, 142–43, 148, 177, 182, 183, 186, 187, 188. *See also* bori
  possession ceremony (*wasa*), 181, 182
power, 235
prison guards
  ambivalent relations with prisoners, 284–85
  monsters and sadists, 277–78, 281–82

prisons
  prisons as hell (*see* hell)
  ranking of prisons, 276
prosperity, 113, 119, 122
psychoanalysis, 42–43
Puar, Jasbir
  on maiming, 206

Q

quantification, 202, 203, 205, 219
Qur'an, 185, 186, 187, 188

R

radical enlightenment, 159
radical evil, 158, 160, 164, 173
Rastafari, 96, 101, 102, 107
reconstituted peasantry, 96
Redeemed Christian Church of God, 114
regression, 43, 48
relativism, cultural and moral, 36
religion, 144–45, 147, 148
repentance movement, 75, 78–80
ressentiment, 171–73
Ricoeur, Paul, 39, 75, 82
Robbins, Joel, 55, 57, 59, 113, 115
Rorty, Amélie, 36–37
Royle, Nicholas, 90
rupture, 112, 113, 114, 115

S

salvation, 76, 80, 81
Samson, 78
Samuels, Annemarie, 63
Santner, Eric, 60
Sapir, Edward, 57, 65
Satan, 111, 112, 113, 123, 124, 127, 128, 178, 179, 185, 187, 194
  Satan's servants, 177, 185, 187
Sderot, 213–14
  Najd, 214
secularization, 136–37, 145
sent sickness, 265–68
settler-colonialism, 200, 203, 212, 217
shadow play, 81–82

shango, 100
siege, 208, 209
Siegel, James, 86, 87, 88
sin, 71, 77, 78, 81, 90
Sinaloa Cartel, 242
slavery, 75
spectacle, 200, 215, 216
spirits
   aljanu, 186, 187, 188, 189, 194
   bori, 181
   Doguwa, 189, 190, 191, 192, 193, 194
   génie tchatcheur (chatty demon), 183, 184
   iskoki, 177, 180, 187
   people of the bush, 180, 186, 188
Spiritual (Shouter) Baptists, 97–100
spiritual attacks, 178, 179, 183, 184, 185, 188, 193
spiritual warfare, 112, 115
state killing, 13, 21–22
Steinbeck, John, 232
structural violence, 24
suffering, 1–27, 133, 138, 142–143, 146–147
suffering slot (Joel Robbins), 55
Suharto, 20, 85, 86, 89
sun/son, 104–6
sunsum, 260, 262, 270
sunsum yaree, 261, 263
symbolic inversion, 98–107

T
taboo, 77
theodicy, 39, 40
torture, 15
   as holistic phenomenon, 287
   as lesser evil, 277
   experience linked to status and collective identity, 281, 292
   importance of ideology to fight torture, 280–81, 286
   interrogative torture, 277
   potentiality of, 292

   spectacular torture, 282–84
   survivor, 275–76, 279–81, 285, 287–88, 290–94
   systematic torture, 275, 278, 281
   terroristic torture, 277, 279
   debate, 277
translation, 77
transvalorisation, 100, 102, 103
Trinidad, 95–107
Turkey, 275–76, 278–85, 287–89, 291–92, 294

U
uncanny, 60, 64, 80, 90–91
US–Mexico security, 237–38

V
victimhood
   torture survivors as victims, 281, 294
violence, 21–26, 35–36, 141, 246
   and evil, 225–48
   theory, 233–36
visuality/visualization, 213, 216

W
Walser, Martin, 275, 276, 278, 292
Weber, Max, 194
Weisglass, Dov, 208
Weizman, Eyal, 202
witch craze, 84–87, 89
witchcraft, 3, 10–11, 14, 134, 137, 259
   accusations, 133–34, 139–44
   and feminists, 146
   and the law, 137, 145–46
   maita, 196, 197, 192
womb, 259

Z
Zaltzman, Nathalie, 42–43
Zande, 10–11
Zionism, 203, 206, 217–18

www.ingramcontent.com/pod-product-compliance
Lightning Source LLC
Chambersburg PA
CBHW072145100526
44589CB00015B/2091